RICHARD HENRY LEE:
STATESMAN OF THE REVOLUTION

RICHARD HENRY LEE

Richard Henry Lee

Statesman of the Revolution

By

Oliver Perry Chitwood

WEST VIRGINIA UNIVERSITY LIBRARY
MORGANTOWN
1967

McClain Printing Company
Parsons, West Virginia

The publication of this book was
made possible by a grant from the

WEST VIRGINIA UNIVERSITY
FOUNDATION

A publication of the University's 100th Anniversary Year

TO

JULIA ELIZABETH

RANDOLPH BEURY

JANS CHRISTIAN

PETER PERRY

Foreword

In 1911-14, James C. Ballagh published two volumes of Richard Henry Lee's letters running from 1762, when he was thirty, to shortly before his death in 1794. In 1943 Edmund C. Burnett contributed to the *Dictionary of American Biography* a good but perforce limited biographical sketch of Lee, and he has, of course, been touched upon in uncounted histories and biographies of the period from 1764, when he emerged as a leader in the Virginia House of Burgesses, to his resignation from the United States Senate in 1792. But the only full-length biography of this great Virginia statesman has been the uncritical, inadequate *Memoir of Richard Henry Lee* by a grandson and namesake, published in 1825.

Now that the long-needed, new biography of Lee has at last been written, it is fortunate, indeed, that it comes from Oliver Perry Chitwood. As a native of Virginia and a graduate of the College of William and Mary, he is naturally sympathetic to Lee, and also, as the thousands of readers of Chitwood's classic *Justice in Colonial Virginia* and *A History of Colonial America* can testify, is a scholar of the first water and a profound student of the period in which Lee was a leading figure.

Though the evidence concerning Lee's personal life is rather meagre, that of his political career is very rich, and Professor Chitwood has used it to the full, and with a fine sense of balance and impartiality. Furthermore, besides presenting us with an admirable biography of Lee, he gives an extremely valuable study of the work of the Continental Congress, during most of whose sessions from the assembling of the First Congress at Philadelphia in September 1774, to the closing days of the Second at New York City, thirteen years later, Lee was an outstanding figure. The Silas Deane-Arthur Lee controversy, in which Richard Henry Lee was much involved, is also fully discussed, and a careful analysis of Lee's *Letters of the Federal Farmer* (1788) brings out clearly his powerful argument against adopting the proposed Constitution without sweeping antecedent amendment.

This is a work which readers in general will find interesting and highly informing, and students of the period from 1764 to 1792 or any part of it, indispensable.

BERNHARD KNOLLENBERG

Preface

This work is a study of the career of Richard Henry Lee, with emphasis on the role he played in the American Revolution. He supported the cause as a brilliant speaker and an ardent patriot. He was among the leaders in initiating revolt, in supporting military operations, in declaring independence, in forming the French Alliance, and in creating the first federal union. He performed useful service in the transition of Virginia from colony to commonwealth, and certainly must be numbered among the most effective in guiding our first federal republic in its brief career. In addition he assisted in formulating our public land policy and the plan of government for our territories, in launching the second republic, and in adding the Bill of Rights to the Constitution. The Continental Congress honored him with its presidency.

His place in written history, however, is not in keeping with this record. His career has been outlined in several published works, but these do not give a full-length portrait of the man. Two older biographies by his grandsons are inadequate, and several later well-written accounts are only to be found in one-volume works on the Lee family. There is a very good account of the part played by Lee in the Revolution—"Richard Henry Lee and the American Revolution" (1939) — by John Carter Matthews. But this work has never been published; the manuscript is in the Alderman Library, University of Virginia, and I have leaned heavily on it in the preparation of this biography. The object of this study is to examine more carefully the reputation of Richard Henry Lee and possibly to accord him a more proper place in public opinion.

O. P. C.

Acknowledgements

In collecting and organizing material for this biography, I have had the valuable assistance of a number of persons, to all of whom I wish to extend my earnest and sincere thanks. To Mr. J. E. Fields, of Joliet, Illinois, for the use of Lee Letters in his possession; to Mr. Robert O. Dougan, Librarian, Henry E. Huntington Library and Art Museum, for the privilege of quoting from a letter in that library; to Mr. Herbert C. Schultz, Curator of Manuscripts, and Miss Helen S. Mangold of the Department of Manuscripts, of the same library, for furnishing me with photostatic and microfilm copies of Lee Papers in the Huntington Library; to Mr. James T. Babb, Librarian, and Mrs. Zara Jones Powers, a former member of the staff, for xeroxed copies of Lee Papers in Yale University Library; to Mr. Howard Henry Peckham, Director of William L. Clements Library (University of Michigan), for copies of letters to and from Richard Henry Lee; to Mrs. Cazenove Gardner Lee of Washington, D. C., for copies of the original Lee portraits in her possession; to the Colonial Studio, Richmond, Virginia, for a photograph of Stratford; to Colonial Williamsburg, for pictures of Raleigh Tavern and other historic buildings; and to Dr. Robert F. Munn, Director of Libraries, West Virginia University, who was exceedingly obliging in procuring books and photostats and microfilms of manuscripts. Important aid was also furnished by the late Reverend Edmund Jennings Lee of Shepherdstown, West Virginia, a direct descendant of Richard Henry Lee. From him I received a copy of an unpublished letter written by his ancestor and a print of the original portrait of him painted by Charles Wilson Peale (see frontispiece).

In like manner I wish to express my deep appreciation of the gracious courtesy shown me, as well as the helpful service rendered, by staff members of the following libraries and manuscript depositories in which I have worked: Boston Public Library, Library of the Massachusetts Historical Society, Houghton Library (Harvard), Annmary Brown Library (Brown University), Library of the New York Historical Society, New York Public Library, Library of Princeton University, Library of the Historical Society of Pennsylvania, Library of the American Philosophical Society, Library of Congress, National Archives, Alderman Library (University of Virginia), Library of the Virginia Historical Society, the Virginia State Library, the Library of the Institute of Early American History, Carnegie Library of

Pittsburgh, the Library of Stetson University, and the Library of West Virginia University. My thanks are also due to Harper and Row for allowing me to quote, without the use of quotation marks, from my work, *A History of Colonial America*, published by them.

I also acknowledge with thanks my indebtedness to the scholars who read part or all of the manuscript and proposed some useful changes in style. This list includes Dr. Ludwell Lee Montague, historian of the Lee Society, who read the first three chapters and suggested some useful changes; my daughter, Dr. Elizabeth Anne Appel, Alexandria, Virginia; three members of the History Department of West Virginia University—Professor Wesley M. Bagby, Professor Elizabeth Cometti, and Associate Professor Edward M. Steele, Jr. Each of the four last-named went over the entire manuscript carefully and thoroughly and suggested many useful changes as to method of expression. Mrs. Agnes C. Chitwood performed valuable service in style revision and proof correction. Very important also has been the contribution made by Dr. Bernhard Knollenberg, historian of the American Revolution. Not only did he perform the valuable service of writing the Foreword, but he also read the whole manuscript, both the first and final copies and made helpful suggestions.

In putting the manuscript in final form and seeing it through the press I had the the valuable assistance of Dr. James W. Hess, of the History Department, and Professor Donovan H. Bond, of the School of Journalism, both of West Virginia University. They made important revisions in the manuscript and read the proof, both galley and page. Miss Ashley Doherty prepared the index and helped with the correction of proof.

O. P. C.

Contents

Chapter I

A History-Making Clan

Until a half-century ago it was generally held that the members of the upper class of colonial Virginians were in large measure descendants of the English gentry. Later scholarship has either rejected or at least aroused serious doubt as to the correctness of this view. It seems therefore that the colonial Virginia gentry in general owed the blue tinge of their blood to achievement rather than to heredity. In the case of the historic Lee family it came in to some extent by both channels. The founders of the Lee clan in Virginia were exceptionally successful in acquiring wealth and in winning prominence in public affairs, but they could also point to a line of upper-class, or at least high middle-class, ancestry that extended almost to the Norman Conquest.

The ancestor who transplanted the Lee family from England to America was Richard Henry's great-grandfather, Richard I, son of Richard and Elizabeth Bendy Lee of Nordley Regis, Shropshire, England. This Richard could trace his ancestry to Sir Thomas Lee, son of Regner de Lega, Sheriff of Shropshire in 1201. Soon after his arrival in Virginia, Richard Lee married Ann Constable, a member of the household of Francis Wyatt, newly appointed governor of Virginia.[1]

Richard Lee was evidently in good standing with Governor Berkeley, Wyatt's successor, and to this relationship he doubtless owed his rapid advancement in public offices. He became Attorney General of the colony in 1643 and Secretary of State in 1659. In the meantime he had served for several years (1651-52, 1660-64) as a member of the Council, one of the highest positions in the government below that of governor.[2] Membership in the Council became almost hereditary in the Lee family, for from Richard's death until the Council was ended by the Revolution each generation of his descendants was at one time or another represented in this body.

1

When the breach between Parliament and King Charles I widened into a civil war (1642), the Puritan Revolution, Richard Lee, along with most of his fellow patricians in Virginia, supported Governor Berkeley in his loyalty to the crown.[3] But Richard Lee was a realist; when opposition to Parliamentary authority on the part of Virginia seemed hopeless, he yielded to the inevitable and swore allegiance to the Commonwealth. When Governor Berkeley surrendered to the commissioners sent over by Parliament (1652), the terms of the capitulation probably were negotiated by Lee and William Claiborne, representing respectively the Virginia and the Commonwealth governments.[4]

The land-grant system in colonial Virginia made it easy for men of means to acquire great tracts of land. Every immigrant was allowed fifty acres for himself and fifty acres for each member of his family and for every other person transported by him. Shipowners, who bore the cost of transporting criminals sent over by the British authorities and emigrants who were unable to pay their passage, received headrights, as they were called, entitling them to fifty acres for each person transported. These headrights were transferable, and by transportation and purchase Richard Lee was able to get headrights with which he obtained a landed estate which ultimately exceeded 16,000 acres.[5]

At the time of his death Richard Lee was probably the richest man in Virginia. In addition to large landed possessions, he had other important business interests. He was engaged in the tobacco trade, owning a warehouse and countinghouse in London, as well as being part owner in the ships used in this trade. In pursuit of this interest he made frequent trips to England. After several temporary residences elsewhere Richard Lee established his home on Dividing Creek, an estuary of Chesapeake Bay, in what later became Northumberland County. He also acquired a fine estate in England at Stratford-Langton, Essex County, near London, now a part of London, going there to live in 1661. After three years' residence in the homeland as a country gentleman with the title of "Esquire," he returned to his Virginia plantation and died at Dividing Creek in 1664.

Richard Lee was survived by six sons and two daughters. After his father's death, John, the oldest son, settled down on his plan-

2

tation, "Machodoc," on the Potomac in Westmoreland County, an estate bequeathed him by his father. He died unmarried at the age of thirty-one.[6]

After the death of his brother John, Richard II, now head of the Lee family, who had probably been living on his estate (Paradise) in Gloucester County, moved to Machodoc which became his permanent home. This Richard had a deep interest in literary pursuits, with a large library to support it. In the lengthy Latin epitaph on his tombstone in the family graveyard at Mount Pleasant is this statement: "He was very skillful in the Greek and Latin language and other parts of polite literature." His grandson, William Lee, stated that Richard II had attended Oxford University, where he made a brilliant record as a student. He is not, however, listed in the University records.[7]

Following his father's precedent, Richard II was active in the public affairs of Virginia. He served for a number of years as a member of the Council and held the offices of colonel of the militia cavalry for the counties of Westmoreland, Northumberland, and Stafford, and Naval Officer and Receiver of Customs for the Potomac.[8]

The second Richard was strongly conservative in both his political and religious views. He was therefore not only a firm believer in the established church but an ardent advocate of Stuart rule. This identified him with the autocratic policy of Governor Berkeley which led to Bacon's Rebellion. Listed by Bacon as one of Berkeley's advisers chiefly responsible for his misrule, Lee was imprisoned for more than seven weeks. His estates probably would have been confiscated had not the rebellion ended with Bacon's death.[9]

When James II was deposed in the Revolution of 1688 and William and Mary were put on the throne of England, Richard Lee remained loyal to the dethroned James, despite the latter's Catholicism. He at first refused to take the oath of allegiance to the new sovereigns and was deprived of a lucrative office and his seat in the Council. Later, seeing that William and Mary were just rulers and that the people of Virginia, including his aristocratic neighbors, were contented and prosperous, he accepted the new regime and took the oath of allegiance. He then regained his membership in the Council and apparently thereafter enjoyed the full confidence of the government. A few

3

months after his death (March, 1714), Lieutenant Governor Spotswood in a report to the Commissioners of the Customs (July, 1714) spoke of him as "a Gentleman of as fair character as any in the Country for his exact justice, honesty, and unexceptionable Loyalty in all the Stations wherein he has served in this Government."[10]

Richard Lee II had seven children, six sons and one daughter. The oldest son, John, died at an early age, and Richard III was then first in line of succession. He received by his father's will that part of the Machodoc estate which had been the family residence. Richard III was at the time a tobacco merchant living in England with an English wife and he never transferred his residence to Virginia.[11]

In making his will Richard II had been influenced to some extent by the law of primogeniture—then theoretically in effect in Virginia—and therefore Thomas, the fifth son, did not receive nearly so large a landed estate as did the oldest heir, nor was he given an opportunity for education commensurate with his exceptional ability and marked interest in learning. His formal training did not go beyond the instruction offered by the home tutor. These deficiencies as to landed possessions and education he resolved to remedy by his own efforts. He was remarkably successful in both these endeavors—in winning a self-education and in securing land grants. Fortunately for this latter aim, his uncle, Edmund Jennings, was appointed agent of the Fairfax family for the Northern Neck of Virginia, and as such was manager of a proprietary domain of 5,000,000 acres.[12] At the time of his appointment Edmund Jennings was in London; he did not come to Virginia until several years later. In this interim (1713-1716) Thomas Lee acted in his place as agent for the Fairfax proprietary. His relationship with Edmund Jennings and his own connection with the proprietorship were circumstances favorable for acquiring lands and he became one of Virginia's largest landowners.

In 1744 Thomas Lee and William Beverley were sent to Lancaster, Pennsylvania, as representatives of the colony to negotiate an agreement with the Indians. By skillful diplomacy and the use of gifts they were able to induce the Six Nations to sign a treaty granting to Virginia the lands west of the Allegheny Mountains. This treaty strengthened England's claim to the

4

Northwest and expanded the area of Virginia into that of an empire. This bargain was considered by a modern author (B. J. Hendrick) as better than the one by which the Dutch bought Manhattan Island (in 1626) for twenty-four dollars.[13]

The Virginia planters at once decided to take advantage of the opportunity thus offered them by pre-empting these western lands. In a few years several large grants were made to groups of petitioners. Prominent in the list of these groups was the Ohio Company of Virginia, formally organized in 1748 with Thomas Lee as president. Two of his sons (Philip Ludwell and Thomas Ludwell), other relatives, and two of George Washington's brothers were original shareholders. A few years later other shareholders were added, including Richard Henry Lee. This company was formed to colonize the West and to forestall the advance of the French. Following the King's approval in council of the petition for this land, the governor and Council of Virginia issued a grant for 200,000 acres of land in the Ohio River region. The company's exploration of the area began about the time of Thomas Lee's death (1750).[14]

True to the family tradition, Thomas Lee took an important part in political affairs. He served for a time in the House of Burgesses and in 1734 became a member of the Council. After a fifteen-year term of service, he was made (1749) president of the Council. Soon afterward, when William Gooch gave up the governorship on account of ill health, he automatically became acting governor.[15]

In 1722 Thomas Lee married Hannah Ludwell, whose family held high rank among the Virginia gentry. Her mother belonged to the noted Harrison clan and her father, Philip Ludwell II, and his forbears had been prominent in the public affairs of the colony. Her paternal grandfather, Philip Ludwell I, was a close friend of Sir William Berkeley and gave loyal support to the governor's policy in Bacon's Rebellion. Later he was governor of Albemarle settlement and then of both the Carolinas.[16]

For a few years after his marriage Thomas Lee lived at the old homestead at Machodoc, under lease from his brother, Richard III. He was forced out of this residence by a fire that destroyed the mansion house (1729). The fire was the work of a "pernicious crew of transported felons." Lee, as justice of the peace, had on complaint made to him issued a warrant for their

5

arrest. It was in revenge for this action that they had set fire to the building. A white servant girl was burned to death in her bed, and Lee, his wife, and three children were saved by getting out at a window "with nothing but their Shifts and Shirts on their backs, which was all they saved, not two minutes before the House fell in."[17]

Before the fire at Machodoc, Thomas Lee had purchased the Cliffs Plantation, on the Potomac thirty-eight miles above its mouth, which, after additional purchases had been made, comprised more than four thousand acres. Here he built Stratford, named for his grandfather's English estate, and by 1730 had occupied it as his permanent home. This noble brick structure stood on a plateau about a mile from the Potomac. With its eighteen rooms and large hall it was a mansion quite worthy of the proud social position of a Potomac baron. Close to the main building there were a number of outbuildings, such as the kitchen, stables, law office, lumber room, schoolhouse, and servants quarters. Crepe myrtle, fig bushes, and beautiful shade trees adorned the yard, and boxwood, flower beds and vegetable gardens dotted the adjacent grounds. In this setting the gracious Hannah Lee presided over the many social activities of Stratford.[18]

One of the outbuildings still standing is the small brick schoolhouse in which the older sons and probably the older daughters were instructed by private tutors. A schoolroom on the first floor of the mansion seems to have been used for the younger children in later years. Prominent in the list of tutors employed by Thomas Lee was Dr. William Douglass (who numbered among his pupils Thomas Jefferson and James Monroe) and the Reverend Mr. Craig, an able Scotch Presbyterian minister, who instructed them not only in the rudimentary subjects but also in the ancient languages. Although Mr. Craig imposed on his pupils a rigid schedule of school hours and exercised a parental authority over them, not sparing the rod, he won and retained their affection and respect.[19]

One serious responsibility with which Thomas Lee was faced was that of making a proper disposal of his great estate. In keeping with the practice of the day, he apportioned his property among his children in a carefully written will.[20] In so doing he adhered to the principle of primogeniture only to the

6

extent of making Philip Ludwell, the oldest surviving son, the most favored legatee, leaving him Stratford and other large tracts of land. The daughters and two youngest sons did not receive any land but had substantial legacies in personal property. To the other three sons he made liberal bequests in land and personal property. While none of the children fared as well as Philip Ludwell, all were well provided for.[21]

All of the Lee brothers took seriously their obligation to be active in public affairs. Philip Ludwell was elected to the House of Burgesses in 1756 and the following year was appointed to the Council, on which he served until his death (1775). As County Lieutenant he was in control of the militia of Westmoreland County. He was the only one of the brothers who did not take part in the Revolutionary movement.[22]

The second of the six sons to reach maturity was Thomas Ludwell, who performed useful public service as a member of the Virginia House of Burgesses, two Virginia conventions (1775, 1776), the Committee of Safety, and the Virginia Senate. He also signed the Westmoreland Association, a mutual pledge of opposition to the Stamp Act written by Richard Henry Lee and signed by one hundred and seventeen citizens of the Westmoreland area (February 27, 1766).[23] Just before his death Thomas Ludwell was appointed one of the five judges in the General Court. His career was cut short by his death in April, 1778. John Adams quoted Chancellor Wythe as saying that Thomas Ludwell Lee was by far the most popular man in Virginia and "the delight of the eyes of Virginia."[24]

Next in the order of age came Richard Henry, who was born January 31, 1733. All the modern authorities examined in this study give 1732 as the year of Richard Henry's birth, but according to the record in the Lee family Bible, 1733 is the correct date.[25] Along with his brothers, Richard Henry received his basic schooling at the hands of private tutors, as was the custom among big planters of Virginia. In his twelfth year he was sent to England to study at an academy at Wakefield, run by the Reverend Benjamin Wilson, the vicar of Wakefield, said to be the one made famous by Goldsmith. Here he stayed for seven years. His older brothers, Philip Ludwell and Thomas Ludwell, were also in the homeland, studying law at the Inner Temple in London. At the death of their father, all three were called home

7

and their formal education was ended. Richard Henry traveled on the Continent for some months before returning to Virginia.[26]

On his return from Europe, at the age of eighteen, Richard Henry Lee took up his residence at Stratford and made it his home for six years or more. During the first four years he seems not to have had any public duties to engage his attention, and he used the leisure thus afforded in wide and serious reading and study.[27] This interest in books continued with him throughout his life and was a most valuable supplement to his formal education.

It is highly improbable that Richard Henry during these early years spent all of his time poring over books. In easy reach of Stratford were a number of homes of the "barons of the Potomac" which were centers of enjoyable social life. In a few years he found a wife in the home of one of these barons. After he and Philip Ludwell had lived together as bachelors for about six years, Richard Henry married (December, 1757) Miss Anne Aylett, the daughter of William Aylett and stepdaughter of Colonel James Steptoe of Homony Hall. She was a sister of the future wife of his brother Thomas Ludwell and a half-sister of Elizabeth Steptoe, who later became the wife of his brother, Philip Ludwell. Richard Henry's first wife died December 12, 1768, leaving four children.

A monument to her was put up by Richard Henry in Nomini Church. The inscription written by him ended as follows:

> Was there so precious a flower
> But given us to behold it waste,
> The short-lived blossom of an hour
> Too nice, too fair, too sweet to last.[28]

The responsibility of caring for four little children must have been a difficult one for Richard Henry, and some months after the death of the first Mrs. Lee he decided to marry again. Writing to brother William (May 18, 1769), he said: "I wrote you before, that it had pleased heaven to deprive me of my dearest Mrs. Lee. But she taught me to love above all things, the married state. I have endeavored therefore and soon hope to repair my loss in great measure, by carrying the good and lovely

Mrs. [Anne] Pinc/k/ard to Chantilly. In this, you see I consult not fortune, but the happiness and safety of my poor little Children as well as myself."[29]

He married again in June or July, 1769. His second wife was the widow of Thomas Pinckard and daughter of Colonel Thomas Gaskins, Sr. She had at least one child, a son, at the time of her remarriage. By this second marriage Lee had three daughters and two sons. This second union, as well as the first, was a happy one. Some months after his second marriage he spoke of his wife as being "a most tender, attentive and fond mother to my dear little girls."[30]

In his will Richard Henry made the following reference to his wives:

> I desire to be decently, privately, and frugally buried in the family burying ground at the burnt House [Mount Pleasant] as it is called, and as near to my late ever dear wife as 'tis possible to place mine without disturbing her remains, and upon her left, so that my present dear Mrs. Lee may be laid, when she dies, on my right; and so my body be placed between those of my dear wives.[31]

Richard Henry continued to live at Stratford for a few years after his first marriage. He then established a home of his own on an estate of about 500 acres on the Potomac, three miles below Stratford, and gave it the name "Chantilly." Before taking this step he had built a dwelling house and outbuildings and had established orchards and gardens on the plantation.[32]

Philip Ludwell Lee owned this plantation and Richard Henry lived there under lease to his brother and his heir to the end of his life. One naturally wonders why Richard Henry made his home on a leased estate when he had large land holdings in another county, Prince William, now Fauquier. The reason for so doing, it is said, was that Philip Ludwell was so attached to his younger brother that he insisted on his living near him.[33] Furthermore, the prospects for social enjoyment and political advancement were brighter in his old home county than they would be in "the remote frontier district" in which his own landed estate was located.

Francis Lightfoot and William, the fourth and fifth surviving sons, respectively, of Thomas Lee, were not sent away to school, but the good instruction received from the home tutors plus supplementary self-education apparently afforded them ample training. Francis Lightfoot inherited lands in Loudoun from his father's estate and made that county his home for some years. In April, 1769, he married Rebecca Tayloe and shortly thereafter they moved to Richmond County. They lived here in a home to which they gave the Indian name "Manokin".[34]

Like his brothers, Francis Lightfoot had an exceptionally successful career. Although he yearned for the quiet of private life, he devoted the greater part of his mature years to public affairs as a member of the House of Burgesses, two Virginia Revolutionary conventions, the Continental Congress, and the Virginia Senate.[35] He was one of the signers of the Westmoreland Association and of the Declaration of Independence. Dr. Benjamin Rush, who served in the Continental Congress with him, thought that Francis Lightfoot had "a more acute and correct mind" than his brother Richard Henry. He said: "I seldom knew him wrong eventually upon any question."[36] John Adams considered him "sensible and patriotic" and "a man of great reading well understood, of sound judgment and inflexible purpose in the cause of his country." According to Washington, Francis Lightfoot was regarded by the Lee family as the one who had the soundest judgment of all the six brothers. His niece, Nancy Shippen, considered him "the sweetest of the Lee race."[37]

The two youngest sons were William (born August, 1739) and Arthur (born December, 1740). Early in life William went to England and became a successful tobacco merchant trading with Virginia. For the management of his financial affairs in Virginia he leaned heavily on his brothers, Richard Henry and Francis Lightfoot.[38] Rising rapidly to prominence in the homeland, William was at one time one of the two sheriffs and later an alderman of London. These connections, however, did not lessen his interest in the American cause or weaken his opposition to British policy toward the colonies. Before leaving for England he signed the Westmoreland Association and later supported the Revolutionary movement at considerable financial sacrifice,[39] serving as the agent of Congress at Nantes, France, and undertaking abortive missions to the courts of Berlin and Vienna.[40]

In 1769 William Lee married Hannah Philippa Ludwell, daughter of his uncle Philip Ludwell III. Through this marriage he came into possession of "Greenspring." He returned to Virginia in 1783 and spent the last dozen years of his life at "Greenspring." During this period his eyesight was failing and he finally became totally blind.[41]

Arthur was abroad in school for some years after his father's death. He studied at Eton and then went to the University of Edinburgh, where he took courses in polite literature, science, and medicine. After graduating in medicine with high honors (1764), he practiced for two years in Williamsburg, Virginia. But since his chief interest was in law and public affairs, he later gave up the medical profession and took up the study of law in Lincoln's Inn and the Middle Temple. After a lengthy course of study he entered upon the practice of his new profession in London (1775).[42]

Arthur was probably the most brilliant of the Lee brothers. He was an able writer, and although he regarded England as the "Eden of the world and the land of liberty and independence,"[43] he used his pen in ardent support of American rights. He was for several years a member of the Virginia House of Delegates and was in attendance as a member of Congress for two and a half years. He was elected by Congress in July, 1785, to the Treasury Board and he served in this office until the end of the Confederation period.[44] But his main contribution to the Revolutionary cause was his service abroad as diplomatic agent of Congress.[45]

The Lee brothers were bound together by strong ties of affection. The correspondence that Richard Henry carried on with Arthur while Arthur was abroad shows exceptional warmth of feeling on both sides. The note of affection was especially strong in the letters that Arthur wrote to Richard Henry in the early period of Arthur's career as a medical student in Edinburgh. A feeling of nostalgia probably added fervor to this correspondence.[46] That there was also a deep mutual affection among Richard Henry, Francis Lightfoot, and Thomas Ludwell is evident from Richard Henry's general correspondence, though not many of his letters to them have been preserved. As the distance between their homes was not too great for the interchange of visits and they saw each other fairly often, their correspondence was probably of a very limited nature. The nearness of their homes doubtless also explains why no letters from Richard Henry to Philip Ludwell have come down to us.

So strong was this family tie that an attack on one of the brothers would usually bring them all into the fray. When Arthur and William were assailed in Congress on their records as representatives abroad, Richard Henry defended them with great bitterness.[47]

It may be, however, that Philip Ludwell was not included in this family solidarity. It is true that he did not sign the Westmoreland Association, for if he had done so he would probably have been expelled from the Council. Furthermore, he remained loyal to the home government until his death. But there is no sign in the correspondence of Richard Henry that Philip Ludwell's nonsupport of the Revolutionary cause had alienated the former's affection for his brother. This charitable attitude may have been due to the fact that Philip's death occurred (1775) before the Anglo-American quarrel had become an irrepressible conflict and when even leaders of the opposition to British policy were confessing loyalty to the homeland. At one time, however, there was some ill feeling between William and Philip Ludwell regarding the disposal of their father's estate.[48]

The documents of the period give little information regarding the Lee daughters. Hannah, the oldest of the three sisters, married Gawin Corbin, the scion of an old and wealthy family, who died leaving her a widow in her early thirties. From one of her letters to Richard Henry (1778) it would seem that, like her brothers, she did her own thinking and did not always accept ready-made conventional opinions. In this letter she protested against the taxing of widows since women did not have the right to vote. This, she contended, was taxation without representation.[49] She was probably the first Virginia woman to advocate women's suffrage.

Hannah also broke with the traditions of the Virginia patriciate in her religious affiliation. When she became a Baptist and refused to attend the services of the Anglican Church, the grand jury reported a presentment against her to the Westmoreland County Court (May 29, 1764).[50] What action, if any, the court took on this indictment could not be determined in the course of this study. It must have caused embarrassment, however, to brother Richard Henry, then president of the court, though it did not disturb their cordial social relations. Nor did her religious nonconformity and her unconventional opinions cause her to lose her place in the society of the Virginia gentry. Her home continued to be frequented by "throngs of the most congenial and enlightened society of the time."[51]

The youngest daughter, Alice, while staying in England at the home of her uncle, Philip Ludwell III, met and married William Shippen, Jr., a young man from Philadelphia who was a medical student in London. Young Shippen afterwards attained eminence as a surgeon in Philadelphia and a professor of surgery and anatomy in the Medical School of the College of Philadelphia, an affiliate of the University of Pennsylvania. He was one of the founders of this medical school, which opened in 1765 as the first medical college in British America. He had attended Princeton College and had become a fine classical scholar and a finished orator.[52] Richard Henry cherished a deep affection for his brother-in-law and stayed at his home when he was a member of the First Continental Congress and during a part or all of the time when he was attending his last session of the United States Senate. Dr. Shippen was also on friendly terms with Washington and John Adams, who were welcome visitors at the Shippen home. It was at the urgent request of Washington that Dr. Shippen became Director General of military hospitals in the Continental Army.[53]

Alice Lee Shippen seems to have been a lady of exceptional charm, and she made a favorable impression on her distinguished guests. Louis Guillaume Otto, an attaché of the French legation, spoke of her as "expressing upon all her features that heavenly mildness which is the characteristic of her Soul." John Adams regarded her as a "religious and reasoning lady."[54]

The last half of the eighteenth century was a notable era in the history of Virginia, for during this period she had an unusually large number of illustrious sons, among them the five Lee brothers, sons of Thomas Lee of Stratford. John Adams termed them ". . . intrepid and unchangeable, who, like the Greeks at Thermopylae, stood in the gap, in defense of their country, from the first glimmering of the Revolution in the horizon, through all its rising light, to the perfect day."[55]

13

Chapter II

A Promising Young Solon

The wealthy planters of colonial Virginia, especially those of the eighteenth century, seemed to feel that their position carried with it the duty to take the lead in securing for their fellow countrymen a wise and just political system. And few of the Virginia patriciate of that day were influenced more by a sense of *noblesse oblige* than was Richard Henry Lee.

Lee began his public career in his early twenties as a justice of the peace in Westmoreland County.[1] At that time the position of justice of the peace, one of dignity and responsibility, attracted the leading men of the county. Acting separately, the justices performed minor judicial functions similar to those performed by their successors of today. The whole group met once a month as a county court. At these joint sessions the more important cases, both civil and criminal, were tried. The county court also had many other duties, and was the main administrative and legislative authority of the county.[2]

Lee performed his duties with such diligence and success that some of his fellow justices in a petition to the governor requested that the rule of seniority be waived and that Lee be made president of the court. This may have been done, for some years later (by 1762) he was acting as presiding justice.[3]

In 1758 Francis Fauquier came to Virginia as lieutenant governor. He called for a new election of the House of Burgesses, and the new Assembly met on September 17, 1758, at the capital, Williamsburg. It was at this time that Richard Henry Lee became a member of the House of Burgesses, representing his home county of Westmoreland. He retained his membership in this body until it was superseded by the revolutionary House of Delegates (1776).

At that time the activity of the House of Burgesses was to a considerable extent under the control of the governor and had been for nearly a century (since 1662). He issued the calls for the election of Burgesses and could prorogue or dissolve the house and thereby determine the length of the terms of membership. By the use of his veto power he could prevent the passage of any measure which he might consider objectionable.[4]

The Virginians were strongly opposed to these restrictions on their legislative assembly. Richard Henry Lee was especially disturbed by them. In a long letter to brother Arthur (December 20, 1776) he pointed out the objections to these limitations, using in support of his position a lengthy quotation in the original French from Montesquieu. ". . . our Forefathers," Lee said, "in framing the Constitution of this Country, had in view the excellent pattern furnished by the Mother Country." "In Britain," he continued, "the three simple forms of Monarchy, Aristocracy, and Democracy, are so finely blended that the advantages resulting from each species separately, flow jointly from their admirable union." In Virginia "the legislative power is lodged in a Governor, Council, and House of Burgesses. The two first appointed by the crown, and their places held by the precarious tenure of pleasure only . . . and the just equilibrium totally destroyed by two parts out of three of the Legislature being in the same hands."[5]

Despite these restrictions, during the last twenty-five years of its existence the Virginia House of Burgesses was an effective body for legislation. The House was composed of two representatives from each county and one each from the four boroughs of Jamestown, Norfolk, Williamsburg, and the College. It was considered by its members as the Virginia counterpart of the British House of Commons. While the remuneration received by the Burgesses was small, the high honor of the position, along with other compensations, made it very attractive. The Burgess was free in his person, servants and estates (both real and personal), from all arrests, attachments and "all other processes whatsoever save for treason, felony, or breach of the peace." If an outsider should use "abusive and scandalous language" in speaking about a member he could be arraigned before the House and sent to jail if found guilty.[6]

At the time Lee was first elected as a Burgess, the right to vote was confined to freeholders owning one hundred acres of unimproved land or twenty-five acres with a house on it. Voting qualifications in Williamsburg and Norfolk were more liberal than they were in the counties. Voting was oral and usually lasted only one day. A non-freeholder attempting to vote was liable to a fine of five hundred pounds of tobacco, and a freeholder who was qualified to vote in a Burgess election and failed to do so was subject to a fine of two hundred pounds of tobacco.[7] Although the Burgesses were virtually all of the landed gentry, they were dependent upon the yeomanry for their election. To win the favor of voters, candidates had to be lavish in their expenditures for drinks and other campaign attractions.[8]

The educational level of the Burgesses was high for a popular assembly. Nearly half of them had attended institutions of college or university rank, including a few who had studied in universities in England and Scotland. Forty had been students at the College of William and Mary and ten had read law at the Inns of Court. Others who had not been to college had had good schooling at home. There were no political parties in the House.[9]

It was a group of exceptionally able men with whom Lee now found himself associated. In this his first session, he numbered among his colleagues George Mason, George Washington, and two of his brothers, Francis Lightfoot and Thomas Ludwell Lee. Another brother, Philip Ludwell Lee, was at the same time a member of the Council.[10]

Although the House of Burgesses wielded more influence in legislation than did the Council, a seat in the Council was a more coveted position. The Council acted as the governor's Cabinet and was the supreme court of the colony and the upper house of the Assembly. Councillors received a good salary (considerably more than the meager compensation allowed Burgesses) and were in a favored position for securing lucrative offices.[11]

So attractive was the position of Councillor that Richard Henry Lee preferred it to his seat in the House of Burgesses. In August, 1762, he wrote to two of his friends in England, asking them to use their influence in favor of his appointment to the Council, but the expected vacancy did not occur.[12] Some years later (July, 1770, and early in 1773) he again indicated a desire to be in the Council, because, he said, the opportunity for doing good was better there than in the lower house; but in each of these later attempts he failed to receive the coveted honor, although brother William supported one, and probably both, of

16

them. William not only exerted his influence in British governmental circles but supplemented his efforts with a promise of money to an influential lady, apparently to win her support.[13]

When the tall Burgess from Westmoreland County arrived at Williamsburg (September, 1758) to take his seat in the House, the little capital of slightly more than three hundred houses was entering upon its golden age. It was the political and social center of the Old Dominion. When Lee walked up Duke of Gloucester, the broad and level main street, from the Capitol[14] to the College of William and Mary, seven eighths of a mile, he passed on the right Raleigh Tavern, already a noted center of social activity, where Jefferson was to dance with Miss Burwell, his "fair Belinda." It was also soon to become the meeting place for Revolutionary leaders and to contest with Faneuil Hall for the title of "Cradle of Liberty." He next saw, on the left, the powder magazine (known as the "Powder Horn"), which was destined to play an important part in the controversy with the mother country. Going on he came to the Palace Green, with the governor's palace in the background; and just beyond he saw Bruton Parish Church, the place of worship for many of Virginia's noted leaders.[15] He also saw several private homes which were soon to become of historic interest by their association with the Revolution. One of these private mansions was Ludwell House, formerly his grandfather's town house, at that time owned by his uncle, Philip Ludwell III.

Richard Henry was active in this first session of the Assembly and continued to take a prominent part in its work as long as he was in attendance, serving on numerous special committees and on several important permanent committees.[16]

His first speech, so far as we can ascertain, was on the motion to levy a heavy duty on slaves brought into Virginia. In November, 1759, two acts were passed by the House, one of which amended the several acts laying a duty on slaves imported into the province from Africa, and the other imposing a duty on slaves from Maryland, Carolina, and the West Indies. Lee was first-named on the committees that drafted one or both of these bills and was delegated in both cases to carry the bills up to the Council after they had been passed by the Burgesses.

The House journal gives no hint as to the nature of the discussion over this important issue. From other sources, however, we learn that the "new men"—those who had few or no slaves—opposed the increase in duty on slaves as it would put the price of slaves beyond their reach and greatly increase the value of those already owned by the big planters.[17] It may be, therefore, that Governor Fauquier was right in thinking that some of the latter group were influenced in their opposition to the further importation of slaves as much by self-interest as by humanitarian considerations.

In his speech on this occasion, Lee argued as follows: The importation of slaves into Virginia "has been, and will be attended with effects, dangerous both to our political and moral interests." Some of the neighboring colonies, though settled much later than Virginia, had outstripped her in improvement. "The reason for [this unhappy truth] seems to be this: that with their whites they import arts and agriculture, whilst we, with our blacks exclude both. Nature has not partially favored them with superiour fertility of soil, nor do they enjoy more of the sun's cheering and enlivening influence; yet greatly have they outstript us."

Furthermore, he continued, the slave was a dangerous security risk. Owing to the injustice to which he was subjected he could never be a loyal member of the society to which he was attached. Slaves therefore "must be natural enemies of society, and their increase consequently dangerous." It was this danger that hung over ancient Greece and Rome, and some of their greatest convulsions "were occasioned by the insurrections of their slaves." He ended his speech as follows:

> Nor, sir, are these the only reasons to be urged against the importation. In my opinion, not the cruelties practised in the conquest of Spanish America, not the savage barbarity of a Saracen, can be more big with atrocity, than our cruel trade to Africa. There we encourage those poor, ignorant people, to wage eternal war against each other; not nation against nation, but father against son, children against parents, and brothers against brothers, whereby parental, filial, and fraternal duty is terribly violated; that by war, stealth, or surprise, we Christians may be furnished with our fellow-creatures, who are no longer to be considered as created in the image of God as well as ourselves, and equally entitled to liberty and freedom by the great law of nature, but they are to be deprived, for ever de-

18

prived, of all the comforts of life, and to be made the most wretched of the human kind. I have seen it observed by a great writer, that Christianity, by introducing into Europe the truest principle of humanity, universal benevolence, and brotherly love, had happily abolished civil slavery. Let us, who profess the same religion, practice its precepts; and by agreeing to this duty, convince the world that we know and practice our true interests, and that we pay a proper regard to the dictates of justice and humanity![18]

This speech was not merely an argument against the slave trade but was also a vigorous attack on the whole institution of slavery. When he implied that Negroes as well as whites were "entitled to liberty and freedom by the great law of nature," Lee appeared in the role of a crusader for human rights. These sentiments were far in advance of those held by most of Lee's Virginia contemporaries and were to some extent followed up by gestures toward practical action. As business representative of William Lee, Richard Henry at a later date made suggestions as to the management of the former's estate in Virginia. In one of his letters to his brother (June 25, 1778) he suggested that it was a good time for William to sell his James River plantation, the one objection, he said, being the humanitarian reason for not selling slaves.[19] He was a member of the committee that framed the Ordinance of 1787, which provided a form of government for the Northwest Territory and apparently did not oppose the clause in the Ordinance prohibiting slavery in the territory.[20] Although he saw much in the new Constitution to condemn, he was careful to state his approval of the clause allowing Congress to prohibit the importation of slaves after January 1, 1801.[21]

Except for his legislative activities and expressions of views, Lee did not in actual practice go beyond the standard of his day in his attitude toward slavery. In 1782 he owned forty-three slaves and later thirty-seven over the age of twelve, all of whom he left in his will to his heirs.[22] Furthermore, a statement in one of his letters shows that at one time he considered going into the business of selling slaves for his brother William and was kept from doing so by the latter's unwillingness to offer satisfactory terms or his inability to produce the slaves. This statement, part of a postscript to a letter written by him to William on July 12, 1772, was as follows: "I have just seen yours to the Squire about Negro consignments. . . . As the planters are nearly out of debt and Negroes have become valuable here, I should be extremely glad to be employed on reasonable terms, but those you mentioned are really too hard."[23]

A few months before Richard Henry offered to sell slaves for William, he had taken part in an action of the Virginia Assembly wholly out of keeping with what one would expect of a would-be slave dealer. The King issued an instruction (December 10, 1770) to the governor of Virginia, commanding him "upon pain of the highest displeasure to assent to no laws by which the importation of slaves should be in any respect prohibited or obstructed."[24] The House of Burgesses had passed in November, 1769, an act levying a fifteen per cent duty on all slaves brought into the colony[25] and naturally took steps to have this instruction changed. On April 1, 1772, it voted an address to the King, prepared by a committee of which Lee was a member. In this address the Burgesses implored the King "to remove all Restraints on his Governors from passing Acts of Assembly, which are intended to check this pernicious Commerce [the importation of slaves]."[26]

When Arthur and William learned of the action of the Virginia Assembly in voting this address to the King, they thought that Richard Henry had had a leading part in the passage of the measure. Arthur thereupon wrote to his older brother advising and censuring him in the following terms:

> I was exceedingly surprised the other day to be told that your assembly had last session sent a petition to the king concerning the slave trade. I could not believe it, till I saw the petition itself, and my surprise was still greater, when from the style of it I conceived it to be your production.
>
> As to your being forward in opposing the importation of Negroes, it should be conducted in your situation with great wariness. You are at once an object of envy and hatred to some. Our brother here [William] is endeavoring to get you some Negro consignments, and should he succeed it will certainly wear an awkward appearance, that a strenuous opposer of this trade should be an agent in it. You will consider this circumstance and act accordingly.[27]

20

William also rebuked his brother for his inconsistency. In writing to him (February, 1773) he asked how he (William) could do anything toward procuring Negro consignments for him when he (Richard Henry) had just sent to the King a petition from the House of Burgesses against the importation of slaves.[28]

Apparently Richard Henry's younger brothers were wrong in thinking that he had taken a leading part in the action of the Assembly against the slave trade. In defense of his position Richard Henry in a letter to William (May, 1773) made the following statement: "I was in no way concerned in the assembly business about addressing the king concerning the nonimportation of slaves.* You know in general I have always thought the Trade bad; but since it will be carried on, I do not see how I could in justice to my family refuse any advantage that might arise from the selling of them."[29] Whether William regarded his reply as a satisfactory explanation of or a rationalizing effort to justify the inconsistency between profession and practice cannot be determined. At any rate, there is no evidence to indicate that Richard Henry ever acted as his brother's agent in the sale of slaves.

As a member of the House of Burgesses Lee usually advocated a policy of liberalism. In the session that convened in the fall of 1762 he was chairman of a committee that brought in a bill for revising the law for voter qualifications in Burgess elections. The proposals of the committee, after having been amended in committee of the whole, were adopted by the House. They lowered the property qualifications for voting and made compulsory the exercise of the voting franchise.[30]

In this same session he also made a report favoring a bill for the relief of insolvent debtors. The measure, as finally passed, was similar to a modern bankruptcy act. Debtors, by complying with its provisions, could be relieved from imprisonment for debt. The bill was passed in December. The British merchants were already having trouble collecting the debts due them by Virginia creditors and this measure would have increased their difficulty. So they brought pressure on the Board of Trade,

*The fact that he was a member of the committee would seem to indicate that he was to a considerable extent involved in the action of the Assembly.

21

which led to a recommendation of repeal by the governor. In obedience to this recommendation the House voted a repeal of the act (May 24, 1763).[31]

In response to the call of Lieutenant Governor Fauquier, the Assembly met in January, 1764, this time mainly to consider the request of General Amherst that Virginia raise a force of 500 men in defense of her frontier against the Indians. The House of Burgesses refused to accept this proposal and appointed a committee consisting of Peyton Randolph, Richard Bland, Edmund Pendleton, and Richard Henry Lee to prepare "an humbel Address" to the governor explaining why it could not comply with this request. In its report the committee stated that the House could make no appropriation without issuing more paper money and that would be objectionable to the British merchants. Under such circumstances, Virginia would have to rely upon the militia for the protection of the frontier. Lee seems to have been greatly pleased with this action of the Assembly. In a letter written the day after the Burgesses had given the request a negative vote, he spoke of "our glorious resolution" of yesterday to defend ourselves with militia and "have no further concern with Regulars."[32]

In 1764 British merchants trading in Virginia appealed to the Board of Trade in England to take steps that would lead to the payment of their sterling debts in sterling money. Acting on an instruction of the Board to this effect, Lieutenant Governor Fauquier presented the proposal to the Assembly (October 30, 1764). To the serious disappointment of the lieutenant governor, the Burgesses voted down the suggestion and gave their reasons for so doing in a report which had been put into final form by a committee of which Edmund Pendleton was chairman and Richard Henry Lee a member. In this report the Burgesses stated (November 9, 1764) that they had given "great attention" to the complaint of the British merchants to the Board of Trade relative to their currency, and that they had revised the laws relating to paper money and the rate of exchange. This method of payment, they felt, was fair to the merchants and better than payment in specie, which would entail transportation costs; besides, they had no specie. In his reply to this report the governor expressed dissatisfaction with this action of the House and indicated that the Board of Trade would not be satisfied with the excuses offered and that serious consequences might result from this noncompliance with its wish and expectations.[33]

When Lee became a member of the House of Burgesses, John Robinson was the Speaker, which position he held for approximately twenty-eight years. He had a reputation for sound political knowledge, was adept in parliamentary procedure, and presided over the House with great dignity. Under Robinson's chairmanship, according to Edmund Randolph, one of his younger contemporaries, "the decorum of the house [of Burgesses] outshone that of the House of Commons." In acting as chairman of the Assembly he coupled a kindliness of manner with dignity and fairness and thus held the affection as well as the respect of the members. Fauquier in reporting his death to the British authorities spoke of him as "the darling of the Country" and deservedly "for his great integrity, assiduity and ability in business."[34]

Owing to the heavy indebtedness caused by the French and Indian War, Virginia issued a great deal of paper money in the form of treasury notes. Taxes were levied to provide a fund for their redemption. At that time the Speaker of the House was also Treasurer of the Province. It was, therefore, the duty of Robinson to burn the war notes as they came into the Treasury for redemption. If Robinson had destroyed this paper currency, as the law required, he would have left the colony without an adequate supply of money. Furthermore, he would have missed an opportunity to extend much needed financial aid to his fellow Virginians. Nearly all the planters were in debt and many of them—including some of the largest landholders—were threatened with bankruptcy and imprisonment for debt. There had been two bad seasons in succession (1757-1758) for tobacco, their only money crop. To the suffering from hard times was added the burden of heavy taxation brought on by the French and Indian War.

So Robinson disregarded the law and put the paper money back into circulation by lending it to those who were in sore financial difficulties. Apparently this illegal action was prompted by goodness of heart and not by the desire to mend his political fences, advance his financial interests, or strengthen his personal popularity. He probably thought that the hard times

23

through which the colony was then passing would soon give way to prosperity and these loans could be repaid. Or if the worse came to the worst, he probably believed that he could make good from his own substantial estate the shortages of those debtors who could not meet their obligations. Among the debtors thus favored were a number of the leading planters in Virginia.[35]

That the Treasurer had taken such liberties with the colony's money was not definitely known until after his death; but in the last year of his life a suspicion had arisen in the minds of some of the leading Burgesses, among them Richard Henry Lee, that irregularities existed in the handling of public funds. This suspicion was aroused by the large amount of paper money that remained in circulation. Robinson had so long been elevated above criticism that to question his integrity or to accuse him of mismanagement would almost be considered *lese majesty*. And yet Richard Henry Lee took the lead in calling for an investigation of Robinson's accounts. His proposal must have fallen like a bombshell into the dignified Assembly. According to a tradition handed down by his grandson, "the Speaker fixt his eyes with a dark and terrible frown upon Mr. Lee. The members opposed to his motion turned their faces from him with haughty and disdainful airs, but these things had no other effect than to animate Mr. Lee to strains of indignant eloquence." The motion, ardently supported by Patrick Henry, was finally adopted although it was opposed by some of the most able and influential members of the House.[36] Robinson probably could have sidetracked this investigation by clever parliamentary practice, but instead of so doing "he met the charge with an air of magnanimity and defense."[37]

A committee was appointed by the House of Burgesses (May, 1763) to investigate the redemption of paper currency. This committee consisted of Richard Bland, Richard Henry Lee, and Benjamin Harrison. The committee made a prompt report in which there was no charge of irregularities.[38] On December 19, 1764, Richard Henry Lee made a motion providing for another committee to investigate the Treasurer's accounts. This motion was carried, despite the opposition of Robinson's friends, and a committee of eight members was appointed, with Edmund Pendleton as chairman and Lee a member. The committee did not make its report until the next session, at a time (May 29, 1765) when Lee was not in attendance. According to this report there had been no irregularities in the office and there was a substantial balance of funds in the Treasurer's hands. Pendleton and two other members of this committee were accused of whitewashing their friend Robinson.[39] However, as there is no proof of this charge, the failure to uncover the shortage in the Treasurer's accounts was probably due to the perfunctory examination made by the committee.

A few months after Robinson's death (May, 1766), a third committee was appointed to examine the Treasurer's accounts. The membership of this committee of eleven included both Richard Henry and Francis Lightfoot Lee, as well as Patrick Henry. The report of the committee showed that the Treasurer's account was more than £100,000 short, due to loans made to various persons.[40]

The death of John Robinson left vacant both the Treasurership of the province and the Speakership of the House of Burgesses. At that time the Speakership was a position of honor only, and no salary went with it. As a compensation for this unrewarded service, the Speakership was coupled with the lucrative office of Treasurer of the Colony. This latter office was held by Robinson during the entire period of his Speakership. When the House first met after the death of Robinson, it proceeded to the election of a Speaker. Archibald Cary presented the name of Peyton Randolph for the place, and Lee nominated Richard Bland. Randolph was elected.

The House then considered a motion offered by Lee for separating the Speakership from the Treasurership. Edmund Pendleton led the fight for continuing the old plan and Patrick Henry supported Lee's proposal. After considerable discussion in committee of the whole, the House passed the resolution (November 12) for the separation of the two offices. This action was acceptable to the Board of Trade, which had previously indicated the wish that the two places might be filled with different officials. To compensate the Speaker for the loss of income derived from the Treasurership, a salary of £500 a year was attached to the Speakership.[41]

In his speech in favor of the motion, Lee gave his views as to the principles on which government should be based. He started

25

out with a reference to Solon and then followed with a modest apology:

> Very insensible indeed should I be, did I not fully feel, how rash it may seem in a young Man to find fault with any part of the Constitution of his Country; . . . But I hope Sir that the sentiments which I shall deliver on this occasion will not be measured by the age of him who gives them, but that they will be determined by Reason and Experience, those two Sovereign Directors, to which the old as well as young, should pay obedience.

This introduction was followed by a discussion of abstract principles in substance as follows: "Government was originally instituted for the greater happiness and benefit of Mankind," and those lawgivers who have adhered most closely to first principles "have so wisely tempered restraint with Liberty as to leave Mankind in full possession of every power to do good while the privilege of doing wrong was only taken from them." This is "that glorious Liberty which nations in all ages have so warmly contended for" and which the best leadership has always "studied to secure on the most sure and lasting foundations." To safeguard this precious liberty we should give heed to this maxim: "That the powers of government and those Posts or Places by which these powers are executed should be so divided among different Individuals as to prevent the acquisition of too great influence, too much power in the hands of one man." For owing to the corruption of human nature, in the past "those who have possessed the power have seldom wanted the inclination to destroy the Liberties of Mankind and to erect their own greatness on the ruin of their Fellow-creatures." He then pointed to the experiences of ancient Athens, Sparta, and Rome, and the modern states of Holland and England as confirmatory of the soundness of this principle.

He concluded his argument as follows:

> If then, wise and good men in all ages have deemed it necessary for the security of liberty to divide places of power and profit, if this maxim has not been departed from without either injury or destroying freedom, as happened to Rome with her Decemvirs and her

Dictator, why should Virginia so early quit the path of wisdom and seal her own ruin so far as she can do it, by uniting in one person the only two great places in the power of her Assembly to bestow?[42]

To what extent this oration influenced Lee's colleagues we cannot say with certainty. The passing of the motion by a vote of 68 to 29 suggests, however, that Lee's eloquence was not in vain.[43]

In taking his stand against a popular idol and in fighting for the separation of the Speakership from the Treasurership, Lee was probably acting from a sense of duty. Instead of this high motive, however, his enemies attributed to him the low one of selfish ambition—the wish to be Speaker. Governor Fauquier seems also to have held this opinion, for in a report to the Board of Trade he stated that Lee wanted to be in the chair and thought that "his opposing Government a likely means to seat himself in it."[44] But Lee was not a candidate for the honor when a new Speaker was chosen.

During this his first septennate in the House of Burgesses, Lee won his spurs as a legislator, both as a hard-working committee member and as a polished speaker who often leaned toward idealism. Even at this early period in his public career he had the courage to take a bold stand against imperial policies which he considered unfair to Virginia. But his greatest display of courage came with the attempt to secure honesty in the financial administration of the colony, and this worthy effort cost him the favorable opinion of some influential leaders. His action in the Robinson affair led to his first clash with the planter aristocracy, as he sacrificed class feeling to public policy. It was a preview of the part he later played in the initial stages of the controversy with the homeland when he, in cooperation with such radicals as Patrick Henry and Thomas Jefferson, ran ahead of his aristocratic associates in opposition to British rule.

Chapter III

Radical Conservatism

Richard Henry Lee, like his well-to-do neighbors, was interested in securing large land grants in the West. In pursuit of this aim he and three of his brothers, Thomas Ludwell, Francis Lightfoot, and William, and George Washington and two of his brothers, along with other stockholders of the Ohio Company, took a prominent part in the organization of The Mississippi Company of Virginia (June, 1763). This company asked for a grant of two and a half million acres of land west of the Allegheny Mountains, 50,000 acres for each of fifty stockholders.

Although Arthur Lee, acting as its agent, pressed the claim of the company in England, he was never able to obtain the grant. The area requested in the first petition was located north and south of the Ohio river at its junction with the Mississippi. Later (1768) the company substituted for the original petition a request for the same amount of land farther east but still west of the Allegheny Mountains. The friction that developed between the British and colonial authorities caused by the approach of the Revolution was unfavorable to land grants in the colonies, and the petition of the Mississippi Company of Virginia, as well as the requests of other later companies, was never granted. Richard Henry Lee, however, was still hopeful as to the successful outcome of the petition of his company as late as April, 1774.[1]

The part played by Lee in the Robinson investigation was his last important activity in the House of Burgesses concerned solely with the provincial affairs of Virginia. Although he was to remain a member of this body for nearly a decade longer, during that time his public service as a Burgess was devoted mainly to steering the colony in its opposition to British policy. Indeed, he had entered upon this type of activity in the House before the report had been made on the last investigation into the affairs of the Treasury.

An early opportunity to express his views on colonial rights was afforded by the Parson's Cause. In 1758 there was a bad season throughout the greater portion of Virginia, and the crop of tobacco was short and its price unusually high. If taxes, fees, and salaries were paid in tobacco at the old rating, salaried officials would gain at the expense of the planters. To remedy this situation the Assembly in 1758 passed for the second time a Two-Penny Act, permitting the payment of taxes, fees, and debts contracted while the act was in effect (with certain exceptions) in money at the rate of two pence for every pound of tobacco that was due. The act was to be in effect for one year only. This evaluation of tobacco was less than one half of the current market price.[2]

The ministers of the established (Anglican) church contended that this act worked a severe hardship on them for it allowed the vestries to pay their salaries at a greatly reduced rate. They therefore brought their grievances to the notice of the Privy Council and that body had the law vetoed by the King in council.[3] In the meantime the Virginia vestries had assumed that the law was valid and had been making payments according to its provisions. The clergy, however, contended that the veto of the King had made the act void from the beginning. Accordingly, some of them brought suit against their vestries for arrears in salary. The most noted of these suits was the one brought by the Reverend James Maury, November, 1763, in the Hanover County Court for back pay against the collectors of his vestry. It was in this case that Patrick Henry made his first great oration. The court decided against the legality of the act; but the jury, acting under the spell of Henry's eloquence, gave the plaintiff only one penny in damage.[4]

Richard Henry Lee, not being a lawyer, did not take part in any of the parsons' suits, but he did prepare a paper in defense of the act of 1758, in which he argued in part as follows: The fact that the governor's assent was contrary to his Majesty's instructions did not invalidate the act, which he had previously signed. The governor could dispense with his instructions in "extraordinary emergencies," the propriety of which he might be called on to explain. The people considered the governor's assent as "virtually that of the Crown, and by his assent the law is in force till his majesty's disapprobation arrives and is rati-

29

fied, consequently everything done in the colony then conformably thereto is legal." The usual practice, he continued, had been for the veto of a measure by order of the Privy Council not to be retroactive.[5]

Lee's action on the Two-Penny Act was a step toward a more vigorous fight which he was soon to begin in favor of American rights. The occasion for his assuming this role was an innovation in British imperial policy, introduced after the close of the French and Indian War. The Treaty of Paris (1763) which ended the Seven Years War, including the French and Indian War, proved to be an important turning point in the relations between Great Britain and her colonies. The war had left England mistress of the seas and the possessor of a worldwide empire. It also had doubled her national debt and increased the tax burdens of her people. There was a rapid growth in industry in the mother country and the British manufacturers were now more anxious than ever to enjoy the exclusive right to buy raw materials and to sell finished products in the colonies. It was thought that the new conditions called for a new policy of imperial administration, which could link the various parts of the empire more closely. The commercial and industrial regulations were to be enforced more effectively and the colonies were to be called on to share the burdens of imperial taxation. This meant for America an abandonment of the policy of "salutary neglect." In short, the mother country was attempting to assume an authority over the colonies in their adulthood which she had not maintained in their childhood.

Such an experiment would have been hazardous even if times had not changed. But recent events had caused the colonies to desire a looser rather than a closer identification with the empire. The war with the French and victory over the western Indians had freed the Americans from the French menace and had to a great extent relieved them of the danger of Indian attack. They therefore no longer felt the need of British protection so strongly as they had done before the treaties of peace had been signed. During the war they had also incurred new financial obligations and they felt little inclined to add to these burdens by accepting imperial taxation.[6]

The British authorities, apparently unaware of this strong feeling on the part of the colonials, decided to leave in America seventy-five hundred British soldiers—a great increase over the pre-war strength—to protect the people against the Indians, to keep the French in Canada quiet, and in general to safeguard the interests of the empire. A secondary consideration was that the presence of regular troops in the possessions would strengthen the hand of the royal governors and aid in the enforcement of the laws against smuggling. The British Ministry decided that the Americans should bear a portion of the cost of maintaining this army.[7] The colonials had not asked for these soldiers and did not want them, especially if they were to be taxed for their support. There were no American commissioned officers in this military force and few of the soldiers were trained in Indian fighting. The British troops were therefore not suited to protect the colonials against Indian attack. In the opinion of Cortlandt Skinner, Attorney General of New Jersey, the presence of these troops instead of quieting the Indians would have the opposite effect. John Dickinson thought that the formidable force established in the midst of peace "was to bleed her [America] into obedience."[8]

It is more than likely, however, that the main reason for increasing the size of the British army in America was that in the opinion of the King and Ministry an adequate defense of the empire called for an increase in the army. But the British people were opposed to such an addition to the military home force. There would, however, probably be no serious opposition to the plan if these additional troops were to be stationed in the colonies with the extra expense borne by the colonial taxpayers. Such troops, available for service anywhere in the empire, would be available for use in any future wars with France or Spain.[9]

In pursuance of this new policy, the House of Commons in committee of the whole (March 17, 1764), passed a resolution proposed by George Grenville, the Prime Minister, indicating its intention to enact a law providing for the collection of stamp duties in America, but deferred final action until the next session of Parliament.[10] It was announced that the revenue accruing from the stamp duty would be used toward the partial support of the troops stationed in the American colonies. Coupled with the resolution was the promise that if the Americans would

31

devise some other means of raising revenue, the British government would accord the plan due consideration.[11]

It was this declaratory resolution that aroused the Virginians to their first serious opposition to British colonial policy.[12] Lee at once took a strong stand against the proposal. In a letter to a gentleman in London (May, 1764), he argued ably and at length against the right of the British Parliament to tax the colonies, contending that the original settlers brought with them to America all the rights guaranteed to Englishmen by their constitution, and that these rights had passed down to their descendants. He held that "the right to be governed by laws made by our representatives, and the illegality of taxation without consent" were among the firmly established principles of the British constitution. He ended his letter as follows: "My mind has been warmed, and I hardly know where to stop."[13]

Soon after the Virginia Assembly met (October 30, 1764), the House of Burgesses took under consideration the British declaratory resolution and after considerable discussion voted (November 14) to appoint a committee of eight to draft an address to the King, a memorial to the House of Lords, and a memorial to the House of Commons. Prominent members of this committee were Lee, Peyton Randolph, Edmund Pendleton, George Wythe, and Landon Carter. On November 30, the report of the committee was presented, and after more than two weeks of debate, the address and memorials, with some modifying amendments, were adopted by both the House and the Council.[14] Lee was largely responsible for this important step taken by the Virginia Assembly. He probably offered the motion for an address to the King and memorials to the Lords and Commons[15] and doubtless wrote the Address to the King and the Memorial to the Lords.[16]

In the Address to the King and the Memorial to the Lords and Commons, the Burgesses declared their "firm and inviolable attachment" to the "sacred person and Government" of the King. They took the position, however, that it is a fundamental principle of the British constitution "that the people are not subject to any taxes but such as are laid on them by their consent, or by those who are legally appointed to represent them." The colonials on coming to America brought with them these rights. Furthermore, the right of self-taxation was confirmed by royal charter and established by practice. Even if it were proper for Parliament to impose taxes on the colonies, the exercise of this power at this time would ruin Virginia and injure Britain by curtailing colonial trade. As a result of the war Virginia had contracted a debt of nearly half a million pounds and was still at great expense protecting the frontier. Owing to the tax burden they were already carrying, along with the lack of specie and the instability of the tobacco market, the Virginians were already in straitened financial circumstances. The proposed tax would add to these burdens and greatly reduce their ability to purchase British products, causing the substitution for them of goods produced at home.[17]

Since no plan for raising revenue in America was suggested by the colonial authorities, Grenville went ahead and had Parliament vote on the Stamp Act. The bill, approved by the House of Commons in February and by the House of Lords in March, 1765, received royal assent on March 22. William Pitt was opposed to the measure, but was absent on account of illness when the vote was taken. Although Isaac Barré made a strong speech against the bill and a few others opposed it, the House voted five to one in favor of the tax.[18] The passage of the bill aroused little interest in England. It was in fact extending to America a policy already in effect in the homeland, for Britain had a stamp tax very similar to this one.[19]

The Stamp Act was to go into effect on November 1, 1765. It provided that a stamp duty be levied on a long list of articles and transactions. The articles to be taxed included certificates or diplomas issued by academies, colleges or universities; dice and playing cards; pamphlets, almanacs, calendars and newspapers; bills of lading; such legal instruments as liquor licenses and licenses and franchises granted by the governor or other public officers; probates of wills and letters of administration and guardianship; and bonds, warrants for land surveys, land conveyances and appointments to office. The money collected from the sale of these stamps was to be paid into his Majesty's treasury and used by Parliament from time to time "for the purpose of defraying the expenses necessary for the defense, protection, and security of the said colonies and plantations."[20]

By passing this tax measure, the British government had unconsciously created an issue of supreme importance between

33

Great Britain and her dependencies. The colonials were insisting that the power to impose internal taxes upon them resided not in Parliament but only in their colonial assemblies and that this principle had been generally recognized prior to that time. The British ministry, on the other hand, contended that Parliament had the right to tax British subjects in the colonies as well as in the homeland. The claim was also made that by a sort of legal fiction the colonies enjoyed "virtual representation." Nor had the British government forfeited this right of taxation by its failure to exercise it in the past. This idea was thus expressed by Dr. Samuel Johnson: "We do not put a calf into the plough; we wait until it is an ox."[21]

Although the colonial leaders had strongly protested Grenville's proposal for taxing America, the passage of the Stamp Act did not at first arouse a great storm of opposition. An attitude of reluctant acquiescence seemed to prevail. So wise an observer as Benjamin Franklin believed that his fellow countrymen would accept the measure and swallow it as a bitter pill. While under this impression he even went so far as to recommend a friend for the appointment as stamp agent for Pennsylvania.[22] Even Richard Henry Lee, much to his subsequent regret, at one time asked his friends in England to use their influence toward securing for him an appointment as stamp agent.[23]

From this attitude of hesitation and acquiescence the colonies were aroused by the stirring oratory of Patrick Henry and the resultant action of the Virginia House of Burgesses. When the question arose in the House as to what action should be taken on the Stamp Act, Henry, a new member, at once offered some very radical resolutions against it. These resolutions were considered too extreme by the patrician conservatives in the Assembly—even by some who afterwards became leaders in the patriot cause—and a violent debate ensued.[24] According to Thomas Jefferson, the opponents of the resolutions held that the same sentiments had been expressed in more conciliatory form in the resolutions adopted at a previous session—those that had been written by Lee and Landon Carter—and an answer to them had not yet been received. Richard Henry considered it an absurdity to accord credit to Patrick Henry for giving the first breath to liberty in America since he was not at the meeting of the Assembly that took this important step. As reported by Carter, Lee said: "*Haec ego primus tentavi tulit alter honores*" ["I was the first to try this, but another received the honors"]. Henry supported his resolutions by a bold and eloquent oration which, in the opinion of his conservative opponents, sounded a note of treason.

Henry's eloquence, together with the sound reasoning of an able colleague, prevailed over the opposition to the extent of securing the passage of five of his resolutions (May 30, 1765). One of the resolutions adopted declared that the General Assembly of Virginia had the sole power to tax the inhabitants of the colony "and that every Attempt to vest such Power in any [other] Person or Persons . . . has a manifest tendency to destroy British as well as American Freedom".[25]

Patrick Henry's resolutions, published in newspapers and scattered abroad, had a great influence in stirring up opposition to the Stamp Act throughout the colonies. This opposition found expression in town meetings, discussion in newspapers and pamphlets, and in various other ways. In several colonies merchants entered into agreements not to buy any more goods from Great Britain and the West Indies, except a few specifically exempted articles, until the Stamp Act was repealed. Opposition groups known as "Sons of Liberty" were organized in the seaport towns of all the continental colonies.[26]

Richard Henry Lee did not attend this session of the Assembly. Why he did not meet his responsibility as a Burgess we do not know. He may have thought that during this short session nothing would be before the Assembly important enough to justify the trip from Westmoreland County to Williamsburg. Certainly it was not due to a feeling of unconcern toward the Stamp Act, for Lee soon became as radical as Henry in opposition to this measure.[27]

Under the provisions of the Stamp Act, stamps were required for use in all civil cases in the colonial courts. The local courts, therefore, had only the alternatives of not handling civil cases, keeping open without stamps in defiance of the Stamp Act, or accepting its objectionable terms by using stamps. Rhode Island was the only colony in which all the courts were kept open. In Virginia and other colonies, some of the county courts were opened in defiance of the Stamp Act, but most of the local courts were closed to civil actions until the act was repealed. Westmoreland County Court, over which Richard Henry Lee presided, was promptly closed with the resignation of all the justices.[28]

Some of the radical leaders, feeling that the closure of the courts was a passive acceptance of the Stamp Act, favored the opening of the courts without the use of stamps as a bold protest against the unjust measure. Others felt that with the courts closed and the consequent suspension of debt collection, British merchants and manufacturers would be threatened with serious loss and would bring pressure on Parliament to repeal the Stamp Act. This argument was especially appealing to Virginians, owing to the high indebtedness of the planters to British creditors. Richard Henry Lee gave it as the main reason for his advocacy of the "shutting" of the courts.[29]

About the time that Lee in the House of Burgesses was engaged in a strenuous fight against the declaratory resolution, he showed a willingness to act as agent for the sale of stamps. According to his own account, given in an article in the *Virginia Gazette* (August 8, 1766), early in November, 1764, he was informed by a gentleman of the intention of Parliament to lay a stamp duty in America. This informant made a friendly proposal to use his influence in procuring for Lee the office of collector.[30] Having not fully reflected on the nature of the proposed law, Lee considered the collectorship only in the light of a beneficial employment. He therefore accepted the offer of his friend, who wrote a letter in the interest of Lee's candidacy. Lee also wrote a letter to the same purpose.

A few days later, after having given more thought to the nature of his application, Lee decided that he had acted unwisely, since he now considered it improper for any American to be concerned in such an affair. He then decided to "exert every faculty I possessed both in public and private life, to prevent the success of a measure I now discovered to be in the highest degree pernicious to my Country." He referred to his support in the House of Burgesses of the Address to the King, the Memorial to the Lords, and the Remonstrance to the House of Commons, implying that he had an important part in preparing these documents. This latter action, he said, took place "long, very long" before his application could possibly have reached England and before the Stamp Act was passed.[31]

Lee's temporary interest in the stamp agency did not lessen his objection to the Stamp Act, which was bitter and on occasion led to extralegal action. One victim of his zeal was George Mercer, who had accepted the appointment of stamp agent for Virginia. Mercer had fought in the French and Indian War with a fine record which had won him the rank of lieutenant colonel. After the war he went to England and at the time of the passage of the Stamp Act was acting as the agent of the Ohio Company and the Mississippi Company of Virginia in their efforts to obtain large grants of land in the West. Since the Lee family, including Richard Henry, was interested in these companies as stockholders, one would expect that Richard Henry would have had a charitable attitude toward any mistakes that Mercer might make, especially since Lee himself had taken a misstep in the same direction.

Lee's objection to the Stamp Act was so strong, however, that it overrode such considerations. He gave vent to his opposition by acting as leader in his home county of Westmoreland in a dramatic performance expressing bitter disapproval of Mercer as stamp agent. This exhibition took place at Montross, the county seat, on a court day in September, 1765, before a large crowd assembled from all parts of the county. According to an eyewitness, a procession, made up largely of Negroes and the "ragtag and bobtail," marched down the street led by two of Lee's slaves armed with long clubs and dressed in the livery of John Wilkes, noted English radical.[32] A contemporary newspaper reports that, as a part of the performance, the images of George Grenville and George Mercer "were carried in a cart to the gallows, and were publicly hanged, with the acclamations and applause of a large concourse of people, of all ranks and denominations." On the breast of Grenville's effigy was inscribed, *"I am G—— G——————, the infamous projector of American slavery."* In each hand there was a placard; on one of them was inscribed: "Money is my God"; on the other: "Slavery, I love." There was also an inscription on the breast of the Mercer image stating that he was stamp agent.[33]

Lee also wrote the "dying words" of Mercer and had them published in the *Virginia Gazette* (September 25), in which he was represented as accepting his punishment as just for the following reason: ". . . for it is true that with parricidal hands I have endeavored to fasten chains of slavery on this my native country, although, like the tenderest and best of mothers she had long fostered and powerfully supported me. But it was the inordinate love of gold which led me astray from honour, virtue, and patriotism."[34]

Soon after this demonstration in Westmoreland, George Mercer arrived at Williamsburg with a supply of stamps. The General Court was in session and there were a number of gentlemen present from different parts of the province. In less than an hour after his arrival, when on his way to see the governor, Mercer was met by a great number of gentlemen who insisted on knowing whether he would act on his commission. Prudently yielding to this pressure, he announced next day that he would not serve. His answer was published that night in the *Virginia Gazette*. The *Gazette* stated that Mercer's declaration gave such satisfaction that he was borne out of the Capitol gate, "amidst the repeated acclamations of all present." "Then he was conducted to a public house, and an elegant entertainment ordered to be provided. . . . Here he was acclaimed with the sound of drums, French horns, etc. . . . At nightfall the whole town was illuminated, bells were set ringing, and other signs of rejoicing were carried out. . . . In short, we never had so much, and so general rejoicing upon any occasion, in so short a time and to crown the whole, there will be tomorrow night a splendid ball."[35]

Lee's action against George Mercer aroused the bitter enmity of John and James Mercer, his father and brother, respectively, and they made a vigorous attack on Lee in the columns of the *Virginia Gazette*. Lee entered the contest with one strike against him, for his earlier mistake in applying for the stamp agency gave the Mercers the chance to say that the pot was calling the kettle black.

On July 18, 1766, the *Virginia Gazette* published a letter from "An Enemy of Hypocrisy." The author of this article was doubtless John Mercer, who later had a signed statement in the same newspaper. James Mercer also published articles against Lee in the *Gazette*, one of great length. In these published statements Colonel George Mercer was defended and Lee attacked as follows: In the fall of 1764 Colonel Mercer went to Ireland and while he was there Parliament passed the Stamp Act. During his absence from England the stamp agency for Virginia was secured for him by the Virginia agent and other friends. On his return to England three months later Mercer received notice of his appointment. He had been away from America for twenty-two months and therefore could not have known of the sentiment in Virginia against the Stamp Act.

In the first of these articles the author gives an alleged "Confession" of Lee enclosed within quotation marks, but it was not an actual statement by Lee. According to this article, Lee admitted that he had accepted the offer of a friend to have him appointed receiver of a tax to be levied and that he, Lee, had also written letters in support of his candidacy. The author also declared that "The Confessor [as he called Lee] never discovered his considerations of the consequences of the act until he was assured his application was not attended with success, so it is to be presumed his patriotick spirit was set on fire by envy and disappointment."[36]

Lee's explanation of his application for the stamp agency was written before the article by "An Enemy of Hypocrisy" appeared, but its publication in the *Virginia Gazette* was a few weeks after the publication of the latter article.[37] John and James Mercer did not accept Lee's newspaper article as an adequate justification of his application for a stamp agency. In his articles in the *Virginia Gazette* against Lee, James Mercer not only elaborated on Lee's mistake in applying for the place of stamp collector, but he also accused him of having made a false statement regarding the application. It was generally reported, he said, that Lee had denied applying for the office. According to this report, continued James Mercer, Lee had told John Monroe that Colonel Corbin had offered him the commission and he had rejected it with scorn. Shortly after this article was published, John Monroe replied to it in a statement in the *Virginia Gazette*. He said that the report referred to by James Mercer as to what had passed "between Col. Lee and myself is an absolute falsehood."[38]

Lee's strenuous opposition to the Stamp Act did not end with his star role in the Montross drama. It was rekindled by the bold attitude of Archibald Ritchie, a Scottish merchant of

Hobb's Hole, in Essex County. Ritchie had a ship loaded with grain to go to the West Indies. If this vessel were not allowed to go he would suffer a loss which would hurt his Scottish conscience. Besides, he resented the meddling in his business affairs by a group of self-appointed leaders. Accordingly, he declared before a crowd on court day that he intended to clear his vessel on stamped paper and that he knew where he could get it. Enraged at such impudence and alarmed at the consequences that might follow his defiance, a group of citizens in Essex County assembled at the county seat and overawed Ritchie into declaring that he had cleared his ship without the use of stamps. This met the demands of the mob and it dispersed.

Lee, however, was not satisfied with Ritchie's repentance. He felt that "the great resentment of the people" could be appeased only after Ritchie had shown them "in public his real sorrow for having offered so great an injury to the community."[39] In keeping with this idea, a number of gentlemen met at Leedstown (now in Westmoreland County) to consider what further action should be taken against Ritchie. They adopted on February 27, 1766, a series of resolutions, known as the Westmoreland Association, which had been written by Richard Henry Lee. In these resolutions the signatories declared all due allegiance and obedience to the King but boldly asserted their rights as British subjects. Under these rights they could not be tried except by their peers and could not be taxed except by a parliament in which they were represented. Since the Stamp Act directed that their property be taken without their consent, expressed by their representatives, and in many cases deprived British-American subjects of the right of trial by jury, they were resolved at every hazard to prevent the execution of the said Stamp Act. It was also agreed that if any abandoned wretch should assist in carrying out this law by using stamped paper, or by any other means, they would promptly "convince every such Profligate that immediate Danger and Disgrace shall attend their Prostitute purpose." They promised that each one would notify others of any attempt to use stamps and that they would restore any associator to his liberty and property if he should be deprived of either on account of his activity growing out of his membership in the Association.

40

The Association was immediately signed by all those present and by others later. The one hundred and fifteen signatures represented all, or nearly all, of the leading families of the county and some from nine neighboring counties. At the head of the list stands the name of Richard Henry Lee and below there are the signatures of three of his brothers, Thomas Ludwell, Francis Lightfoot, and William. The list also includes the names of five Washingtons, four of whom were brothers of the General.[40]

At the same meeting a declaration was voted, to be signed and sworn to by Ritchie, the offending merchant. If he should refuse to sign, he was to be stripped to the waist and drawn to the public pillory at the tail of a cart and to be kept there for an hour. If he still persisted in not signing, he should be brought to Leedstown, where the whole company would decide on the final action to be taken.

Next day the signers went to Hobb's Hole, where they were joined by a large number from the adjacent counties south of the Rappahannock River. They came to call Ritchie to account. The Sons of Liberty, to the number of four hundred, drew up in two lines in the main street of the town, while some gentlemen were sent to Ritchie to have him come before the main body and sign the declaration. After some hesitation he took the oath, expressing remorse for what he had said and done and promising not to use any stamped paper.[41]

Soon after the Ritchie affair, there was published a pamphlet under the title of an "Address to the Good People of Virginia," signed by "A Virginia Planter." It had been written by Lee before Ritchie had fully yielded to the demands of the mob. In the "Address" he argued that the colonials, like all other Englishmen, cannot be taxed except by an assembly in which they are represented. He continued:

> Now one of the best things that Englishmen enjoy is, that their property, *their* property, *their* living shall not be taken from them, *nor any part of it,* except by the consent of those members or burgesses whom they shall choose at their elections to represent them. Because if the burgesses . . . do wrong, and lay taxes without reason, the people can turn them out at the new elections. This reasonable right, you know, my countrymen, we

have all along enjoyed. . . . And if the Stamp Act should go down here, the people of England will go on to tax us every year *because the more they tax us, the less necessity will there be to tax themselves.* . . .

He therefore suggested that Ritchie be severely punished if he should carry out his intention to clear his vessel on stamped paper.[42]

There was also strong opposition to the Stamp Act in England. The decline in the purchase of English goods by the colonials and the stoppage of payment of their debts to English creditors were serious blows to British merchants and manufacturers. Memorials from them were sent to Parliament from most of the leading towns in England. The military weakness of the British forces in America and the fear that a conflict with the colonies would bring in France and Spain as their allies were additional reasons for repeal. In recognition of these untoward circumstances Parliament early in March, 1766, repealed the Stamp Act. With the act of repeal was coupled a resolution, known as the Declaratory Act, asserting that Parliament had full power to make laws binding on the colonials "in all cases whatsoever."[43]

So pleased were the Burgesses over the repeal that they seemed to disregard the objectionable Declaratory Act. The Burgesses, therefore, in their address to the governor, drafted by a committee of three of which Lee was a member, expressed fulsome thanks and appreciation for the removal of this heavy burden, and gave assurance of devoting their lives and fortunes in defense of the King's sacred person, crown and dignity, and of their conviction of the necessity of a close connection between Great Britain and her colonies.[44]

Lee was also appointed to a committee by the House with instructions to prepare inscriptions for a statue and an obelisk to be erected respectively in honor of the King and the British patriots who had brought about the repeal of the Stamp Act. But it was not long before the enthusiasm had cooled off and neither the statue nor the obelisk was ever erected. Lee was anxious for the citizens of Westmoreland County to show their appreciation of the fight that Lord Camden and William Pitt had made against the Stamp Act. He called a public meeting in the county which voted thanks to Lord Camden and raised money to pay for a portrait of him to be hung in Westmoreland courthouse. Lord Camden never sat for the portrait and Lee returned the money to the subscribers. But William Pitt seemed more appreciative of the thanks of the Americans, for he sat for a portrait by Charles Wilson Peale, which Edmund Jennings, Esq., of London, had ordered for Westmoreland County. This life-size portrait of Pitt standing was sent over in the care of Richard Henry Lee, and now hangs on the wall of a small museum near the courthouse at Montross.[45]

The Stamp Act, along with the opposition aroused by it, was the first step toward the American Revolution. The Virginia leaders were especially bold in this clash with British authority and therefore had a leading role in this the first act of the Revolutionary drama. Bancroft said: "Virginia rang the alarm bell for the continent."[46] He could have added that Richard Henry Lee and Patrick Henry pulled the rope.

Chapter IV

Loyal Opposition

The period of more than a year (from March, 1766, to May, 1767) between the repeal of the Stamp Act and the passage of the Townshend Duty Act by Parliament was one of calm in Virginia. Nothing came up to disturb the harmony between the government of the Old Dominion and that of the homeland. Fauquier, the popular lieutenant governor, was on such good terms with his assembly that it looked as if the popularity he enjoyed on his accession had lengthened into a second honeymoon. The leaders in Virginia and the colonials generally seemed not to be seriously disturbed by the fact that with the repeal there was coupled a resolution asserting the right to tax the American colonies. Apparently they took the view, as Dr. Franklin had predicted, that while this measure was unconstitutional it was only a face-saving gesture and the right asserted would never be exercised.[1]

In their opposition to the Stamp Act the American leaders had made a distinction between an "internal" tax—that is, one collected inside the colonies—and an "external" tax—one collected at the ports. Townshend, therefore, thought that they would submit to an external tax, and so he secured the passage of a law by Parliament (the Townshend Duty Act) imposing a duty on glass, lead, paper, and tea imported into the colonies (May, 1767). One serious objection to the measure was the provision that a part of the revenue to be raised under it was to be applied to the support of the civil government in those colonies in which it should be found necessary. The revenue accruing from the act could, therefore, be used in paying the salaries of colonial judges and governors. Prior to this time these officials in the Northern colonies had to look to the assemblies for their salaries; but if their salaries were provided for by a regular fund they would be entirely free from the control of the people's representatives.

44

Another one of the unpopular Townshend Acts provided for the establishment of a board of customs officials in America. The British ministry hoped that this arrangement would encourage commerce between the mother country and the colonies and facilitate the collection of the duties imposed on commodities exported from or imported into the overseas possessions. Also objectionable was an act of Parliament (June, 1767) which suspended the assembly of New York because it had refused to make adequate provision for the quartering of the soldiers who were to be stationed there. The Americans considered this act a high-handed measure, and one that struck at a fundamental principle of their liberties. For if Parliament could suspend one provincial assembly it might suspend or abolish any or all of them. Acquiescence in such a practice would involve the giving up of the American contention that the colonial assemblies were independent legislative bodies, acting as little Parliaments in their respective provinces.[2]

The Townshend Duty Act worked a special hardship on the merchant class, and the opposition to it was strongest in the commercial colonies in the North. Organized resistance began in the Massachusetts assembly, under the leadership of Samuel Adams; although he was not a merchant and his own pecuniary interests were not directly affected by the measures, he and his radical followers were more ardent in their opposition to them than were the merchants. A petition to the King was drawn up and letters were sent to the other colonies, asking them to join in expressing disapproval of the law. These letters met with a sympathetic response in many of the colonies. Agreements were entered into by the merchants of Philadelphia, New York, and Boston, and by some of the planters of the Chesapeake and southern provinces, not to import British goods until the obnoxious measures were repealed.[3]

When the Virginia Assembly met in March, 1768, it was confronted with the unpopular Townshend Acts. Lieutenant Governor Fauquier had died since the last meeting, and John Blair, president of the Council, was acting as governor. Petitions from Westmoreland County and other counties protesting against the Townshend Acts showed that the people of Virginia would support the Assembly in vigorous opposition to these objectionable measures.[4] Encouraged by this popular sentiment, the Burgesses early in the session took a determined stand against the Townshend Acts. After a few days of discussion, the House by a unanimous vote adopted (April 14, 1768) a petition to the King, a memorial to the House of Lords, and a remonstrance to the House of Commons. Next day, these documents were approved by the Council.[5] The statements in these papers were extravagant in their professions of reverence for the King and of loyalty to the British empire. But underneath this courtesy of expression there was a vigorous protest against these recent acts. The softness of the glove did not conceal the hardness of the hand that it covered.

Richard Henry Lee had taken no part in the framing or adoption of these resolutions, for he was not in attendance during this session, owing to a serious accident which befell him in the spring of that year. While he was hunting swans his gun exploded and the four fingers of one hand were blown off. We may safely assume that Lee would have supported these resolutions if he had been present when they were voted on, although, in the beginning, he was not as violent in his opposition to the Duty Act as might have been expected. In a letter of March 27, 1768, to a "gentleman of influence in England," he spoke of the measure as not literally a violation of our rights but as arbitrary and unjust. He was, however, vigorous in his denunciation of the billeting act as it affected New York. In this same letter he spoke of this "oppressive measure" for he could not agree to call it a law. The act suspending the legislature of New York, he said, *"hangs, like a flaming sword,* over the heads, and requires, *by all means to be removed."*[6]

One way in which Richard Henry opposed the Townshend Acts was to cooperate with his brother Arthur and John Dickinson of Pennsylvania in newspaper and pamphlet propaganda against them. In December, 1767, John Dickinson began the publication in the *Pennsylvania Chronicle* of a series of articles known as "The Farmer's Letters." In these letters, which were later published in pamphlet form (1768), Dickinson made a vigorous attack on this new British imperial policy. Arthur Lee, who was then practicing medicine in Williamsburg, was inspired by the able arguments of these articles to enter the lists in defense of colonial rights. He thereupon published in the *Virginia Gazette* (February 25–April, 1768) a series of ten articles, entitled "The Monitor's Letters." His purpose in publishing these letters was, he said, to aid "The Farmer's Letters" "in alarming and informing" his fellow countrymen.[7]

Richard Henry considered the letters of Arthur Lee and John Dickinson so important that he had them reprinted as a single pamphlet with a preface of his own.[8] In the preface he gave as the reason for a reprint of the two series of letters the fact that the previous publication had been only in gazettes and their importance to the cause of liberty called for a wider reading.[9] Referring to Great Britain's claim of the right to tax the colonials without the consent of their representatives, he said that the exercise of such power "would indeed reduce America to a state of slavery, more deplorable and more ignominious than has ever yet been known in the world."[10] He sent three copies of this brochure to his brother William with instructions to have them neatly bound in London and presented, one each to Colonel Barré, Lord Shelburne, and Mrs. Catherine Macaulay, the historian.

In the fall of 1768, Norborne Berkeley, Baron of Botetourt, came to Virginia as governor. His arrival marked a turning point in the administration of the province. The practice since 1705 had been for the governor, usually a British nobleman, to remain in England, receiving a large portion of the salary of the office and with the remainder employing a substitute with the title of lieutenant governor, who would reside in Virginia and perform all the duties of the office.[11] In his first speech before the General Assembly (May 8, 1769) Governor Botetourt gave assurance from the King that Virginia's chief governor would hereafter reside in the colony. This speech was very pleasing to the Burgesses, and they responded to it with a most gracious resolution—so gracious that its extravagant expressions of loyalty to and affection for the King sound obsequious to modern ears. Lee was a member of the committee which drew up this address to the governor.[12]

The new governor had entered upon his administration under auspices that appeared most favorable, and yet he had assumed a responsibility which it was impossible to discharge to the satisfaction of both the British government and the people of Virginia. He was bound by his instructions to uphold British authority; he was prompted by his emotions, and probably by his principles, to protect colonial rights. He was thus put in the embarrassing position of having to hold with the hare and run with the hounds. Richard Henry Lee seems to have sensed this difficulty right in the beginning. Writing to John Dickinson on November 26, 1768, he said: "Our long expected Governor has at length arrived, his lordship's good sense, affability, and politeness give general pleasure, but how his political opinions may agree with those of Virginia remains to be known."[13]

The appointment of Botetourt as governor and the conciliatory attitude of the British government toward Virginia were intended to discourage the Old Dominion's support of Massachusetts in the controversy with the home government. This purpose was shown when Governor Botetourt expressed the wish that no resolutions be passed by the Virginia Assembly sustaining the cause of Massachusetts. In this attempt the governor was unsuccessful, for on May 16, 1769, the House in committee of the whole adopted some resolutions in line with the position that Massachusetts had taken. A committee of six, of which Richard Henry Lee was a member, was appointed to prepare an address to the King. Next day the report of this committee was brought in and unanimously adopted.

In this address the Burgesses declared that they were ready "at any Time, to sacrifice our Lives and Fortunes in Defense of your Majesty's sacred Person and Government." They pointed out, however, how unfair it was to the colonials to have them sent to England for trial, thus subjecting them to unfair and unnecessary hardships and depriving them of the right of a just and fair trial. They ended their statement as follows: ". . . we presume to prostrate ourselves at the Foot of your Royal Throne, beseeching your Majesty, as our King and Father, to avert from your faithful and loyal Subjects of America, those miseries which must necessarily be the Consequence of such Measures."[14]

The amiable governor now saw that he was called upon to drive a double team, the two parts of which were pulling in opposite directions. This action on the part of the Burgesses left him with only two alternatives—to disobey his instructions or dissolve the Assembly. He naturally chose the latter alternative. He called the Burgesses upstairs to the council chamber, saying "I have heard of your Resolves and augur ill of their effect," and ordered the House to be dissolved.[15]

On the day on which the Assembly was dissolved the members withdrew to the house of Anthony Hay in Williamsburg and proceeded to take action against the Townshend Duty Act. Peyton Randolph, who had been Speaker of the House of Burgesses, was unanimously chosen chairman of the body. It was proposed that an association be formed and a committee was chosen to prepare regulations for such an association.

This committee made its report next day (May 18, 1769). The resolves embodied in the report had been written by George Mason, who was not present, and were said to have been offered by George Washington. The report declared that the signatories were "deeply affected with the Grievances and Distresses, with which his Majesty's *American* Subjects are oppressed," and they dreaded the evils which threatened the ruin of themselves and their posterity by reducing them "from a free and happy People to a wretched and miserable State of Slavery. . . ." They attributed the evil situation into which the colony had fallen to the recent acts of Parliament, especially the Duty Act, which, they declared, were ruinous to trade and prevented the payment of debts to British merchants. They had unanimously entered into these resolutions with the hope that "the Merchants and Manufacturers of *Great Britain* may, from Motives of Interest, Friendship, and Justice, be engaged to exert themselves to obtain for us a Redress of those Grievances, under which the Trade and Inhabitants of America at present labor."

Passing from protest to action, the signatories unanimously entered into an agreement, or association, whereby they would not at any time hereafter import any merchandise that was then or would later be taxed by Parliament for the purpose of raising a revenue in America, except paper not exceeding eight shillings per ream. They also promised that until the act of Parliament imposing duties on tea, paper, glass, etc., should be repealed, they would not import from Great Britain or any other country in Europe (except certain articles produced in Ireland) any of a long list of articles and would not after November next import any slaves nor purchase any that had been imported.

These resolves received eighty-nine signatures, with that of Peyton Randolph heading the list. Other prominent signatories were Richard Henry Lee, George Washington, Patrick Henry, and Thomas Jefferson. After signing the agreement the

Associators marched in a body from the Capitol to Raleigh Tavern to drink toasts. Some of these toasts were as follows: "The King"; "The Queen and Royal Family"; "His Excellency, Lord Botetourt, and Prosperity to Virginia"; and "A Speedy and lasting Union between *Great Britain* and her Colonies."[16]

In a letter to Lord Shelburne (May 31, 1769) Lee assured him that the action of the Assembly in adopting this Association was not seditious, as it would appear to some, but only a manly and necessary assertion of rights founded on reason, guaranteed by the English constitution, and sanctified by possession for nearly two hundred years. The American people he continued, "are certainly loyal, very warmly attached to their mother country, and who wish its prosperity with unfeigned heartiness."[17]

When the new Assembly met on November 7, 1769, the governor announced in his speech that his Majesty's administration intended at the next session of Parliament to take off the duties on glass, paper, and colors. This announcement seemed acceptable to the Burgesses, although they were disappointed in that the repeal of the Duty Act was to be only partial—with the duty on tea continued. There was, however, no note of dissatisfaction in their resolution of thanks to the governor, which contained the usual extravagant declarations of loyalty to and affection for the King.[18] Before the Assembly adjourned on December 21, the Burgesses gave "a ball and elegant entertainment at the Capitol" for the governor and Council and the gentlemen and ladies of Williamsburg, "who [the ladies] were chiefly dressed in Virginia cloth, and made a genteel appearance."[19]

When the Burgesses received notice of the partial repeal of the Duty Act, the Conservatives thought that the colonials should meet the British half-way and accept the partial repeal as a final settlement. The radicals, however, were opposed to this view. Prominent among the dissenters was Richard Henry Lee, who was displeased with the action of the Burgesses in accepting the British announcement as a removal of their grievances. He regarded this move on the part of the British ministry as "a shallow impotent plan of tyranny." The partial removal of the Duty Act, he said (July, 1770), instead of appeasing the colonials had inflamed all North America and had produced a general determination to be most firm in opposition.[20]

The disappointment among the Burgesses over the retention of the duty on tea, which had been covered up with politeness in the vote of thanks to the governor, later found expression in their decision to form another association and to appoint a committee to prepare "a most humble and dutiful Petition" to the King asking him to take into "his Royal Consideration the Grievances under which his faithful Subjects of Virginia still continue to labor."[21] On June 22 a number of merchants and political leaders met in Williamsburg and signed articles of association, promising not to import a long list of British commodities until the full repeal of the Duty Act. After the ceremony of signing at the Capitol was over, the whole body, led by Peyton Randolph, the moderator, marched to Raleigh Tavern for the enjoyment of drinks and for the offering of patriotic toasts. The last of these toasts was: "May the Rose flourish, the thistle grow, and the Harp be tuned to the cause of American liberty."[22]

Committees were formed in various counties for the enforcement of this agreement; but in a few months the spirit of opposition had cooled considerably and when the time appointed for a second meeting arrived (December 14, 1770), there were so few present that they did nothing but adjourn until the next summer. According to William Nelson, this decline in interest was due to the defection of the Northern colonies.[23]

On June 27, 1770, Richard Henry Lee, as chairman of a committee of Burgesses, presented to the House the petition which it had been instructed to frame. In accordance with the instructions given to the committee, the petition expressed strong disapproval of the use of admiralty courts in the trial of colonials and of the continuance of the tax on tea. The partial repeal of the Duty Act, it stated, only lifted the duty of British manufactures and left it on the foreign commodity of tea. The petition was unanimously accepted that same day.[24]

After the adoption of the petition by the House of Burgesses in June, 1770, there was both in Virginia and in the other colonies a let-up in the opposition to British policy. During this time Lee had a partial release from political agitation and was able to turn his attention to other interests. He devoted some effort to business pursuits and some to church affairs.[25] One serious question with which he was concerned was that of religious tolerance. The English Toleration Act of 1689, which granted tol-

51

eration to Protestant Dissenters, was not reenacted by the Virginia Assembly, but there was a sort of recognition and acceptance of it. Some Dissenters, such as the Quakers and Presbyterians, enjoyed freedom of worship, but not the Baptists and some other religious orders. Naturally these Dissenters were not happy under such conditions, and groups of Baptists from time to time petitioned against this discrimination.

Soon after the House of Burgesses convened in February, 1772, petitions from Baptist groups came before the House asking that they "be treated with the same kind of indulgence in religious matters as Quakers, Presbyterians and other Protestant Dissenters." The Committee for Religion, of which both Richard Henry and Francis Lightfoot Lee were members, reported (February 25, 1772) that these petitions were reasonable. A bill was offered and was passed through second reading which extended to all Protestant Dissenters the benefits of the toleration acts. This bill did not, however, provide for complete religious freedom. It prohibited Baptist Dissenters from holding preaching services at night and from teaching or preaching publicly or privately to "any Slave or Slaves the Unfitness or Unlawfulness of Slavery." Nor were they allowed to receive into membership any slave without the permission of the owner of the slave.[26]

The Baptists, along with some other Dissenters, sent in new petitions stating that the clause in the proposed bill forbidding night meeting was unfair, and was inconsistent with the law of England and the practice of the Anglican Church. It would be a hardship to some Baptist workers who could not attend day services as conveniently as they could those held at night. The House voted (June 13, 1775) to lay the last of these petitions on the table,[27] and no further action on them or on the proposed bill was ever taken by the colonial Assembly. Complete religious freedom, therefore, had to wait until after the colonial government was superseded by that of the new commonwealth.

Lord Botetourt died on October 15, 1770, at the "Palace" in Williamsburg. The next governor was John Murray, Earl of Dunmore, who arrived in Williamsburg early in 1772.[28] At first he was very popular. Lady Dunmore had exceptional charm, which was a great aid in directing the social life at the "Palace" toward a popular administration. But Dunmore lacked the personal qualities and political acumen needed to guide the colony through this difficult period. "A forthright man with a single-track mind, . . . he had no vision of the colonists' cause, and met the emergency with force rather than by finesse."[29] In November, 1775, after his feeling toward England had been raised to white heat by the Revolutionary War, Richard Henry Lee gave this unfavorable appraisal of Dunmore: "If Administration had searched thro' the world for a person best fitted to ruin their cause, and procure union and success for these Colonies, they could not have found a more complete Agent than Lord Dunmore."[30]

After the partial repeal of the Townshend Duty Act, there was a breathing spell in the quarrel between the colonies and the mother country. A wise and tactful policy on the part of the British government at this juncture might have put an end to all serious opposition in America. But wisdom and tact were not characteristic of British policy at that time.

One of the serious mistakes in British policy was the inept handling of the *Gaspee* affair. The *Gaspee* was a British ship used along the coast of Rhode Island to enforce the revenue laws; that is, to prevent smuggling. When it ran aground near Providence (June, 1772) a mob attacked it, overpowered the crew, and burned the vessel. The British authorities appointed a special commission to investigate the case with the idea of having the perpetrators of the crime sent to England for trial. The commissioners were unable to secure evidence sufficient to support an indictment, and so no further action was taken. But the announced intention of the British government to have Americans accused of crimes sent to England for trial aroused a strong protest in the colonies, especially among Virginia leaders, who regarded this as a violation of a fundamental right.[31]

Having seen a newspaper account of the *Gaspee* affair, Lee wrote to Samuel Adams (February 4) for a full and correct account of the event.[32] Inasmuch as the Assembly was to meet soon, he wanted to be armed with full information regarding the *Gaspee* event and with instructions from his constituents that would strengthen him in the stand he planned to take in the House of Burgesses. Accordingly, he arranged to have a meeting of Westmoreland citizens in February on court day. At this meeting the voters instructed Lee to take a firm stand against the British position in the *Gaspee* affair.[33]

When the Assembly met in Williamsburg (March 4, 1773) Lee found among his fellow Burgesses a group of progressives, including Patrick Henry, Francis Lightfoot Lee, Thomas Jefferson, and Dabney Carr, who were willing to support him on the *Gaspee* question and to formulate a plan for intercolonial correspondence. These liberals held a caucus to agree upon resolutions to be offered in the House. This meeting was described by Jefferson as follows:

> Not thinking our old & leading members up to the point of forwardness & zeal which the times required, Mr. Henry, R. H. Lee, Francis L. Lee, Mr. Carr & myself agreed to meet in the evening in a private room of the Raleigh to consult on the state of things. There may have been a member or two more whom I do not recollect. We were all sensible that the most urgent of all measures was that of coming to an understanding with all the other colonies to consider the British claims as a common cause to all, & to produce an unity of action; and for this purpose that a commee of correspondce in each colony would be the best instrument for intercommunication: and that their first measure would probably be to propose a meeting of deputies from every colony at some central place, who should be charged with the direction of the measures which should be taken by all. We therefore drew up the resolutions. . . .[34]

The report of the caucus in the form of resolutions, probably drawn up by Jefferson, was presented to the House in committee of the whole by Dabney Carr. Henry and Lee both spoke in favor of the resolutions. On March 12 the committee of the whole reported out resolutions in line with those suggested by the caucus and they were unanimously adopted by the House. These resolutions provided for the appointment of a standing committee of correspondence consisting of eleven members. Prominent in the list of appointees were the Speaker, Peyton Randolph (first-named), Patrick Henry, Richard Henry Lee, and Thomas Jefferson.[35]

The committee was charged with obtaining as promptly as possible all information regarding acts of Parliament and the British administration affecting the colonies and to correspond with sister colonies to share this information with them and receive information regarding their proceedings. A copy of these resolutions was to be sent to all of the other colonial assemblies with the request that they appoint committees or persons to communicate with the Virginia committee. This standing committee was also to inquire into the action of the court of inquiry lately held in Rhode Island, which claimed authority to transport overseas Americans charged with offenses committed here. The committee selected a subcommittee of three consisting of Peyton Randolph, Robert Carter Nicholas, and Dudley Digges to carry on the correspondence.[36] Within a year all colonial assemblies except that of Pennsylvania had appointed similar committees of correspondence. These committees were not very active, however, until after the Boston Tea Party.

The Virginia organization was the first of the intercolonial committees of correspondence,[37] and Lee was the first of the Revolutionary leaders, so far as we know, to propose such a committee. In a letter to John Dickinson (July 25, 1768), he had suggested that committees of correspondence for all the colonies be formed and "that a private correspondence should be conducted between the lovers of liberty in every province."[38]

The organization of intercolonial committees of correspondence was the most important step up to that time taken by the colonies toward effective unified opposition to British policy. "Thus in these two sets of committees, local and provincial, the foundation of American independence was laid." Lee rightly considered the organization of committees of correspondence as the initial step toward that union and mutual understanding of the colonies "on which the political salvation of America so eminently" depended.[39]

This action of the Virginia Assembly in favor of committees of intercolonial correspondence had important repercussions in England. William Lee probably was referring to this action when, in writing to Richard Henry from London (January 1, 1774), he said that "the last resolves of the Virginia Assembly have struck a greater panic into the Ministers than anything that has pass'd since the stamp act."[40]

Also in New England events were now pushing colonial opposition to British rule to new heights. To punish her for the Boston "Tea Party," Parliament enacted several severe measures against Massachusetts, including the Boston Port Act, which closed the harbor of Boston to commerce, except for the bare necessities, until the tea that had been destroyed was paid for.[41] Boston responded to this measure with an appeal, voted in town meeting, to the people of all the colonies to cooperate with her in stopping all commerce with Great Britain. This appeal at first had a cold reception in the North, but, as Bancroft said, fortunately "warmer hearts beat below Mason and Dixon's line."[42] Even before this appeal reached Virginia, the House of Burgesses had taken a decided stand against the Boston Port Bill.

At the session of the Virginia Assembly which met on May 5, 1774, the leadership of the House of Burgesses was taken over by a small group of liberals—Patrick Henry, Thomas Jefferson, Francis Lightfoot Lee, Richard Henry Lee, and others. Feeling "the necessity of arousing our people from the lethargy into which they had fallen as to passing events," according to Jefferson's report, this group decided that Virginia should take another long step forward in opposition to British oppression. Accordingly, they met as a caucus and "cooked up a resolution" for "appointing the first day of *June*, on which the [Boston] *Port Bill* was to commence, for a day of fasting, humiliation, and prayer." To give greater emphasis to the proposition, they had Robert Carter Nicholas, "whose grave and religious character was more in unison with the tone of our resolution," present their resolve (May 24, 1774).[43] The resolution was unanimously adopted that same day by the House and published in the *Virginia Gazette* two days later. The resolution as finally adopted also provided that the members of the House should assemble on June 1 and "go in a body, with the Speaker and the mace," to Bruton Parish Church to attend religious services. The Rev. Mr. Price was appointed to read prayers and Richard Henry Lee was to request the Rev. Mr. Gwatkin to preach "a sermon suitable to the occasion." The governor responded to this defiant challenge by promptly dissolving the Assembly.[44] The day of fasting was observed throughout the colony. No food was eaten between the rising and setting of the sun by those who observed the fast.

The day after the dissolution, eighty-nine former members of the House met at Raleigh Tavern with Peyton Randolph as chairman. There they adopted resolutions declaring the attack on Massachusetts to be an attack on all the colonies, which should be opposed by the united action of all. To effect such co-operation they recommended that the Virginia Committee of Correspondence communicate with the committees of other colonies as to the expediency of appointing delegates from the several colonies to meet annually in a general congress "to deliberate on those general measures which the united interests of America may from time to time require." These former Burgesses (they were no longer members of the Assembly) also strongly urged their fellow countrymen to cease importing or using any products of the East India Company, except saltpetre and spices, "until the grievances of America are redressed."[45]

Lee wanted his colleagues to take even more vigorous action against the Boston Port Act than they had taken at the Raleigh Tavern meeting. On the day before the House was dissolved he prepared a set of seven strong resolutions to be presented to the House. One of these resolutions declared that the blocking of the harbor of Boston was "a most Violent and dangerous Attempt to destroy the constitutional liberty and rights of all British America." Another provided for the appointment of delegates by the House to meet delegates from the other colonies in a general congress "to consider and determine on ways the Most effectual to Stop the Exports from North America and for the adoption of such other methods as shall be most decisive for securing the Constitutional rights of America against the Systimatic [sic] plan formed for their destruction."

If these resolutions had been offered, so he thought, they would have been adopted by a large majority. But Lee refrained from proposing them on the advice of "many worthy members who wished to have the public business first finished" and suggested that he offer his resolutions later, as a sudden dissolution of the Assembly was not expected. At the meeting of the dissolved Burgesses at Raleigh Tavern he again made his proposal for a continental congress. They declined to take action, however, on the ground that they had no legal authority.[46]

Two days after the meeting at Raleigh Tavern, Peyton Randolph received a letter from Boston imploring the cooperation of the sister colonies in its "most piteous and melancholy situation." The communication suggested that the most effectual assistance to Boston which the other colonies could give would

57

"arise from a general Association against Exports and Imports, of every kind, to or from *Great Britain.*" Most of the dissolved Burgesses, including Lee, had by that time left Williamsburg; but the twenty-five that were still there met promptly (May 30) and agreed to the suggestions received from Boston. They expressed the opinion that Virginia probably would enter into an association against importations, and also exportations "after a certain time." They made it clear, however, that this statement was not to be considered as a commitment, for they had no authority to bind the colony. They also voted to send dispatches to the late representatives asking them to meet in Williamsburg on August 1 in convention to pass on these important questions.[47]

Governor Dunmore's next step was to call for the election of a new House of Burgesses to meet on August 11. This election was held in July.[48] The convention met in Williamsburg on the appointed date (August 1, 1774) and was in session for six days. All of its members were also members of either the old or new House of Burgesses. The convention adopted twelve resolutions which provided for an association or an agreement for nonintercourse with Great Britain. The members declared that after the first day of November they would not import any slaves nor any articles produced in Great Britain except medicine. They promised not to import any more tea and not to use that already in their possession. Nor would they purchase any of the other products of the East India Company if Boston were forced to pay for the tea destroyed in her harbor. They also resolved not to export any products to Britain after August 10, 1775, if their grievance had not been righted by that time. They recommended that Virginia farmers devote less attention to the cultivation of tobacco and more to the production of those articles that could serve as a basis of manufactures.[49]

They also promised that they would "most cordially and firmly join" with other counties in Virginia and the other colonies on this continent, after some future date hereafter to be agreed upon, to stop all exports to Great Britain and the West Indies and all imports thence until the acts against Massachusetts and the "several Acts laying Duties on America" had been repealed. The Williamsburg Convention chose seven delegates to represent the colony in a general congress to be held in Philadelphia on the first Monday in the following September.

When the business was finished those in attendance went to the tavern for dinner, where numerous toasts were offered and drunk. The first of these was "God bless the King, may he long reign the King of a free and happy people." Another was "Union of Great Britain and the Colonies." Other toasts expressed sympathy for the people of Boston and admiration for the British friends of America, such as Lord Chatham and Lord Shelburne.[50]

By August 1, meetings had been held in thirty-one counties of Virginia. Twenty of these had declared for absolute nonintercourse, though only eight favored the suggested moratorium on British debts.[51] That Westmoreland would be one of the counties to share in this movement was to be expected in view of the prominent part that it had played in opposing British policy. Even before the Williamsburg Convention met, Lee had called (June, 1774) a meeting of the citizens of Westmoreland County and "harangued" in strong terms against the English ministry and offered some vigorous resolutions, which expressed warm sympathy for the people of Boston, gave assurance of support, and urged them to persevere in their opposition. A committee of correspondence was appointed for the county, and of this committee R. H. Lee was a member.[52]

Virginia had now come to the parting of the ways. Loyal opposition was at the point of becoming actual rebellion. Henceforth leadership in the Old Dominion, despite protestations to the contrary, was concerned mainly with the organization of the revolutionary movement. It is true that the conservative leaders still hoped for a settlement of the controversy that would keep the colonies within the empire. They supported the nonimportation agreement with the expectation that it would lead to a removal of their grievances. This hope, however, was based on an optimism not warranted by circumstances.

Chapter V

The Birth of the Union

On September 5, 1774, forty-three delegates representing eleven states assembled in Philadelphia for the first meeting of the Continental Congress. The members met at the City (or Smith's) Tavern at ten o'clock, and walked to Carpenter's Hall, which was selected as their permanent place of meeting. Later arrivals brought the membership to fifty-six, with all the colonies except Georgia represented. Peyton Randolph of Virginia was unanimously elected president of the assembly and Charles Thomson secretary. The Virginia delegation, headed by Randolph, chairman of the Virginia Convention and Speaker of the House of Burgesses, included, in the order of their selection, Richard Henry Lee, George Washington, Patrick Henry, Richard Bland, Benjamin Harrison and Edmund Pendleton.[1]

In the instructions to their representatives the members of the Virginia Convention desired them to express "our Faith and true Allegiance to his Majesty King George the Third, our lawful and rightful Sovereign; and that we are determined, with our Lives and Fortunes, to support him in the legal Exercise of all his just Rights and Prerogatives." They declared that they sincerely approved "of a constitutional Connexion with Great Britain" and most ardently wished for "a Return of Intercourse of Affection and commercial Connexion that formerly united both Countries, which can only be effected by a Removal of those Causes of Discontent which have of late unhappily divided us."[2]

Four of Virginia's delegates—Randolph, Bland, Harrison and Lee—arrived at Philadelphia by September 2. Patrick Henry and Edmund Pendleton had gone as far as Mount Vernon by the thirtieth of August, and next day they and Washington left on horseback for Philadelphia, arriving there on the fourth of September.[3] Lee also had been invited by Washington to join him at Mount Vernon, but instead he had ridden directly with his three associates to Philadelphia, making the trip in four and a

60

half days. They traveled about thirty-five miles a day, and usually covered one third of the day's journey before breakfast in the cool of the day.[4]

To Lee, who had spent years in England and traveled in continental Europe, city life probably did not offer many new experiences; to most of his colleagues the contrast between life on a Virginia plantation and that now confronting them must have seemed most thrilling. Philadelphia, with its population of thirty thousand, was the largest city in North America. Its paved streets and brick sidewalks were a decided contrast to the muddy roads of the Old Dominion. Furthermore, they were all looking forward to the activities of the Congress. The frolicsome Harrison said that he would have come if he had had to walk, and Bland declared that he would have made the journey if it had been to Jericho.[5]

Lee took lodging in the home of his brother-in-law, Dr. William Shippen, Jr. He had hardly had time to get settled when John Adams, whom he had met for the first time the evening before at the tavern, came around to the Shippen home to have breakfast with him. From this initial association stemmed a lifelong friendship between the two.[6]

The assembly was delayed a few days in its opening owing to the late arrival of some of its members. This waiting period afforded opportunity for a social commingling of the delegates with mutual pulse-feeling and appraisals. One of these early social events was a meeting on the first Saturday night at the home of Thomas Mifflin. After "an elegant supper," John Adams, Lee, Harrison, the two Rutledges, and several others had a gay time drinking toasts. Among the toasts were "Unanamity to the Congress"; and "Union of Britain and the Colonies on a Constitutional Foundation." Adams said that "Lee and Harrison were very high" and that "Lee had dined with Dickinson, and drank Burgundy the whole afternoon."[7]

Throughout the session such social functions continued to offer relaxation to the otherwise seriously concerned delegates. In his diary Adams speaks of at least a half-dozen occasions on which he and Richard Henry dined together. Once in referring to guests who had spent the evening at his lodging, Adams said that "Colonel Lee staid till twelve o'clock and was very social and agreeable."[8]

61

The first Congress was an exceptionally capable body. Most of the members were among the leading men in their respective colonies, especially in the cases of the Virginia and Massachusetts delegations. John Adams said that the gentlemen from Virginia appeared "to be the most spirited and consistent of any." The fact that Virginia had so strongly supported Massachusetts in her opposition to British policy may have influenced Adams in forming such a high opinion of the delegation from the Old Dominion. Later, however, he removed Benjamin Harrison from this honor roll and made a very unfavorable appraisal of him, calling him another "Sir John Falstaff, excepting in his larcenies and robberies."[9] A favorable impression also was made on others of their contemporaries by these first representatives of the Old Dominion. Caesar Rodney, in speaking of them, said ". . . more sensible, fine fellows you would never wish to see."[10]

Among the Virginia representatives who had a high rating with their colleagues, Lee held a prominent place.[11] Even Silas Deane, who later became a bitter enemy of the Lee family, spoke of Richard Henry in complimentary terms. In a letter to his wife he said that Patrick Henry and Lee were "styled the *Demosthenes* and *Cicero* of America."[12] Lee stood especially high in the esteem of John Adams, who regarded him as "a masterly man." He had won this favorable estimate partly by his personal charm, but mainly by his advanced political views. Lee held that the colonies had not been founded by any act of Parliament or the King, except insofar as they had consented to colonization. "There is now," he said, "no other legislative over the Colonies but their respective Assemblies." He even denied the right of the crown to issue charters.[13]

Lee at once indicated that he favored a vigorous policy on the part of Congress and outlined to Adams what, in his opinion, Congress should set as its goal. It should demand the repeal of every revenue law, the Boston Port Act, the act for changing the constitution of Massachusetts, the Quebec Act, and also the removal of all British troops from the colonies.[14] Congress should force the British government to redress these grievances by a resolution against any further importation into the colonies of any dutiable articles. Such action, he thought, would bring the relief they sought. "He is absolutely certain," said Adams, "that the same ship that carries home the resolution will bring back the redress." He also thought that Congress should declare to the King that the American colonies could never be happy so long as Lords Bute, Mansfield, and North were his confidants and advisers. Lord North's whole administration, he said, had been a blunder. Lee was opposed, however, to any action against the navigation laws; if such action were taken, he feared that every man in Great Britain would be united against it, since the kingdom could not exist without these laws. He seemed willing to allow the British government the right to regulate colonial commerce as a compensation for the protection afforded the colonies by the British fleet.[15]

After having effected a permanent organization, Congress agreed upon rules of procedure and the method of voting. The rules provided that the doors were to be kept closed while Congress was in session and members were to consider "themselves under the strongest obligations of honour, to keep the proceedings secret, until the majority shall direct them to be made public." It was then proposed that in "determining questions in this Congress" each colony should have one vote, since Congress did not have the "proper materials for ascertaining the importance of each Colony."[16]

This latter proposal stirred up a warm debate, giving Patrick Henry and Richard Henry Lee an opportunity to display their oratory. Henry, in one of the most eloquent addresses of his career, contended that the representation in Congress should be based on the number of freemen. In this oration was his oft-quoted statement: "The distinctions between Virginians, Pennsylvanians, New Yorkers, and New Englanders, are no more. I am not a Virginian, but an American." This sounded as if the great apostle of the doctrine of localism had gone over to the camp of the nationalists. But such was not the case. He was skillfully manipulating a catch-phrase to give his own state a stronger voice in federal affairs.[17]

The plan did not give the larger colonies a proportionate voice in federal legislation, especially in the case of Virginia, which had the greatest area and largest population of any of the colonies. Lee therefore favored proportional representation, but he supported the plan for equal representation. He argued that however just proportional representation might be, the information was not available for making such an apportionment. The final decision was that each colony should have one vote.[18]

On September 6, Congress appointed a committee to state the rights of the colonies, the several instances in which these rights had been violated, and the most suitable means to be employed in restoring them. This committee was at first composed of two delegates from each of the colonies represented in Congress, but shortly afterwards the three most populous colonies—Massachusetts, Pennsylvania, and Virginia—were each given an additional member. Virginia's representatives on this committee were Richard Henry Lee, Edmund Pendleton, and Patrick Henry.[19]

The committee for two days engaged in what John Adams termed "a most ingenious, entertaining debate." The two points around which most of the controversy turned were the authority of Parliament over the colonies and the law of nature as the basis of colonial rights. Lee warned that if the colonials rested their rights on the charters alone it would be a weak foundation, for the right of the King to grant such charters had been questioned. The Americans, he thought, should lay their rights "upon the broadest bottom, the ground of nature." "Life, and liberty, which is necessary for the security of life," he said, "cannot be given up when we enter into society." Colonial rights, he contended, were "built on a fourfold foundation: on nature, on the British constitution, on charters, and on immemorial usage." There was marked disagreement among the delegates as to what authority they should concede to Parliament; whether they "should deny the authority of Parliament in all cases"; whether they should "allow any authority to it" in the internal affairs of the colonies; or whether they "should allow it to regulate the trade of the empire with or without any restriction."[20] After considerable discussion in both a general committee and two subcommittees the report of the general committee, known as the Declaration of Rights, was adopted (October 14).[21]

This Declaration consisted of a lengthy preamble followed by twelve resolutions in which the rights and grievances of the colonies were pointed out. In the last resolution, there was a pledge to enter into a nonimportation, nonconsumption, and nonexportation agreement or association. There was also a provision for preparing an address to the people of Great Britain, a memorial to the inhabitants of British America, and a loyal address to his Majesty. The most important clause in this historic document was the statement in the preamble to the effect that the rights of the inhabitants of the English colonies in North America were based on "the immutable laws of nature, the principles of the English constitution, and the several charters or compacts."[22] The principles embodied in the declaration were virtually the same as those for which Lee had been so earnestly contending.

In the meantime Congress had adopted some other measures which proved to be long steps toward revolution. It soon developed that the delegates were divided into two groups, the conservatives and the liberals, or radicals. According to Joseph Galloway of Pennsylvania, dean of the conservatives, the two parties were in balance for the first three weeks, but after that the radicals were in control.[23] One of the first victories scored by the radicals was in securing the endorsement by Congress of the "Resolves" that had been adopted by Suffolk County (the county in which Boston is located). The tone of these resolves was unusually bitter. They spoke of arresting "the hand which would ransack our pockets" and of disarming "the parricide which points the dagger to our bosoms." The measures (the Coercive Acts) recently passed by Parliament were to be "rejected as the attempts of a wicked administration to enslave America." On the other hand, loyalty to the King was affirmed and "affection to his majesty" professed.[24]

The "Suffolk Resolves" were brought to Congress by Paul Revere. When Peyton Randolph finished reading the Resolves, "the hall exploded." "Men swarmed to the Massachusetts delegation cheering and shouting." Lee at once offered resolutions expressing sympathy for Massachusetts and approval of her opposition as expressed in the Suffolk Resolves and providing for the continuation of contributions from all the colonies for the relief of the distress of Boston. "Long and warm disputes ensued between the parties," and the resolution endorsing the Resolves was promptly and unanimously passed (September 17).[25]

Although the endorsement of the Suffolk Resolves was a decided victory for the radicals, the conservatives, led by Joseph Galloway, were still hopeful that colonial rights might be upheld without a break with the mother country. It was to secure such a result that Galloway offered a plan of union for the colonies (September 28, 1774). He and the other advocates of his plan contended that it would afford security to American rights and provided for a much needed union of the colonies.

The Galloway Plan provided for establishing in America a general legislature for all the colonies, to consist of a President-General appointed by the King and a Grand Council composed of representatives chosen by the colonial assemblies for a term of three years. The Grand Council would meet once a year or oftener if occasion should require. The assent of the President-General would be necessary for the passage of any act and he would carry out the acts of the Grand Council. Measures affecting the colonies would be initiated by the Grand Council or the British Parliament, but would have to be approved by both bodies before being effective. Each colony was to retain its existing constitution and governmental authority.[26]

The Galloway Plan received some support in Congress but not enough to win acceptance. Its opponents urged that Congress had no authority to take this radical step, for under such a union as was proposed by the plan the right of self-government in the colonies would be sacrificed. Richard Henry Lee, credited with the first speech against the plan, argued as follows: "How did we go on for one hundred and sixty years before the year 1763? We flourished and grew. This plan would make such changes in the Legislature of the Colonies, that I could not agree to it without consulting my constituents." Patrick Henry declared that it would "liberate our constituents from a corrupt House of Commons" only to throw them into the arms of an American legislature that might be bribed by Great Britain. The plan was finally rejected (October 22, 1774) and an order was voted to expunge from the minutes both the plan and the rule referring it to further consideration.[27]

Early in the session the question of the British colonial army came before Congress. Lee not only was opposed to taxing the colonials for the support of a British army stationed in America, he also advocated the return of these forces to England. Accordingly, he offered (October 3, 1774) a resolution declaring that it was unnecessary for Britain to keep an army in America, as the colonies were able and willing to arrange for their own defense, and recommending that each of the several colonies provide for a well-disciplined and well-armed militia for its own protection. It was quite unreasonable, the resolution stated, that the mother country should have to be at the expense of maintaining standing armies in America.[28]

Lee's proposal, too strong for the majority of Congress, was softened by amendment before it was passed. As finally adopted, it was as follows: The members of Congress do assure his Majesty that the militia in the several colonies, if put on a proper footing, would be amply sufficient for defense in time of peace, and that they are desirous of putting the militia on such a footing immediately. In case of war, they would provide the further forces necessary. Lee was so displeased with the watering-down of his original resolution that he voted against the amended one.[29]

The leaders in Congress, especially those of the more radical group, felt that it was not enough to issue a declaration of their rights and to send petitions and memorials to England urging a redress of their grievances. They insisted that the British government should be pressured into righting the injustices to America by a threat to the economic interests of the English people or at least to an influential group of them. American trade was an important source of wealth for British merchants and manufacturers. By adopting a nonintercourse policy Congress could, they contended, dry up this source of gain. To ward off such a danger the merchants and manufacturers, who had the ear of Parliament, would demand a repeal of the laws objected to by the colonials. The American leaders seemed to think that the most important nerve in the body is the one that leads from the pocketbook to the heart. They were of the opinion, therefore, that they could reach the hearts of the British merchants by touching their pocketbooks.[30] With this loss of trade confronting them, the merchants and manufacturers would agitate in favor of the repeal of the objectionable laws. In support of this view its advocates could point to the fact that nonintercourse, though not carried out throughout the colonies, had been an important factor in forcing the repeal of the Stamp Act and the partial repeal of the Townshend Duty Act.

It was therefore to be expected that Congress would consider a policy of nonintercourse with the homeland as the most effective means of bringing the English government to terms. As the first step toward this objective, Congress resolved unanimously (September 22) to request the merchants and others in the several colonies to send no more orders for goods to Great Britain and to delay or suspend orders already sent, until Congress announced a definite policy.[31]

A few days later, Richard Henry Lee made a motion for nonimportation, which gave rise to considerable discussion as to the date on which nonintercourse should begin and whether nonintercourse should include nonexportation and nonconsumption, as well as nonimportation. It was decided (September 27) that after the first day of the following December "there should be no importation into British America from Great Britain or Ireland, of any goods, wares or merchandizes, . . . as shall have been exported from Great-Britain or Ireland; and that no such goods, wares or merchandizes imported after the first day of December next, to be used or purchased." Some members of the Congress, especially the radicals, held that nonintercourse would not achieve the results desired unless it included nonexportation as well as nonimportation. Accordingly, Congress passed a supplemental resolution declaring that on and after September 10, 1775, the exportation of all commodities to Great Britain, Ireland, and the West Indies ought to cease unless the grievances of the colonies had been removed by that time.[32]

An exportation agreement like this was hard on the Chesapeake and Southern colonies as they were dependent upon the European market for the sale of their staples. Virginia therefore wanted to postpone its operations until the fall of 1776, and South Carolina insisted that rice and indigo not be included in the list of commodities covered by the nonexportation pledge.[33] Despite these objections, the resolution passed and a committee of five, of which Lee was a member, was appointed to "bring in a plan for carrying into effect, the nonimportation, nonconsumption, and nonexportation resolved on."[34]

When the committee made its report on October 12 the South Carolina delegates (at least four of them) renewed their demand that indigo and rice be excepted from nonexportation because, they contended, the economic life of their province was dependent upon the exportation of these products. They declared that unless this exception was made South Carolina would not join the Association, as the proposed agreement was called. This

68

breach in the union was prevented by a compromise which exempted rice from nonexportation. Virginia also yielded her insistence upon a later date for the beginning of nonexportation. Agreement therefore was reached and the Association was signed October 20. Richard Henry Lee's name headed the list of Virginia's six signatories, including all the members of the delegation except Peyton Randolph, who was absent on account of illness.[35]

In this document the Congressional delegates declared themselves to be "his majesty's most loyal subjects" and then gave a list of objectionable measures in colonial policy, both as to legislation and administration, that the British government had adopted since the end of the French and Indian War. This policy was characterized as "a ruinous system of colonial administration." The Virginia delegation had been instructed to limit its complaints to measures adopted since the first of 1763. It was doubtless for this reason that no grievances prior to this date were listed.

The main terms of the Association were as follows: That after the first day of December next, they would not import either directly or indirectly any commodities produced in Great Britain or Ireland, certain listed articles from the British West Indies, foreign indigo, or wines from Madeira or the Western Islands. Nor would they import any slaves after the first day of December next, or purchase any that had been imported after that date. It was also agreed to stop at once the consumption of any tea imported on the account of the East India Company or any on which a duty had been paid. From and after the first day of March next they would not "purchase or use any East-India tea whatever."

The Association further promised to encourage frugality and economy, promote agriculture and manufactures, and "discountenance and discourage every species of extravagance and dissipation, especially all horseracing, and all kinds of gaming, cockfighting, exhibitions of shews, plays, and other expensive diversions and entertainments." The first part of this statement is quite similar to one in the Virginia Association, but the taboo on amusements sounds like a New England contribution.

There was also the promise that after September 10, 1775 (if the late objectionable acts of the British Parliament had not

69

been repealed), they would not export any commodities directly or indirectly, "to Great Britain, Ireland, or the West Indies except rice to Europe." The reason given for this later date for the beginning of exportation was the "earnest desire . . . not to injure our fellow-subjects in Great-Britain, Ireland, or the West Indies." The members of the committee must have had their tongues in their cheeks when they inserted this clause. Every member of Congress knew that the delay in nonexportation was in consideration for "their fellow subjects" of Maryland, Virginia and the Carolinas and not for those of Britain, Ireland, and the West Indies.[36] This dubious statement, however, could have been good propaganda in winning the sympathy of the British people for the American cause.

For the enforcement of the agreement it was recommended that in every county, city, and town a committee be chosen by the voters to "observe the conduct of all persons touching this association" and publish in the gazette all violations. Also the committees of correspondence were to inspect the customhouses for violations. They also promised not to trade with any colony or province in North America that would not accede to or did hereafter violate this Association.[37]

Later (October 11, 1774) Congress appointed a committee, consisting of Richard Henry Lee, William Livingston and John Jay, to prepare an address to the people of Great Britain and a memorial to the people of British America. Lee was assigned to prepare the draft of both the address and the memorial. After a two-day discussion, resulting in the addition of amendments, Lee's draft of the memorial to the people of the twelve colonies represented in Congress was adopted.[38]

This memorial was a long, well-written document. Although it expressed strong disapproval of British colonial policy, its tone was not unreasonably severe. It listed alleged grievances to which the colonies had been subjected since the end of the French and Indian War, with the conclusion that these grievances indicate "that a resolution is formed, and is now carrying into execution, to extinguish the freedom of these colonies by subjecting them to a despotic government."

Owing to this threat to American freedom, the memorial continued, Congress was faced with the unfortunate dilemma "of being silent and betraying the innocent, or of speaking out and censuring those we wish to revere. In making our choice of these distressing difficulties, we prefer the course dictated by honesty, and a regard for the welfare of our country." The method of opposition suggested was the peaceable one of nonintercourse. If this method should prove ineffectual, then the American people "must inevitably be reduced to chuse, either a more dangerous contest, or a final ruinous, and infamous submission."

A favorable opinion was voiced of the piety, generosity and good sense of the English people, and the hope expressed that they would take sides with their American brethren against *"our open* and *their own secret* enemies," whose intrigues for several years "have been wholly exercised in sapping the foundations of civil and religious liberty." There also was indicated the wish and expectation that the bond which held the colonies to the homeland *"may never* be dissolved."[39]

Lee was also a member of a committee of three appointed to prepare an address to the people of Quebec and a letter to each of the British American colonies which were not represented in Congress. These reports were promptly drafted by the committee and were adopted by Congress after amendments had been added. The letter to outside colonies was a short paper about a half-page in length. Along with the letter went documents giving the measures adopted by Congress and the recommendation that these colonies adopt these measures with all seriousness.[40]

The address to the people of Quebec as finally adopted pointed out the injustices of the Quebec Act[41] and suggested that the people of Quebec cooperate with their fellow Americans in opposition to British tyranny. It asked this province to join the union with the other colonies by sending delegates to the next meeting of the Congress (May, 1775).[42] There is no statement in the *Journal* to show what part, if any, Lee had in preparing the address. We know, however, that he was strongly opposed to the Quebec Act and denounced it in Congress as one of the worst of all the measures objected to by the colonials. The attempt to extend the jurisdiction of the Province of Quebec to the Ohio, he maintained, was especially objectionable to Virginia, for it would rob her of territory that rightfully belonged to her.[43]

In the meantime Lee had performed another important duty which had been placed upon him—that of writing an address to the people of Great Britain. On October 18 he presented to Congress his draft of this address. According to Thomas Jefferson, who received his information from Benjamin Harrison and Edmund Pendleton, Lee's report was most disappointing.

When it was read in Congress every countenance fell and a deep silence endured for many minutes. At length it was laid on the table for perusal and consideration till the next day, when first one member and then another arose, and paying some faint compliments to the composition, observed that there were still certain considerations, not expressed in it, which should properly find a place in it. At length Mr. Livingston (the Governor of New Jersey), a member of the Committee, rose and observed that a friend of his had been sketching what he had thought might be proper for such an address, from which he thought some paragraphs might be advantageously introduced into the draught proposed; and he read an Address which Mr. Jay had prepared *de bene esse* as it were. There was but one sentiment of admiration. [Lee's] address was recommitted for amendment, and Mr. Jay's draught reported and adopted with scarce an alteration."[44]

A careful reading of Lee's paper leaves one uncertain as to the reasons for its unfavorable reception. Its indictment of British policy followed the usual line of complaint, listing as grievances taxation, the Quebec Act, the withdrawal of the right of trial by jury for some Americans by having them sent to distant American courts and to England for trial, and the subversion of the charter of Massachusetts. Loyalty to the British empire and allegiance to the King were declared, though not in as extravagant terms as was employed in some of the other declarations.

In a rather lengthy discussion of these grievances he contended that the royal charters granted and confirmed to the first settlers and their posterity all the rights of the free people of England. One violation of these rights was the attempt to tax the colonials by act of Parliament, since they were not represented in that body and could not be on account of distance. "We would certainly be Slaves," he continued, "if we were not exempted from such Taxation . . . we would be unworthy of the british ancestry which is now our boast, if we did not esteem our constitutional liberty far above the possession of Life, disgraced with the Shackles of Slavery."

He was bitter in his opposition to the Quebec Act, which, he said, would establish a colony with a despotic government and the Roman Catholic religion on the western border of all the colonies. It is well known, he declared, from the teaching of history,

> that this bloody and intolerant religion is at such fatal variance with Protestantism, that the inhabitants of that now greatly-extended Country will thereby be well-fitted both from civil & religious Principles to carry Slaughter and destruction into the free protestant Colonies whenever they shall be encouraged by a wicked Ministry to do so.

Despite the strong opposition expressed toward British colonial policy, it was made clear that the Americans had no thought of separation from the homeland. They were therefore grieved to learn that "some malignant Spirits in Great Britain" were charging them "with designing independency and wanting to dissolve all connection with the parent state." The whole history of the colonials and their "uniform tenor of conduct" was, he continued, "directly in the teeth of this assertion." If Parliament should repeal the objectionable acts and allow the colonies to return to the status they had at the end of the last war, all opposition on the part of the Americans would cease and they would be "intent on promoting the common interests and happiness of the United Empire." To this hopeful possibility he attached this final note of caution:

> But this most desirable connection between Great Britain and the Colonies, supported by such a happy intercourse of reciprocal benefits, must be interrupted, if the people of America are distressed and ruined by unconstitutional Taxes. Their Liberty and antient rights being taken away, no encouragement to industry will remain, but ignorance and idleness the constant Attendants on Slavery will overrun this great Continent, hitherto the seat of freedom, virtue, and growing Science.[45]

The address as written by Jay and finally accepted by Congress was a vigorous assertion of colonial rights and an enumeration of the grievances which the American people had recently suffered at the hands of the British ministry. The English people were warned that if the Ministry should be successful in its unfair practices toward the colonies and would with its armies be able to enslave the Americans, it would then be in a position to enslave the British people. Along with complaints of injustice there went a strong statement of allegiance, coupled, however, with the threat of strenuous opposition to the encroachment upon their rights.

The grievances complained of by Jay were much the same as those listed by Lee, but the tone of opposition of the former was less colorful and emotional and therefore less provocative than that of the latter. Jay also gave greater emphasis than Lee to the exclusion of the British people from blame for the objectionable measures, although Lee had made no complaint against them. For example, Jay, too, was strongly opposed to the Quebec Act and made a severe attack on the Catholics, whose intrigues, he declared, "for several years past have been wholly exercised in sapping the foundations of civil and religious liberty." He expressed the hope that the British people, in whom the Americans "repose high confidence" for "their piety, generosity, and good sense," would not, as "the defenders of true religion and the assertors of the rights of mankind, . . . take part against their affectionate protestant brethren in the colonies, in favour of our open and *their own secret enemies.*"[46]

The objection of Congress to Lee's paper may have been due to the fear that its indictment of British American policy was too boldly expressed and might induce in the Ministry a more aggressive instead of a more favorable attitude toward the colonies. Furthermore, it is probable that Congress did not view his paper with as much disfavor as Jefferson's report indicates. Jefferson was describing from memory an event that took place more than thirty years earlier. He had obtained his information from two of Lee's colleagues, one of whom (Harrison) was his chronic enemy, and any account by him of the part played by Lee on any occasion would not likely be flattering to his old adversary.[47]

On October 1 Congress voted to send a loyal address to the King entreating his interposition for the removal of colonial grievances, and Patrick Henry was chosen to prepare the document. His draft was not acceptable and after debate was recommitted. John Dickinson was added to the committee, and he

74

rewrote or radically revised Henry's paper. The new draft was presented on October 25 and after further debate was approved.[48]

Congress voted that the petition to the King be sent to the various colonial agents and by them presented to the King. These agents were instructed to invoke the aid of influential Englishmen who were favorable to the American cause. Richard Henry Lee and John Jay were appointed to prepare a letter to be sent to the colonial agents.[49] This letter was written by Lee. It was read, discussed, and adopted on October 26 and then sent by the acting president of Congress, Henry Middleton, to the seven colonial agents.[50]

The petition was presented by Arthur Lee, Franklin, and one other colonial agent to Lord Dartmouth, Secretary for the Colonies, to be transmitted by him to the King. Later, Lord Dartmouth informed Arthur Lee and Franklin that his Majesty had received the petition "very graciously" and was pleased that it was so "decent and respectful."[51]

A few days before it adjourned, Congress voted (October 22) that another Congress should be held at Philadelphia on May 10, 1775, unless the grievances complained of should have been redressed in the meantime. The first Congress had lasted less than two months, but in that short time it had made a record of outstanding significance. It had started the colonies on the road that led to independence and federation. "As the Declaration of Rights was in an important sense a forerunner of the Declaration of Independence, so the Association stands out as an important step toward the creation of an organic union among the colonies."[52]

Chapter VI

Organizing Revolt

The Continental Association was adopted by all the thirteen colonies except New York and Georgia and in these provinces it was enforced in some communities. Local committees were everywhere active in compelling compliance with the nonintercourse agreement. Expecially was this the case in Virginia. According to Governor Dunmore, by the end of the year 1774 a committee had been formed in every county in the colony. These committees were to inspect the books of merchants, watch the conduct of every inhabitant, and punish violators by stigmatizing them and thus turning them over to mob violence. They had no legal authority, but being supported by public opinion, they were able to wield a power as great as that conferred by law. If violators were not pressured into obedience by social ostracism they could be brought to terms by that favorite weapon of the mob—tar and feathers. Even the provision against extravagance and improper amusements seems to have been enforced. A lady in Virginia was advised not to give a ball that she had planned. At another time some men, also in the Old Dominion, were called up for having taken part in a horse race and were forced to make amends for their "enormity."[1]

Westmoreland County was active in enforcing the policy of nonintercourse. On June 22, 1774, before the First Continental Congress had met, there was a meeting at the county seat at which sympathy for Boston was expressed and the right of the colonies to be free from taxation except by their provincial assemblies was affirmed. Those present at the meeting also promised to join the inhabitants of other counties in Virginia and other colonies on the continent to stop exports to and imports from Great Britain and the West Indies until the Duty Act and all the recent acts against Massachusetts were repealed. Richard Henry Lee was in attendance at this first meeting, and the resolutions adopted by it sound like a production of his pen.[2]

After the Association was adopted by Congress another committee of which Lee was a member was appointed by the Westmoreland organization to carry out the provisions of the Association in that county. One important act of the committee was the disciplining of David Wardrobe for a letter which he had written to a friend in Scotland which had been published in the *Glasgow Journal* (August 14, 1774). The committee considered the statements made in the letter as unpatriotic and had him before it for an explanation. At first Wardrobe showed no sign of yielding but later made an abject apology.[3]

These restrictions on individual freedom met with opposition in some cases. One of the protestants is said to have made this complaint: "If I must be enslaved, let it be by a KING at least, and not by a parcel of upstart lawless Committee-men. If I must be devoured, let me be devoured by the jaws of a lion and not gnawed to deth by rats and vermin."[4]

Opposition to British policy was not confined to the enforcement of the nonintercourse agreement. The colonials were also now making military preparations. Every county in Virginia was arming a company of men. The courts of justice had been closed again and, according to Governor Dunmore, there was "not a Justice of the Peace in Virginia that acts except as Committee-man." The committees were chosen by the voters in mass meeting and were composed of former justices of the peace, vestrymen, and other leading citizens. Since the county courts were in suspension, these committees took the place of the local government. Their activities consisted not only in enforcing the Association but also in punishing unpatriotic actions or expressions of opinion.

A second state convention was called, this time to meet at the little town of Richmond, "at a safe distance from Dunmore."[5] The convention met in St. John's Church on March 20, 1775, and adjourned March 27. Every county was represented, as well as the towns of Norfolk, Jamestown, and Williamsburg. Peyton Randolph was made chairman by unanimous choice. The convention gave a vote of thanks to the delegates to the First Continental Congress and elected delegates to the next Congress. It also adopted a resolution stating its wish "to see a speedy return of those halcyon days" when the Virginians lived as "a free and happy people."[6]

77

The expression of this "pious wish" was very objectionable to Patrick Henry, and he promptly countered this honeyed statement by offering resolutions for bold opposition. These resolutions provided that this colony be immediately put into "a posture of defence" and that a committee be appointed to prepare a plan for "arming and disciplining such a number of men as may be sufficient for that purpose." The conservatives opposed this step. They feared that the threat of force would alienate their Whig friends in England. They still hoped that the policy of nonintercourse would suffice to bring about a removal of their grievances. Furthermore, they felt that Virginia "was in no condition to go to war with the first military and naval power in the world." Prominent among the liberals who supported Henry's motion were Lee, Jefferson, and Washington. The resolution was passed by a vote of 65 to 60. To prepare this plan of defense a committee of twelve prominent citizens was appointed, with Henry and Lee as first- and second-named, respectively. George Washington and Thomas Jefferson were also members.[7]

It was in support of his resolution that Patrick Henry made his most noted speech, the one which ended in this oft-quoted peroration: "Is life so dear, or peace so sweet, as to be purchased at the price of chains and slavery? Forbid it, Almighty God! I know not what course others may take; but as for me, give me liberty or give me death!" The effect of the speech was too profound to be followed by applause, but a general feeling was expressed by the cry, "to arms!"[8]

Lee followed Henry with an oration which was received by the convention as a worthy supplement to Henry's fiery appeal. According to one of Lee's contemporaries (Edmund Randolph), it "fanned and refreshed with a gale of pleasure."[9]

Thomas Marshall afterwards gave to his son, John, the Chief Justice, an account of Lee's speech, which was relayed to William Wirt by the Chief Justice as follows: Lee agreed that Britain could bring a powerful force against the Americans, and discussed the advantages and disadvantages of both parties. He even admitted that in military strength the calculations were in favor of Britain. But, despite these discouraging admissions, the address ended on this high note of optimism: We are assured, he said, in Holy Writ that " 'the race is not to the swift, nor the battle to the strong' and if the language of genius may be added to inspiration, I will say with our immortal bard: 'Thrice is he armed, who hath his quarrel just! And he but naked, though lock'd up in steel, Whose conscience with injustice is oppressed'."[10]

The adoption of Henry's resolution and the appointment of a committee to carry it out were not mere dramatic gestures but real steps toward preparation for war. In its report the committee recommended the organization of cavalry units in the Tidewater region and of companies of riflemen in the Piedmont and mountain sections, all to be furnished with suitable arms and ammunition.[11]

The convention also appointed a committee of thirteen to prepare a plan for the encouragement of arts and manufactures in the colony. The membership consisted of both conservatives and radicals. Among the latter were Henry, Lee, and Washington. The committee promptly reported a series of resolutions (15), all of which were unanimously adopted. In these resolutions it was recommended that as few sheep as possible be killed for mutton in order that more wool might be available for cloth-making; that the manufacture of steel, nails and wire, and of cotton, woolen and linen goods be promoted; that colonial manufactures be used in preference to all others; and that the brewing of malt liquors in Virginia be encouraged so as to lessen the consumption of foreign liquors.[12]

In February, 1775, the House of Commons had passed a resolution which was generally considered as Lord North's peace proposal. This resolution declared that Parliament had authority over the colonies and the right to tax them. If, however, any colony should offer a plan for contributing its proportion for the common defense and should "engage to make provision also for the support" of its civil government and the administration of justice, and if this plan should be acceptable to the King and Parliament, the British government would not levy any tax or duty against that colony except to continue the duties needed for the regulation of commerce.[13]

Virginia, along with the other twelve colonies, rejected this proposal, an action that was most acceptable to Richard Henry Lee. He had written to his brother, Francis Lightfoot, who was a member of the House of Burgesses, urging him to take a decided stand against the proposed peace plan. The Virginia Assembly also refused to reopen the courts of justice and showed its rebellious mood by unanimously endorsing the proceedings of the Richmond Convention and the First Continental Congress.[14]

Since the opposition in America was now approaching rebellion, the British government decided that no more arms and ammunition should be sent to the colonies. The next step would be to remove military supplies from those colonies which were threatening revolt. In line with this policy Governor Dunmore on April 20, 1774, had the gunpowder in the public magazine in Williamsburg taken out in the dead of night and transferred to the *Magdalen*, lying in the James River.

This act raised the spirit of opposition throughout Virginia. In a number of counties "men reached for their arms" with the intention of marching to Williamsburg and forcing the governor to restore the gunpowder. In the meantime, Dunmore had threatened that if any insult were offered the captain of the *Magdalen* he would arm his own slaves and set free all other Negroes. And if the magistrates and others professing loyalty to him did not come to his assistance he would consider "the whole Country in an actual state of Rebellion," and he would "not hesitate at reducing their houses to ashes and spreading devastation" wherever he could reach.[15]

Among the military groups that threatened to march on Williamsburg was a body of some six hundred cavalrymen from several counties of northern Virginia, assembled at Fredericksburg. They organized a council of war, probably on January 25, or 26, for on the latter date the council sent Mann Page, Jr., to Williamsburg to inquire if the powder had been restored. Page returned at once bearing a letter from Peyton Randolph stating that a satisfactory settlement would be reached and entreating the assembled troops to return home. Soon afterwards Randolph and Edmund Pendleton, on their way to the Continental Congress, arrived at Fredericksburg and gave the same advice in person. Thereupon, the council of war, which had been in session three days, advised the company to disband, and this action was promptly taken. On disbanding, the soldiers pledged each other to be in readiness, "at a moment's warning, to reassemble, and by force of arms, to defend the law, the liberty and rights of this or any sister Colony from unjust and wicked invasion." The declaration ended with the sentence: "God save the liberties of America."[16]

According to two authorities on this event (David John Mays and John Richard Alden), the troops at Fredericksburg also had been influenced to disband by Washington and Richard Henry Lee. This statement is supported by several contemporaries, including James Madison and John Marshall. The latter said that Lee presided over the council of war.[17] But the strongest evidence is against this view. Washington's *Diary* shows that he was at Mount Vernon or Alexandria during the entire period of the assembly at Fredericksburg. And a letter by Lee (April 25) shows that he was at home at the time, or only one day before, the Fredericksburg meeting began. If he had planned to take part in this council he would in all probability have stated this intention to his close friend, Landon Carter, to whom this letter was addressed.[18] Furthermore, in all the Lee papers, the Ballagh *Letters*, and the manuscript collections examined there has not been found a single letter from Lee advising action on this important occasion. It is therefore certain that Washington was not at the Fredericksburg meeting and very probable that Lee was not in attendance.

More persistent was another effort to regain the powder. A body of militia, under the command of Patrick Henry, marched from Hanover County toward the colonial capital to force Dunmore to give up this ammunition or pay for it. The governor was so frightened that he sent forward money to pay for the powder, and the troop turned back before it reached Williamsburg.[19]

Under such conditions, the governor did not feel certain as to his personal security. Lady Dunmore and her children were put on board the *Fowey*, a British warship. Dunmore remained at the "Palace" for a short time under the protection of an armed band of British seamen and slaves. Later (June, 1775) a battle was fought at Great Bridge, near Norfolk, between British and Virginia troops. The patriots were successful in the engagement and they forced Dunmore to leave Norfolk and to take shelter on a British vessel.[20]

In this unsettled state of affairs the colonial assembly could not be expected to function normally. Before adjourning in June, 1775, the House of Burgesses voted to meet again on

81

October 12. When it assembled at that time less than a quorum were present and the house adjourned without transacting any business. Two other abortive attempts at meeting were made (March 7 and May 6, 1776), but both of them failed from the lack of a quorum. It was in this undramatic way that this noted body ended its historic career. It was spared the death pangs that so often attend the passing of long-established institutions and died quietly in its sleep.[21]

The Second Continental Congress met in Philadelphia on May 10, 1775, the date set by its predecessor. In the beginning the membership of the second Congress was in the main the same as that of the first, and Virginia's distinguished delegation had been returned without change; but later Thomas Jefferson was named to fill the vacancy caused by the return of Randolph to Virginia to preside over the House of Burgesses. Other prominent new members were John Hancock of Massachusetts and James Wilson and Benjamin Franklin of Pennsylvania. As Georgia now had a representative, chosen by one parish, all thirteen colonies were represented.[22] After spending a night at Mount Vernon, Lee and Washington proceeded to Philadelphia and arrived there on the evening of May 9.[23] They and Benjamin Harrison had supper at the house of Joseph Reed the first night after their arrival in Philadelphia, and until early morning they discussed plans for the defense of the Delaware River against British warships.[24]

The second Congress was in effect a continuation of the first. Peyton Randolph and Charles Thomson were re-elected as president and secretary, respectively, and the old rule of secrecy was continued and strengthened. When Randolph was called back to duty in Virginia he was succeeded as president by John Hancock. The Congress started off under promising auspices. There seemed to be general agreement as to the main objectives. In the opinion of Richard Henry Lee there "never appeared more perfect unanimity among any set of men."[25]

When the second Congress began its first session, hostilities had started in Massachusetts, and the representatives from that colony asked Congress to take over their war and thus accept it as a continental conflict. Lee was prominent among those who held that the clash of arms in the North was an American, not merely a New England, war. Congress showed a willingness to comply with the request of Massachusetts, and voted (June 14) to raise ten companies of riflemen as a reinforcement for the army around Boston. These troops were to be paid by Congress and were to serve for one year "unless sooner discharged." Next day Congress appointed Washington to the command of "all the continental forces, raised, or to be raised, for the defense of American liberty." Lee was made chairman of a committee of three to draft Washington's commission and instructions. This committee promptly reported a commission and a list of instructions for the commander-in-chief, and Congress at once accepted both without change. Congress also directed Lee's committee to prepare the form of a commission for major generals, brigadier generals, and other officers in the army.[26]

Although in the first Continental Congress Lee had failed to meet the expectations of his colleagues when he wrote the first draft of the Address to the People of England,[27] he was appointed (June 3, 1775) chairman of a committee of three to prepare an Address to the Inhabitants of Great Britain. At the same time John Dickinson was first-named on a committee to report a petition to the King. These documents were prepared in due course, the former by Lee, the latter by Dickinson, and were adopted by Congress early in July.[28]

The Address written by Lee is a bold statement of the rights of the colonials and the grievances they had sustained at the hands of the British Ministry. Running through it all, not like a silver thread but a knotted cord, is regret that the British people have not supported their American brethren in the championship of freedom. It refers to the wounds that the colonials had received "fighting by your Side for the extention of the Empire," and expresses grief "that rash and inconsiderate Councils should precipitate the destruction of an Empire, which has been the envy and admiration of Ages." It lists as colonial grievances the denial of trial by jury, the annulment of colonial charters, the destruction of American commerce, the establishment of a despotic government in a neighboring province (Quebec), and the "rigorous Acts of Oppression which are daily exercised in the Town of *Boston*." The hope of coming to terms with the mother country had well-nigh been destroyed by the British military attack on America. "Can Men deliberate," it continued, "with the Bayonet at their Breast? Can they treat with Freedom, while their towns are sacked . . .?" The Ministry is now making the attempt "to reduce us by the Sword to a base and abject submission."

The Address pointed out to the British people that if the Americans were deprived of their freedom the loss of British freedom would follow. "Soldiers who have sheathed their Swords in the Bowels of their *American* Brethren, will not draw them with more reluctance against you." "Your liberty will be the price of your victory; your ruin, of your defeat." On the other hand, the Americans have every confidence in the ultimate success of their cause. Owing to their favorable geographical position, they could never be conquered by the British. "We can retire beyond the Reach of your Navy, and, without any sensible Diminution of the Necessaries of Life, enjoy a Luxury of being Free."

Official London opposed the measures of which the colonials complained. The sheriffs of London, along with Benjamin Franklin, Arthur Lee, and other prominent Americans located there, had signed a petition to the House of Lords against the bill then before Parliament to punish Boston for the destruction of the tea.[29] In appreciation of this aid to the American cause Congress ordered the committee charged with the duty of writing the address to the British people also to prepare a letter to the Lord Mayor of London. Lee, as chairman of this committee, prepared the text of this letter, which was approved by Congress on July 8, 1775. In the London letter the twelve colonies expressed their thanks to the Lord Mayor and the body of which he was the head for the "virtuous and unsolicited resentment" they have shown over the violation of American rights. "North America, my Lord," it declared, "wished most ardently for a lasting connection with G. Britain on terms of just and equal liberty. . . . A cruel war has at length been opened against us," and while we will defend ourselves, "we still hope that the mediation of wise and good Citizens, will at length prevail over despotism and restore peace and harmony on permanent principles to an oppressed and divided Empire."[30]

Both the "Petition to the King" and the "Address to the People of Great Britain" proved to be empty gestures. Arthur Lee and Richard Penn sent (September, 1775) a copy of the petition to the Secretary of State for America. When they pressed the Secretary for the King's answer they were told that the King would not give an answer.[31]

Shortly after adopting the "Address to the People of Great Britian" and the "Petition to the King," Congress broke an important strand in the cord that held the colonies to the mother country. This act was the adoption of a measure (July 26, 1775) for creating an independent American postal system.[32] The colonial post office had been under provincial management until 1691, when Thomas Neale was granted a patent giving him a monopoly for twenty one years of the postal business in all the British possessions in America. Acting on this patent, Neale appointed a deputy postmaster general in America who established an intercolonial postal system. The postal service under Neale's authority was carried on with a financial loss, and in 1707 he surrendered his patent to the British Royal Postal System.[33] Even before the beginning of the quarrel with the homeland, there had arisen considerable dissatisfaction with the Royal Postal Service in America, owing to the arrogance displayed by postal officials and the high rates charged for handling mail. This feeling of dissatisfaction grew quickly into a rebellion as a result of the policy carried out by the imperial post office after the controversy arose over the Stamp Act. According to John C. Fitzpatrick, "the Royal-Post Office interfered in every possible way that could block the efforts of the Colonies to obtain unanimity of action. It delayed and suppressed news and mishandled mail. Letters were opened, read, and destroyed, and the information thus obtained was transmitted to the royal authorities."[34]

The progressive leaders in Congress felt that the only way to put an end to this intolerable situation was to organize an American postal system to supersede the Royal Mail Service. Lee took the lead in the movement by which the colonial postal system was transferred from British to American management. He moved that the ministerial post be stopped since a post had been established from New Hampshire to Georgia. John Langdon of New Hampshire seconded the motion; Thomas Willing of Pennsylvania opposed it, on the ground that it was going back beyond the line which the patriot leaders had originally set for themselves—that of 1763. It will be early enough, he said, to throw aside the royal post "when the time comes that we shall throw everything aside." Dr. John Zubly of Georgia also opposed the resolution stating that in Georgia they had received news from the King's post that they could not have obtained in any other way. R. R. Livingston also said that the royal post was a convenience.

In support of his motion, Lee argued as follows: "When the Ministry are mutilating our correspondence in England, and our enemies here are corresponding for our ruin, shall we not stop the ministerial post?" "No intelligence comes to us, but constant intelligence to our enemies." Robert Treat Paine was of the opinion that the ministerial post would die a natural death. ". . . it has been," he said, "under a languishment a great while; it would be cowardice to issue a decree to kill that which is dying; it brought but one letter last time. . . . " To this Lee replied, "Is there not a Doctor, Lord North, who can keep this creature alive?"[35] Lee's motion was adopted and in May a committee was appointed to devise a plan for an American postal system. Lee, as a member of this committee, proposed the creation of a post office department that would have charge of the business of conveying and distributing letters throughout the colonies.[36] This proposal was accepted by Congress on July 26, 1775. The independence of the American postal system thus came nearly a year ahead of political independence.

In establishing the American post office, Congress did not appropriate the machinery of the Royal Mail Service, but took over and developed a postal system that had been organized by William Goddard, an enterprising newspaper publisher. Goddard, the owner of the weekly *Maryland Journal and Baltimore Advertiser*, had been upholding the rights of the colonies with courage and enthusiasm. Owing to his severe criticism of British policy, his newspaper was refused the use of the mails. Whereupon he formed a plan for delivering copies of his weekly by sending out his own riders, who covered routes extending from Maine to Georgia. His riders were more reliable than those of the Royal Mail Service, and it was not long before the people living along their routes began to entrust them with their letters and small packages.[37]

On July 12, Congress appointed a committee of five to devise ways and means to protect the trade of the colonies. Lee and Franklin as members of this committee each offered a plan in the committee's report of July 21, 1775. Lee proposed that, since recent acts of Parliament had forbidden the colonies to export their produce to any place other than Great Britain, Ireland, and the British West Indies, after a certain number of months (if recent acts of Parliament for restraining colonial trade were not repealed) all customhouses in the thirteen colonies be closed and all the ports of the confederacy be thrown open to all foreign countries to purchase American produce and to import and sell free of duties all products and manufactures except tea and the merchandise of Great Britain, Ireland, and the British West Indies. He also proposed that the colonies stop all exportation by themselves after a certain date in order to keep the ships and armies of our enemies from being supplied with our produce and also to compel a speedy and just settlement of the dispute between the colonies and Great Britain.[38]

Lee had earlier opposed including the British navigation laws in the list of colonial grievances. He was now, however, willing to violate these acts by encouraging the exportation of American goods to foreign ports. He argued as follows: "We shall be prevented from exporting, if British power can do it. We ought to stop our own exports, and invite foreign nations to come and export our goods for us. I am for opening our exportations to foreigners, further than we have."[39]

Lee's proposal was not accepted but it was finally decided that exports should be allowed, even encouraged, to the foreign West Indies in exchange for saltpetre and war supplies. Rice still could be exported to foreign countries, except Great Britain and her possessions. With these exceptions, there was to be no exportation from the colonies to foreign ports prior to March 1, 1776, without the permission or order of Congress.[40]

If Congress had fully accepted the original recommendation of its committee on colonial trade and had opened up unrestricted trade with other powers it would have meant defiance of the British navigation laws and entrance upon the road to independence. And yet the war could not be carried on without arms and these could be had through foreign trade only, for the British government had forbidden the export of arms to the American colonies. Accordingly, it was decided to open the door to foreign trade only to the extent of allowing war supplies to be secured.

Lee also had a share in an effort to end a serious conflict that had grown out of a boundary dispute between Pennsylvania and Virginia. In northwestern Virginia, or southwestern Pennsylvania, the settlers had taken up arms in defense of their alleged landed rights. To end this serious threat to federal unity, Congress referred this problem to a committee composed of members from both states. Prominent among Pennsylvania's representatives were Benjamin Franklin, John Dickinson, and James Wilson. Virginia's representatives were Patrick Henry, Richard Henry Lee, Benjamin Harrison, and Thomas Jefferson.

In its report, made July 25, 1775, the committee indicated deep concern over the disturbances that had arisen but expressed no opinion as to which side was right. It made, however, a strong appeal for a truce in the controversy so that a united front might be presented for the good of "our common country." The committee also recommended that all armed bodies be dismissed and that all who had been in confinement for taking part in the contest be released.[41]

In 1779 the two states appointed a joint commission which settled the disputed question by extending the Mason and Dixon Line due west to five degrees of longitude west of the Delaware River and thence due north to Lake Erie. The agreement was ratified by both states and the lines were run by a joint commission, which completed its work in 1786. Virginia had waived her claims on condition that the land grants already made by her be validated.[42]

Congress adjourned on August 1 and three days later Lee left Philadelphia to take his seat in the Virginia Convention. He arrived at Richmond on August 11 and at once entered upon his duties as a member of the Convention, which had been in session since July 17. On the day of his arrival the Convention elected Virginia's delegates to Congress for another term. In the seven-member group Lee came second—next to Peyton Randolph—in the number of votes received.[43]

Lee was in attendance in the Convention less than two weeks, for on August 22, he was called away "to settle the accounts of the militia lately drawn out into actual service." In this short time, however, he performed some useful services for the Old Dominion. He was a member of two committees, each of which framed an important ordinance. One offered a plan for encouraging the production of saltpetre, gunpowder, and lead, the refining of sulphur, and the providing of arms for the colony. The other made a recommendation, which was accepted by the Convention, for creating a Committee of Public Safety.[44]

After an absence of a few weeks in Virginia, Lee returned to Philadelphia (September 24) and resumed his seat in Congress. For the period of three months (until he again left Congress, December 23) he was engaged as usual in committee work. One important committee of which he was a member prepared an answer to two letters that Congress had received from the commander-in-chief. In addition to joining in this official communication, Lee at the same time (September 26) sent a personal letter to Washington reporting some of the recent developments in Virginia and expressing in strong terms his approval of the way in which Washington was managing the war. His letter sounded a note of unwarranted optimism as to the prospective outcome of the fight for their rights. He expressed the belief that the enemies of the American cause in England would "shortly meet with a total overthrow. The entire failure of all their schemes and the rising spirit of the people . . . clearly denote this."[45]

In this session Lee also took an important part in the initial effort to create a federal navy. Congress voted (October, 1775) to fit out four vessels. Lee was a member of the committee appointed to contract for the construction of these ships and conducted much of its official correspondence. In November the committee, in a letter written by him, instructed Silas Deane to go to New York and buy two ships and have them fitted out and furnished with crews.[46]

The creation of the federal navy was a further step toward separation from England; it was opposed by the conservatives who still hoped for a settlement of the quarrel with the mother country and feared that the establishment of a continental navy would block the road to reconciliation. Despite their opposition, Congress voted (December 10) to appoint a committee, composed of one representative from each colony, to "devise ways and means of furnishing these colonies with a naval armament." Lee was the Virginia representative. The committee in a prompt report stated that thirteen ships could be made ready, probably by the end of March, and recommended that a committee be appointed to carry out this plan. Congress accepted the proposal and chose Lee to represent Virginia on the new committee. By December 22 the committee had chosen a list of officers for the fleet, among whom was Lieutenant John Paul Jones.[47]

Writing from Philadelphia (November 29, 1775) to Mrs. Catherine Macaulay, the historian, Lee said with optimism: "No doubt is entertained here, but that this Congress will be shortly joined by Delegates from Canada, which will then complete the union of 14 provinces." America is determined, he continued, to prepare for defense both by sea and land. He admitted that the colonies were not then in a position to meet the British force at sea, but "as Hercules was once in his cradle," so the infant American navy would in time (by next spring he hoped) be in condition "to annoy our enemies greatly, and to afford much protection to the Trade of North America."[48]

On December 23, 1775, Lee left Congress to return to his home in Virginia after three months of hard work on the floor and in committees.

Chapter VII

Secession from the Empire

Authorities on the American Revolution apparently are not certain as to the exact date at which colonial dissent crossed the line that separated loyal opposition from the demand for independence. It was a jagged line and was reached by the majority of the people in some colonies earlier than in others. More than likely, the leaders, especially the radicals, were converted to independence some time before they professed this faith in their public utterances or even in their private correspondence. If they had declared this belief before the general public was ready for it they would have been uttering true prophecy. But every age either repudiates or stones its prophets; and the Revolutionary leaders, even the most liberal among them, were politicians, not martyrs. There is even a conflict in the evidence as to when such radical leaders as Samuel Adams, John Adams, and Richard Henry Lee became advocates of independence.[1]

In the early stages of the opposition to British policy there was in the leadership of Virginia no expectation or desire for separation from the mother country. Protests against British policy, although of strong tone, all were expressed in the most respectful terms and allegiance to the empire was emphasized. Perhaps we should credit these expressions of loyalty to conventional politeness; and yet, after making due allowance for exaggeration in the overcautious protestations, we can still note in them a pride in Virginia's membership in the empire. Even such drastic measures as the nonimportation agreements were adopted with the hope—certainly on the part of the conservative leaders—that these associations would cause a redress of their grievances and thus prevent an assertion of independence.

When war broke out in April, 1775, a majority of the colonials were still opposed to separation from the empire. They hoped that the fight would be a brief one and would end in a recognition of their rights by the British government; but feeling between the mother country and the continental colonies grew in bitterness as the war progressed, and the desire for independence developed rapidly. The growth of this feeling was greatly promoted by British policy. In August, 1775, the King issued a proclamation declaring that America was in a state of rebellion and should be treated as such.[2] This was followed by an act of Parliament prohibiting all trade and intercourse with the continental colonies as long as they were in a state of rebellion. The opponents of this act in England and the radical colonials contended that it was a formal abdication by the British government of its connection with the colonies and was thus a virtual declaration of their independence. John Adams stated that the King, by this act, had declared America independent.[3]

Under such circumstances it was both inconsistent and unwise for the colonies to continue to declare their loyalty to the empire. To profess loyalty to a government against which they were waging war was to continue to sit on the limb at which they were sawing. The choice was to quit sawing or get off the limb. America chose the latter alternative.[4] Among the Virginia leaders, Richard Henry Lee was one of the first to advocate independence, but we cannot say just when he first took this stand.

In his conversion to an advocacy of independence, Lee probably was strongly influenced by Thomas Paine's *Common Sense*. His friend, Colonel Landon Carter, spoke of Lee "as a prodigious admirer, if not partly a writer," of this treatise.[5] Lee seems to have taken a stand in favor of independence early in 1776, and possibly before the end of 1775; for on February 3, 1776, John Page wrote to Lee stating his agreement with him on independence.[6] Lee had come to feel that the British government was an incurable despotism. Writing to Carter (April 1) he said: "As well, dear Sir, might a person expect to wash an Ethopian white as to remove the taint of despotism from the British court."[7]

By April, 1776, Lee was urging an assertion of independence. In a letter to Patrick Henry (April 20) he declared that the "late act of Parliament had to every intent and purpose dissolved our government, uncommissioned every magistrate, and placed us in the high road to Anarchy." "We cannot be rebels excluded from the King's protection and Magistrates acting under his authority at the same time." It was therefore necessary for Virginia to declare her independence and form a government of her own. Virginia was urged to take this step not only on account of the necessity imposed upon her by these developments but as an example to other colonies. If Virginia should take this stand, he felt that North Carolina, Maryland, Pennsylvania, and New York would follow. Quoting Shakespeare, he said, "There is a tide in the affairs of men," with the inference that the colonies were then on such a tide. We are, he continued, a people engaged in war with a powerful nation, without taking any steps to secure the friendship or even the neutrality of foreign nations. We cannot pay taxes and carry on the war effectively without being able to sell our produce. We cannot do this unless we can trade with foreign countries. These foreign countries will not negotiate with us for trade so long as we consider ourselves subjects of Great Britain. "Honor, dignity, and the customs of states forbid them until we take rank as an independent people."[8]

The main reason for delay by Congress in issuing a declaration, he said, was that "we are heavily clogged with instructions from these shamefully interested Proprietary people, and this will continue until Virga. sets the example of taking up Government, and sending peremptory orders to their delegates to pursue the most effectual measures for the Security of America."[9]

Lee soon participated in an important move taken by Congress toward independence. In May, 1776, Congress passed a resolution, sponsored by Lee and John Adams, recommending that those colonies in which new governments had not been established adopt such forms of government as would best serve their safety and welfare. John Adams was greatly pleased with this action. "This day," he said, "the Congress has passed the most important resolution that was ever taken in America." He considered it a virtual declaration of independence. A committee of three, Adams, Edward Rutledge, and Lee, was appointed to prepare a preamble to this resolution. The suggestions offered by the committee were sent out promptly to the states.[10]

During the first third of 1776 sentiment in favor of independence grew rapidly in Virginia as it did in the other colonies; therefore, when the convention met at Williamsburg on May 6,

1776, it was in the mood to move rapidly toward separation from the empire. The resolutions adopted in the counties showed that the people throughout the colony were in favor of independence. With such support, the convention felt free to take a radical stand in favor of separation.[11]

The convention was organized with Edmund Pendleton as president. A resolution was unanimously adopted which instructed the Virginia delegates in Congress to propose a declaration of independence and to support whatever measures might be deemed wise and necessary for foreign alliances and a confederation of the colonies. The convention also unanimously adopted the Bill of Rights and the state constitution.[12]

According to Thomas Ludwell Lee, a member of the convention, the action of the convention gave "infinite joy" to the people of Richmond. "The exultation here," he said, "was extreme, the british flag was immediately struck on the Capitol, and a continental hoisted in its room. The troops were drawn out, and we had a discharge of Artillery and small arms."[13] The action by the Virginia convention also was most acceptable to Richard Henry. Writing to Landon Carter on June 2, 1776, he said that it was not choice but necessity that called for independence as the only means by which foreign alliances and federation for internal peace and security could be obtained. Nor did he see any danger to American liberties (as some feared) from an alliance with a despotic power like France.[14]

Lee had advised the Virginia Convention to establish a new government to prevent the lawlessness that would result when it was known that government had been annulled by the last "wicked act of Parliament." For "we cannot be in rebellion," he said, "and without the king's protection, and Magistrates acting under his authority, at the same time."[15] He also suggested a plan of government for Virginia. George Wythe had written to John Adams (January, 1776) asking him for suggestions as to new state constitutions. Thomas Paine in his *Common Sense* had suggested a plan of government for the states and one for the United States. Adams considered Paine's proposals foolish and dangerous. In response to Wythe's request, and with the hope of counteracting this danger, Adams wrote a pamphlet entitled *Thoughts on Government,* in which he outlined a scheme of state government. Lee was so pleased with Adams' plan that he had it published, first in New York and then in the *Virginia Gazette*. By revising and publicizing Adams' plan and issuing a broadside of his own, Lee outlined a constitution for the prospective commonwealth.[16]

The instructions issued by the Virginia convention were brought to Philadelphia by Thomas Nelson, Jr., and were presented to and read by Congress on May 27,[17] but no further action was taken on them until June 7. On that day Lee offered the following resolutions:

> Resolved, That these United Colonies are, and of right ought to be, free and independent States, that they are absolved from all allegiance to the British Crown, and that all political connection between them and the State of Great Britain is, and ought to be totally dissolved.
>
> That it is expedient forthwith to take the most effectual measures for forming foreign Alliances.
>
> That a plan of confederation be prepared and transmitted to the respective Colonies for their consideration and approbation.[18]

John Adams supported the resolutions in a strong address,[19] and according to tradition Lee made a great speech in their favor. No authentic report of Lee's speech has come down to us, but in Charles Botta's *History of the War of the Independence of the United States of America* is given what the author seemed to accept as the substance of this oration.[20]

The alleged speech, as reported by Botta, was in line with Lee's known views, and ended in a burst of eloquence:

> Why then, do we longer delay, why still deliberate? Let this most happy day give birth to the American republic. Let her arise, not to devastate and conquer, but to re-establish the reign of peace and of the laws. The eyes of Europe are fixed upon us; she demands of us a living example of freedom, that may contrast, by the felicity of the citizens, with the ever increasing tyranny which desolates her polluted shores. She invites us to prepare an asylum where the unhappy may find solace, and the persecuted repose. She intreats us to cultivate a propitious soil, where that generous plant which first sprung up and grew in England, but is now withered by the poisonous blasts of Scottish tyranny, may re-

vive and flourish, sheltering under its salubrious and interminable shade all the unfortunate of the human race. . . . If we are not this day wanting in our duty to country, the names of the American legislators will be placed, by posterity, at the side of those of Theseus, of Lycurgus, and of all those whose memory has been, and will be dear forever to virtuous men and good citizens.

Modern historians are inclined to the view that Botta was indebted for this text partly to tradition and partly to his own creative imagination. Although the oration, with its smooth style, apt figures, and references to Greek, Roman, Dutch, and Swiss history, has a ring similar to that of Lee's known speeches, the one long, involved sentence raises some question as to its genuineness.

Lee's resolutions were debated in committee of the whole for two days (June 8 and 10) and it was decided to postpone further consideration of them until July 1. The reason given for this delay was that New York, New Jersey, Pennsylvania, Delaware and Maryland "were not yet matured for falling from the parent stem, but they were fast advancing to that state."[21] Prominent among those who were opposed to immediate adoption of the resolution for independence were James Wilson and John Dickinson of Pennsylvania, Robert R. Livingston of New York, and Edward Rutledge of South Carolina. They were in favor of independence, they declared, but were opposed to taking the step at that time.

At the appointed time the resolution for independence came up again for consideration, and after two days of discussion in committee of the whole it was adopted on July 2 without a dissenting vote.[22] The resolution as finally accepted was the one originally offered by Lee. Furthermore, that part of Jefferson's noted document that declares the independence of the colonies is in the exact words of Lee's motion. So Lee was the real author of the declaration of independence (written with a small "d"), although Jefferson deserves credit for the authorship of the Declaration of Independence. July 2 was regarded by John Adams as the real day of independence, and he felt that it would be chosen as the date for annual celebration.[23]

In the meantime Congress had appointed (June 11) a committee to draft a declaration of independence. This committee was composed of Thomas Jefferson, John Adams, Benjamin Franklin, Roger Sherman, and Robert R. Livingston, with Jefferson as chairman.[24] It was the custom then as now for the mover of a resolution to be selected as chairman of the committee provided for by the motion. That Lee was not appointed to this important place is one of the events for which we do not have a satisfactory explanation. The explanation given by Lee's contemporaries is far from convincing.

The immediate reason or excuse for leaving him off the committee was that he was absent from Congress when the committee was preparing the Declaration. He left Philadelphia for Virginia on June 13, 1776, and so was present when the committee was chosen; but he did not return until after the middle of August.[25] Why he left at this time is one of the puzzles that the student of history has some difficulty in solving. His grandsons said that he had been called home by the illness of his wife,[26] but in none of his extant letters does Lee give this as a reason. On the contrary, he said that he had left Congress to attend the Virginia Convention at Williamsburg so as to take part in "the formation of our new government."[27]

It is true that he had been elected a member of the Virginia Convention, and, like other Virginia leaders, he probably considered state affairs more important than federal. Peyton Randolph seems to have held this view, for he gave up the presidency of Congress to preside over a short session of the Virginia House of Burgesses. It is quite likely, therefore, that Lee was willing to forego the opportunity to help write the declaration in order to have a hand in the establishment of the government in his home state.

Furthermore, he was urged to follow this course by friends on whose judgment he relied. John Page had written to him on February 20, saying: "I think you had better attend the Assembly. You will be more wanted here [Williamsburg] than at the Congress."[28] George Mason also wrote to him making this suggestion: "I need not tell you how much you will be wanted here on this occasion. I speak with the sincerity of a friend, when I assure you that, in my opinion, your presence cannot, must not be dispensed with. . . . All your friends anxiously expect you."[29] Richard Henry's brother, Francis Lightfoot, in urging him to come to Williamsburg expressed the fear that if affairs at Williamsburg were "not regulated and directed by a skillful hand," the good intentions of the members "might dissipate in idle fumes or be blasted by the arts of sly timidity." Thomas Ludwell wrote that all of his (Richard Henry's) friends thought that his presence at Williamsburg "is of the last consequence."[30] Patrick Henry and Augustine Washington also wrote to him expressing the hope that he could attend this session of the Assembly.[31]

A pamphlet attributed to Carter Braxton, entitled *An Address to the Convention of the Colony and Ancient Dominion of Virginia on the Subject of Government*, proposed an aristocratic plan of government sharply at variance with the trend toward democracy.[32] Lee said that the ideas of "this Contemptible little Tract" were so unsound and so badly organized and expressed as to "put it out of danger of doing harm."[33] But despite his protestations to the contrary, he may have feared that some of the objectionable proposals of Braxton's plan might be embodied in Virginia's constitution. So, all things considered, patriotism seemed to beckon him to Williamsburg rather than to Philadelphia.

In his efforts to serve both his state and the confederation in their movements for independence, Richard Henry Lee came near to slipping between two stools. Before his arrival at Williamsburg in 1776 Virginia already had adopted her famous Bill of Rights, but he was there in time to vote for the adoption of the new state constitution.[34] In Congress he not only missed the opportunity to draft the final Declaration of Independence, but he left Philadelphia before his own resolution for independence had been voted on.

On July 4, 1776, Congress adopted Jefferson's Declaration by a vote of twelve colonies after some important changes had been made in the first draft.[35] Two weeks later (July 19) Congress voted that the Declaration be engrossed on parchment and signed by members of that body. On August 2 all members present signed the Declaration, and those who were absent later attached their signatures. In the list of final signers were both Richard Henry and Francis Lightfoot Lee.[36]

If Lee ever harbored any deep regret over losing the author-ship of America's best-known public document, he failed to re-veal this in his extant correspondence. Dying (1794) before the new republic gave promise of becoming the world's greatest power, he may never have fully realized how important an op-portunity he had missed. While he may have been slightly jealous of Jefferson,[37] no evidence has been found indicating that Lee harbored ill will toward him. He expressed a high opinion of Jefferson's work in writing the Declaration, and their relations continued to be most friendly. When Jefferson sent him a copy of the Declaration, Lee expressed regret that Jefferson's original draft had been "mangled" by revision. "However," he continued, "the Thing is in its nature so good, that no Cookery can spoil the Dish for the palates of Freemen."[38]

Although Lee did not win the prestige that went with the authorship of the Declaration of Independence, he did as much as any leader of the period in promoting the movement that led to the separation of the colonies from the empire, and the British authorities seem to have appreciated the part he played in in-fluencing America to take this important step. At the time the Declaration was adopted, Richard Henry's son Ludwell was at school at St. Bees in England. Young Lee later reported to the author of Lee's *Memoir* that the ministerial newspapers, in an-nouncing the adoption of the Declaration, headed their column as follows: "Richard Henry Lee and Patrick Henry have at last accomplished their object: The colonies have declared them-selves independent of the mother country." Ludwell was twitted by his associates with statements like this: "We shall yet see your father's head on Tower Hill." Ludwell, evidently a chip off the old block, replied: "You may have it when you can get it."[39]

Just why the Lees and others of the Virginia aristocracy played so important a role in launching the Revolution is a fact that historians have had difficulty in explaining. At first glance it would seem that this class instead of taking the lead would have been most reluctant to follow in a movement that ulti-mately resulted in separation from the homeland. For at the be-ginning of the seventeen sixties they were bound to the mother country by the strongest economic, social, and sentimental ties. They looked to British money lenders for the credit needed in carrying on their farming and business ventures and depended largely upon British markets in disposing of their tobacco. They also belonged to the Anglican church, followed the English fashions in dress, and adopted the conventions of the gentry in their social customs. Moreover, they felt pride in belonging to an empire that was the greatest power in the world. For the English constitution they had a respect that amounted almost to reverence. The literary and educational ideals of the mother country were accepted without question. Shakespeare and the other masters of English poetry and prose were held in the highest esteem. In short, they regarded themselves as Englishmen away from home. Before the controversy over taxation arose, not only the conservatives, but also the radicals among the gentry felt a strong attachment to the empire. Such bonds of loyalty could have been broken only by strong counteracting forces.

One explanation that has been offered is that the planters were deeply indebted to British creditors and that separation from the empire would have the effect of erasing this indebtedness. It is true that many, if not most, of the Virginia planters were heavily in debt to British creditors at the outbreak of the Revolution. Thomas Jefferson thought that the debt of Virginia was nearly as much as that of all the rest of the colonies.[40] As has been seen, in the Old Dominion there was a suspension of these debt payments in 1765 and later, resulting from the closure of the courts in civil suits. This proved to be an effective weapon in the fight against the Stamp Act since British creditors brought pressure to bear on the Government in favor of the repeal of measures objectionable to the colonials. A large proportion of the Virginians favored the cancellation of British debts; most of the dominant class were not thinking of repudiation, however, but were intending ultimately to pay their debts to foreign creditors. They therefore regarded the initial nonpayment only as a political weapon. Some of the prominent leaders were even opposed to using the temporary nonpayment of British debts as a political weapon.[41]

Opposition to the payment of British debts was strong enough to induce the Assembly to pass an act (May, 1782) declaring that the debts due British creditors were not recoverable.[42] When news of the treaty of peace reached Virginia there was at first a strong feeling of indignation against the clause in the treaty which provided for the payment of pre-Revolutionary debts.

George Mason occasionally heard this question: "If we are now to pay the debts due to British merchants, what have we been fighting for all this while?"[43]

Congress formally ratified the peace treaty January 14, 1784, and then urged each state to repeal all laws preventing the collection of British debts.[44] Acting in line with this recommendation, James Madison offered in the Virginia House of Delegates (June, 1784) a resolution declaring that all laws then in force that prevented "a due compliance with the stipulations contained in the definitive [peace] treaty" should be repealed. A motion in favor of Madison's resolution was defeated, with Richard Henry Lee supporting and Patrick Henry opposing it.[45] In December, 1787, when Lee was no longer a member of the House, the Virginia Assembly passed a bill repealing all acts that prevented the recovery of debts due British subjects, but the act was to be suspended until Great Britain had given up the western posts and returned the slaves taken away from Virginia by the British army.[46] In the beginning there was no expectation or intention that opposition would bring about separation from the homeland. Nothing in the way of cancellation of debt could therefore be expected. In the light of these facts and others brought out by recent research, authorities on the debt question are very doubtful as to its being an important issue in bringing on the Revolution in Virginia.[47]

A more reasonable explanation can be found in the character and traditions of the Virginia gentry. They always had been quick to uphold their political rights and in doing so had several times gone to the length of deposing governors. Indeed, the contest between this privileged class and the King's representative had at times been not unlike the ancient struggle in England between the King and the nobility. So the Virginia barons were not contending for new privileges but old rights. It was not a case of the common people clamoring for the elimination of old abuses, but mainly that of the gentry fighting to preserve old principles.

In the beginning the leaders were contending not for the natural rights of man but for the prescriptive rights of Englishmen. Some of the radical leaders (probably Lee among them) were influenced even from the beginning by the doctrine of natural rights proclaimed by the French philosophers, but such views played no significant part until the movement had taken a turn toward independence. In its earlier stages the opposition was led in the main by men who asked only for a redress of their grievances and hoped that the measures adopted by them would bring about this result. They did not foresee that the movement could not be kept within the limits defined by them. They did not realize that by sowing the wind they would reap the whirlwind. Furthermore, the conservatives, who originally intended to confine their dissent to loyal opposition, were borne along with the tide in both feeling and action; and when independence was finally declared they accepted separation as the logical outcome of unexpected developments. It must have been with mixed feelings, however, that the leaders, both radicals and conservatives, viewed this important step. With the joy that came with the freedom to set up house for themselves must have been mingled sorrow at the final departure from the parental roof.

In adjusting their political principles to the adverse circumstances, the Virginia patriciate had to make a violent break in their sentiments and social traditions. With the Lee family this wrench was especially severe. The aggressive policy of Richard Henry and four of his brothers in the Revolutionary cause was a reversal of the precedents set by their forbears, who were strongly conservative and against the revolutionary movements of their day.[48]

As we view in retrospect the events of the decade preceding the Declaration we can see that separation from the empire was the logical outcome of the developments of the period. Even if the colonies had not had any serious grievances against the mother country, they still would have been within their rights in demanding independence; for America had reached adulthood and no longer needed to be tied to the apron string of the motherland. According to Dr. Lawrence Henry Gipson, the Revolution was not caused by the "deeds or misdeeds" of the radical American leaders or the policy of George III and his ministers, but was due to "the growth of nationalism and a sense of self-sufficiency in the colonies after 1763."[49]

While the time had come for American independence, the manner in which it came was one of the tragic blunders of history. The political bond with the homeland should have been broken but the sentimental and economic ties need not have been severed. A proper solution would have left America in a relationship with England similar to that sustained today by Canada and Australia. That such an adjustment was not reached was due in part to the ineptness of the British government; but the main reason that the controversy developed into conflict was that at that time world opinion accepted the right of a parent state to rule over its colonies in a condition of dependence. If England had then had the same attitude toward colonialism that she has recently shown, there would have been no Revolutionary war. To blame her for this view, however, would be to expect her to have adopted in the last quarter of the eighteenth century principles that were not generally accepted until near the middle of the twentieth.

Chapter VIII

War Diplomacy

Lee's absence from Congress, occasioned by his attendance at the Virginia convention, was only a temporary break in his Congressional career. Returning to Philadelphia late in August, 1776, he resumed activity in the federal assembly and continued his membership until late in May, 1779. During this time, although he was absent at intervals—some of them of considerable length—because of ill health, the demands of his private affairs, or attendance in the Virginia House of Delegates, he was able to take an important part in the achievements of Congress.[1] One of these services was the part he played in the diplomacy that led to foreign aid and the French Alliance. To secure foreign aid was one strong reason for a declaration of independence. In pursuance of this aim, Congress on September 18, 1775, established a secret committee of nine to contract for the importation of gunpowder. Later in the same year (November 29) it appointed another secret committee—this one with a membership of five—to correspond with the friends of America in Great Britain, Ireland, and other parts of the world.[2] These two committees were at first known respectively as the Secret Committee (which later became the Committee of Commerce) and the Committee of Correspondence. "This [latter] committee was the embryo of an American foreign office." It was later superseded by the Committee for Foreign Affairs and still later (1781) by the Secretary of Foreign Affairs.[3]

By October, 1776, Lee had become a member of the Committee of Secret Correspondence and was active in its service. For the next two years his name frequently appears as signatory to letters sent by the diplomatic committee and often it heads the list of signatures. He wrote some of the important letters sent by the diplomatic committee to the American commissioners in France, and the original manuscripts of these letters were in his handwriting.[4] He was also a member of special committees that had to do with foreign affairs.[5]

In an effort to maintain secrecy in the management of foreign affairs Congress adopted resolutions (August, 1778) instructing the Committee of Secret Correspondence to keep secret from all but members of Congress, "under like obligation of secrecy," all information that it might receive from correspondence. Lee voted against these resolutions on the ground that the injunction of secrecy was not generally obeyed and that these provisions imposed restraints on the honorable members of the committee which were disregarded by the others. He was also opposed to the secrecy with which Congress conducted other affairs. Later (April 21, 1779) he moved that the doors of Congress be open and the motion was referred to a committee of which he was chairman. Apparently, nothing came of this attempt, for in October of the same year he spoke of the secrecy of Congress as an objectionable practice.[6]

On December 12, 1775, the Committee of Secret Correspondence sent a request to Arthur Lee, who was then in London as the agent of Massachusetts, that he sound out the European powers, especially France, as to their attitude toward the American cause.[7] Early in January, 1776, two Frenchmen, Penet and Pliarne, came to Philadelphia and entered into negotiation with the Secret Committee of Commerce to furnish military supplies and other materials to the Americans. They also intimated that the French government would not interfere with American trade with France. Influenced by these strong hints, Congress, on the recommendation of both secret committees, in March, 1776, appointed Silas Deane as its commercial representative in Europe. He was to go to France to find out the attitude of the French government toward American independence and toward prospective treaties of alliance between France and the American colonies.[8]

Deane and Arthur Lee were able to secure valuable supplies for the continental army. During the first two and a half years ninety per cent of the powder came from Europe, most of it from France.[9] Unfortunately Deane did not confine his activity to procuring supplies; he also made some other commitments that embarrassed Congress and brought serious criticism upon himself. He and William Bingham, American agent in Martinique, encouraged too many foreign soldiers to go to America and claim positions as officers in the American army.

While some of these foreigners did good service, many of them proved a serious embarrassment to Washington. Not only was there a language difficulty; but if Washington had assigned them the commands called for in their commissions, he would have discriminated unfairly against American officers and aroused their jealousy and just opposition. Generals Knox, Sullivan, and Greene announced that they would resign if Congress should confirm the Deane contracts. Washington wrote to Richard Henry Lee, pointing out the difficulties presented by these commissions and appealed to him for help.[10]

Congress was placed in a difficult position by these contracts, and on one occasion refused to comply with an agreement made by Deane with some French soldiers, although they had already come to America. Disgusted with this refusal, the soldiers returned to France. Lee rightfully felt that such action on the part of Congress and its foreign representative would have an unfavorable effect on public sentiment in France.[11]

The action of Congress in declaring the independence of the colonies did not destroy the hope of the British government of coming to terms with the rebellious Americans. On September 6, 1776, General Sullivan, a paroled American officer, presented to Congress a request from General Howe for a conference with a committee of Congress with the view to ending the war by agreement. Richard Henry Lee opposed such a conference, feeling that it would only serve to weaken the American cause. Congress, however, voted to meet the request by appointing a committee composed of John Adams, Edward Rutledge, and Benjamin Franklin to confer with Howe. Lee was placed in nomination for membership on the committee but was not chosen. He and Rutledge were tied on the first ballot and then Lee announced that he would not serve.[12] In their conference with General Howe the commissioners insisted on the recognition of the independence of the American states as a necessary condition of peace. Howe had no authority to negotiate on this basis and the conference ended in deadlock.[13]

It will be recalled that Lee's motion (June 7, 1776) for independence included this provision: "That it is expedient forthwith to take the most effectual measures for forming foreign alliances." In furtherance of this proposal a committee on foreign alliances was duly appointed. On July 18, 1776, this committee reported an elaborate "Plan of Treaties," which with slight modification was adopted September 17, 1776. The plan was written by John Adams, with liberal borrowings from European treaties of the eighteenth century. This draft, with a few changes, became the text of the Treaty of Amity and Commerce afterwards made between France and the United States (1778) and the model for nearly all the treaties of the United States prior to 1800.[14]

The adoption of this plan was followed by the creation of a commission with instructions to offer a treaty of amity and alliance with the French government. Lee's name, along with five others, including that of Lafayette, was in the original list of nominees for the place of commissioner to France, but Lee's name was dropped before the vote was taken, apparently at his request; as he stated in a letter to Samuel Adams, he felt that others were more able than he to discharge the duties of this responsible office.[15] Silas Deane, Benjamin Franklin, and Thomas Jefferson were appointed as members of the commission. Jefferson declined the appointment and Arthur Lee was chosen in his stead.

The Committee of Secret Correspondence gave instructions to the commissioners, directing them to point out the necessity of a speedy declaration of war by France and of European assistance for securing American independence. The French government must be made to see that if the Americans were defeated, the American soldiers, being trained to the use of arms, would be compelled by Britain to aid in the conquest of French American possessions. By this time Richard Henry had become a member of the Committee and his name appears as signatory to these instructions,[16] which were probably written by him.

The American commissioners for a time were not accorded official recognition. Not until the surrender of Burgoyne at Saratoga (October, 1777) gave hope of success to the Americans did Vergennes and the French king decide to risk war with Great Britain. This they now did by signing (February 6, 1778) a treaty of commerce and one of a defensive and offensive alliance between the United States and France. By the Treaty of Alliance, France agreed to recognize the independence of the States and aid them in their fight for independence.[17]

Lee felt that the French Alliance placed American independence beyond all doubt. Writing to John Page the day after Congress received these treaties, Richard Henry said:

> There appears a magnanimity and wisdom in his most Christian Majesty exemplified in these Treaties with France, that does him great honor. It was surely magnanimous not to take advantage of our situation so as to obtain unequal advantage. . . . If England were wise she would immediately acknowledge our Independence and make as France has done a Treaty with us, which, if agreed to on her part without making war on France, might give peace to the world.[18]

Congress ratified these two treaties by a unanimous vote on May 4, 1778, and appointed a committee of three, of which Lee was first-named, to prepare a form of ratification.[19] Two days later the committee reported a draft but it was recommitted and Gouverneur Morris was added to the committee. A second draft, submitted in the afternoon of the same day, was adopted.[20]

The surrender of Burgoyne at Saratoga not only put a new face on American relations with France but also opened up an opportunity for Congress to come to terms with Great Britain. The British government, anxious to end the war, made peace proposals through Lord Howe and General Clinton. Each of these military commanders sent a letter to Congress, dated May 27 and June 3, 1778, respectively, along with the three acts of Parliament giving the terms of the British proposal.[21] The reply of Congress to these letters (June 6), drafted by a committee of which Lee was a member, was probably mainly the work of Lee, for in the Lee papers there is in his handwriting an answer similar to the one adopted by Congress. In this reply it was stated that when Great Britain should be disposed to put an end to the "Unprovoked and cruel war against the United States" Congress would be willing to negotiate a peace on the basis of American independence and a due regard for sacred treaty commitments.[22]

Shortly after the reply to the letters of Lord Howe and General Clinton had been sent, Congress received a letter from the three British commissioners proposing a peace settlement. There was in this letter a reference to the French alliance as an "in-

sidious interposition of a power which has, from the first settlement of these colonies, been actuated with enmity to us both."
After some discussion Congress adopted (June 17) a reply reported by a committee of which Lee was a member. The reply
expressed strong disapproval of the charge against "his most
Christian Majesty" but declared that notwithstanding this unjust attack on France and the savage manner in which the British had conducted the war, Congress was willing to enter upon
peace negotiations, with the explicit recognition of American
independence by the British government and the withdrawal of
its fleets and armies.[23]

Lee regarded the peace offer presented by the British commissioners as "a combination of fraud, falsehood, insidious offers,
and abuse of France, concluding with a denial of Independence," which he considered the *sine qua non* of an acceptable
agreement.[24] And yet he was in favor of answering it. He drew
up a reply similar to the one presented by the committee but it
is not known whether it was presented to Congress or to the
committee only. In his draft, which was in the form of a vigorous letter to Lord Howe, Lee said that the "unprovoked and
cruel war" rendered it impossible for the states ever to go back
under British dominion. But to stop the effusion of blood they
were willing to negotiate with Great Britain as an independent
nation whenever "the King of G. B. shall be seriously disposed
to peace." He also expressed "the highest resentment" over the
indecent reflection the commissioners had made on the French
king.[25]

Lee's bitterness toward Britain seems to have been increased
rather than lessened by this overture of peace. This is seen in his
attitude toward an unwise motion that was made in Congress in
August, 1778. This motion was as follows: "Resolved that Congress will not in any degree, negotiate with the present British
commissioners in America, for restoring peace." The motion was
defeated, and Richard Henry alone of the Virginia delegation
voted for it. Evidently, he had a very low opinion of the British
commissioners. In writing to John Adams (October 29, 1778) he
said: "Never did Men cut a more ridiculous figure than the British Commissioners have done here."[26]

In July, 1778, Monsieur Gérard, the French minister to the
United States, arrived in Delaware Bay on the *Languedoc*, com-

manded by Count D'Estaing, who was in charge of the French fleet sent to aid the Americans. Congress, now turning its attention toward a proper welcome for the French envoy, decided to roll out the red carpet for him. Richard Henry, along with four other committee members appointed to meet Gérard and escort him to his lodgings, went down to Chester, Pennsylvania, to welcome him. They were taken out to the ship in a barge rowed by twelve "Oarsmen dressed in Scarlet trimmed with silver." Gérard met them at the gangway and congratulations and compliments were exchanged in the ship's cabin. Returning to shore, the committeemen and the French retinue drove in four coaches, each drawn by four horses, to Philadelphia, where they were greeted with a fifteen-gun salute. After having been assigned temporary quarters, Gérard dined with the committee, the President, and the other members of Congress.[27]

Lee was seated near Gérard at the dinner and was able to converse "largely with him." His appraisal of the French Plenipotentiary as reported to his brother Francis Lightfoot was as follows: "Mons. Gérard . . . is as grave as a Frenchman can be, and he is a wise well bred Gentleman." He also considered him perfectly acquainted with the politics of Europe.[28] Later, Lee reversed his high opinion of the French representative.[29]

On July 14 Gérard asked for a formal meeting with Congress, and Lee was first-named on a committee of three "to report to Congress on the time and manner of the public reception of Mons. Gérard. . . ." The committee made a prompt report which was adopted after four days of discussion.[30] Congress later arranged a formal reception of the French minister. Before the reception was held, Gérard sent Congress a copy of the speech that he intended to deliver at his public reception. Lee was named as the first of a committee of three to which this speech was referred.

Congress set August 6 as the time "for giving audience to the Hon. Sieur Gérard" and appointed Lee and Samuel Adams "to wait upon the Hon. Sieur Gérard and conduct him to the audience."[31] At the appointed time, Gérard appeared before Congress and had his secretary present his credentials to the President of Congress. The letter of credence was read by the Secretary of Congress, first in French and then in translation. "Imme-

110

diately after the reading of the letter Mr. Lee arose and presented the minister to the President of Congress, who also arose." After a mutual salutation Gérard delivered his address.[32]

Lee's record in diplomacy was marred by an unpleasant experience with Silas Deane. Deane's unwise policy in promising military commissions had aroused opposition in Congress to his activities abroad.[33] This dissatisfaction caused Congress to recall him for a report on the European situation. The resolution for his recall was offered by Lee and was passed by a unanimous vote (November 2, 1777). As Deane suspected, the desire for this information was only the ostensible, not the real, reason for his summons home. A week later John Adams was appointed as Deane's successor.[34] Apparently, Deane did not receive word of his recall until after the treaties with France had been signed. Accordingly, he stayed on and returned home on the same ship with Gérard.

Congress was so engrossed with the ceremonies attendant on Gérard's reception, that for a time it seemed to overlook the Deane affair. Deane requested the privilege of appearing before Congress to give an account of his stewardship and was granted an audience on August 15, 1778. He did not finish his defense the first day and six days later he again appeared before Congress to complete his report. By this time he was faced with charges more serious than those of having acted unwisely in issuing commissions to French officers, having been accused by Arthur Lee of misapplying public funds and of other improper activities.[35]

In his report Deane made extravagant claims for his own achievements and downgraded those of Arthur Lee. This report let loose a violent controversy which split Congress into two bitter factions, the partisans of Lee against the advocates of Deane. For some months Congress was paralyzed as to constructive action by this division.[36]

Deane tried repeatedly to induce Congress to investigate his case and pronounce a verdict. Congress, busy with other important matters, was slow to take final action. Besides, Deane's enemies favored delay as a part of his punishment. Feeling that this delay was unjust to him, he finally made a direct appeal to the public by publishing in the *Pennsylvania Packet* (December 5, 1778) an address "To the Free and Virtuous Citizens of

America." In this article he not only defended his own conduct but made a vituperative attack on four of the Lee brothers. He blamed Arthur for the failure of his mission to Madrid and for having allowed his papers to fall into the possession of the British envoy when he was in Berlin.[37] He declared that Arthur, by a letter to someone in England, had reported the signing of the French treaties on the very day that they were signed. Arthur was able to prove this a false accusation.[38] To these charges Deane added the accusations that Arthur had "an undignified hatred" of the French nation, was opposed to the treaty of alliance with France, and had been "dragged into the treaty with the utmost reluctance." Arthur Lee, continued Deane, was under suspicion by some of the best and most influential friends that America had abroad. This arose from his association with Lord Shelburne, to whom it was thought he disclosed American secrets.[39]

In this diatribe Deane accused William Lee of having been dilatory in meeting his public responsibilities and spoke of Francis Lightfoot and Richard Henry as his avowed personal enemies. He was especially severe in his attack on the latter, whom he charged with having had several meetings with Dr. Berkenhout, who was accused of being a British spy. Richard Henry had also, Deane declared, assured the British Commissioners that by the alliance with France "America was at liberty to make peace without consulting her ally, unless England declared war against France," a doctrine which he "constantly and persistently" maintained.[40]

Deane's article seems to have given him an initial advantage in the contest with the Lees. General William Whipple, a friend of the Lees, in a letter to Dr. Brackett (March 7, 1779) said that Deane's publication "operated very violently in his favor in this city [Philadelphia] at its first appearance; but," he continued, "at this period I do not know of anything that would injure a man's reputation (among honest men) more than to be his advocate." The men whom Deane had tried to calumniate were, he said, the most faithful servants of America.[41]

Deane's publication added fuel to a flame that was already throwing off too much heat. His enemies contended that his newspaper article was an insult to Congress, while his friends maintained that it was a legitimate defense against an attack on

112

his character. Among those who regarded Deane's article as an insult to Congress was President Henry Laurens, a strong supporter of the Lee faction. He suggested the appointment of a committee to report on the letter. Congress failed to do this and he resigned the presidency (December 9, 1779). Among the reasons given for his resignation was the failure of his effort to arouse Congress to a vindication of its honor. Laurens' successor was John Jay, who belonged to the pro-Deane faction.[42] Richard Henry in a letter to Laurens (June 20, 1779) said that there were few private clubs of gentlemen in the world that would allow themselves to be insulted in the way that Congress had been by Deane.[43]

Richard Henry naturally came to the defense of his brothers and himself. Coupled with this defense was a violent attack on Deane. When he made the motion for Deane's recall, however, he apparently had not been prompted by any feeling of bitterness; on the contrary, at that time he seemed inclined to make an excuse for Deane's mistakes. In a letter to Samuel Adams (November 23, 1777) he said that Deane was acting on his best judgment when he made these distressing contracts and that circumstances may have forced him to carry them further than he originally intended; but after Congress had taken such a strong position against these commitments it would have been out of all character to have retained him in this diplomatic position. "Yet this is a matter," he continued, "of great delicacy and I am not well satisfied with the whole of it."[44] Writing to Arthur, he said that since Congress already had recalled him, it was not necessary to say much about Deane. His recall "will prevent all future machinations from him, at least in Europe," Lee said. "Our friend Mr. Adams," he added, "is a wise and worthy Whig, who will not form cabals for any private or sinister purpose."[45]

Richard Henry gave up this charitable attitude toward Deane after the latter had made his attack on the Lee brothers. He was now bitter in his outspoken enmity toward Deane, using a pen which seemed to have been dipped in gall. In a letter to Arthur (October 27, 1778) he referred to Deane as follows: "This Wretch would rise upon the ruin of the first, the finest, and most uniform friends of this Country and of France."[46] These excoriations were set forth in private letters and in newspaper articles over an assumed name. Nor was this bitterness a sudden explosion of bad temper; on the contrary it flattened out into cold malice of long duration. Eight months later (August, 1779) we find him speaking of Deane's "atrocious misconduct" and "infamous libel," which, he said, had done more injury to the American cause than a reinforcement of 20,000 men to the army of the enemy. Deane's misappropriation of funds, he contended, was "downright robbery."[47]

Richard Henry's most elaborate defense of the family honor and attack on Deane was published in the *Virginia Gazette* and later reprinted in the *Pennsylvania Packet* or the *General Advertiser*. This article, in the form of a letter to Deane under date of January 22, 1779, and signed "Economis," is a closely knit argument in answer to Deane's charges against the Lees and a severe indictment of Deane. His accusations against Deane included the following: He had exceeded his instructions by entering into contracts "with a host of officers from the ensign to the major general." The promises he made to these gentlemen as to commands, pay, and pensions, "astonished Congress, enraged the army, and produced a heavy expence for defraying the charges of their return to France." He jeopardized the favorable opinion of the French Court by sending out vessels to cruise on the English coast after the French Court had indicated its disapproval of such a course. The prizes taken by sailing cruises which he sent along the coast of England, "against the desires of France and the orders of Congress," were consigned to private hands "instead of being delivered to the agents of the U.S." He had used his official position to engage in private speculation and had never shown his account concerning his public expenditure.[48]

Richard Henry then accused Deane of having traduced the character of Arthur and William Lee by "misrepresentations and calumnious innuendos," for his accusations against them were without foundation. He again took up Deane's attack on himself because of his relations with a certain Dr. Berkenhout. The latter had represented himself to Lee as being strongly in favor of the independence of America, and Lee, believing that his professions were sincere, had showed a friendly attitude toward him. Later Dr. Berkenhout was arrested on charges of being an agent of the British ministry but was released for lack of evidence.[49]

Deane's accusations against Arthur Lee called for an official answer and Arthur sent to the president of Congress (under date of February 10, 1779) a statement, accompanied by vouchers in answer to the charges made against him by Deane.[50] There was a strong anti-Lee faction in Congress, and a motion was made for Arthur's recall, which was hotly discussed for several days. The vote was a tie—four states for the motion and four against it, with four divided (May 3, 1779). Although the motion failed to carry, the vote per poll was against Arthur, being twenty-two yeas for the motion and fourteen against it.[51] Later (June 10, 1779) a motion for Arthur's recall was passed. The alleged reason for this action was to enable Congress the better to "enquire into the truth of the several allegations and suggestions made by the said Arthur Lee, in his correspondence with Congress, against the said Silas Deane."[52] It was, however, more than a year before Arthur Lee returned to the United States and appeared before Congress (August, 1780). In the meantime he had sent in his resignation with a statement in his defense. His letter was held up, apparently by James Lovell, his friend, until after it was seen how Congress would act in the Deane affair. So it was not until October 13, 1779, that a copy of the letter was read in Congress. The letter was listened to with grave attention and apparently produced a very favorable impression.[53] Congress took no further action in Arthur's case.

Richard Henry declared that Congress had acted unfairly and unwisely in its handling of this unfortunate controversy. It had, he thought, rewarded the libeller (Deane) and dishonored as much as it could the man (Arthur Lee) who had adhered diligently to the honest duties of his station. By its treatment of Arthur Lee, Congress had announced to future ministers, he continued, "that zeal, ability, and integrity are qualities which they do not intend their servants shall practice without incurring their utmost displeasure."[54]

No clear-cut decision was ever reached by the Continental Congress in this long-drawn-out controversy. A later action of the Federal government, however, was a verdict to some extent in Deane's favor. In 1842 Congress voted an appropriation of $37,000 to his heirs as compensation for the expenses incurred by Deane as commissioner to France.[55]

The disagreement between the two factions in Congress as to the truth of the charges and counter-charges has been handed down to modern scholars, who are also divided into pro- and anti-Deanites. Of recent writers, Dr. Julian P. Boyd contends (and with strong evidence supporting his view) that Deane, while acting as commissioner to France, had intrigued with Dr. Edward Bancroft, whom he knew to be a spy for the British authorities, and in so doing kept the English ambassador to France fully informed as to the negotiations between the American commissioners and the French foreign office. Deane had also aided in fitting out privateers, and, as a means of promoting his financial interests, had furnished his business partners in England with information in violation of the strictest commitment of secrecy.[56]

The Deane-Lee controversy was one of the most unfortunate affairs that afflicted the Continental Congress during its entire career. It was "a virulent poison in the bloodstream [of Congress], destined seriously to affect the body politic for years to come."[57] By dividing the membership into two hostile groups it hampered the efficient activity of a body that was already not strong enough to meet its responsibilities. The controversy also adversely affected the chief actors in the unfortunate drama, putting an end to the diplomatic careers of Arthur Lee and Silas Deane and smearing the reputation of the former to some extent[58] and injuring that of the latter to a greater extent.[59] It also had a serious and unwholesome effect on Richard Henry. In his correspondence he continued to attack Deane, defend his brother, and criticize Congress for not taking more vigorous action against Deane. He contended that Deane should have been censured by Congress and there should have been "a thorough extirpation of those cancerous ramifications with which he has overspread our affairs in every part." He contended that the failure of Congress to take action against Deane would be construed as approval of his conduct. How "will the honor of congress stand," he said, "if they allow that wicked insulter and injurer of America—Silas Deane, to go uncensured." Deane should, he contended, be required before leaving America to give security for a fair settlement of his accounts and a refunding of the amount due the government by him.[60]

This fight added to the list of Richard Henry's personal and political enemies and caused bitterness to crowd out to some extent the amiable and charitable feelings which were more characteristic of him. This bitterness was directed not only toward Deane but was also extended to his supporters, whom he classified as Tories, grafters, or those who were hoping to get the positions held by Arthur and William Lee. In one of his letters to Arthur he made this bitter appraisal of Deane's supporters: "For my part I believe a wickeder set never sprang from the corrupt compost of avarice, ambition, envy and fraud."[61]

For months this controversy used up much of his time and energy. Gout and weariness added to the impairment of his efficiency. It is no wonder, therefore, that he became tired of public life and resigned his seat in Congress.[62] Thus he closed a half-decade of useful service in that body on a note of disappointment and bitterness.

While Lee was participating in the ceremonies attending the royal reception accorded Gérard by Congress, the auspices were pointing to most agreeable personal and official relations between him and the French representative. This augury proved to be false prophecy. For later on, Gérard, in Lee's opinion, had become an extreme partisan of Deane, and had thereby put himself in Deane's class. He even spoke of Gérard as being a greater enemy of Arthur than was Deane.[63]

In letters to his friend Henry Laurens (August, 1779), then a member of Congress, Richard Henry asked him to prevent any action by Congress complimentary to Gérard on his departure for France. If such an attempt should be made he wanted Laurens to call for the yeas and nays. Lee felt that the handling of the Deane case by Congress had been a masterpiece of wrongdoing. To make its mistake a perfect one all Congress had yet to do was to "Bedaub his [Deane's] friend and supporter G——— with praises on his going away."[64]

Lee's enemies used his quarrel with Gérard as the basis for a charge that he had an unfriendly attitude toward France and was opposed to the French alliance. This accusation was without foundation, for he had all along been an advocate of the French alliance and had put forward every effort to bring it about. Even before he offered the resolution for independence he had declared that a foreign alliance was absolutely necessary and should be sought at once.[65] And as early as April, 1776, he had expressed the fear that while the colonies were hesitating as to foreign alliances Great Britain might secure the aid of these powers in conquering the colonies by offering them portions of her American possessions.[66] Later, in a letter to Samuel Adams (July 29, 1776) he expressed the hope that no time would be lost in sending ambassadors to France and other European courts. When France had publicly received our ambassadors, he continued, most of the other European powers would quickly follow.[67] Congress undoubtedly must have felt that Lee was favorable to foreign alliances, for when it chose a committee of five (December 24, 1776) to prepare a plan for obtaining foreign assistance, Lee was appointed on the committee.[68]

With such a record it is no wonder that he resented this false accusation in the strongest terms. Writing to Arthur (February 11, 1779) he said that he would rather cease to live than agree that the United States should desert her ally. He felt "infinite gratitude and reverence" for France. "You know perfectly well how long and how ardently my Soul has panted after this connection with France. Perhaps there was not another man in America so enthusiastically strenuous for the measure as myself. . . . And now a pack of rascals would insinuate (for their private purposes) that I would injure the measure that I have been so uniformly and warmly promoting." As he viewed it, the charge of his having coalesced with the enemies of America against her friends would, in the eyes of those who knew him, be like that of accusing a miser of having leagued with another person to rob himself of his own gold. One of his strong arguments in favor of a declaration of independence had been that as long as the colonies claimed membership in the British empire they could not expect to make foreign alliances. Furthermore, he saw no danger to our liberties (as some feared) from an alliance with a despotic power like France.[69]

Lee was also anxious for Spain to come into the war as an ally of the United States. When Spain declared war on Britain he expressed hopeful satisfaction over this favorable turn in American affairs. He also favored a treaty of alliance between Spain and the United States, believing that it would bring speedy victory for the patriot cause. "The declaration of Spain effectually secures the downfall of G. Britain," he believed, concluding: "A mighty empire crumbled to dust."[70]

The military and naval assistance which resulted from the alliance with France was a most important factor in the winning of American independence. It was Lee's motion (offered in June, 1776) that started the ball forward and his efforts that did much to keep it going until it reached the goal.

Chapter IX

Strenuous Statesmanship

The incomplete *Journal* of the Second Continental Congress gives no hint as to Lee's oratorical efforts, but it devotes a great deal of space to his contribution to routine action during his membership. Since the Federal government did not have a separate executive, Congress at this time performed its administrative duties through committees. In the index of the *Journal* for the years 1777 and 1778 there are ninety-five references to Lee's activity on committees, as chairman or member. This list included a number of special committees and the following standing committees: Intelligence, Navy or Marine, Commerce, and Secret Correspondence. At one time (October, 1778) he was chairman of the Marine Committee.[1]

Among the duties assigned committees to which he belonged were those of considering means of raising ten million dollars to carry on the war; conferring with Generals Washington, Gates. and Mifflin upon the best measures of support for the American cause in Canada; concerting with these same generals a plan of military operations; examining letters from Washington conveying important information from England along with the treaties that the British government had made with German princes for troops, and publishing such portions of these papers as might seem advisable to the committee; cooperating with the executives of Pennsylvania and the officials of Philadelphia in suggesting steps to be taken if the enemy should attempt an attack on Philadelphia; considering ways and means of speedily reinforcing Washington's army; and reporting as to whether the King of Portugal had violated the laws of neutrality in forbidding United States ships to enter his ports and in ordering those already there to depart. In June, 1778, Lee was appointed on a committee of three to prepare a form for the ratification of the Articles of Confederation.[2]

Lee frequently acted as the spokesman of Congress or its committees in writing reports and other papers; in conducting correspondence with Washington and other military leaders; and in preparing instructions for American representatives abroad and for other agents of Congress. His friendship for Washington especially qualified him to act as a liaison agent of Congress in its relations and communications with the commander-in-chief. From the partial report of the *Journal* and the writings of his contemporaries we know that he consistently voted and spoke in favor of a vigorous prosecution of the war.[3]

By the middle of December, 1776, the military situation had become most gloomy for the American cause. Washington had retreated across New Jersey with great losses by desertion and the expiration of terms of enlistment. He had taken his remnant of an army across the Delaware River near Trenton after a continuous pursuit by the British forces under General Howe. The temporary protection afforded his army by the river barrier gave Washington a breathing spell, but there was serious danger that Howe would transport his troops across the Delaware and annihilate the patriot army.

It looked as if the British might soon capture Philadelphia and this threat caused serious alarm in the city and great fear in Congress. "The near approach of the enemy to that city [Philadelphia]," said William Whipple, "struck such panick in all orders of the people there, except Tories . . . that the contagion seized the nerves of some members of Congress." Congress voted December 12, 1776, to adjourn, to meet on December 20 in the town of Baltimore.[4]

In coming to this decision, the members of Congress were acting like practical politicians rather than idealistic heroes. But running away is seldom a dignified movement, and they were criticized by some of the friends of the patriot cause. In defense of their action it was stated that Generals Mifflin and Putnam had advised the removal, since they could not guarantee Congress protection against attack. The enemy was only a few miles away and there was no adequate force to stop their advance. If Congress had remained and some of its members had been captured it would have been a serious blow to the American cause. Samuel Adams and Richard Henry Lee said that they were opposed to the move. Lee, writing shortly afterwards (January 1, 1777) said: "The removal from Philadelphia was not a measure of mine, but had my hearty disapprobation so long as disapproval availed anything; but when go they would, I endeavored to put the best face on it."[5]

There was disagreement among the representatives as to whether Baltimore was a suitable place for the meeting of Congress. After having become settled in Baltimore, Samuel Adams stated that he preferred it to Philadelphia for the deliberations of Congress. In writing to John Adams (January 9, 1777) he said, "we have done more important business in three weeks than we had done . . . at Philadelphia, in six months." This favorable opinion of the new location, however, was not concurred in by all the members. Some of them complained of the high prices, the dirtiness and isolation of the town, and the bad condition of the streets. At times when the representatives rode to the place of meeting, their horses had to plough through deep mud. Benjamin Rush in a letter to Robert Morris (February 8, 1777) made this complaint: "We live here in a Convent, we converse only with one another. We are precluded from all opportunities of feeling the pulse of the public upon our measures."[6]

Attendance at the Baltimore session was small. Dr. E. C. Burnett said that the members "sat through the gloomy winter, much of the time no more than a 'rump' Congress." But Lee was not one of the delinquents. He was in Baltimore ready to take his seat on January 20, the time set for the opening meeting, and on the first day was appointed on a committee to answer important letters, three of which were from Washington. Mrs. Lee had come down from Philadelphia and remained in Baltimore until the recess of the session, when he "carried" her home, from which she had been absent for six months.[7]

In the resolution by which Congress had voted to adjourn to Baltimore was this important provision: ". . . that, until the Congress shall otherwise order, General Washington be possessed of full power to order and direct all things relative to the department, and to the operations of war." A committee of which Lee was first-named was then appointed to take into account the state of the army. The committee made a prompt report and Congress adopted its recommendation by passing another act (December 27, 1776) which gave Washington full power to raise additional troops and engineers for the army; to fix their pay; "displace and appoint all officers under the rank of brigadier general, and to fill up all vacancies in every other department in the American armies, to take, wherever he may be, whatever he may want for the use of the army, if the inhabitants will not sell it, allowing a reasonable price for the same; [and] to arrest and confine persons who refuse to take the continental currency, or are otherwise disaffected to the American cause." These powers were to be exercised by Washington for a period of six months, "unless sooner determined by Congress."[8]

The same committee then prepared a letter, which, after amendment, was adopted by Congress (December 30) and sent out to the states. The letter declared that Congress would not have vested such powers in the Commander-in-chief "if the Scituation of Publick Affairs did not Require at this Crisis a Decision and Vigour, which Distance and Numbers Deny to Assemblies far Remov'd from each other and from the immediate Seat of War."[9]

One important problem with which Congress grappled during the Baltimore session was that of rising prices due to inflation. A committeee representing the New England states had met at Providence, Rhode Island, and adopted resolutions recommending regulation of prices. This proposal, which was presented to Congress on January 28, 1777,[10] gave rise to a lively discussion for several days in committee of the whole, with Francis Lightfoot Lee as chairman. There was a difference of opinion as to the main cause of inflation, whether it was the result of the circulation of paper money or because of the intrigues of economic royalists, and whether the regulation of prices either by Congress or state legislature could be effective. Though it was evident that prices were too high, the members of Congress were not in agreement as to the advisability of attempting to regulate them. James Wilson thought the effort would be abortive, saying that there are certain things "which Absolute power cannot do." Dr. Benjamin Rush, in opposing the resolution for fixing prices, declared that the attempt of government to regulate prices had in all ages and all countries been a failure. Prices, he argued, could be regulated by governmental action temporarily but not permanently. The attempt to regulate them would not reach the deep disorders of the economic situation. "The continent labors," he continued, "under a universal malady. From the crown of her head to the Soal of her feet She is full of disorders. She requires the most powerful tonic medicines. The resolution before you is Nothing but an Opiate. It may compose the continent for a night, but She will soon awaken again to a fresh sense of her pain and misery."

Lee answered Rush's objections as follows:

> Mr. President, The learned Doctor has mistook the disorder of the continent. She labors under a spasm, and Spasms he knows require palliative medicines. I look upon the resolution before you only as a temporary remedy. But it is absolutely necessary. It is true the regulations formerly recommended by Congress were not faithfully carried into execution, but this was owing to the want of effective governments. New and regular governments have been instituted in every part of America, and these will enable all classes of people to carry the resolutions into execution.[11]

After a week's consideration the house referred the proceedings of the New England conference to a special committee of five, on which Lee was first-named. Ten days later (February 15) the house adopted a resolution approving the plan of price regulation that the New England states had agreed upon for themselves. The resolution also recommended that the other states "adopt such measures as they shall think most expedient to remedy the evils occasioned by the present fluctuating and exorbitant prices." The states were not to act individually but in groups.[12]

The effort of Congress to regulate prices proved to be much ado about nothing, for the plan was not carried out. Congress therefore recommended (June 4, 1778) that those states which had adopted the plan repeal all such laws.

Shortly afterwards a committee of which Lee was a member recommended that Congress request the states to put an embargo on exports of food stuffs, to last from June 10 to November 15, 1778. The reason for this action was to keep sufficient food within the United States to supply the army and prevent the enemy from procuring supplies from captured ships. This recommendation was accepted by Congress.[13]

Congress adjourned on February 27 to meet in Philadelphia on March 4, but it was not until the 12th that the new session had a quorum for the transaction of business. Richard Henry Lee was one of the latecomers. After he had "carried" Mrs. Lee back to Chantilly, he took a rest for about a month. Returning early in April, he resumed strenuous activity, but only until June 15.[14] At that time he had to return to Virginia, not merely to mend but to rebuild his political fences. His enemies in the Virginia assembly had brought charges against him and had succeeded in defeating him for another term; he therefore hastened to Williamsburg to defend himself. Taking his seat in the House of Delegates, of which he was an elected member, he made such a fine defense of his record that he received the thanks of the two houses of the Assembly, and was reelected to Congress.[15]

On August 22, 1777, Congress was informed that General Howe had advanced far up the Chesapeake Bay and was posing a serious threat to Philadelphia. This danger gave Congress such a fright that at once it again conferred almost dictatorial powers on Washington. He was authorized "to proceed in such manner, as shall appear to him most conducive to the general interest."[16] This action of Congress and that of the preceding December were the longest steps toward a dictatorship ever taken in this country. Only extreme danger could have induced this waiver of individual liberty by men who had led in the revolt against the mother country for a violation of their financial rights.

The British threat eventuated in a real setback to the American force. Howe defeated Washington at Brandywine Creek (September 11), and two weeks later took Philadelphia. Soon after the battle of Brandywine, Congress voted that in case it should be necessary to leave Philadelphia, it should adjourn to Lancaster, Pennsylvania. Four days later a letter came from Colonel Alexander Hamilton, one of Washington's aides, advising Congress to remove from Philadelphia. At once the members, without a vote but by general agreement, left the city on horseback to assemble again at Lancaster. But Lancaster did not offer entire safety, and, as Henry Laurens said, "hearts were still fluttering in some bosoms." Therefore, after one day's meeting here, Congress moved over to York, putting the Susquehanna River between it and the enemy.[17]

With his active interest in military campaigns, Lee was unavoidably brought into the controversies between American generals. One such dispute was over the relative merits of Generals Philip Schuyler and Horatio Gates. Congress had to decide which of these generals should lead the forces in opposing the advance of the British general, Burgoyne. Both Schuyler and Gates were eager for this great opportunity. The New Yorkers ("Yorkers") supported Schuyler and the New Englanders ("Yankees") strongly opposed him. In March, 1777, he was reprimanded by Congress on a flimsy charge made against him by the New Englanders and was deprived of his command of the Northern Army. Two months later Congress reversed this action by voting a vindication of him and reinstating him in his command (May 22, 1777). The vote was 6 to 4, with one state divided and two states not represented. Virginia gave her vote in favor of vindication and reinstatement, but Lee voted in the negative. In so doing he was acting in agreement with Samuel Adams and the Massachusetts delegation. Later, dissatisfaction arose over Schuyler's failure to stop the British and he was superseded by Gates.[18]

Instead of being discouraged by the initial success of Burgoyne's invasion of New York, Lee predicted that this success would serve to bring him into the country to encompass his ruin.[19] Nor was Lee greatly disturbed by the British victories at Chadd's Ford and Germantown, believing, he said, that the former would prove a Pyrrhic victory for Howe and the latter would result in the weakening of his army. Even the capture of Philadelphia by the enemy seemed to cause him no serious alarm. Although it would produce an unfavorable impression in Europe he thought it would mean little in America. He even hoped that the occupation of Philadelphia (which he considered "an attractive scene of debauch and amusement"), by giving the British troops comfortable quarters, would cause a relaxation in discipline and render them less formidable. "To Hannibal's wintering in Capua," he said, "is ascribed his loss of Rome." This hope was apparently realized, for Dr. Franklin (borrowing a figure from a Roman historian) afterward said: "Howe has not taken Philadelphia so much as Philadelphia has taken Howe."[20]

The Congressional session at York, from September 30, 1777, to June 27, 1778, was a low period in the career of this body.

The attendance was so poor that at times nothing could be done for lack of a quorum. Often the number present did not exceed thirteen and sometimes only nine states were represented. The work of the body was carried on by a faithful few steadfast, overworked representatives, usually ranging in number from seventeen to twenty-one. Richard Henry Lee was in attendance at York during the first two and the last two months of the session. In one of his letters (October 8, 1777) he stated that he was crowded with business a hundred times as much as he could discharge with propriety. Relentless attention to his duties brought on illness and rapidly increasing eye trouble.[21]

York was a small inaccessible town, lacking in the comforts of Philadelphia. Each morning the delegates met in a room in the courthouse which was heated by a very large wood stove with a pipe extended to the rear of the room. President Hancock and Secretary Thomson sat at the judge's desk with the members arranged in rows in front. Although the cost of living was high the fare was poor.[22] Cornelius Harnett, a representative of North Carolina, wrote (November, 1777) to Thomas Burke, a former member, to this effect: "For God's sake endeavor to get some Gentleman appointed in my stead. I can not stay here any longer with any pleasure." A month later, he wrote to another friend, saying: "Believe me it [York] is the most inhospitable scandalous place I ever was in. If I once more can return to my family all the Devils in Hell shall not separate us."[23]

Shortly after Congress had assembled at York the tedium of the daily routine was relieved by the reception of the glorious news of Burgoyne's surrender. In a spirit of gratitude for this great victory, Congress appointed a committee of three, of which Lee was a member, to frame a recommendation to the states that they set apart the coming December 18, 1777, as a day of thanksgiving. The committee promptly brought in a report in line with this suggestion, which apparently had been written by Samuel Adams. This recommendation was accepted by Congress and thus became the first Thanksgiving Proclamation ever announced by the general government.[24]

Lee was one of the earliest and most persistent of the advocates of a union of all the colonies. As early as July, 1768, he had stated, in a letter to John Dickinson, that the union in counsel and action of all the colonies was undoubtedly necessary if they were to succeed in their struggle against the unjust policy of Great Britain. It must therefore have afforded him great satisfaction to be able to include in his motion for independence (June 7, 1776) a provision for organizing a federal union. Five days later a committee consisting of one representative from each state was appointed to prepare a plan of union. Since Lee was expecting to leave Congress (he did leave next day), he was not put on the committee, and Thomas Nelson was the Virginia representative.[25] On July 12, 1776, the committee reported a draft of articles of confederation which had been written by John Dickinson.[26]

While Lee had no part in framing the original draft of the Articles, he was active in the debates in favor of confederation and did all he could to bring it to fruition. "This great bond of Union," he said, "will more effectually than anything else, produce present strength, credit, and success; and secure future peace and safety. Nor can any human plan more conclusively establish American Independence." These considerations, he thought, should urge the friends of America to effect "a firm and persevering union" as quickly as possible.[27]

The text of the constitution proposed by the committee became the subject of heated discussion, which continued, off and on, for more than two years, due to differences of opinion, the stress of war, and interruptions occasioned by the demands of the war. Prominent among the disagreements were the questions of apportioning taxes and representation among the states, and of fixing the western boundaries of those states claiming to extend to the Mississippi River.[28] One group contended that federal taxes should be apportioned among the states on the basis of their free population, and the other on that of their total population. As to representation in Congress, one party contended for equal representation of the states and the other for the apportionment of representatives according to numbers or according to land values.

On October 7, 1777, an amendment to the Articles was offered providing for representation on the basis of one representative for each fifty thousand white inhabitants, the three states having the smallest population (Rhode Island, Delaware, and Georgia) each having one vote. The motion was defeated, but Virginia and Pennsylvania voted aye, with both the Lees—Richard Henry and Francis Lightfoot—voting for the amendment. Two other resolutions—one apportioning representation on population and the other on the amount of taxes paid into the federal treasury—were voted on and also defeated. Both measures received the support of all the Virginia representatives.[29] On that same day the provision of the original draft giving each state one vote was adopted by a large majority. Richard Henry Lee and the other Virginia delegates voted no.

The original draft of Article XI provided that federal contributions should be apportioned among the states according to population, counting all persons except Indians not taxed.[30] This provision was changed to base contributions by the states to the federal treasury on the value of surveyed lands with buildings and improvements. According to John Adams, this change was mainly due to the Southern delegates, especially to Richard Henry and Francis Lightfoot Lee. The Virginia representatives all voted aye on the proposal. Next day a resolution to give Congress the exclusive right to fix the western boundaries of states claiming to extend to the Mississippi River or the South Sea was offered and defeated. The Virginia delegates voted against this proposed amendment.[31]

In the discussions over the mooted points in the Articles of Confederation, Lee usually took the stand that one would expect of an advocate of states' rights. On one occasion, however, he cast a vote which was apparently on the side of nationalism. Burke, of North Carolina, offered an amendment declaring that all sovereign powers are in the states separately. This amendment was passed but was opposed by Richard Henry Lee.[32]

On November 10, 1777, several propositions were laid before Congress as additional provisions of the Articles of Confederation. That same day Congress appointed a committee of three, of which Lee was a member, to take these suggested changes into consideration and report as to which should be incorporated in the draft already agreed upon. The committee made its report next day. After two days of discussion a few significant additions recommended by the committee were adopted. Important among these new articles were the provisions for the extradition of criminals from one state to another; the acceptance in full faith by each state of the records, acts, and judicial proceedings of every other state; and the freedom of debate in Congress and exemption from arrest of members while in attendance at and in going to and from the place of meeting.[33]

On November 13, 1777, Congress appointed a committee of three "to revise and arrange the articles of confederation agreed to and prepare a circular letter to the respective states to accompany the said articles." Lee was first-named on this committee and in all probability was the author of the circular letter. The report of the committee, made next day, was promptly adopted, apparently without change. Finally (November 15, 1777), the new frame of government was adopted, but the constitution was not to go into effect until it had been ratified by the legislatures of all the states.[34]

The circular letter was a well-worded document of moderate length. It asked the states in considering the constitution to take into account the difficulty of adjusting a plan of union to the political views of all the states. The plan, it said, "was the best which could be adapted to the circumstances of all," and the only one which afforded "any tolerable prospect of a general ratification." It urged the states to ratify it as quickly as possible. "Every motive loudly calls upon us to hasten its conclusion." When ratified and put into effect it will "confound our foreign enemies, defeat the flagitious practices of the disaffected, strengthen and confirm our friends, support our public credit, restore the value of our money, enable us to maintain our fleets and armies, and add weight and respect to our councils at home, and to our treaties abroad." "It seems," it continued, "essential to our very existence as a free people, and without it we may soon be constrained to bid adieu to independence [and] to liberty and safety."[35]

The delay of some of the states in ratifying the Articles of Confederation was a great disappointment to the advocates of union. In a private letter (June 20, 1778) Lee wrote: "The friends of the future happiness and glory of America are now urging the Confederation to a close, and I hope it will be signed in a few days."[36] A weighty problem connected with the question of ratification was that of the unoccupied lands of the West. At the beginning of the war, eight states laid claims to lands west of the Allegheny Mountains on the basis of royal charters. Five states (Rhode Island, Pennsylvania, New Jersey, Delaware, and Maryland) made no claim to the West. The "landless" states insisted that the other states should surrender their claims to the West and thus cede this vast area to the United States.

So anxious was Lee for the consummation of the union that he was willing for Virginia to give up her claim to the West if this sacrifice would bring the constitution into operation. As early as November, 1778, he suggested to Governor Patrick Henry that Virginia cede to the Union her lands west of the Ohio River on condition that the ceded territory be organized into a new state and Virginia be compensated for the expense incurred in the wars against the western Indians and for the conquest of the Illinois region. This sacrifice on the part of Virginia would, he contended, inure to her advantage. If the state extended over too great an area it would be difficult, he thought, to maintain an effective republican government. It would also be a "benefit in point of economy," he argued, "from having a frontier State to guard us from Indian wars and the expense they create."[37]

Later (September, 1780), in a letter to Samuel Adams, Lee expressed his deep concern for the consummation of the union: "The confederation alone can give us system, strength, and respectful consideration." He thought that Congress should open negotiations on the cession of the western lands. He hoped that Virginia would cede the territory northwest of the Ohio on the following terms: That the ceded lands be sold fairly and the purchase money applied to extinguishing the Continental debt; that not fewer than two or three states be established in the territory; and that Virginia be reimbursed for the expense incurred in wresting the country from the British. If this were done Maryland would have no excuse for staying out of the Confederation. If she should still refuse, then the other states should confederate "without the refractory sister."[38]

In January, 1781, the Virginia Assembly passed an act ceding to the Union the lands west of the Ohio River but connected with the act of cession two important conditions: Congress must declare null and void all land purchases from the Indians and all grants by royal commission that were inconsistent with the chartered rights and laws of Virginia. Congress must also guarantee to Virginia her possession of the Kentucky region.[39]

Richard Henry was a member of the House of Delegates when this action was taken and it must have afforded him great satisfaction to be able to report the result to his friend Samuel Adams. Writing to him (February 5, 1781), he pointed out that Virginia had made a great sacrifice for the sake of the union. The territory which she offered to cede, he said, was greater in extent and better in climate and soil then the remaining area of the state. If this cession was accepted by Congress under the terms laid down, it would be "a means of perfecting our Union by closing the Confederation—and thus our Independency will be secured in great measure."[40] Congress was unwilling to comply with these conditions and refused to accept the cession on Virginia's terms. In September, 1783, it voted to receive the grant if Virginia would waive the two above-mentioned objectionable conditions. Later in that same year the Virginia Assembly agreed to the terms demanded by Congress, and the latter on March 1, 1784, accepted the cession.[41]

By the beginning of 1779 all the states but Maryland and Delaware had ratified the constitution. In February of that year Delaware ratified it, but Maryland held out for two years longer. The main reason for this long delay on the part of Maryland was the refusal of the landed states to surrender their claims to western lands. Finally (1781) New York turned over to the federal government her shadowy title to western lands, and it was expected that the other six states having claims in the West would surrender them to the Confederation. Relying on this expectation, Maryland accepted the constitution on March 1, 1781, and it went into effect on that date.[42]

While the adoption of the Articles of Confederation was an important step forward, it fell far short of meeting the problems of the new union. The federal government still showed a serious shortcoming in the management of its financial problems. This failure was due not so much to the mistakes of Congress as to the inherent weakness of the general government. Many measures were passed to put the currency on a firm basis, but they could not be carried out because of the failure of the states to do their part. As a member of finance committees Lee took a leading part in formulating financial measures and he deplored the rapid depreciation of both state and federal paper currency.[43]

When Lee left Congress in November, 1778, having been excused because of ill health, he was still deeply concerned over the financial situation. In writing to Patrick Henry (November 15), he spoke of the paper money situation and the disagreement among the states as the great dangers to the patriot cause. The loss of American liberty, he said, was threatened "from the state of our currency [more] than from all other causes." Later (June, 1779) he expressed his concern as follows: "The inundation of [paper] money appears to have overflowed virtue and I fear will bury the liberty of America in the same grave." He attributed the cheapness of the paper money to the overissues by Congress and the states and to counterfeiting. He thought the punishment for counterfeiting should be death. The law had been too mild. Counterfeiting exceeds other crimes, he said, to the same extent as parricide exceeds murder.[44]

Lee's earnestness in support of the war and his willingness to make sacrifices in pursuit of this aim caused him to advocate measures which one would expect a Virginia patrician to oppose. Such a stand was his vote in favor of two resolutions passed by Congress (October, 1778) to discourage theater-going and other diversions in which the Virginia gentry freely indulged. These resolutions were as follows:

> Whereas true religion and good morals are the only solid foundations of public liberty and happiness:
> Resolved, That it be, and it is hereby earnestly recommended to the several states, to take the most effectual measures for the encouragement thereof, and for the suppressing of theatrical entertainments, horse racing, gaming, and such other diversions as are productive of idleness, dissipation, and a general depravity of principles and manners.
> Whereas frequenting play houses and theatrical entertainments have a fatal tendency to divert the minds of the people from a due attention to the means necessary for the defense of their country, and the preservation of their liberties:
> Resolved, That any person holding an office under the United States, who shall act, promote, encourage or attend such plays, shall be deemed unworthy to hold such office, and shall be accordingly dismissed.[45]

The Virginia delegation was divided on these motions, but Lee voted for them. In doing so he was acting more like a Massachusetts Puritan than a Virginia Cavalier.

Lee's statesmanship was in the main free from sectionalism. More than once he supported measures that his colleagues in the Virginia delegation considered unfair to their state, as in his refusal to support a request of Governor Edmund Randolph that Congress reimburse his state for the expense that she had lately incurred in sending out an expedition against the Indians on both sides of the Ohio. A proposal was made in Congress by which the way would have been left open for compensation to Virginia and Lee voted against it on the ground that the expedition had not been authorized by Congress.[46]

In putting the interests of the whole country above those of his own section he was laying himself open to the charge of disloyalty to the South. So much was this the case that James Lovell said (June 13, 1779) that Richard Henry Lee and Henry Laurens of South Carolina were squinted at as monsters by the people south of the Susquehanna River, because they advocated policies in which the Southern states had no interest.[47] This was a harsh appraisal of his real attitude, for he was always alert to the rights of the South and quick to oppose measures that he considered unfair to that section. It was in line with his desire to protect the rights of the Southland that he opposed giving Congress power to regulate the trade of the union. This power would be dangerous in the extreme to the Southern or staple states, he maintained, for their lack of ships would expose their freightage and produce to a most pernicious monopoly.[48]

The first period of Lee's long career in Congress ended in May, 1779. His strenuous service had taken a heavy toll of his vitality and had brought on a physical and spiritual fatigue that called for a change of work. His earlier enthusiasm as to American prospects was undergoing a pessimistic slump. In writing to his friend, George Mason (June 9, 1779), he sounded a note of despondency over the condition of affairs—the avarice, extortion, and fortune-seeking of all classes. He felt that in public life there was a woeful lack of wisdom, integrity, and industry in both counsel and execution.[49] In a letter to Thomas Jefferson (May 3, 1779) he expressed the hope that Jefferson and his other friends would not blame him for sending his resignation to the Assembly. He had neglected his health, he said, by continued and close application to his duties, and "a long neglected numerous family demands some attention." Furthermore, he had been persecuted "by the united voice of toryism, peculation, faction, envy, mali[ce], and all uncharitableness." He added, however, that he would be willing to make the sacrifice of staying on if he had such associates as Jefferson, Mason, and Wythe.[50]

Lee's decision to take a long vacation from Congress at that time, was, therefore, a wise one. Smarting under the indignity to which Congress had, as he thought, unjustly subjected his brother Arthur, he had lost confidence in many of his colleagues. Whenever a statesman gets under a juniper tree, as did the prophet of old, with the feeling that many, if not most, of his colleagues are worshippers of Baal, he may be ready to ascend to Heaven in a chariot of fire, but he is not in condition to play an effective role in the rough and tumble of practical politics. Lee needed a vacation from public affairs to have time to listen to the still small voice of hope and optimism.

Chapter X

A Prophet in His Own Country

During the period from August 1, 1774, to July 5, 1776, the Old Dominion adopted a series of measures that brought her into the war, severed the bond that had held her to the homeland, and organized a government for a new commonwealth. These measures were adopted by five state conventions. Lee was a member of four of these bodies, but his duties in Congress at the time limited his attendance to a short term for each.[1]

The state government was to a considerable extent modeled after that of the colony. The new legislative assembly, like the old colonial assembly, was a body of two houses. The House of Delegates was the larger body, and was closely patterned after the House of Burgesses. The upper house, the Senate, however, was very different from the colonial Council, for its membership, like that of the House of Delegates, was chosen by the voters. Lee served for a number of years as a member of the lower house and for a short period was Speaker.[2]

As a member of the Virginia assemblies, Lee furnished useful leadership in the organization of the new commonwealth, but his services apparently were not fully appreciated by all of his fellow Virginians. Indeed, the attitude of some of them toward him confirms the truth of the Biblical adage that a prophet is not without honor save in his own country and among his own people. For during the greater part of his career he had the ill will of some of the prominent leaders in the Old Dominion. This enmity had started in the main with Lee's call for an investigation of Treasurer Robinson's accounts and had persisted throughout later years.

Of fellow Virginians who were hostile to him, Carter Braxton held a leading place. In a letter to his Uncle Landon Carter (October 16, 1776), Braxton, without calling any names, referred in a malicious way to Lee as follows: "Upon the whole it does appear to me as if the two Suns that had shone with so much Influence lately in our political Hemisphere were much in their decline and as the Int of this poor Country seem so indespensably to require it, I hope they will soon sett to rise no more."[3]

His enemies charged that he was soft on piracy, and that as a member of the Committee of Secret Correspondence he had opposed reporting its proceedings to Congress in order to hide his embezzlement of public funds.[4] He also was accused of having favored New England to the injury of Virginia. In a long letter to Governor Patrick Henry (May 26, 1777), Lee declared that this accusation was ridiculous since the interests of Virginia were not in conflict with those of New England; on the contrary, the interests of both could be best served by mutual cooperation. The delegates from New England had, he continued, shown love and respect for Virginia. That section along with Virginia had taken the lead against tyranny. To stir up jealousy between these two sections would be to promote dissension in the patriot cause and thus invite defeat. Furthermore, he said, "I defy the poisonous tongue of Slander to produce a single instance in which I have preferred the interests of N. E. to that of Virginia." He ended his defense as follows: ". . . I have served my Country, Sir, to the best of my knowledge and with fidelity and industry, to the injury of my health and fortune, and a sequestration from domestic happiness—I shall rejoice to find that others are employed who will do the business better than I have done, and I shall be ever happy in the reflection, that those Malignants who would represent me as an enemy to my Country cannot make me so."[5]

Although Lee's detractors could not make such accusations stick, they found a point to attack in his management of his landed estate in Fauquier County. Instead of having overseers to supervise farming operations on these lands, he had leased them for a money rental.[6] With the outbreak of war, owing to the restrictions on foreign commerce caused by the non-intercourse agreements entered into by the colonials and the restrictions on trade imposed by the British government, along with the dangers and difficulties occasioned by the war, exportation from the colonies had virtually come to an end. Lee's tenants therefore were unable to turn their wheat and tobacco into money, except at a very low price, and so could not pay their

137

rent. The situation had, therefore, become embarrassingly unfair to Lee. Simple justice demanded that a new arrangement be made with his tenants.

In August, 1775, he suggested to Colonel Marshall (father of the Chief Justice), one of his tenants, a new plan by which the tenants would pay their rent in tobacco at prices fixed by mutual agreement. Colonel Marshall "very much approved" the proposal and agreed to present it to his fellow tenants. But he went into the military service and could not carry out his purpose. Later (1776) Richard (?) Parker, acting as Lee's agent, was able to get all the tenants but two or three to agree to pay their rent in tobacco. At that time paper currency had been issued only in small amounts and had not gone far, if at all, toward depreciation. Yet for more than a year Lee had received little or nothing from his leased estate.

In offering his renters these new terms Lee doubtless considered that he was granting them a favorable concession, a view supported by the fact that in August, 1776, the tenants of Loudoun County petitioned the Virginia Convention to have their money rents changed to produce.[7] This new arrangement, if it had been effectively carried out, also would have been a most salutary policy from Lee's own point of view. For when inflation ran wild, because of the overissue of paper money by Congress and the state governments, he would have been protected to some extent against the loss that he would otherwise have sustained. Nor is it entirely unlikely that he had an eye to this eventuality when he proposed the new plan, whether he was motivated mainly by generosity toward his tenants or by an honest self-interest.

Apparently the new arrangement did not afford the anticipated relief, for Lee's rent agent, Joseph Blackwell, wrote him on January 16, 1777, that he had had great difficulty in collecting his rent, owing to the fact that "a sett of Vile men" had been aspersing Lee's character and telling his tenants that he was trying to depreciate the value of the paper currency. They had made some of his tenants so bold that they would not pay their rent until forced to do so by law. Blackwell said that he had all he could do "to silence your Enemies and put your Character in a fair light but there is too many of them to be silenced by me."

He urged Lee to come to see his tenants and look after his interests. Lee said that the trouble was all brought on by "Malicious enemies, Pseudo Patriots, and a few Knavish Tenants."[8]

By circulating malicious reports against him, Lee's enemies had been able not only to cause him serious trouble with his tenants but to build up a springboard from which they could leap to an attack against him in the Virginia Assembly. In a letter from Henry Lee ("Light-Horse Harry"), probably written in October, 1776, Richard Henry received warning of a plot to deprive him and his brother Francis Lightfoot of their seats in Congress. These enemies, Henry Lee thought, had been trying to ruin Richard Henry in both his public and private life from the beginning of his career in the House of Burgesses.[9]

When the Virginia Assembly was called upon to elect its delegates to Congress for another year (May, 1777), Jefferson offered a bill limiting the tenure of the Virginia representatives to two years in succession. If the resolution had passed without amendment both Richard Henry and Francis Lightfoot Lee would have been disqualified for reelection. But the bill was amended and as passed provided that no person "shall hereafter serve as a member of Congress for three years successively."[10] Just what prompted Jefferson to take this action we can only conjecture. William Wirt Henry, the biographer of Patrick Henry, thought that he did it out of enmity to Lee.[11] A more charitable opinion of Jefferson's motive is probably correct, but he was called home by the illness of his wife and so took no part in the election which was calculated to humiliate Lee.[12]

On May 22, 1777, the Assembly of Virginia elected by joint ballot of both houses its representatives to the Continental Congress. George Mason was chosen to fill the unexpired term of Thomas Nelson, who had resigned, and also for a full term of one year. Four other delegates (one of whom was Francis Lightfoot Lee) were chosen for the regular term beginning on August 11. Richard Henry Lee had been elected as a member of the Assembly, but was not in attendance at that time as he was then in his seat in Congress. His name was on the list of candidates for Congress, but the vote received by him was very small. The highest vote he received on any of five ballots was eleven and the lowest two.[13]

139

Lee's enemies had scored an initial victory, but in less than a month this victory was superseded by defeat. Mann Page, Jr., and Lee's brother, Francis Lightfoot, expressed their protest by sending in their resignation as members of Congress.[14] No action was taken on these resignations.

A short time later, George Mason wrote (June 14) to George Wythe, Speaker of the House of Delegates, declining his appointment as a member of Congress. One reason given was that he should not leave home since a large family of children needed his care. Besides, he had been elected to the Virginia House of Delegates and he felt that he should not give up this position without the consent of his constituents, "and such of them as I have had the opportunity of consulting are averse to it." The following cryptic statement at the end of the letter indicated that he had another important reason for refusing the appointment: ". . . I must acknowledge I have other reasons for declining the appointment; which to avoid offence, I forbear giving." Mason's biographer was certain that chief among these "other reasons" was his resentment over the mistreatment that Lee had received at the hands of the Assembly.[15]

When Lee heard of the action of the Virginia Assembly, he wrote to John Page as follows: "It has been a wicked industry, the most false, and the most malicious that the deceitful heart of Man ever produced. I am not on my own account affected with this malice of my enemies, because I have long panted for retirement from the most distressing pressure of business that I ever had conception of. But my principal concern arises from the dreadful example my case presents to cool the ardor of patriotism, and prevent the sacrifice of private ease to public service. I ought at least to have been heard in my defence."[16]

Lee promptly left Congress for Williamsburg, and a few days later (June 20) took his seat in the Virginia House of Delegates. He at once demanded an investigation of certain charges "injurious to his reputation and public character, which as he was informed had in his absence been alleged against him." The House voted to give him a hearing, and the Senate on the same day accepted the invitation to attend the inquiry. Several witnesses were examined and then Lee addressed the Assembly.[17] Not a word of this speech has come down to us, but, according to tradition, he spoke with such eloquence "that every heart was melted by its power, and that every eye was in tears." One of his hearers, Colonel John Banister, a member of the Assembly, spoke of Lee's answer as follows: "Certainly no defence was ever made with more graceful eloquence, more manly firmness, equalness of temper, serenity, calmness and judgement, than this very accomplished speaker displayed on this occasion."[18]

When Lee had ended his defense the Senate withdrew and the House passed this resolution: "Resolved, That the thanks of this House be given by the Speaker to Richard Henry Lee, Esq., for the faithful services he has rendered his country in the discharge of his duty as one of the delegates from this State in General Congress."

The speaker, George Wythe, thereupon reported to Lee the order of the House (tradition says, in tears), prefacing the resolution by a statement of his own:

> Sir.—It is with particular pleasure that I obey this command of the House; because it gives me an opportunity, whilst I am performing an act of duty to them to perform an act of justice to you. Serving with you in Congress, and attentively observing your conduct there, I thought that you manifested to the American cause a zeal truly patriotic; and, as far as I could judge, exerted the abilities you are distinguished for to promote the good and prosperity of your own country in particular and of the United States in general. That the Tribute of praise deserved may reward those who do well, and to encourage others to follow your example, the House has come to this resolution.

In response, Lee thanked the House for its "candor and justice" and the Speaker "for the obliging manner" in which he reported the resolution of the House. "I consider," he continued, "the approbation of my country, Sir, as the highest regard for faithful services, and it shall be my constant care to merit that approbation by a diligent attention to public duties."[19]

The Senate also voted that "as a just tribute due to Richard Henry Lee, esq., our worthy delegate in General Congress," the Speaker "present him the warmest thanks of the House for his unwearied diligence and fidelity in discharge of that important trust."[20] The Speaker, Archibald Cary, reported this resolution to Lee, who replied to it by letter (June 23, 1777) as follows:

Sir,

As nothing can be more valuable to a citizen than the approbation of his countrymen, so I have received with singular pleasure the honourable testimony that the House of Senators has been pleased to give of my conduct in Congress as a delegate from this commonwealth.

That community which is willing to acknowledge the fidelity of its servants can never want such as are zealous to promote its best interest, honest and diligent in discharge of their duty.

It shall be my care, sir, to deserve, on all occasions of public trust, the reward that the honourable Senate have now conferred upon me.

I am, with the sentiments of duty and respect for the honourable House,

> Sir, your most humble servant,
> Richard H. Lee[21]

A few days later, the Assembly selected Lee by a large majority on the first ballot to fill the full-term vacancy in the Virginia Congressional representation occasioned by Mason's refusal to accept election.[22]

Later that same year (October 7), William Booth wrote to Lee, warning that at the next meeting of the Assembly there was to be a severe attack made upon him. After receiving this information Lee wrote a long letter to Speaker Wythe justifying his action with reference to his tenants and asking him to use his discretion as to whether he would defend him in case an attempt should be made in the House to his prejudice. "I have no doubt Sir," he said, "but that you will on all proper occasions, as well upon principles of justice to injured character, as on account of the long friendship that has subsisted between us, place this matter in the clear light that your abilities enable you to do."[23] However, no attempt to smear him was made at the next session of the Assembly.

Lee returned to Congress in August, but a few months later he had to leave (December, 1777) on account of ill health. After a tiresome trip from York, where Congress was in session, he arrived at Chantilly for a short period of rest and recuperation. He then went to Williamsburg to take his seat in the Virginia Assembly, arriving there about the middle of January, 1778.[24] The session was far advanced and he was in attendance for only about two weeks. He was very active during this short period, serving on important committees and once as chairman of the committee of the whole.[25] The Virginia Assembly, like the Continental Congress, devoted much of its time to the consideration of military affairs. As a member of the House of Delegates Lee consistently advocated measures that would provide an effective home defense and give adequate support to the Continental Army.

Later in this year (May, 1778) the Virginia Assembly gave him another mild slap in the face. When it chose the seven delegates to Congress, Richard Henry's name was next to the last on the list. Francis Lightfoot fared better as he had the fourth place.[26] Patrick Henry, then governor, wrote to Richard Henry (June, 1778) expressing sympathy for him on seeing the order in which the balloting placed the delegates in Congress. "It is in an effect," he said, "of that rancorous malice that has so long followed you through that arduous path of duty which you have invariably traveled since America resolved to resist her oppressor."[27]

In May, 1779, the Virginia Assembly voted to make Richmond instead of Williamsburg the seat of government, which was "more safe and central than any other town situated on navigable water." In the spring of 1780 the Assembly held its first session in the little town.[28] At this time Richmond was a small, crude village, though its warehouses even then were filled with tobacco and other farm products for export.[29]

Lee was not a member of the Assembly during the two sessions held in 1779, but in the spring of 1780 he again took his seat in the House of Delegates. Not returning to Congress until 1784, for more than four years he was free to devote much time to affairs in his home legislature as a member—often chairman—of both special and permanent committees. He was a member of the Committee of Privileges and Elections and chairman of the Committee of Propositions and Grievances. As chairman of special committees he presented to the House a number of important bills.[30]

In March, 1780, Congress voted to call in and destroy the old continental currency at the rate of one fortieth of its face value. The plan for redeeming the old notes was for the states to pay their tax quotas to the Federal government in the old currency at this reduced rate. New notes bearing five per cent interest and redeemable in specie in six years were to take the place of the old notes. The states were to set aside specie as a fund for the redemption of the new notes. The success of the plan therefore would depend on the willingness of the states to assume their share of this responsibility.[31]

In June, 1780, the Virginia House of Delegates took under consideration this proposal of Congress. A motion was made providing that the act of Congress be accepted; that Virginia assume her proportion of the continental debt and speedily discharge it by taxes or otherwise; and that the state establish certain funds for the redemption of her portion of the new paper money to be issued by Congress. The motion was strongly opposed by Patrick Henry and was defeated by a vote of 25 ayes to 59 noes, with Richard Henry voting aye. Another motion then was made providing for the redemption of Virginia's quota of the old paper money at the rate of forty dollars in paper for one in specie. This proposal also was defeated by a vote of 28 ayes to 53 noes, with Lee again voting aye. Next day Henry obtained a leave of absence for the rest of the session. There were additional changes in the personnel of the House, and two weeks later Lee and Mason were able to have the Assembly reverse its action and accept the Congressional plan, but they were unsuccessful in the attempt to provide for the redemption of Virginia's paper money.[32]

In the autumn session of the Assembly (1780), its acceptance of the Congressional plan was attacked and a bill was introduced making legal tender the new currency to be issued under the recent act of Congress and also that issued by Virginia that year. After two days of debate the bill was passed with Henry and Lee leading respectively the fight for and against it. The assembly also voted, over Lee's opposition, another issue of paper money at the rate of forty dollars in paper to one in specie. Virginia's certificates almost totally collapsed after this act. Sixty dollars in paper were now rated at one in specie.[33]

In November, 1781, after the surrender of Cornwallis, the Virginia Assembly adopted a plan for solving her paper money problem. It provided that after a certain date the paper currency should cease to circulate as money. In the meantime, however, it could be used in the purchase of gold and silver bonds

144

paying six per cent interest. For this purpose the paper currency was to be valued at 1000 to 1. There was little opposition to this proposal as Patrick Henry and other leaders had come around to its support. So 1781 saw the end of paper money in Virginia.[34]

At the end of 1780, the Virginia Assembly voted to send a special agent to Congress and General Washington. The principal candidates for the position were Richard Henry Lee and Benjamin Harrison, Speaker of the House of Delegates. On the first ballot the vote was a tie. Then, after "much debate and perplexity," Lee withdrew and Harrison was chosen. To be thus thwarted by his old enemy must have been rather a bitter pill for Lee to swallow. Nor did Harrison get much satisfaction from his victory. He was so disgusted with the vote that he told Carter Braxton he believed he would resign the appointment; but on second thought, he decided to accept the mission and proceeded to Philadelphia.[35]

When the Assembly met in short session March 2, 1781, it was thus faced with a vacancy in the Speakership. Richard Henry Lee was nominated for the place by Mann Page and was elected without opposition. As Lee was Speaker, he did not serve on any of the committees and his name is not mentioned in the *Journal* after the account of his election as Speaker. This session ended on March 22, and with it ended Lee's speakership, for Harrison had returned from his mission to Congress and was again elected Speaker. The journal for this short session is so incomplete that we know very little as to what measures were considered and adopted.[36]

The Assembly met again this same year in Richmond on May 7. After a three-day session it hastily adjourned because the British army was approaching Richmond. Two weeks later the Assembly met in Charlottesville; but inasmuch as the British were overrunning a good part of the state, even this frontier town was not a safe refuge. The Assembly again adjourned and the members sought safety in flight to Staunton. Apparently Lee was not in attendance during this runaway session.[37]

This fugitive assembly had to its credit at least one important measure looking to an improvement in federal finances. In February, 1781, Congress adopted a resolution asking the states to vest in Congress the power "to levy for the use of the United States, a duty of five per cent *ad valorem* . . . upon all goods, wares and merchandises of foreign growth and manufactures, which may be imported into any of the said states. . . ."[38] Such a tax would have afforded the general government a source of revenue not dependent upon dilatory action of the states. But the resolution to be effective required the assent of every state legislature. The Virginia Assembly, after some days of deliberation and discussion, voted in favor of this grant of authority to Congress.[39] The proposal was also promptly accepted by all the other states except Rhode Island.[40]

The fall session of the 1782 Assembly was scheduled to meet in Richmond on October 21, but is was not until the 9th of November that the House of Delegates had a sufficient number present for organization.[41] The latecomers were taken into the custody of the sergeant at arms and were fined unless they could give a good excuse for their tardiness. Thomas Jefferson, Richard Henry Lee, and Patrick Henry were among the delinquents. On November 4, Lee appeared under the custody of the sergeant at arms, but it was ruled that there was good reason for his absence and he was admitted without a fine.[42] At this session the Assembly rescinded its previous acceptance of the proposal that Congress be given power to levy a five per cent duty on goods imported from foreign countries. The reason given for this reversal of its former action was that to grant this power to Congress would be to violate the spirit of the Confederation.[43] Lee was not a member of the House of Delegates when it accepted the resolution of Congress, but was in attendance at the time the endorsement was rescinded. Governor Harrison accused the Lees (Arthur and Richard Henry) of being responsible for Virginia's repeal of the impost.[44] Edmund Randolph also blamed them, saying that the Lees were thought to have been motivated in their action by the desire to pique Robert Morris. "The tenor of their daily language," he said, "justifies the suspicion—their character for malice confirms it."[45]

In a letter to General William Whipple (July 1, 1783), Richard Henry gave his reasons for supporting repeal as follows: Such a tax would endanger liberty and would "strangle our infant commerce in its birth." Instead of considering this new policy as "too little and too late" (as it was), he termed it "too early and too strong an attempt to over leap those fences established by the Confederation to secure the liberties of the respective States." This, he contended, would do away with the

146

present excellent plan of leaving the apportioned sum to be levied by the states and would give "the all important power of the purse" to an aristocratic assembly. "For give the purse, and the sword will follow, and . . . that liberty which we love and now deserve will become an empty Name." "Let us be cautious how we introduce such radical defects into our system. . . ." In taking this step, Lee was departing from his earlier record regarding financial policy. As a member of Congress and the Virginia House of Delegates, he had generally supported efforts to keep the state and federal monetary systems on a sound basis. He later changed to some extent his position on the impost, owing to the "unpardonable remissness" of the states in meeting their quotas of the federal revenue.[46]

At this session of the Assembly (October-December, 1782) the enemies of the Lees brought a new charge against Richard Henry. Delegate John Mercer presented statements from Colonel Samuel Griffin, James Mercer, and Meriwether Smith as follows: "That it was the public conversation in Philadelphia, that there is *a British party on the continent* at the head of which are Messrs. [Samuel] Adams, [Richard Henry] Lee, and [Henry] Laurens."[47] This accusation was referred to the Committee of Privileges and Elections for examination. After considering the committee's report, the House, in committee of the whole, unanimously agreed that the evidence presented did not touch the public or private conduct of Lee "or induce the most distant suspicion of his want of attachment to the interests of his country; but that on the contrary, this committee do bear testimony to the world, that the uniform rectitude of his public conduct entitles him to the fullest confidence, and warmest approbation of his country." This report was at once adopted unanimously by the House.[48]

Richard Henry's vindication may not have been as complete as the unanimous vote in his favor would indicate; at the next session of the Assembly the House of Delegates refused to accord him for a second time the highest honor at its disposal. When the House chose its Speaker (May 12, 1783) the two candidates for the office were John Tyler (future father of a President of the United States), nominated by Patrick Henry, and Richard Henry Lee, nominated by Mann Page. Tyler was elected by a vote of 61 to 20. A year later Lee nominated Tyler, who was re-elected Speaker.[49]

There was another meeting of the Assembly during the last months of 1783. Richard Henry Lee, along with Richard Lee, was elected to the House of Delegates as a representative of Westmoreland, but apparently R. H. Lee was prevented by illness from attending this session. Early in January, 1784, he spoke of not yet having recovered sufficiently from his illness to take part in public affairs.[50]

He attended the next session of the Assembly but again illness cut his attendance to a very short period, probably little more than a week. He was appointed to three standing committees, but his only special assignment recorded was that of cooperating with other members of the committee to prepare, in concert with a committee of the Senate, an address expressing the thanks of the General Assembly to General Washington for the services rendered by him to his country.[51]

It was unfortunate that Lee's illness came at this time, for his support was badly needed for an over-due reform—the revision of the state constitution. The constitution of 1776 had been hastily framed and adopted under emergency conditions and was seriously in need of revision. Under this constitution the executive and judiciary were too dependent upon the legislature, and there was an unfair distribution of seats in the Assembly and an undue limitation of the suffrage.[52]

A resolution, strongly supported by James Madison, called for the election of representatives to a constitutional convention. This convention could either endorse or revise the constitution. In either case the constitution would have the vote of the people behind it. Madison was at first encouraged in his purpose by the arrival of Richard Henry Lee, who was for calling a constitutional convention. But the day before the question came up for final action Lee had to leave on account of illness, and Patrick Henry was more violent in his opposition than was expected. Consequently, after two days of debate the attempt failed (June, 1784).[53]

As a member of the House of Delegates, Richard Henry Lee had played a major role in the organization of the commonwealth government, yet Virginia never conferred upon him her most honored state office—that of governor of the commonwealth. He was a candidate for the governorship in 1786 and was defeated by Edmund Randolph.[54]

148

Chapter XI
Home Defense

Lee's services to his home state, in addition to legislative counsels and activity, included effective military advice and service. Early in his career he was chosen an officer in the Westmoreland militia, and on the death of his brother Philip Ludwell (1775) he succeeded to the command of the local militia, with the title of colonel. Under his command the untrained citizen soldiers of the Westmoreland militia proved an annoyance to the attacking British regulars. Admiral Graves, who led the invasion in the Potomac region, was reported to have said: "I never set my foot upon Westmoreland, that the militia are not upon me directly."[1]

As a member of the House of Delegates, he also offered and supported measures looking to the defense of the state against outside attack. The House appointed him to a committee to investigate naval conditions. Lee made the report, which contained six recommendations for the protection of the coast, Chesapeake Bay, and the navigable rivers. These proposals were adopted by the Assembly in January, 1778.

These resolutions provided that armed vessels should be stationed at the mouth of Chesapeake Bay and at the mouths of navigable streams to prevent the entrance of enemy ships. A tender was to cruise in the Bay and one in the ocean near the mouth of the Bay to give notice of the approach of British ships. The coastal trade was to be protected by two galleys stationed in harbors off the Eastern shore. Inasmuch as Maryland and North Carolina also were in need of such protection, it was suggested that these two states be asked to cooperate with Virginia in these measures. On learning that the British warships in the Potomac River were receiving supplies and livestock from the Virginians and the Marylanders, Lee had written to the governors of Virginia and Maryland (December, 1777) suggesting that this practice be stopped by Virginia and Maryland galleys in the Potomac.[2]

Lee had hardly become settled at Chantilly after his return from Congress, in May, 1779, when ten British ships came up the Potomac to a point just below his home county of Westmoreland. Making a landing here, they burned a warehouse with from two to three hundred hogsheads of tobacco and three private houses and carried away several slaves. Lee mustered the Westmoreland militia, but found the militia unarmed and reluctant to make the needed resistance. By persistent appeals to the state government he procured arms, powder and lead, and had the lead made into bullets. The militia then resisted the enemy with spirit.[3] He felt, however, that the use of local militia was not the proper method of defense. It took the men away from their farm work to the detriment of their crops. Besides, these invasions could not be properly met without the aid of ships. He therefore asked General Whipple to send two frigates from the federal navy to patrol the Chesapeake Bay.[4]

He also appealed for state aid. In a long letter to Governor Jefferson (July 8, 1779) Lee suggested a plan to secure Virginia against British invasion. "In Virginia," he said, "we have properly two frontiers, one bordered by a wilderness, the other by a Sea; into both of these issue savages, and into the latter the most savage. Our people on the former, have by long experience acquired the means of securing themselves with a good degree of success against their human brutes. The eastern frontier has not yet been so successful."

He advised that the Old Dominion station armed vessels to engage the enemy at their landing points. Virginia, he pointed out, has more than 1,000 miles of shore on navigable waters, but the mouth of Chesapeake Bay is only twenty miles wide. Boats should be stationed at the mouth of the Bay with spy boats out at sea to give notice of the approach of British vessels. In this way her armed ships could meet and defeat the invaders before they would have time to commit depredations. Such a method of defense, he argued, would be better than that afforded by forts. For if the forts were weak they would easily be captured by the British; if they were strong they would afford protection only for the small area around them.[5]

In the last days of December, 1780, Benedict Arnold appeared in the Chesapeake Bay with a squadron of ships, carrying sixteen hundred soldiers. Lee wrote to Washington for the aid

COLONEL THOMAS LEE, father of Richard Henry Lee.

HANNAH LUDWELL LEE, mother of Richard Henry Lee.

STRATFORD, home of Colonel Thomas Lee about one mile from the Potomac in Westmoreland County, was the early home of Richard Henry Lee. It was built in 1730 or earlier.

RALEIGH TAVERN in Williamsburg was a center of social activity and a meeting place for Revolutionary leaders. The original building was erected about 1740 and burned in 1859.

of ships, saying that Arnold had ascended the James River as far as Jamestown. Arnold's purpose, he thought, was to plunder and divert Virginia's attention from the Southern war. In Lee's opinion, a ship of the line and a frigate or two, sent with speed and secrecy to Chesapeake Bay, could apprehend the plunderers and leave the Virginia forces free to engage in the Southern operations.[6] On March 27, 1781, Lee wrote to Governor Jefferson reporting with approval a proposal which Baron Von Steuben had offered in a conference with Lee at Williamsburg. As a means of keeping the British forces separated, it was suggested that Von Steuben lead his men south and cooperate with General Greene or at least prevent the British troops in Virginia from joining Cornwallis. This plan was not adopted, however, as it did not fit in with the strategy that Greene had planned.[7]

In the spring of 1781, it looked as if northern Virginia might be the scene of British invasion. A British tender was grounded on the shore of the Potomac close to Lee's home. Wanting the arms it contained, Lee led the Westmoreland militia in an unsuccessful attack on it (April 9). Since he expected retaliatory attacks by the British, he wrote to Governor Jefferson for more flints and ammunition to replenish his limited supply.[8]

Lee's fear of a raid by the British was strengthened by a letter (dated May 10, 1781) from General Weedon, in which the General stated that northern Virginia might soon expect an attack by the enemy. This warning acted as an alarm bell to Lee. Writing to his brother Arthur (June 4, 1781) he said: "We and our property here are now within the power of the enemy." Lee made plans for calling out the militia of Westmoreland County and the adjacent region. He moved his residence from Chantilly to Epping Forest in Lancaster County to insure the safety of his family. Here, in the midst of a dense forest, his family was safely out of the reach of the British. It was expected that the British would carry out the same kind of depredations along the Potomac that they had practiced on the James River. The big planters were especially alarmed, for the British claimed that they left the poor unmolested and plundered only the rich. Owing to the lack of ships on the part of the Virginians, the British by the use of their ships could baffle them with a force one tenth that of the defenders.[9]

General Weedon followed up his warning with another letter (May 31, 1781) requesting Lee, as County Lieutenant of Westmoreland County, to draft a fourth of his militia and appoint a time and place for the meeting of his force with those of the four lower counties. This was done and Westmoreland Court House was appointed as the rendezvous. Cornwallis had crossed the James River and Lafayette had abandoned Richmond and fallen back toward Fredericksburg to protect the arsenal at Falmouth. Lafayette wrote to Weedon for more troops. Thereupon Weedon promptly called upon Lee to draft and send to Lafayette half the militia of Westmoreland County and to forward his request to the lieutenants of the other counties of the Northern Neck. Lee received this letter Saturday, June 2, and issued orders for a general muster to be held two days later. On the appointed date a number of men were drafted, and three days later two hundred were on the march to Falmouth under command of Colonel Augustine Washington.[10] General Weedon was pleased with Lee's co-operation. Writing to him on June 15, 1781, he expressed himself as being happy "in having an officer in the lower parts that gives satisfaction" and spoke of "well knowing your prudence and activity in time of alarm."[11]

Lee felt that the Old Dominion was not getting the assistance either from the Continental Army or from the American ally, France, that the situation demanded. In a letter to his brother Arthur (June 4, 1781) he made the following complaint: "We have received next to no assistance from our Sister States or from our Ally, whilst our vet[e]ran regulars" are in the Continental army with Greene in the South. They constitute a considerable part of Greene's strength. The people feel that they have been abandoned and "are exposed to the infinite acts and fraud of our enemies and of our internal Tories."

Richard Henry had reason to be alarmed at conditions in Virginia. Her situation, he declared, demanded immediate and effectual aid, else her resources would fall to the enemy and be used by them to overthrow the liberties of North America. He admitted that Virginia had nine times as many men as the enemy threatening her but they were dispersed and unarmed. British troops, under the command first of Arnold and then of Cornwallis, were penetrating far into the interior. The legislature, which had adjourned to Charlottesville, had not been able to get a quorum before the members dispersed to escape capture by the enemy. Governor Jefferson's term had expired and he gave up the office although no successor had been provided. He contended that his authority as governor had ceased with the end of his one-year term. Mr. Digges, the lieutenant governor, had been captured and released on parole. Thus the Old Dominion was without a state executive.

With the state government suffering from a temporary paralysis, the enemy was operating almost at will. Lee was especially disturbed by the British depredations in Westmoreland—the taking away of slaves and the destruction of corn, cattle, and tobacco. He appealed to Congress to send Washington immediately to Virginia with two to three thousand troops and give him dictatorial power until the legislature could convene and a governor could be appointed. Congress should also strongly recommend that the extraordinary authority conferred on Washington be continued by the Virginia Assembly, when convened, for six, eight, or ten months.

Lee also sent a letter to Washington urging him to assume this responsibility. In this letter he said: "Our country [Virginia] is truly, Sir, in a deplorable way, and if relief comes not from you it will probably not come at all." "It would be a thing to weep [over?]," he continued, "if the goodly fabric of human freedom, which you have so well labored to rear, should in one unlucky moment be leveled with the dust."[12]

Washington replied that he was very well acquainted with the distress of Virginia but thought that the plan suggested by Lee for her relief was "a greater proof of your unbounded confidence in me than it is that the means proposed would be found adequate to the end in view were it practicable to make the experiment." He said too, for reasons which he could not safely give in a letter which might be intercepted, that he could not leave the joint command. He had a plan which he felt would cause the British either to withdraw from New York or from Virginia except Portsmouth. If he could see Lee, he believed he could convince him in a half-hour's conversation that his plan was advisable. But he dared not trust it in writing.[13] Washington's plan was the one which resulted in the American victory at Yorktown and the ending of the war.

While his home state was in the midst of this crisis, Lee was also devoting his energies to promoting the general military effort. One such service was an attempt to stop desertions from the army. A number of men had deserted from the French army and navy and the commanders wished to capture them. The Governor of Virginia directed Lee to give such orders to the ferrymen of Westmoreland County as would put an end to this leakage in the armed forces. All foreigners looking like soldiers or seamen trying to cross the ferries were to be examined with great strictness. Lee carried out the order in accordance with these instructions.[14]

Washington's decision to move south against the British forces in Virginia gave great satisfaction to Lee. In a letter to Washington (September 17, 1781) he congratulated him on the bright prospects of the American cause. As he saw it, only two things could prevent the success of Washington's plan—naval aid from Europe to the British or the lack of supplies for the American forces. The former was not at all probable, but it was, he thought, a disgrace that in a land of abundance the American military and naval efforts were handicapped by a lack of provisions. He suggested that millers be promised payment in specie for flour furnished by them and that provision be made for commandeering half the beef and bacon in every family for the use of the army.[15]

When he received word of the arrival in Virginia waters of the French fleet under Count de Grasse, Lee went around Westmoreland County in person and secured contributions of live cattle, poultry, butter, vegetables, etc., making a liberal contribution himself. He loaded these supplies in a schooner which with a very cordial letter he sent to the Count.[16]

Richard Henry saw in the coming of the French fleet the opportunity for the Old Dominion to solve her two greatest problems—the security of her waters and the stabilization of her currency. The French ships could be used, he thought, to capture the British vessels and thus remove the danger to Virginia's waters. By using the captured vessels as transports, and one or two French frigates as convoys, Virginia could export her public tobacco to Holland and obtain specie with which to buy up her paper currency. This should be done as soon as possible, before the price of tobacco was brought down by competition.[17] But the plan was not adopted, although Lee in his correspondence continued to urge it. Objections of a practical nature, the lack of money to start the plan, the difficulty of getting sailors, etc., were urged against it.

154

On the eve of Yorktown, Governor Nelson directed Lee to impress supplies for the army and send horses to aid in the Yorktown campaign. In response to this order he at once dispatched "discreet active men" along the Potomac and Rappahannock rivers to impress corn and fodder, and sent ten horses to Williamsburg, although at the time he was "but a feeble convalescent from an attack of the gout." But the victory at Yorktown made it unnecessary to collect the supplies and apparently they remained with the owners.[18]

Lee's grandson stated that the British tried to capture Richard Henry and were thwarted by one of the managers of Lee's estate. According to another account, the British broke into the Lee house at midnight and were misled by the slaves, who reported that Lee had gone to Philadelphia, although he was only a few miles from the Chantilly mansion.[19]

When word came that Cornwallis had surrendered at Yorktown, Lee was greatly pleased but probably not surprised, for his optimism had led him to expect such an outcome. Writing to Washington a week before the surrender, he said: "We are anxiously waiting for the rejoicing time to come when Ld. Cornwallis and his people will be your prisoners." Lee, with other statesmen and the officers of the French and American armies, attended a great peace ball at Fredericksburg (November 11) to celebrate the victory. The occasion was honored by Mary Ball Washington, who came in leaning on the arm of her distinguished son.[20]

The British raids did not cease with the surrender of Cornwallis, but continued in northern Virginia until late in the fall of the next year. Indeed, Lee's reports of the devastations of 1782 sound very much like those of the previous year. Writing to Governor Harrison, July 9, 1782, he said that on the previous Friday a party of the enemy consisting of one hundred men, black and white, had landed at a plantation on the Potomac in a county adjoining Westmoreland. They took away Negroes, committed other robberies, and announced that they would soon return for other attacks since they knew that the militia were unarmed.[21] Lee appealed to Governor Harrison to take steps to put an end to these piratical excursions.[22]

Even if the militia were supplied with arms it would not be an adequate defense, he maintained, for they were so dispersed that they could not guard against sudden attack. The "pirates" (as he termed the British invaders) were growing more dangerous since they had adopted the plan of arming black men. The only adequate defense would be by water. He suggested that two vessels be sent up the Chesapeake Bay. The need for them was especially great now since the French fleet (as he supposed) had gone and the French frigates had left the Bay. Later (September 6) he again wrote to Governor Harrison about the British depredations. These "pirates" would land in the night, plunder houses two or three miles from shore, and return to their vessels with safety. It is very unfortunate for this country, he continued, "that no exertions are made to defend its honor and interest upon the water within the very bowels of the state."[23] It was not long, however, before Lee was relieved of these fears; a few months later the preliminary treaty of peace was signed with Great Britain.

Chapter XII

Indian Summer of the Confederation

Lee had left Congress at the end of his first period of service with a bad taste in his mouth. He had incurred the enmity of some of his colleagues and he had a rather low opinion of the body in general. In writing to brother Arthur a year and a half later he expressed the hope that Arthur would find in "Congress now more justice, impartiality and patriotism than" he "left it possessed of."[1]

In April, 1780, when William Ellery nominated him for a seat on the Federal Court of Appeals, his enemies were strong enough to defeat him.[2] His friend, James Lovell, had earlier in January refused to nominate him, saying: "I would not risque Coll. R. H. Lee in the present Temper of the House, though I think him extremely well calculated. . . . I found a Number of Virulentissimes still cocked and primed at the very Name of Lee."[3]

Early in 1783, his enemies circulated a report which represented the Lees, Samuel Adams, and Henry Laurens as being at the head of a pro-British party. Congress, however, voted unanimously in committee of the whole (January 7, 1783) to express the "fullest confidence and warmest approbation of R. H. Lee," and this action was confirmed by the house.[4]

In June, 1784, Lee was again elected to Congress for a one-year term.[5] On the first of November, the time set for the opening of the session, only Lee and six other delegates, representing five states, were in attendance. The members were so slow in arriving that it was not until the end of the month that enough states were represented to organize and elect a president. Lee was "much grieved" at this lack of interest. The rainy weather and the muddy streets of the village of Trenton, where the session began, added to his depression. On November 30, with nine states represented, the house elected Lee as its president on the

157

twelfth ballot. Congress continued to meet at Trenton until December 24, when it adjourned to convene in New York on January 11.[6]

Lee was proud of this new honor and lived in a style worthy of his high position. In one of his letters he spoke of the "old President" as being rigged out by his tailor "into a young beau." He arranged for suitable living quarters, and rented ["hired"] a house which he spoke of as being "very spacious and elegant" and "provided with every accommodation." It was the one in which Washington later resided as President.[7]

Slaves were taken up from Chantilly for service in the New York home, but apparently were not capable of properly managing the domestic activities of the presidential mansion. The president, therefore, had Dr. William Shippen, Jr., send him a head servant from Philadelphia. Lee did not take his family with him to New York. Accordingly, for thirteen months continuously he was away from his family, except that one of his sons was with him at least part of the time. And yet he seems to have performed his ceremonial functions satisfactorily without the aid of his wife and daughters. Robert Hunter, a young Scotsman then touring the United States, called on President Lee and was deeply impressed with the hospitality accorded him. He was introduced to the president by his friend, Mr. "Rosawelt [Roosevelt]."[8]

In December, 1784, Congress decided to send a minister to Spain "for the purpose of adjusting the interfering claims of the two nations respecting the navigation of the Mississippi, and other matters highly interesting to the peace and good understanding which ought to subsist between them." Lee voted for this resolution[9] and advocated the appointment of Jefferson to this important mission, pointing to the great importance of the affairs with Spain. In so doing he was opposing Jefferson's appointment to the court of France. Monroe accused Lee of acting from selfish motives, attributing to him the desire to get Jefferson out of the way as a possibility for either the French or British mission, so that one of these positions could go to himself or one or both of them to his friends, especially R. R. Livingston or Arthur Lee. Monroe, he said, had been assured by Lafayette and Marbois of the French government's wish that Jefferson should succeed Franklin, who had asked permission to give up

158

his post and return home. Lee was not successful in this effort, for Jefferson was chosen (March 10, 1785) as the representative of the United States to the court of Versailles.[10]

On December 23, 1784, Congress considered a motion providing for the appointment of three commissioners to lay out as the seat of the federal government a district "on the banks of either side of the Delaware" River, not less than two nor more than three miles square. Samuel Hardy made a motion, seconded by James Monroe (both of Virginia), striking out the words, "on the banks of either side of the Delaware" and putting in "at Georgetown, on the Potomac." This amendment failed, but Lee and the other Virginia delegates voted for it. On the same day the original motion was passed after having been amended so as to make New York the temporary capital with the Virginia delegation voting for the bill as amended.[11]

During the year of Lee's presidency of Congress, two attempts were made to amend the Articles of Confederation. In January, 1785, a committee under the chairmanship of James Monroe brought in a report recommending that the 9th article be amended to give Congress authority to control commerce.[12] Lee led the opposition to this proposal and was the main speaker against the report when it was considered in committee of the whole. While the *Journal* gives no report of speeches made in Congress, we know from his correspondence something of his objections. His line of reasoning was as follows: The eight Northern states owned nearly all the American ships. If the federal government had control of commerce, these Northern states, with the cooperation of one Southern state, could gain a monopoly of American shipping and place the South at the mercy of the North. "The Spirit of Commerce," he declared, "is a spirit of Avarice," and he feared that the remedy would be worse than the evil, "bad as the last may be." The proposal failed to get the approval of Congress.[13]

The other proposal was concerned with changing districts within existing states into new states. The effort was unsuccessful with Lee and Grayson, the only representatives from Virginia, voting against it.[14]

The most important measure adopted by Congress during Lee's presidential term was the Land Ordinance of 1785. The sale of western lands if properly managed would be a source of

159

much-needed revenue. Congress was aware of this opportunity but did not take advantage of it until this ordinance was passed. Action by Congress was hastened by the advice of Washington, who had made a journey to the west in the fall of 1784 and noted that squatters were settling there and that this would prove a hindrance to the legal occupation of the region. In writing to Richard Henry Lee (December 14, 1784) he advised that Congress adopt as quickly as possible a system of land sales for the West. In reply Lee said that Washington's suggestions were wise and just and would "certainly have great weight when that business shall be discussed in Congress," which Lee thought would be as soon as the negotiations with the Indians were concluded.[15]

A land ordinance had been presented to Congress in May, 1784, but no action had been taken on it at that time. Early in March, 1785, it was again presented, and after considerable discussion and some amendment, it was adopted by a unanimous vote of the states (May 20). One important amendment to the original draft was the deletion of a clause which provided that one section in every township should be reserved for the support of religion. This clause was a step toward the union of church and state and was regarded by James Madison as smelling strongly "of antiquated Bigotry." Lee and the other Virginia representatives voted in favor of retaining the religious provision. There was also a clause in the original ordinance reserving to the federal government one-third of all gold, silver, lead and copper on land sold to individuals. A motion to strike out this clause, made by James Monroe (April 20, 1785), was lost with Lee voting against it. The Virginia delegation unanimously supported an amendment that safeguarded the claims of officers and soldiers to whom the state had made grants of land in the region northwest of the Ohio.[16]

The Land Ordinance of 1785 provided that from time to time considerable areas of land were to be surveyed and divided into townships, rectangular tracts six miles square. Each township was to be divided into thirty-six sections of 640 acres each. Section sixteen in every township was to be reserved for the use of schools and the rest was to be auctioned off to the highest bidder. The minimum single purchase was to be one section and the minimum price one dollar an acre. Because few individual settlers could raise such a large sum, most of the land was sold to speculators who could cut up the land into smaller tracts and sell them on credit. Lee expected that the sale of western lands would eventually discharge nearly all the public debt.[17] The Land Ordinance of 1785 initiated the land-grant system which, with some modification, was followed by our government for three quarters of a century.

Absence from his family was not the only bar to Lee's enjoyment of the presidency; his old enemy, ill health, had returned to torment him. In August, on leave of absence from Congress, he visited "the Calybeate waters in Pennsylvania" for rest and recuperation, and after two months returned to his duties with his health much improved. Samuel Holten, a delegate from Massachusetts, acted as chairman of Congress during his absence. While away, Lee also kept in touch with the secretary, who sent him the papers which required his signature.[18]

At the end of his term as president, Lee, accompanied by his son and his servants, left New York for his home in Virginia. On the way they stopped for one night to enjoy the hospitality of General Washington. Robert Hunter, mentioned above, was at Mount Vernon at the same time. According to his report, the General received his guests in an informal and cordial manner and after a few glasses of champagne became quite merry.[19]

Lee was re-elected to Congress in November, 1785, but because of ill health he was not in attendance at any time during this one-year term. In July, 1787, he entered Congress to perform his last service in that body.[20] By this time the old Congress was nearing its end and was showing all the symptoms of senility. In its later years, especially after the signing of the final peace treaty (1783), the Continental Congress had become little more than a shadow of its former self. Gone were the enthusiasm and pioneering activity of the first session. The removal of the danger presented by the war left the states without a common purpose strong enough to hold them together in effective unity of action. Each state was concerned more with upholding its own rights than with creating an efficient general government. The Articles of Confederation had put Congress on a constitutional basis but had not increased the authority of the Union.

One ominous sign of the decline in importance of the federal government was the poor attendance at the sessions of Congress, due in part to the participation in the Constitutional Convention of many Congressmen. In August, 1787, owing to these absences only five states were represented in Congress.[21] But despite its weakness, Congress in 1787 adopted one of the most important measures of its career. This was the Northwest Ordinance, which provided for the government of the Northwest Territory.

Congress had already adopted a plan for the government of all the western territory. This plan was embodied in the Ordinance of 1784, which had been written by Jefferson; but it was not to go into effect until all the western lands had been ceded to the general government. Before all the cessions had been made this plan was superseded by the Ordinance of 1787 and so was never carried out.[22] In Jefferson's original draft of the Ordinance there was a provision prohibiting slavery in the western territory after 1800. This clause was stricken out by a vote of 6 to 3, with two states divided. Virginia's vote was against this provision, since Jefferson was the only member of the delegation present who supported it. Next year a resolution was passed by Congress (March 16, 1785) declaring that there should be no slavery or involuntary servitude in any of the states carved out of this western territory. Lee, then president of Congress, voted no, along with the majority of the Virginia delegates.[23]

When Lee arrived at New York (July, 1787) for his final term in Congress he found that that aging body had been dillydallying for some time with the problem of establishing a government for the Northwest Territory. On the day he took his seat (July 9) a committee of five, including Nathan Dane and Lee. was appointed to report a plan for the temporary government of the Northwest Territory. Two days later the committee reported an ordinance for the government of the Territory,[24] which included the article prohibiting slavery in the territory. The Ordinance was passed (July 13) after only a few verbal changes had been made in Dane's draft. Lee and the two other delegates from Virginia voted in the affirmative and apparently raised no objection to the anti-slavery clause.[25]

This new measure applied not to the entire West, as did the Ordinance of 1784, but only to the Northwest Territory—a vast area lying between the Ohio River and the boundary of Pennsylvania on the east, the Mississippi on the west, the Ohio on the south, and the Canadian border on the north. The Ordi-

162

nance consisted of governmental provisions and a bill of rights. By the latter the inhabitants were guaranteed freedom of worship, the benefits of the writ of habeas corpus and trial by jury, and exemption from unusual and excessive punishments. Judicial proceedings were also to be in accordance with the common law. Private contracts were not to be interfered with, and no one was to be deprived of life, liberty, or property "but by the judgment of his peers or the law of the land." There was to be no slavery or involuntary servitude in the entire territory.[26]

The Ordinance of 1787 provided that the whole region was to be governed temporarily as one Territory but later was to be divided into not less than three nor more than five districts. The Territory was at first to be governed autocratically by a governor and three judges appointed by Congress. As soon, however, as the Territory attained a population of 5,000 adult males, this autocratic government would end with the addition of a legislature with a lower house chosen by the people and an upper house selected by Congress from nominations made by the lower house. At this stage the Territory could send a delegate to Congress to take part in the deliberations of that body but without power to vote. Whenever any one of the three to five districts into which the Territory was to be divided had a free population of 60,000, that district was to be admitted into the Union as a state on an equal basis with the older states.[27]

The Ordinance of 1787 inaugurated a policy in the government of our territories which has been followed in principle ever since. The new Territory was not to be treated as a colonial dependency but as an integral part of the country. The new states to be carved out of the Territory would be put on the basis of political equality with the original thirteen. This wise decision settled at once the question whether the young nation should have a colonial system. Lee was pleased with the governmental provisions of the Ordinance which, as he thought, were "much more tonic" than were those of the eastern state governments.[28]

In this last year of his membership in Congress, Lee and his Virginia colleagues took a vigorous stand on foreign policy. The piratical states of Algiers, Tunis, and Tripoli were exacting tribute from American and European ships operating in the Mediterranean Sea. As a means of upholding the rights of American seamen in that region, Grayson of Virginia moved "That the

Minister plenipotentiary of the United States at the Court of France be directed to form a Confederacy" with the European powers who were then at war or might be disposed to go to war with Algiers, Tripoli, and Tunis, with the purpose of protecting the citizens of the contracting parties in the free navigation of the Mediterranean Sea. The agreement was to provide against a separate peace on the part of any of the contracting parties and to assure that in case of future aggression the whole confederacy would resume hostilities. The resolve carried, with Lee and the other two Virginia delegates voting aye, July 27, 1787.[29]

These were high-sounding words for the weak confederation, and the Secretary for Foreign Affairs, to whom the motion had been referred for report, had the good sense to realize it. In his report to Congress he pointed out that the government was inefficient; that the federal navy was weak and rapidly declining; and that the public revenue received was inadequate to the exigencies of the union. Under such conditions it was highly probable that the quota of force expected of the United States would be much greater than it would be able to supply. He therefore advised against the plan, and apparently nothing further was done about it.[30]

Before bidding farewell to Congress, Richard Henry was able once again to show his affection and respect for his old friend, John Adams. In January, 1787, Adams, who was minister plenipotentiary to Britain, had requested permission to return home at any time after February 24, 1788.[31] John Jay, the Secretary for Foreign Affairs, recommended that Adams' request be granted and that his successor be appointed and sent over in time to be briefed by Adams before he left in February. He also suggested that with the acceptance of Adams' resignation there should be coupled a resolution expressing appreciation of his services.[32]

In response to Jay's suggestion, several motions concerned with Adams' request for recall were made, discussed and defeated. Lee's votes on these resolutions showed his friendliness for Adams; but the defeat of one of them indicated that there was considerable hostility to Adams in Congress. This motion was as follows: "That Congress entertain a high sense of the services which Mr. Adams has rendered to the United States in the execution of the various important trusts which they have from time to time committed to him; and that the thanks of Congress

164

be presented to him for the patriotism, perseverance, integrity and diligence with which he has ably and faithfully served his Country." This resolution failed to pass (September 24, 1787), with Virginia's four representatives voting two for and two against it. Richard Henry, of course, voted aye, but his nephew-in-law, "Light-Horse Harry" Lee, voted no.[33] It was not until several months later (February, 1788) that Congress granted Adams permission to return to the United States. Along with the letter of recall went a resolution by Congress expressing appreciation "for the patriotism, perseverance, integrity, and diligence, with which he hath ably and faithfully served his country."[34]

The adoption of the Land Ordinance of 1785 and the governmental Ordinance of 1787 were spurts of activity on the part of Congress which did not arrest the decline in vitality of that decrepit body.[35] So great was the danger that the Congress would be reduced to a nonentity that even Richard Henry Lee, a strong advocate of states' rights, seemed to feel that something should be done to strengthen the union. In a letter to James Madison (November 26, 1784) he stated that many members felt that Congress should call a federal convention to revise the Articles of Confederation so that Congress could perform with "more energy, effect and vigor the powers assigned it." These advocates of a stronger union, he said, contended that a convention was necessary because all attempts at amending the Articles of Confederation made by Congress had ended in failure. Lee himself seemed to be leaning toward this proposal, for in this letter he asked the opinion of Madison as to the advisability of calling a convention. A month later, however, he reported that "the conversation [in Congress] concerning a Continental Convention has ceased for some time, so that perhaps it may not be revived again."[36]

But it was not long before agitation in favor of a constitutional convention again arose in Congress.[37] The first important step toward converting this sentiment into action was taken not by Congress but by a convention (composed of delegates from five states) at Annapolis in September, 1786. This convention unanimously recommended that all the states appoint delegates to a convention to be held at Philadelphia on the second Monday of May, 1787, "to devise such further provisions as shall appear to them necessary to render the constitution of the Federal Government adequate to the exigencies of the Union."[38]

The report of the Annapolis Convention was received by Congress on September 20, 1786. After this report had been under consideration in committee for some months, Congress adopted a resolution (February 21, 1787) which in its final form provided for the calling of a constitutional convention to be held on the second Monday in May, 1787, in Philadelphia "for the sole and express purpose of revising the Articles of Confederation." Any amendments made by the convention were to be adopted by Congress and agreed to by the states.[39]

Virginia was the first state to accept the invitation issued from Annapolis by choosing delegates to the proposed constitutional convention. For this important service she selected seven of her most distinguished sons, including Peyton Randolph, Washington, George Mason, and James Madison. Patrick Henry and Richard Henry Lee were also appointed but both declined. Henry refused to serve because he was not in sympathy with the plan to create a strong general government. In this move he sensed a serious danger to states' rights, or, as he expressed it, he "smelled a rat." It was probably this same feeling that caused Lee to decline the appointment, although he gave other reasons.

When Lee received from Governor Edmund Randolph a notice of his appointment as a delegate to the Constitutional Convention, he declined it "with much regret," saying that his health would not permit him to go northward until the middle of June and by that time his appointment to Congress would take him to that assembly. Besides "so many gentlemen of good hearts and sound minds" had been selected for the convention that he was willing to entrust the outcome to their determination. Later (October 27, 1787), in a letter to Samuel Adams, he said that he considered it improper for a member of Congress to accept a seat in the Convention. To him it seemed inconsistent "that the same Men should in N. York review their own doings in Philadelphia." He was confirmed in this view when members of the Convention came to New York in such numbers that they decided the vote in three states, divided it in two others, and gave individual votes in others. For this reason the Constitution did not and could not, as he contended, have a dispassionate and impartial consideration in Congress.[40]

On his way to New York to attend the Continental Congress, Lee stopped in Philadelphia long enough to get some idea of the work of the Convention then in session. Although strict secrecy was observed as to the proceedings of the assembly, he received the impression that the new government would be not unlike that of the British constitution, with an executive and a legislature of two houses. Apparently, he was willing to accept this form of government. "This departure from Simple Democracy," he said, "seems indispensably necessary, if any government at all is to exist in N. America." Indeed the people had become so disgusted with "the injustice, folly, and wickedness" of the state legislatures and executives that they seemed ready for anything. He hoped, however, that this tendency would be controlled and that the democratic influence would be completely secured by the proper safeguards.[41]

On September 20, 1787, the text of the Constitution was received by Congress. Lee proposed a number of amendments to be incorporated in the Constitution before it would be submitted to the states. He felt deeply that the adoption of the Constitution unamended would "put Civil Liberty and the happiness of the people at the mercy of Rulers who may possess the great unguarded powers given." "The necessary alterations will by no means interfere with the general nature of the plan, or limit the power of doing good; but they will restrain from oppression the wicked and tyrannic." Lee's amendments included a bill of rights, similar to but broader than the first ten amendments later adopted, and other important changes. Among the latter were the following suggestions: There should be a Privy Council of eleven members to give the President responsible advice (about the same as the President's Cabinet of today). The Privy Council, and not the Senate, should cooperate with the President in appointing all officers, civil and military. There should not be such an officer as the Vice-President. A speaker chosen by the Senate should perform his duties as president of the Senate, and the other duties now assigned the Vice-President should be performed by the Privy Council. The number of members of the House of Representatives should be increased and a larger number of votes than a bare majority should be required in the passage of certain laws and in the election of the President by the House of Representatives. Certain changes of a general nature in the trial of civil and criminal cases were also suggested. These proposals were not debated by Congress and were not recorded in the *Journal*.[42]

The friends of the Constitution (according to Madison) admitted that the Continental Congress had the constitutional right to make amendments but urged the expediency of foregoing this right on the following grounds: A discussion of the merits of the new Constitution would consume a great deal of time, and if the plan should be revised by Congress it would no longer be solely an act of the Convention. The revised plan would be sent by Congress to the legislatures, not the conventions, of the states and would require the ratification of thirteen instead of nine states. The unchanged Constitution would also go to the states, and some states might ratify the Congress plan and others the Convention plan. That would mean confusion and probably the defeat of both plans.[43]

These specious arguments against amendments were by no means convincing to Lee, for the danger of having two constitutions before the states could be avoided by calling a new convention. The Philadelphia Convention was easily assembled and another could be held without difficulty. This second convention could incorporate the proposed amendments in the original constitution and present to the states the new plan only. The slight delay occasioned by these changes would not be serious. The country was at peace with the rest of the world and could get along for a short time longer with a government under which it had been living for more than a decade.[44]

On September 27, Lee moved that Congress transmit the new Constitution "to the executive of every state in this Union to be laid before their respective legislatures." This motion failed to pass and was stricken from the *Journal*. Next day a motion was unanimously passed which provided that the state legislatures submit the Constitution to state conventions chosen in accordance with the resolutions of the Philadelphia Convention.[45] The Virginia delegation was divided as to the way in which the Constitution should be submitted to the states. Edward Carrington and Henry Lee wanted Congress to give it a warm endorsement. Richard Henry Lee and Grayson, on the other hand, opposed any statement of approbation by Congress, but agreed to a neutral submission to the states. The advocates of approbation yielded on this point because even one adverse vote would weaken it with the states. So the resolution for submission, with no statement of approval, was passed unanimously.[46] In providing for

168

the ratification of the Constitution and the inauguration of the new government, the Second Continental Congress was performing its last real service. The old government was bowing out to make room for its successor.

The Second Continental Congress had lasted, with interruptions, adjournments, and changes in its personnel, from May, 1775, until the new Constitution went into effect. It had been the organ of the federal government for nearly a decade and a half. It never had authority commensurate with its responsibility. And yet this weak Congress had to its credit a record of achievement with which a more powerful assembly could have been contented. It had carried on a war with the world's strongest power on finances that had been largely pulled out of the air. Along with its military policy went the adoption of other measures which stand out as conspicuous landmarks in American history, including the assertion of American independence, the creation of a plan of federal union, the negotiation of the French Alliance and the treaty of peace, and the system under which our public lands have been disposed of and our territories governed.

Chapter XIII

New Wine and Old Bottles

Lee seems to have been doubtful from the beginning as to the advisability of framing a new constitution or of making radical changes in the Articles of Confederation. He admitted that under the old system Congress could not demand money sufficient for paying the public debt and defraying the expenses of the Federal government. But this defect, he thought, could be remedied by giving Congress compulsory authority in the collection of revenue. He had now come to think that, owing to the unpardonable remissness on the part of the states in meeting their financial quotas, Congress should have the power to levy an impost for a period of time, provided that all revenue raised in this way should be applied to the payment of the public debt of the states. The agents for collecting this impost should be appointed by and be amenable to the states. He also held that the right of issuing paper money should be vested exclusively in Congress. Such a restraint on the states, he thought, was of great importance to the peace and happiness of the Union. His opposition to the unrestricted use of paper money was expressed in these terms: "Knaves assure, and fools believe, that calling paper money, and making it tender, is the way to be rich and happy."[1]

Since his proposed amendments had not been accepted by Congress, and the Constitution had been sent out to the states unchanged, Lee was opposed to its unconditional ratification. Not content with passive disapproval of the new plan, he carried on an active campaign against the Constitution by writing letters to his influential friends. To Washington, George Mason, Samuel Adams and others, he expressed anxiety and fear at the probability that under the new regime the states would lose their identity and individuals their liberty, in a consolidated government. In a letter·to Dr. William Shippen, Jr. (October 2, 1787) he said:

I have considered the new Constitution with all the attention and candor that the thing and the times render necessary, and I find it impossible for me to doubt that in its present state, unamended, the adoption of it will put Civil Liberty and the happiness of the people at the mercy of rulers who may possess the great unguarded powers given. . . . The necessary alterations will by no means interfere with the general nature of the plan, or limit the power of doing good; but they will restrain from oppression the wicked and tyrannic.[2]

A few days later (October 5) in writing to Samuel Adams, he spoke of the proposed government as an "*elective despotism*" (his italics). "Chains," he said, "being still Chains, whether made of gold or iron." He was, however, in favor of accepting the Constitution, properly amended, for it contained "many good regulations." He suggested that the state conventions propose amendments as conditions for their ratification and that these amendments along with the Constitution be reported to Congress and a new Federal convention. This second convention could so weave the proffered amendments into the original plan "as that a Web may be produced fit for freemen to wear." He also suggested as a possible alternative to acceptance of the new Constitution the continuance of the Articles of Confederation revised to give Congress complete power to make treaties with foreign powers, regulate trade, and levy an impost for a limited period.[3]

Writing to Governor Edmund Randolph of Virginia (October 16, 1787), he warned against hasty action in ratifying the Constitution. "Good government," he said, "is not the work of a short time, or of sudden thought." ". . . to say that a bad government must be established for fear of anarchy, is really saying that we should kill ourselves for fear of dying! . . . We should not trust to time and future events to correct errors, that both reason and experience, in similar cases, now prove to exist in the new system." He advised that Virginia propose the necessary amendments, and expressed his willingness to accept the Constitution with these amendments. Lee's letter to Governor Randolph was widely circulated in manuscript and then published. The arguments of this letter and others presented by Lee in pamphlets and newspapers had great influence in Virginia—greater, according to one modern authority, than that of the *Fed-*

eralist papers, which were then in circulation in the Old Dominion.[4]

In a letter to Washington (October 11, 1787) Lee had expressed deep regret at not being able to accept without question the new plan of government. He said that as a result of "long reflection upon the nature of Man and of government" he was led "to fear the danger that will ensue to Civil Liberty from the adoption of the new system in its present form." Washington viewed Lee's fight against the Constitution with strong disapproval. It was Lee's influence, he thought, that had caused George Mason to join in the attack on the Constitution. According to the report received by Washington, Lee had made himself obnoxious in Philadelphia by his declarations against the Constitution. "His conduct," continued Washington, "is not less reprobated in this country [Virginia]."[5]

In writing (May 22, 1788) to Edmund Pendleton, Lee elaborated on his objections to the Constitution in its original form. He said that after the most mature consideration he was forced to conclude that the proposed Constitution would leave the three essential securities against oppression—"the liberty of the Press, the Trial by Jury, and the Independency of Judges . . . under the mere pleasure of the new rulers." He predicted that under the proposed plan the state governments would become "as feeble and contemptible as was the Senatorial power under the Roman Emperors." "The name existed but the *thing* was gone." In this same letter he advised that Virginia make it plain as to what amendments she would insist upon, and if these amendments were not adopted within two years after the first meeting of the new Congress then "Virginia shall be considered disengaged from this ratification." But if the changes he suggested were added as conditions of ratification, then he thought Virginia could safely agree to the Constitution and "the most salutary consequences would ensue."[6]

The most important of all Lee's writings against unconditional ratification of the Constitution were two pamphlets: *Letters from the Federal Farmer to the Republican,* published in 1787, and *Additional Letters from the Federal Farmer to the Republican,* published in 1788. The favorable reception of the first pamphlet prompted the publication of the second. Within a few months after its publication the first *Letters* had gone through

172

four editions, with several thousand copies sold.[7] The *Letters* were Lee's greatest literary achievement. The style was clear and straightforward, but not especially brilliant; there was little in the work to indicate that the author was a great orator. Some of his criticisms were meticulous but many were based on sound principles. Some of his prophecies seem amusing in the light of later events, while others have been fulfilled.[8]

Lee discussed at length the plan of government to be established, basing his observations and appraisals on a minute study of the Constitution. His references to practices in other countries revealed a breadth of knowledge that could have been obtained only by exceptionally wide reading. These citations showed a familiarity with the common law in England and America and the legal and political systems of England and the American states. There were references to the political systems of the continental European countries and of ancient nations, such as Rome, Sparta, and Carthage. He also displayed familiarity with the works of the great writers on political and legal theory, such as Holt, Hale, Blackstone, Beccaria, Mansfield, DeLolme, and Montesquieu, especially the two last-named.[9]

Lee repeated the objections already noted—those given in his personal letters and those on which his proposed amendments had been based—and gave additional reasons for opposing unconditional ratification. Underlying all these discussions was the fear, expressed or implied, that the proposed plan would lead to a centralized government under which the rights of individuals and states would be sacrificed. Yet he considered a purely federal government inadequate and favored a general government that would be partly federal and partly consolidated—a sort of cross between the Articles of Confederation and the new Constitution. But one general government and general legislation for a country as large as ours with different customs, traditions, and beliefs, could not, he contended, extend equal benefits to all parts of the United States.

Apparently the purpose of these booklets was not to defeat ratification of the Constitution but to effect certain important changes by the incorporation of amendments. These amendments could be offered by the states as conditions of ratification or merely as suggestions to be embodied in the Constitution as amendments after the new government had gone into effect. He preferred the former method because, thanks to the discussion that had been going on, the people were alive to the issue; but after ratification this interest might cool off and the addition of amendments would be more difficult.

If his plan should be generally accepted, a new federal convention would have to be called to weave the new material into the original fabric. The advocates of unconditional ratification contended that this procedure would cause great delay and that another assembly could not hope to frame a more acceptable instrument than that prepared by the old convention since the Philadelphia Convention was composed of the ablest men in the states. Lee agreed that the framers of the Constitution were the ablest men in the country, but they had had to act without knowing the opinions and sentiments of the people. A second convention could learn from the proposals of the state conventions the needs and wants of the masses and would thus be in a position to frame a constitution that would meet them.

He admitted that any action taken with reference to the Constitution would involve risks. "Our situation," he said, "is critical, and we have but our choice of evils—We may hazard much by adopting the Constitution in its present form—We may hazard more by rejecting it wholly—We may hazard much by long contending about amendments prior to adoption." "The greatest political evils that can befall us, are discords and civil wars—the greatest blessings we can wish for, are peace, union, and industry, under a mild, free, and steady government."[10]

In the *Letters* Lee began his lengthy discussion of the proposed Constitution by disavowing any objection to an effective general government. The opening statement in the first letter of the series (October 8, 1787) was as follows:

"My uniform federal attachments, and the interest I have in the protection of property and a steady execution of the laws, will convince you, that, if I am under any bias at all, it is in favor of any general system which shall promise those advantages. The instability of our laws increases my wishes for firm and steady government; . . ." But he was not in favor of any government that would not equally preserve the rights of all the people.

The critical situation at that time, he conceded, demanded that a federal government of some sort be established. "We have suffered the present [government] to languish; and whether the federation was capable or not originally of answering any valuable purposes, it is now of little importance. But what was needed was not a change in the principles but only in the forms of government."[11] Besides, many of the evils attributed to the defects of the federal system were the result of a long war. "Our people are like a man just recovering from a severe fit of sickness." The war disturbed commerce and brought in floods of paper money and threw many valuable men out of steady business. But the American people have done more in the past three or four years in repairing the injuries of war and restoring industry than any people have ever done in a like time. He admitted that some of the evils which they were enduring "ought to be imputed to the defective administration of the government," but he was sure "that the evils we sustain, merely on account of the defects of the confederation, are but as a feather" as compared with those from a loss of liberty.[12]

Continuing the discussion, he argued as follows: The Philadelphia Convention was called solely to amend the old constitution, not destroy it. Probably not one man in ten thousand originally had any idea that the old ship was to be destroyed and the people were to be given the alternative of embarking on a new ship or sinking. It was universally supposed that the work of the Convention would have to be accepted or revised by Congress and then ratified by all the state legislatures. The powers granted the federal government under the Constitution are so great that some of them must either be neglected or enforced by military authority. "Neglected laws must first lead to anarchy and confusion; and a military execution of laws is only a shorter way to the same point—despotic government."[13]

Lee's attitude toward the new Constitution was not that of wholesale condemnation. He saw in it some good features, notably the elective principle on which it was based. He also thought that such powers as regulating commerce, coining money, managing the postal system, and conducting foreign affairs properly belonged to the federal government.[14] He approved the provision for a bicameral legislature and the one allowing Congress to prohibit the importation of slaves after 1808, though the latter did not go far enough. It is proper that federal laws should be superior to state enactments, but they should yield to fundamental and inalienable rights, and since they are made by a few men, they should extend to only a few national objects.[15]

175

Lee gave little space to the approved features of the Constitution, devoting nearly all of both booklets to its defects. The Constitution should be modified by amendment, he argued, so as to give the general government such powers as experience and present circumstances direct, "with a reasonable regard to time to come." If in the future it should, "contrary to our expectations," seem advisable to extend these powers, "we can do it far more easily, than get back those we may now imprudently give." The proposed system is untried and its advocates admit that it is in a degree an experiment. Surely then the safe policy is to be cautious in investing it with power.[16]

He pointed out the inadequacy of the federal bill of rights and argued at great length to show that the smallness of the House of Representatives was a serious menace to democracy and good government. Not only would a small body be more amenable to bribery and corruption; it would become an agency for advancing the privileges of the upper classes at the cost of sacrificing the rights of the masses. If there is only one Representative for every thirty to forty thousand inhabitants, very few if any of the common people will be elected as Representatives. Those chosen, therefore, will, in the main, be aristocrats, demagogues, or upper yeomen. Only if the number of seats were increased could the common people have Representatives from their own class.[17]

The adverse criticism of the provisions regarding the Senate were not so elaborate as those for the House. He considered the Senate too small for a legislative branch but too large for an administrative body. The smallness of the Senate exposed the members to the temptation of bribery. Equal state representation in the Senate was unfair, and the provision for cooperation between the executive and the Senate was an aristocratic element. The Senate probably would uphold the rights of the states more than the House and would be more stable in character. But unless some changes are made regarding this upper house it would in a very few years become the source of the greatest evils. To avoid these future dangers, he proposed the following changes, some of them advisable and some absolutely necessary:

A. The term of each Senator should be limited to three or four years. "Men six years in office absolutely contract callous habits, and cease, in too great a degree, to feel their dependance. . . ."

B. The practice of the recall as used in the old Congress should apply in the new, especially in the Senate.

C. There should be rotation in office so far as the legislative branch is concerned. "Even good men in office, in time, imperceptibly lose sight of the people and gradually fall into measures prejudicial to them."

He was not perfectly satisfied with the provision giving the Senate a share in treaty-making. And yet he knew of no better means of checking the power of the President in this respect. So, on the whole, he seemed to accept this as a proper provision. The plan did not present a well-balanced government. The Executive and the Senate were substantially united and this union was unfavorable to democracy in government. The provision against changing that part of the Constitution which provided for equal representation in the Senate was unwise, for the reason that we cannot bind our descendants. The attempt to bind the majority usually results in a breach of contract.[18]

He objected to giving Congress power to levy taxes, duties, imports, and excises. Congress should not have the power to raise internal taxes except by requisition on the states. If, however, a state should neglect to meet its quota, then Congress should have the right to collect the amount with interest. This would mean that the states would collect these internal taxes and not be bothered with Federal tax collectors. He pointed out that to allow the Federal government to impose internal taxes on the states would be inconsistent with the stand that the colonies had taken against the Stamp Act. "I admit," he said, "that it is not probable that any prudent congress will attempt to lay and collect internal taxes, especially direct taxes," but this power is lodged in Congress and could be abused by imprudent and designing men.

He considered some of the provisions regarding the Federal judiciary good, and some "very extraordinary." He approved the provision for life tenure for judges but objected to the one which permitted an increase but prohibited a decrease in the salaries of judges during their lifetime. Fluctuation in prices, due to war and other causes, he observed, might call for increases in salary at some times and decreases at others. This change in the value of money made it desirable that the salary scale be flexible in

177

both directions. Another defect was the exclusion of trial by jury in the Supreme Court and the absence of a provision for trial by jury in civil cases in the other Federal courts. The jurisdiction of the Federal courts should not extend to an action by a citizen or a foreigner against a state, an action in which a foreign subject is a party, or an action between citizens of different states, unless in each case it is of considerable importance.[19]

The President should not be allowed to continue in office indefinitely. He would make a better official and could retire with more grace and dignity if there were a constitutional limitation on the length of his service. Such a restriction would eliminate or greatly lessen the danger of the President's usurping power and becoming a dictator. He "ought to remain in office so long as to avoid instability in the execution of the laws; on the other hand, not so long as to enable him to take any measures to establish himself." One term of seven years, which the Philadelphia Convention first agreed upon, was better than the plan provided for. Furthermore, the President should not have the power to veto legislation acting singly. He should act with the judges in vetoing acts of Congress. The President should not make all appointments to Federal offices. Minor positions should be filled, some by the courts and others by heads of executive departments. In making his appointments the President should in some cases act alone; and in others he should have the advice of a council of state, but not the assent of the Senate.[20]

The power to make uniform bankruptcy laws should not, in his opinion, have been given to the Union. Owing to the size of the country and the diversity of ideas, he felt that the Union would never be able to establish such laws. The provision for a federal district was objectionable. If a federal town is necessary for the residence of the government, it ought not to be so large as ten miles square. Such a federal city, he predicted, would be a dazzling social center, the mistress of fashions, and the fountain of politics. "It will be prone to corruption and slavery." A smaller city would be "pure and chaste, frugal and republican."[21]

The general government was given too much authority in military affairs. The militia of any state should not remain in the service of the Union beyond a given period, "without the express consent of the state legislature." No land forces should be kept up and no appropriations for land forces be made except for one year at a time, and such acts might be required to pass by special majorities. Congress should be limited in raising troops to a given number, say 2,000 in peace time and 12,000 in time of war.[22] Lee also felt that the Constitution should have listed the powers reserved to the states along with those given to the general government. "When we particularly enumerate the powers given, we ought either carefully to enumerate the powers reserved, or be totally silent about them. . . ." The just principle "that all powers not given are reserved, is in effect destroyed by this very constitution."

His final appraisal of the Constitution is summed up in the following statement: "I conceive the position to be undeniable, that the federal government will be principally in the hands of the natural aristocracy, and the state governments principally in the hands of the democracy, the representatives of the body of the people." Congress will be an agency for oppressing the people, and the voters will have no way of helping themselves. The Constitution provides for no adequate checks by the states on the measures of Congress. It is evident, he continued, "that a very great majority of the People of the United States think it, in many parts, an unnecessary and unadvisable departure from true republican and federal principles.[23]

Lee's pamphlets were published about the same time as were the articles written by James Madison, Alexander Hamilton, and John Jay that were afterwards collected under the title of *The Federalist*. These articles, appearing in New York newspapers under the name of Publius, gave able arguments in favor of the ratification of the Constitution. Lee apparently was not trying to answer these arguments, but one statement made in the *Letters* would indicate that he did not consider the essays of Publius as presenting formidable opposition to his views. In one of the *Letters* (under date of January 14, 1788) he refers to "the lengthy writer in New York" saying that he has attentively examined his pieces and comes up with the following appraisal of them: The writer "appears to be a candid goodhearted man, to have a good stile, and some plausible ideas." His arguments seem to move constantly on a smooth surface, but the parts of his work, "like the parts of a cob-house, are all equally strong and equally weak"; his articles appeared to have but little relation to the great question, whether the Constitution is fitted to the condition and character of the people.[24]

Lee objected to the term "Antifederalist" as the name for those who opposed the Constitution or contended for amendments. They should, he maintained, be called Republicans and those who advocated the adoption of the Constitution without amendments should be known as anti-Republicans. But the champions of a strong general government had already appropriated the term "Federalist" and were able to hold on to it, although it was in a sense a misnomer.[25]

Lee did not carry on his fight against unconditional ratification to the last ditch. To do this he would have had to go as a delegate to the Virginia ratifying convention which met in Richmond June 2, 1788. In all probability he could have been elected to a seat as a representative of Westmoreland County, but he was not a candidate. In a letter to General John Lamb (June 27, 1788) he declared that repeated experience had shown that he could not have good health in Richmond.[26] It is difficult to understand why the climate at the falls of the James River was so much worse than that at Chantilly, near the broad Potomac, that a sojourn at Richmond for less than a month would have endangered his health. It is possible that he foresaw a victory for ratification and that he did not wish to make a strenuous fight for a lost cause.

If Lee had been guided solely by personal feeling, he would have had more reason for supporting than for opposing the Constitution. One of the leaders in the fight for ratification was Henry Lee ("Light-Horse Harry"), his second cousin and nephew-in-law. Also his brother, Francis Lightfoot, on whose judgment the family placed much reliance (according to Washington), was decidedly in favor of ratification.[27] On the other hand, prominent among the opponents of ratification were Benjamin Harrison, Lee's chronic enemy, and Meriwether Smith, whom he held in very low esteem. Indeed, Washington in a letter to James Madison a few months later (January 10, 1788) reported Lee as being unhappy with the company that his position had forced him to keep.[28]

George Mason was to be in the Virginia convention and it was a serious disappointment to him that he would not have the support of Lee in his fight against the ratification of the Constitution by Virginia. Furthermore, as Mason stated to Arthur Lee, Richard Henry would be regarded as having deserted a cause which he had declared to be of the greatest importance. Some of Richard Henry's friends, continued Mason, had circulated the report that he had given up all idea of opposing the Constitution because his friends were for it and that he had recommended two violent Constitutionalists as representatives of Westmoreland County in the Virginia Convention. Mason was afraid that these reports would injure Lee's reputation and prevent his election to a second federal constitutional convention, if one should be called.[29]

However sincere may have been Lee's motives, by betting on the wrong horse he lost some of his prestige. The adherents of lost causes are seldom left in favorable positions. Human nature is too much inclined to the belief that "whatever is, is right." The later acceptance of the first ten Amendments was some consolation, for these amendments were in line with his proposals, but they did not go as far as he had suggested.[30]

It may seem a little surprising that leaders like Patrick Henry and Richard Henry Lee, who stood out in front in opposition to British policy, lagged in their support of the movement to establish an effective general government. When the Stamp Act was passed Lee said that the colonials were threatened with Egyptian slavery. He must have felt, therefore, that he and Patrick Henry had played an important part in leading their people out of Egyptian bondage. But their leadership (to continue the borrowed figure) died in the wilderness and they had no part in the conquest of the Promised Land. The boldness of youth had been supplanted by the timidity of late middle age. They magnified in their thinking the possible dangers of the new regime, fearing that the cherished rights gained by the Revolution would be sacrificed by the despotism of a consolidated government. And yet the position of Lee and Henry in opposing the Constitution was not inconsistent with that held by them as Revolutionary leaders. It is true that these former radicals were now conservatives, but they had not undergone any considerable change in their political views. From the beginning they had fought for rights which they maintained were secured to the colonials by the English constitution. In hurling their philippics against George III and the British Parliament they were using radical measures, but their professed aims were conservative. They were then radical conservatives; now they were con-

181

servative radicals, or rather their conservatism was radicalism grown old. They still were sitting in the car of progress, but were trying to handle it in a different way. Formerly their main interest had been in the power of the engine; now their chief concern was with the strength of the brakes.

While Lee, now in his fifties, showed no sign of senility, he had reached the age when new ideas do not win easy rootage in the mind. He had not changed so much as he had failed to recognize the change that had been brought about by new conditions.

Chapter XIV

Wearing the Toga

Supporting the effort to amend the proposed Constitution, Richard Henry Lee became a candidate for the United States Senate. In announcing his purpose to a friend, he assured him "that nothing but the reverence I have for the liberties of my country and a thorough conviction of the danger these will be exposed to by the unamended state of the new constitution, could have induced me to consent again to become a public man. . . ."[1] Other aspirants for the honor were James Madison and William Grayson.

When the Virginia legislature met in the fall of 1788, the Antifederalists were in the majority and they followed the lead of Patrick Henry. The situation was thus unfavorable to Madison. Henry was not only smarting under the defeat that he had received in the state convention at the hands of Madison, but he was hoping and working for a second federal convention that would change the Constitution. This plan could not be furthered by the election of Madison to the Senate. He was also afraid to trust Madison with the amendments that the Virginia convention had proposed.[2]

Henry could easily have won the Senatorial toga for himself, but he declined the honor and assumed the role of king-maker, supporting Lee and Grayson as the first Senators from the Old Dominion. One of Madison's friends, who was a member of the Virginia Assembly, reported Henry's attack on Madison as follows: "Mr. Henry on the floor exclaimed against your [Madison's] political character, and pronounced you unworthy of the confidence of the people in the station of senator. That your election would terminate in producing rivulets of blood throughout the land." When the election came up in the Virginia Assembly, Henry succeeded in having Lee and Grayson chosen. The ballot was Lee, 98; Grayson, 86; and Madison, 77.[3]

Washington was disappointed by this action, for he felt that the new government should be organized by those who had supported the Constitution. He favored Madison's election not only because he was a Federalist but because his brilliant leadership would be needed in Congress. Washington, however, was not greatly discouraged by the election of Lee and Grayson, for he later learned that they would support the new government and would only insist upon such changes as were, in their opinion, necessary to remedy its defects.[4] Madison was elected to the House of Representatives.[5]

On March 4, 1789, the day set for the first meeting of Congress, only eight Senators were present, and it was not until April 6, when Richard Henry Lee took his seat, that a quorum was formed. An organization was effected and John Langdon, of New Hampshire, was elected President *pro tempore*. The Senate then, in cooperation with House members, proceeded to count the votes for President and Vice President; and a Senate committee of which Lee was a member promptly notified Washington and John Adams of their election. Adams at once assumed his duties as Vice President.[6]

On his arrival at New York Lee wrote a cordial letter to Washington stating that he had stopped at Mount Vernon on his way to New York and expressing his satisfaction at Washington's election to the Presidency.[7] One of his first duties was that of taking part in the inauguration. Before these ceremonies could be properly carried out it had to be decided how the President should be addressed. This question gave rise to considerable discussion in each house of Congress. John Adams contended that such an important official should be honored with an impressive title. Lee, temporarily forsaking his democratic principles, agreed. Madison was opposed to the idea; he felt that the use of titles was not in keeping with the nature of our government or the genius of the people, and would diminish, rather than increase, general respect for the government. Furthermore, there was a widespread feeling that no title could add anything to the dignity of Washington; for, as Senator William Maclay said, "it was impossible to add to the respect already entertained for him." Washington seems also to have been embarrassed by the proposal, for he thought that the use of an exalted title would arouse public resentment.[8]

This proposal was referred to a committee of the Senate of which Lee was chairman and to a committee of the House of which Madison was a member. Finally, after due consideration by the two committees meeting jointly and by a conference committee, it was decided to address the chief executive as *"The President of the United States,* without addition of title."[9]

Today it is easy to consider this controversy a tempest in a teapot, but the leaders and voters at the time, or at least some of them, did not view it so lightly. Lee's part in the dispute seems to have caused him a considerable loss of popularity among his constituents. Dr. David Stewart wrote to Washington (July 14) that the proposal was thought to have originated with Lee and Adams. They were, therefore, very unpopular in Virginia—"highly odious"—and neither of them would, as he thought, "ever get a vote from this State again."[10]

Having agreed upon the title to be used in its communication with President Washington, Congress proceeded to arrange for the formalities of inauguration. A committee of three, with Lee as first-named, had been appointed by the Senate to cooperate with a like committee of the House to conduct the inauguration ceremonies in New York's City Hall. On April 30 the joint committee, led by its chairman, introduced the President of the United States to the Senate chamber where he was received by the Vice President. After Washington had delivered his address, each house of Congress, in keeping with the tradition of the British Parliament, replied to the President's speech.[11]

One of the first responsibilities of the new Congress was to provide the federal government with revenue. To meet this urgent need, the House of Representatives, early in the session (May 16) passed a bill levying import duties on certain articles. The measure was taken up promptly by the Senate and a number of amendments were passed. Some of these changes were unacceptable to the House, and a conference committee was appointed, of which Lee was a member. The bill as finally formed by the conference committee was accepted by both houses.[12]

The Senate met behind closed doors until 1794, and the brief report of its proceedings in its *Journal* and the *Annals of Congress* does not cover the speeches made by members. For our limited knowledge of the discussions of the first years, we are largely indebted to William Maclay, a Senator from Pennsylvania, who kept a journal covering the first Congress, but who allowed personal feeling to color his statements. He was especially hostile to Lee, to whom he twice referred as the Ishmael of the Senate. "If I really wished," he said, "to destroy the new Constitution, . . . I would follow exactly the line of conduct which he has pursued." Before he had come in contact with Senator Pierce Butler, of South Carolina, Maclay considered Lee as the worst of men; but after he had encountered the opposition of Senator Butler, he gave the palm of wickedness to the South Carolinian.[13]

Lee objected strongly to the protective duties and any discrimination in rates on articles brought in by ships of foreign powers with whom we might have commercial treaties. Maclay said that Lee spoke an hour and a quarter against the duty on twine. Since Virginia imported her nets from Britain, he contended this impost would be unfair to her people. He also opposed the provision imposing a duty on loaf sugar and according to Maclay spoke against it as follows:

> He said the loaf-sugar of America was bad. It was lime and other vile compositions. He had broken a spoon in trying to dissolve and separate it, and so he must, he said, go on breaking his spoons and three millions of people must be taxed to support half a dozen people in Philadelphia. He pronounced this sentence, especially the part about the spoon, with so tremulous an accent and so forlorn an aspect as would have excited even Stoics to laughter.

His strong opposition to certain import duties, however, did not prevent Lee from offering a motion doubling the rate on salt and delivering a "lengthy harangue" in favor of this increase in duty.[14]

On June 12, Lee, as chairman of the committee for organizing the federal judiciary, reported a bill for establishing federal courts. After considerable debate, a bill was passed on July 17, 1789. The meagre report of the Senate *Journal* leaves us in the dark as to what was the original recommendation of Lee's committee and what revisions were made from the floor. In its final form the bill must have been radically different from the committee report, for when it was passed by a vote of 14 yeas to 6 nays both Lee and Grayson voted in the negative.[15]

Lee's main purpose in going to the Senate, so he declared, was to add amendments to the Constitution; but it was Madison in the House, rather than Lee and Grayson in the Senate, who carried the ball in the amendment contest. Lee, however, voted for all amendments that were adopted by both houses of Congress, and contended for the acceptance of all the other proposals made by the Virginia convention. The lower house, under the vigorous leadership of Madison, seized the initiative in this move to revise the Constitution; the Senate did little more than accept, modify, or reject proposals sent up to it by the House.

Madison took the first step toward the adoption of amendments when on June 8, 1789, he moved that the House go into committee of the whole to consider some amendments that he would propose, following suggestions offered by a number of the ratifying state conventions and especially the forty proposals of the Virginia convention. On August 24, 1789, the House by a two thirds vote agreed to seventeen amendments to be submitted to the State legislatures for ratifications.[16] These proposals encountered considerable opposition in the Senate, which suggested twenty-six changes. The House accepted only ten of these revisions. A conference committee which took up the task of ironing out the differences, reduced the number of articles to twelve. These twelve proposals were approved by the Senate on September 25, 1789.[17]

Madison insisted upon such provisions of the amendment regarding religion as would guarantee not only religious freedom but also the separation of church and state. The wording of the amendment as accepted by the House was very satisfactory to him, and his biographer, Irving Brant, thinks that it was written by him. It declared: "Congress shall make no law establishing religion, or to prevent the free exercise thereof, or to infringe the rights of conscience." The Senate considered this proposal and sent it back to the House "with its vitals cut out." As modified by the Senate, it said that Congress could "make no law establishing articles of faith or a mode of worship or prohibiting the free exercise of religion." Under this provision the federal government could give financial support to churches and church schools. Brant places the blame for this emasculation of Madison's proposal on Lee and the New England Senators. Church and state were still united in the New England states (except in Rhode Island) and the Senators from this section were opposed to a complete separation. Lee, in supporting the Virginia assessment plan in 1784, had showed that he was against an absolute divorce between religion and government.[18]

187

The final draft was prepared by a conference committee of which Madison was chairman. As finally expressed, the amendment declared that "Congress shall make no law respecting an establishment of religion, or prohibiting the free exercise thereof." The provision as thus stated applied only to the federal government and imposed no restrictions on the States as to legislation on religion. Madison had succeeded in getting the conference committee to insert a clause imposing the same restriction on the States, but the Senate rejected this change.[19]

Lee had favored the calling of another federal convention to add amendments to the Constitution, but early in the session (May, 1789) he had come to see that there was no immediate prospect of having another convention since two thirds of the state legislatures had refused to apply for one. The only way open, therefore, for improving the Constitution was by amendment.

He welcomed the twelve amendments proposed by Congress but they did not go as far as he desired. In his opinion, "some valuable rights are indeed declared [in them], but the power to violate them to all intents and purposes remains unchanged." "I am grieved to see too many look at the rights of the people as a miser examines a security, to find a flaw in it."[20] When Lee and Grayson sent a copy of the twelve amendments to the Speaker of the Virginia House of Delegates, they accompanied it with a statement expressing disappointment at their inadequacy: "It is impossible for us not to see the necessary tendency to consolidated empire in the natural operation of the Constitution, if no further amended than now proposed." They had done, they declared, all they could to have Congress adopt all the amendments proposed by the Virginia convention.[21]

In a letter to his brother Francis Lightfoot (September 13, 1789) Richard Henry expressed great dissatisfaction with the proposed amendments. They had passed the Senate, he said, "after having been much mutilated and enfeebled . . . it is very clear, I think, that a government very different from a free one will take place e'er many years [have] passed." The federal government, he thought, would be under the control of the North—the section from New Hampshire to Pennsylvania. "The love of liberty has fled from hence to France." Despite his disappointment, Richard Henry hoped that all the proposed amendments would be ratified; they were a start in the right direction and other desired amendments might follow.[22]

In his attitude toward the amendments, Lee showed that his old fear of standing armies was unabated. On September 4, 1789, the Senate had under consideration a proposed amendment sent up by the House of Representatives. A motion was made to add to this proposal a provision against standing armies in times of peace, "as far as the circumstances and protection of the community will admit; that in all cases the military should be under strict subordination to and governed by, the civil power"; and that no regular troops should be raised in times of peace without the consent of two thirds of the members present in each house. This motion was defeated but Lee and Grayson voted for it.[23]

On one occasion in this first session (September, 1789) Lee took issue with Vice President Adams on the question of whether the President had the right to displace federal officers without the consent of the Senate. The vote in the Senate was a tie. The Vice President, casting the deciding vote, decided that the President had this authority. Lee contended that the Constitution did not confer this power on the President. Furthermore, he did not believe that the Vice President should have a decisive vote in a Senatorial tie.[24]

The most important committees to which Lee belonged during his first session were the committee on titles for the President and Vice President, the conference committee on the impost bill, and the committee on the organization of the federal judiciary. His achievements as a member of these committees were not outstanding.[25]

When the second session convened early in January, 1790, neither Lee nor his new Virginia colleague, John Walker, was present.[26] Lee's name does not appear in the Senate records until more than three months later.[27] This delay was due to illness and the "inclemency of the season." Shortly after resuming his seat in the Senate he came down with a severe case of the influenza which was epidemic at that time. He was confined to his room almost wholly for two weeks with an attack so violent that, as he said, he was nearly dispatched "to that Country from whose Bourne no Traveller returns." The influenza left him in a weakened condition and with a cold that "sticks faster than a blister."

He was thus in attendance for less than half the session. This illness took a heavy toll of his strength and vitality, and he was no longer buoyed up by the enthusiasm of former days. He now seemed to be bored with his legislative duties. In writing to William Lee he reported with apparent relief that this "tedious Session" was to end in August.[28]

An important question carried over from the first session was that of the permanent location of the federal capital. In agreement with the other Congressmen from Virginia, Lee was in favor of a more southerly location for the capital than New York. This city seemed especially objectionable to him and apparently he wanted the seat of government removed from it as soon as possible. He voted (September 25, 1789) for a motion to strike out the provision for continuing the seat of government in New York until the necessary buildings could be erected elsewhere.[29]

By the beginning of the second session there was no hope for either New York or Philadelphia as the permanent seat of the federal government, but both were anxious to be selected as the temporary capital. Virginia and the other southern states wanted the seat of government located permanently on the Potomac River. The northern states were contending for a more northerly location. The Virginia delegates in both houses favored Philadelphia as the temporary capital, hoping that this stand would win the support of the Pennsylvania delegation for the Potomac as the permanent site. Furthermore, they objected to New York as the temporary capital owing to the high cost of living in that city.[30] The Senate finally voted in favor of locating the temporary capital at Philadelphia, and the permanent seat of government "on the river Potomac" in December, 1800, at such a site as Washington should select. Lee and Walker, of course, voted yes on this motion, which was passed by the narrow margin of 14 yeas to 12 nays.[31] Shortly afterwards the House accepted the bill as it had passed the Senate.

The question of the location of the capital was not decided solely on its own merits but became entangled with the financial policy of Alexander Hamilton, Secretary of the Treasury. It was not until after Hamilton and Madison had entered into a log-rolling agreement that a final decision was reached. Hamilton's financial measures included the funding of the domestic and foreign debts of the United States, the assumption by the general government of the state debts, and the creation of a national bank. There was no serious objection to his proposal for funding the domestic and foreign debts, but the assumption of state debts by the federal government encountered strong opposition in both houses of Congress. Madison led the Virginia delegation in the House against it. The Virginians objected to assumption for two main reasons: Virginia had paid off a considerable portion of her debt and assumption would mean that she would have to pay part of it twice. Furthermore, assumption would increase the importance of the federal government and lessen that of the states. The proposal for assumption was defeated in the House by a vote of 31 to 29, with all the Virginia Representatives except one voting against it.[32]

The bill providing for the payment of the domestic and foreign debts of the United States passed the House of Representatives and was received by the Senate on June 2, 1790. The House bill was referred by the Senate to a committee of five of which Lee was chairman. The committee made its report a few days later, but its recommendations were modified by amendments before final action was taken. Lee favored the funding of the bonded indebtedness incurred under the old Congress but opposed the amendment, offered and passed, which provided for the inclusion of the assumption provision in the bill.[33] After this amendment was added and other changes were made, the bill passed the Senate (July 21, 1790) by a vote of 14 yeas and 12 nays, with both Lee and Walker voting nay. The House accepted the Senate amendment and then passed the assumption bill (July 23).[34] This reverse action was the result of a trade by which Hamilton promised to use his influence in favor of the Potomac site for the permanent capital and Madison agreed to soft-pedal his opposition to assumption. Furthermore, the total amount of state indebtedness to be assumed by the federal government would be reduced from the original figure of 25 to 21½ million dollars.[35] In keeping with the agreement two Representatives from Virginia and two from Maryland who had opposed assumption now voted for it, and it was accepted by the House.[36] There is no hint in Lee's letters that he ever heard that they had taken this road to a solution of the problem, although he did refer in one of his letters to a reversal of the four votes on assumption.[37]

191

In the third session of the first Congress Lee was more than two months late in arriving at Philadelphia, the temporary capital. This long delay again was due to illness.[38] Virginia, however, was represented by her recently elected Senator, James Monroe. Early in this session (December, 1790) the House of Representatives received from Hamilton a plan for a national bank, and in less than two months both houses had agreed upon a measure providing for the establishment of the First Bank of the United States.[39] Since Lee did not take his seat until after the Senate had passed the bill, he had no part in its enactment. But he did express opposition to it before leaving Chantilly for Philadelphia. In answer to an inquiry from Monroe, Lee took this stand: "It does not appear to me that the public have any business to become Bankers, because Banks are capable of great abuses, and because such abuse practised by Government leave injured Individuals too much without redress." In support of his position, he referred to an argument against government-owned banks by Adam Smith, giving a specific citation to *The Wealth of Nations.*[40]

Despite his tardy arrival, Lee was in time to take part in the aftermath bank legislation. In February, 1791, a supplementary bank bill was under consideration in the Senate. To this bill an amendment was offered which provided that nothing in the act "shall restrain the Legislature [Congress] from repealing the same, and abolishing the corporation thereby established, at any time after the fourth day of March, One thousand eight hundred and two." The amendment was defeated, but both Lee and Monroe voted for it.[41]

The first session of the second Congress was held in Philadelphia from October 24, 1791, to May 8, 1792.[42] Lee had planned to be present by the time the real work of Congress should begin. He wrote a month ahead of time to his nephew, Thomas Lee Shippen, to engage for him a decent lodging "as convenient to the State house as possible," that his gouty feet might "sustain no injury from the wintry weather." He also instructed young Shippen to "hire" stabling room for his two horses. He hoped to be in Philadelphia about November 10. By that time, he thought, the "important negotiation of compliments" in Congress will be over and "forms will have subsided into business."[43]

Lee was not able to carry out this plan. An injury received when his carriage overturned delayed his arrival in Philadelphia until December 20, 1791, nearly two months after the beginning of the session. During this session he did not take a leading part in legislative activity. His name is listed on a few special committees, none of which was of marked importance.[44] Nor was he chairman of any of these. His most noted act was his motion, previously mentioned,[45] for the Senate to open its doors when engaged in legislative action. Lee also took a prominent part in the adoption of a plan for apportioning membership in the House of Representatives.

This matter was embodied in the first amendment to the Constitution proposed by Congress, but it was not ratified by three-fourths of the state legislatures and so did not become a part of the Constitution. Congress, therefore, still had the responsibility of offering a plan of apportionment. In November, 1791, the House passed a bill providing for a new apportionment of Representatives, to go into effect in March, 1793. This bill was amended by the Senate, and the two houses could not come to an agreement, so the bill died in deadlock.[46]

In February, 1792, the House passed a bill providing for a temporary apportionment of the membership of the House based on the first census, and a permanent apportionment, March 3, 1797, based on a second enumeration to be taken in five years. The basis of representation was to be one Representative for each thirty thousand inhabitants. In the Senate, the House bill was amended so as to provide that after March 3, 1793, the House of Representatives should consist of 120 members, with a specific number allocated to each state. The amended bill was passed by the Senate on March 12 by a vote of 14 to 13.[47]

Lee and Monroe voted against the Senate bill as finally passed. In a letter to "Light-Horse Harry" Lee, Richard Henry said that it would give six eastern states one more Representative each than they would have under a fair apportionment plan based on 30,000 population to one representative. At first the House would not accept the Senate amendments and a conference committee was appointed to adjust the differences. The Senate, however, would not recede from its position and finally the House accepted its amendments (March 23, 1792) and thus agreed to the final passage of the bill.[48]

After much deliberation, Washington, acting on the advice of Edmund Randolph, Jefferson and Madison and against that of Hamilton and Jay, decided to veto the bill. In explanation of his

193

veto Washington pointed out that the bill violated two provisions of the Constitution, namely "that Representatives shall be apportioned among the several States according to their respective numbers. . . . The Constitution has also provided that the number of Representatives shall not exceed one for every thirty thousand, and the bill has allotted to eight of the States more than one for every thirty thousand."[49]

This was the first Presidential veto. The Northern members of Congress were displeased with this action of the President, but most of the Southern leaders expressed satisfaction. The House reconsidered the bill but failed to pass it over the President's veto. The House then passed another apportionment bill (April 10), which provided for one Representative for every 33,000 population based on the census that had already been made. The Senate accepted this act by a unanimous vote, and the President signed it on April 14, 1792.[50]

On February 3, 1792, the Senate received a bill from the House making provision for the protection of the frontiers of the United States. One clause in the bill provided for the raising "for a term not exceeding three years" three additional regiments of infantry. The Senate at first voted to expunge this clause but later rescinded this action. Lee and Monroe voted for the resolution to expunge and against the one to restore the provision. The Senate passed the House bill after having added some amendments (February 23, 1792). Both Lee and Monroe voted against the final passage of the bill.[51]

On April 18, 1792, Lee was elected President *pro tempore* of the Senate. Since the Vice President was absent, he presided over the Senate until it adjourned on May 8, 1792.[52] This was Lee's last public service. Before the beginning of the next session of Congress, he had been forced by ill health to retire from public life.

On October 8, 1792, he sent a letter to the Speaker of the Virginia House of Delegates resigning his seat in the Senate. In his letter of resignation he made the following statement: "The strong sense that I entertain of public duty," he said, "joined to a deep feeling of gratitude for the reiterated goodness of the General Assembly to me, would render the toils of public business a pleasure, altho I am grown gray in the service of my Country; were I not prevented by infirmities that can only be relieved by a quiet retirement."[53]

The two houses of the Virginia Assembly joined in a unanimous vote of sympathy with him in his infirmities, "which have deprived their country of his valuable services" and a wish that he might in retirement, "With uninterrupted happiness, close the evening of a life, in which he hath so conspicuously shone forth as a statesman and patriot." Appreciating his many exertions to promote the public interests, *they are particularly thankful for his conduct as a member of the Legislature of the United States.*[54]

As a Senator, Lee did not add to the prestige earned by his previous career; in fact, his Senatorial record as compared with that made as a Revolutionary leader was anticlimactic.

Chapter XV

Park-Bench Statesmanship

In his correspondence Lee expressed views on numerous public affairs in which he was less directly involved. His opinions often were valuable because they were based on wide reading and experience.

Before Lee left Congress in May, 1779, that body had turned its attention to the peace terms which it would ask of Great Britain, and had reached agreement as to the boundaries which the American peace commissioners would demand. Two important questions still under discussion were the navigation of the Mississippi and the use by the Americans of the fisheries in the Newfoundland waters.

The contest over the fisheries began early in February, 1779, and continued until the middle of August. The Northern Representatives, especially those from New England, demanded that the Americans be allowed the use of these fisheries. Most of the Southern Representatives were unwilling to risk a prolongation of the war on this issue which occasioned one of the longest and hottest parliamentary battles ever fought in the Continental Congress. In July, 1779, Congress adopted a resolution stating that if, after the peace treaty, Great Britain should interfere with the rights of American citizens to engage in the fisheries, Congress would regard it as a violation of the peace, and would uphold the rights of the injured parties by force.[1] France, however, was not willing for the right to the Newfoundland fisheries to be insisted upon as an ultimatum. Gérard notified Congress that his government would not support a prolongation of the war for this purpose. Accordingly, in the instructions (August 14, 1779) for the guidance of the American plenipotentiary in his negotiation of peace terms, he was directed to regard the guarantee of the fishery rights as of great importance but not as an ultimatum.[2]

Lee had left Congress before it had adopted its resolution regarding the Newfoundland fisheries, but in his letters he insisted for some time both on the right of Americans to share in these fisheries and to navigate the Mississippi River. In writing to Henry Laurens and Samuel Adams in the summer of 1779 he said that an acknowledgment of these rights was necessary for a safe and honorable peace. They are, he said, momentous rights, and "Nature and reason have given us both." "These, Sir, are the strong legs on which N. America can alone walk securely in independence."[3] Later (October, 1779, May, 1780) in writing to John Adams, American peace commissioner in France, he expressed the hope that Adams would be able to secure both of these demands and added that without the right to navigate the Mississippi, the vast back country would be so distressed by a lack of outlet to market as to lay the foundation for future wars.[4]

On July 9, 1779, the New York *Evening Post* published an article under the *nom de plume* of Cato, which advocated the acceptance of a treaty without a provision giving Americans the fishery rights, declaring that they would exercise these rights without a clause in the treaty covering them.[5] In a long letter (July 30, 1779) to an unknown addressee, Lee vigorously attacked this position. The fisheries, he contended, were our only nursery of seamen and without them we could not build up an efficient navy. "These Fisheries," he continued, "were first discovered by our Ancestors: they are contiguous to our Coasts; they have been uniformly enjoyed by our Ancestors and ourselves; they are indispensable to our existence, as a people who would carry on an independent Commerce." In a letter to Henry Laurens shortly afterwards he said: ". . . but I will never call the loss of the fisheries and the navigation of [the] Mississippi equitable—And I am sure posterity will execrate those that do."

Lee's advocacy of the fisheries right was one reason for the esteem in which he was held by New Englanders. General William Whipple, writing to him from Portsmouth, New Hampshire (April, 1783), congratulated him on the outcome of the war and declared that the country was indebted mainly to him for the fisheries clause in the treaty. In appreciation of this service, Whipple was sending him a quintal of fish.[6]

Lee later abandoned his fight for the free navigation of the Mississippi River. By July, 1787, he had come to the conclusion that his people could not for many years to come, if ever, gain this right without war with Spain and most likely with France.

He advised against continued agitation for the opening of the Mississippi as it might cause the exchange of the friendship for the enmity of a powerful monarchy and probably the loss of valuable commercial rights. He now thought that the United States could not force the free navigation of the Mississippi for twenty-five years, and it would be unwise to risk the loss of valuable objects for an unattainable aim.[7]

By the terms of the peace treaty Great Britain agreed to give up all her western posts. She retained these posts, however, for some time after the treaty was signed. One excuse the British gave for this violation of the treaty of 1783 was that Virginia had not repealed the act against the recovery of British debts. Lee regretted that Virginia had laid herself liable to this charge and urged action to provide for the payment of these debts.[8]

In letters that Lee wrote after the peace his old bitterness toward England had to a considerable extent given way to a reasonable, charitable attitude. He referred to British encroachment upon our territory in the region of the St. Croix River, restrictions on our trade with the West Indies, and the retention of British forts in the West. Much of this mischief he felt, was due to a misunderstanding of us, fomented by Tory refugees in Britain. He considered that both sides were to blame for the failure of the British to live up to the terms of the treaty. The Americans, instead of showing a spirit of magnanimity toward the British, had assumed an attitude of superiority. Our people had also treated with violence the friends of the British and had held up the payment of British debts. Both sides must act with wisdom and good temper. He hoped that his country would cease to give the smallest cause of offense.

This mild tone, more of sorrow than of anger, was a far cry from his oratory of the middle seventies, which had been ablaze with enmity toward the British government. It ought to be added, however, that he advocated the carrying of a big stick along with soft speaking, for he wanted his country to be prepared for war. Whenever Great Britain, he said, "shall find us just, temperate and prepared, she will be extremely cautious of hostile aggressions, or of unjust treatment of us." In his advocacy of preparedness he quoted with approval the inscription upon the arsenal of Berne, Switzerland: "That people happy are, who, during peace, prepare the necessary stores for war."[9]

Lee's desire for friendly relations with Great Britain did not cause him to approve her policy toward the United States. He complained (October, 1785) that she still held the western posts, still encroached upon the American eastern boundary, and continued commercial restrictions that were detrimental to both countries. Her commercial policy, he said, would have the effect of diverting American trade away from England to other countries. He agreed with John Adams in hoping to see American factories established in the East. As a means of forcing Britain to sign a commercial treaty, he suggested that the United States give preference to American ships and those of countries with which it had commercial treaties.[10]

Lee had great confidence in the ability of John Adams, who had been appointed minister to Great Britain, to restore friendly relations between the two countries. Writing to him (May 28, 1785), Lee expressed hope that the wisdom of Adams and the good sense of the British administration would "extinguish the mischievous discord" that had existed between Britain and the United States and which had been fomented by the enemies of both countries to the injury of both."[11] It was this attitude that gave Lee's enemies the opportunity to accuse him of being pro-British in sentiment.[12]

Writing to Lafayette (June 11, 1785) on the subject of international commerce, he expressed the opinion that the European nations, since they supplied the United States largely with manufactures, were acting unwisely and against their own interests by hampering American trade with them. "For if these restrictions cause our people to sell less of their products they will be less able to buy European manufactures." Furthermore, it would tend to cause them to set up industries at home which would still further lessen their purchases in Europe.[13]

In another letter to Lafayette (October, 1785), Lee spoke of the excellent troops of the King of Prussia but showed his disapproval of the use that was made of them: "A philosophic mind is apt, however, to regret that such fine exertions of human art should so often be employed for the destruction of the human species." He also advocated a sort of league of nations. He posed this query to Lafayette: "Among the many leagues that are formed, why may not one be formed for the purpose of protecting the rights of humanity?"[14]

Like other American statesmen, Lee kept a watchful eye on the political and social upheaval in France. His ideas of freedom were in agreement with the political philosophy behind the French Revolution, and on one occasion, when in a pessimistic mood over the actions of Congress, he said that liberty had left the United States and taken up her abode in France. But when the French revolutionary movement reached the stage of blood-letting and mob violence, he turned against it. When he heard that the Jacobins had confiscated British and Dutch trading vessels in French ports, he expressed the hope that if this report was correct the British lion would "claw these fellows handsomely for their misdoing."

He expressed disapproval of the execution of Louis XVI, "this glorious monarch," in the following strong terms: "His death with the lights I have was cruel, unnecessary and highly impolitic. . . . I had a deep rooted affection for this good King because he so effectually aided us in the day of our distress, and I will say with Queen Elizabeth—'God may forgive his murderers, but I never can.'" He also had a high opinion of Louis as a ruler. The reign of this monarch, he felt, had been eminent in promoting the good of mankind.[15]

When Great Britain was drawn into war with France, Lee's sympathies were with the mother country though he strongly urged neutrality on the part of the United States. The contest in France, he said, had been less for liberty "than for Jacobinism or Anarchy, to favor the views of ambition and avarice; as well might it be said that supporting O. Cromwell was defending the cause of liberty, when he had destroyed it by erecting a despotism in his own country."[16] On January 5, 1794, while afflicted with the illness that a few months later brought on his death, he sent a letter, nearly twelve printed pages in length, to his son-in-law, Richard Bland Lee, a member of the House of Representatives. Despite his weak physical condition, Lee wrote most of this letter himself, using an amanuensis for the rest. The discussion is a strong argument for American neutrality toward the European conflict.

He thought that the new republic was in no position to engage in a war with "many puissant Nations without money Men, Ships or Munitions of war—at a time when the debts of [the] last war are not yet sufficiently provided for—when we are borrowing from Peter to pay Paul." In such a ruinous war everything might be lost and nothing could be gained. Such a war would "inevitably put our existence, as a free people, to the most eminent hazard." To avoid being drawn into conflict we should observe and enforce a strict neutrality, and this should extend to our commercial policy. He deprecated the ill feeling that still existed in the United States toward Great Britain and Spain. During the war, he said, Great Britain did not have a more determined foe than himself; but after peace was made he had done all he could to show his disapproval of a hostile mind. He was hopeful that the wisdom and firmness of "our good President" and the patriotism and good sense "of a very good Majority of the good people of this Union" would keep us out of war. He strongly opposed the movements of Genêt, whose actions went beyond his authority as French minister to the United States. Lee referred to Genêt as "the harsh and premature executor of harsh and unwarrantable orders," and thought that the United States should take a firm position against him. "If something effective is not done in that business," he said, "farewell to the respectability and dignity of our government."[17]

Shortly afterwards (February 12, 1794) in a letter to Thomas Lee Shippen he said: "I too love Liberty, but it is a regulated Liberty, so that the ends and principles of society may not be disturbed by the fury of a Mob or by the art, cunning, and industry of wicked, vicious and avaricious Men." The then rulers of France, he thought, did not care "a groat for Liberty any further than as a great noise about it may conduce to their acquisition of wealth & power. It is impossible that so sacred a thing as liberty can ever be necessarily supported by assassination, murder, deceit, plunder and every species of wickedness that the mind of Man has hitherto been supposed capable of possessing." "I heartily wish the French," he continued, "as much Liberty as they can bare but I do not believe that the present rulers design it for them therefore I hope that in Gods good time they will all be hanged."[18]

Lee's attitude toward the relation of church and state appears somewhat anomalous. He thought that neither tithes nor ecclesiastical courts would do in America, and at one time he showed a liberal attitude toward Quaker pacifism.[19] Yet he later took a stand that was inconsistent with absolute religious freedom.

In 1784 Patrick Henry introduced in the Virginia House of Delegates a resolution for levying a tax for the support of the Christian religion or some Christian church. After the resolution was adopted in committee of the whole (November 11), a bill was drafted in keeping with the resolution. Madison opposed the measure, but Henry, John Marshall, George Washington, and other prominent Virginia leaders favored it. Though not a member of the House, Lee wrote to Madison from Trenton (November 26, 1784) stating that he considered the bill necessary and not a violation of the Virginia Bill of Rights.[20] Later (December 23), after Henry had left the House to assume the governorship, a motion was passed to postpone final action until the next session. In the meantime, a broadside against the measure, written by Madison, was sent out for signatures. The thousands of signatures attached to the remonstrance showed that public sentiment was overwhelmingly against the bill. So when the Assembly met again in the autumn of 1785 no effort was made to revive it.[21]

Lee's support of Henry's bill was based on the contention that it is the function of the state to promote morality; and since religion is the basis of morality, government should encourage religion by providing for its financial support. In support of his position he argued as follows:

> Refiners may weave reason into as fine a webb as they please, but the experience of all times shows religion to be the guardian of morals; and he must be a very inattentive observer in our country, who does not see that avarice is accomplishing the destruction of religion, for want of legal obligation to contribute something to its support.[22]

As a park-bench statesman, Lee also advocated the appointment of a bishop for the Episcopal Church in America, reversing a position which he had strongly held in the earlier years of his career.[23] The Episcopalians had held a national convention at Philadelphia in October, 1785. Lee was pleased that the convention had concluded its session "with great concord," and that the Council was "not disturbed by the mischievous high church principles." This convention had sent an address to the archbishops and bishops of England proposing a plan for the consecration of American bishops. Lee supported this proposal. In a letter (October 24, 1785) to John Adams, then American minister to Britain, he asked Adams to explain to the British court that such action on the part of British archbishops and bishops would not be considered by the Americans as an interference in their affairs. Instead of giving offense, it would come as a friendly assistance to the Christian cause in America.[24] In his reply to Lee's letter Adams stated that the Archbishop of Canterbury was liberally disposed to comply with the request of the Convention. In relaying this report to officials of the Convention, Lee expressed satisfaction with this position of the Archbishop and the hope that this beginning would end "in the right organization of our church, the want of which hath hitherto greatly injured it." For this service the General Convention of the Episcopal Church gave him a vote of thanks.[25]

Lee showed an interest in popular education in a letter (October 13, 1779) to Thomas Jefferson, in which he approved Jefferson's proposed educational schemes and expressed the hope that the Virginia Assembly would "not neglect that noble and best foundation for public liberty, general diffusion of knowledge. . . ." In writing shortly afterwards (December 27, 1779) to an unknown correspondent he spoke of Jefferson's plan as follows:

> . . . our Assembly have digested a System (for the establishment of public Schools and thereby diffusing Knowledge) for the wisest and best [plan] that I believe was ever before devised. Jefferson is the Father of it. When once this System has taken place and produced its natural effects, the internal and external independence of Virginia will rest on the surest Basis. Universal depravity may destroy it but folly cannot.[26]

He was more interested in private than in public schools. The former, he thought, were in a better position than the latter for impressing the minds of the young "with a love of religion and virtue."[27] He gave two acres of land to a classical school, which had been started in Fauquier County by Hezekiah Balch, a Princeton graduate. A large and costly building was erected on the lot and the school was incorporated (November 28, 1788) as

203

Warren Academy.[28] Along with his donation to Warren Academy went this statement of his views on the importance of public education:

> It is certainly true that a *popular government* cannot flourish without *virtue* in the people, and it is as true that *knowledge* is a principle source of virtue. These facts render the establishment of schools for the instruction of youth a fundamental concern in all free communities. I wish that it had been made a primary duty of the legislature, by our constitution, as it has been wisely done by some of the states in this union. Such establishments will be the surest means of perpetuating our free forms of government, for, when men are taught to know, and well to understand, the greatest inherent rights of human nature, they will care not to suffer the hands of vice, of violence, or of ignorance, to rob them of such inestimable blessings.[29]

Lee was a trustee of Fredericksburg Academy and contributed to its financial support. At one time, he seems to have been dilatory in performing his duties as a trustee, for James Mercer, chairman of the board of visitors, advised that Richard Henry and "Light-Horse Harry" Lee resign from the board if their duties forbade their attendance at its meetings.[30]

Lee's correspondence often reflected his views on political principles rather than on specific timely matters. For example, he expressed the conviction that a democratic system to be successful must rest upon an enlightened people. The press, he said, is "the quickest and surest means of conveying intelligence to the human mind." Hence the importance of the freedom of the press.[31]

His writings indicate a great fear of the abuse of power on the part of rulers. "I think Sir," he said in one of his letters, "that the first maxim of a man who loves liberty should be never to grant to Rulers an atom of power that is not most clearly and indispensably necessary for the safety and well being of Society. . . . The fact is that power poisons the mind of its possessor and aids him to remove the shackles that restrain itself."

His apprehensions regarding the abuse of government seem to have been based on his belief in the depravity of human nature. On one occasion when referring to his objections to the Constitution, he said: "If all men were wise and good there would be no necessity for government or law—but the folly and the vice of human nature renders government and laws necessary for the Many, and restraints indispensable to prevent oppression from those who are entrusted with the administration of one and the dispensation of the other."[32]

A lifetime association with men in public life gave Lee a rather pessimistic view of politics and politicians. "I think that generally speaking," he wrote in 1791, "the former may be called the Science of fraud—and the latter the Professors of that Science." He agreed with the aphorism that "truth is the most Unbending and uncompliable, the most necessary, firm, immutable, and adamantine thing in the world." But to be effective it must be made known to the public. He considered human weakness as a partial antidote for human wickedness. "It is happy for mankind," he said, "that depraved hearts are commonly joined with weak heads." One of his sayings was: "Who fails in doing right, fails nobly, because Virtue is its own and very great reward." But he was a realist and agreed with Patrick Henry that "right without power to protect it, is of little avail."[33]

Chapter *XVI*

Lee and His Colleagues

In his long and active participation in the public affairs of Virginia and the union, it was inevitable that Lee should incur some ill will. This antagonism was in certain cases of a personal character and very bitter. There was a breach between Lee and other Virginia patricians which went back to his career in the House of Burgesses. Benjamin Harrison and Carter Braxton were among the leaders whose chronic hatred he incurred by his stand in the Robinson affair. Braxton especially seemed to nurse a grievance in later years.[1] Apparently Lee was not seriously disturbed by the unfriendly attitude of these two fellow Virginians. If he was he seems to have turned the other cheek, for in the sources examined no expression of ill will toward Harrison has been found and only a mild criticism of Braxton has been noted.[2]

James Lovell thought that Edmund Pendleton also had become unfriendly to Lee because of the latter's fight against John Robinson. No evidence to corroborate, but much to contradict, this statement has been found in Lee's private letters and public utterances. In the *Lee Papers* (Alderman Library) there are twenty-two letters from Pendleton to Lee. A number of these were written in the first half of 1777 while Pendleton was recovering from an accident that had temporarily crippled him. The correspondence shows a deep interest on the part of Pendleton in Lee's letters and a warm friendship for him. Preceding all, or nearly all, the signatures is the word "affectionate." John Mays, biographer of Pendleton, stated that he could not recall a single fact or event indicating that Lee and Pendleton were ever on unfriendly terms.[3]

In the list of enemies for whom Lee had bitter feelings Silas Deane held the leading place. Next came those who supported Deane in his quarrel with Arthur Lee. High among the latter stood Gérard, the French minister to the United States.[4] Lee also had a very low estimate of his Virginia "compatriot," Meriwether Smith, whom he regarded as an assistant villain in the Deane drama. In a letter to Henry Laurens (August 1, 1775) Lee spoke of his fellow Virginian in the following terms: "I think with infinite contempt and a good degree of detestation of my Compatriot M.S. [Meriwether Smith]. If he produces papers that can in any manner affect my character, I affirm they are forgeries, and thus I have done with him." In referring to him in one of his letters, he used for him the names "Fiddle" and "Dogberry."[5]

Since Benjamin Franklin was on the side of Deane in his controversy with Arthur Lee, Richard Henry naturally had a low opinion of him and felt that he should be recalled from France. It was even charged by one of his contemporaries that Lee was suspicious of Franklin before the beginning of the Deane controversy. William Bradford in a letter to James Madison (June 2, 1775) stated that Lee was said to have suspected Franklin of being a British spy, since he had not reported information picked up in England and was behaving "more like a spectator than a member."[6] At first he thought that the fame of Dr. Franklin was such that it would be unsafe to remove him; but later he changed his opinion and advised his recall. "I foresee," he said in a letter to Henry Laurens (August 13, 1779), "abuse without end and injury extreme from his continuance." His vices are "no longer restrained by checks from the cautions of his head." A year later he spoke of "the conscious guilt of that old man and the wicked enmity he has practiced." His dislike of the philosopher continued to increase until he finally came to believe that the salvation of America depended upon Franklin's recall.[7]

An occasion for specific complaint against Franklin was afforded by the latter's participation in the trial of a captain of an American ship of war for having disobeyed the orders of the captain of a French privateer. Lee considered this trial an insult to the dignity of the sovereign American state and severely blamed Franklin for the part he played in this affair. He wrote to Samuel Adams (September 10, 1780):

> How long, my dear friend, must the dignity, honor and interest of these United States be sacrificed to the bad passions of that old man under the idea of his being a philosopher? That philosophy which does not rectify the heart is not the kind of wisdom which it

befits republicanism to cherish and to confide in. If this man must be retained in the public service with all his imperfections on his head, let him be sent to some Court, causa honoris, where he can do neither good nor harm, such as the court of the Czarina of Russia.[8]

The ill will generated by the Deane controversy, however, was not all on one side. Some of the Deane party were as violent in their attacks on the Lees as were the latter in their assaults on the Deanites. Some of Richard Henry's enemies were so bitter against him that they were sorry that their military hero, "Light Horse Harry," had to bear the name of Lee. This enmity, Richard Henry said, was due to a "contemptible envy" and the inflexible adherence of the Lee family to the cause of independence.[9]

But during Lee's long service in Congress he gained the admiration and affection of a number of the outstanding leaders in the Revolutionary cause, among them James Lovell, James Searle, Henry Laurens, Dr. James Warren, and Nathan Dane. Lovell's support of Arthur in his contest with Deane endeared him to the Lee brothers.[10] Richard Henry's friends among the military leaders included Generals Horatio Gates, Charles Lee, Thomas Mifflin, William Whipple, James Warren, George Weedon, Lafayette, Washington, and Nathanael Greene.[11]

Lee had both respect and real affection for Lafayette.[12] He first met the French general in the summer of 1777, after having received a letter of introduction to him from William Carmichael, secretary of the commissioners to France. In a letter to his brother William (October 19, 1778) he spoke warmly of Lafayette and asked William to introduce Richard Henry's son, Ludwell, to the Marquis and to charge him to respect Lafayette "as the much esteemed friend of his father."[13]

Although Lafayette at one time apparently thought that Lee had intrigued against Washington, his letters of later years expressed friendship for Lee. In one of these letters, written March 16, 1785, he spoke of his "regard and affection" for Lee and referred to him as "my good friend":

> . . . but the personal tribute of my regard and affection, I can only trust to persons, whose sentiments, my good friend, have been long engraved in my heart. To you I owe my first obligation—and to be obliged to you, has

208

been long to me a more pleasing idea. Highly sensible
of your friendship, and its value, I am happy in every
opportunity to remind you of me. . . . Remember me
most affectionately to all your family and Ludwell in
particular.[14]

Lee and George Mason were usually in agreement on important political issues and were on intimate terms in their
personal relations.[15] Another close friend was Landon Carter of
Sabine Hall. Lee's visits there, he said, always gave him pleasure.
He seemed greatly to enjoy having a pipe with his friend in his
palatial residence.[16] Lee also had friendly social relations with
Robert Carter of Nomini Hall.[17]

James Monroe, though not an intimate friend of Lee, maintained cordial social relations with him[18] and seems to have held
him in high esteem. In a letter to Lee (April 4, 1783) Monroe
expressed his regret at hearing that Lee was thinking of retiring
from the service of his country. He pointed out as friend and
citizen reasons for Lee's continuing in public life. He supported
his plea by the following statement:

In the faithful and able part you have acted upon the
late theatre, decisive and independent as you have
been, you have not failed to make enemies, but the
malignity of the people has not been able to effect the
minds of the public who have looked on with deliberation, and assured by events of the eminent integrity
and propriety of your conduct, have felt themselves
more grateful and warmly interested in your favour, in
proportion as these attacks have been more base and
ungenerous.[19]

There were a few incidents in Lee's and Jefferson's careers
which may have caused a temporary coolness in their relations,
but which apparently did not result in any permanent rift.[20] On
learning from Lafayette that Lee had been elected President of
Congress, Jefferson wrote from Paris (February 7, 1785) con-
gratulating him.[21] When Jefferson was Governor of Virginia Lee
wrote to him endorsing his policy, saying that it was actuated by
"sound whiggism" and philanthropy.[22] Lee also gave his endorsement to the public school system proposed by Jefferson for
Virginia.[23] A like friendly interest in Jefferson was also shown in
his later correspondence. He asked William Short (June, 1785)

to present "my best respects to my old friend, Mr. Jefferson;" and in writing to Monroe (January, 1791) he expressed the wish to be remembered to all his friends—"Particularly to Mr. Jefferson."[24]

It may be, however, that Jefferson did not place so high an estimate on Lee's ability and career. Certainly he did not accord as great a value to his achievements as did Lee's grandson, R. H. Lee, in his *Memoir,* a copy of which he sent to Jefferson. The latter, in a letter to John Adams (December 18, 1825), made this comment on the work:

> You and I know that he [Richard Henry Lee] merited much during the revolution. Eloquent, bold and ever watchful at his post, of which his biographer omits no proof. I am not certain whether the friends of George Mason, of Patrick Henry, yourself, and even of Genl. Washington may not reclaim some feathers of the plumage given him, noble as was his proper and original coat.[25]

The personal feeling that existed between Lee and Patrick Henry was of a changing and elusive quality. Irving Brant states that Henry was the perennial foe of the Lees. Jefferson also represented Henry as having a deep enmity toward the Lees (Arthur and Richard Henry).[26] There are a number of facts, however, that indicate the contrary. It is true that Lee opposed Henry when he was elected the first governor of Virginia. In the House of Delegates they were often on opposite sides of important questions, and on one occasion Henry was instrumental in defeating Lee for the Speakership of the House of Delegates.[27] But these disagreements on policy seem not to have caused any permanent estrangement between them. They stood side by side in their fight on some big issues. Patrick Henry's grandson, William Wirt Henry, says that Henry and Lee were first brought together when Henry supported the motion offered by Lee in the House of Burgesses for separating the Treasurership from the Speakership, and by 1767 they had become fast friends.[28] Lee spoke in favor of the radical resolutions offered by Henry in the Virginia Convention (March, 1775), and owed his election to the United States Senate to Henry's support.[29]

In one of his letters (February 14, 1785) Lee said: "No time or circumstance can ever force from my mind the sincere affections that I entertain for the original friends to the just rights of America. . . ." And it is plainly implied that he considered Henry as belonging to that group.[30] Henry is said to have told Richard Henry Lee's son: "Your father, sir, and myself always agreed upon the great principles of freedom. We differed on some questions of internal policy, but liberty alike we fondly loved."[31]

Richard Henry was also on friendly terms with Henry ("Light-Horse Harry") Lee, his second cousin and nephew-in-law. Young Lee had warned Richard Henry of the plot of his enemies to defeat him for re-election to Congress (May, 1777). Later Richard Henry returned this favor by making an effort to advance the political fortunes of "Light-Horse Harry." In a letter to Francis Lightfoot (July 14, 1787) he asked him to use his influence with the "old Squire," Richard Lee of Lee Hall, in getting him to resign from the House of Delegates "so that his Nephew ["Light-Horse Harry"] may get early into the house of Delegates." "I know," he continued, "that it is like persuading a Man to sign his own death warrant—but upon my word the state of public affairs renders this sacrifice of place and vanity necessary." The "old Squire," however, did not sign his death warrant; his nephew had to wait.[32]

The Lee family placed a high value on the friendship of Henry Laurens, of South Carolina. After Arthur Lee had made his report to Congress, Laurens resigned the presidency in protest of the action, or rather inaction, of Congress. His dissatisfaction with the policy of Congress was due largely to its failure to do justice to Arthur Lee. Richard Henry deeply appreciated Laurens' defense of Arthur, and his letters expressed both affection and respect for him.[33] Thomas Paine also splintered a lance in the cause of the Lees in the Deane controversy, and his advanced views as to independence were very acceptable to Richard Henry. Of the friends for whom Lee had the deepest affection, his brother-in-law, Dr. William Shippen, Jr., held a leading place.[34]

High in the list of Lee's personal and political friends stood Samuel and John Adams. It was at the first session of the Continental Congress that Richard Henry first met both of them. Since all three were strongly opposed to British policy, they at once became political allies as well as personal friends. A great aid to this friendship was the support that both Adamses gave to Arthur Lee in his quarrel with Silas Deane.

Communication between Richard Henry and Samuel Adams, however, had begun before their meeting in Philadelphia. Lee had written to Adams in February, 1773, introducing himself as Arthur's brother.[35] From that time until near the end of his life, Lee kept up an intermittent correspondence with Adams. Lee spoke of him as "a friend I much esteem," and was proud of the fact that Adams considered him an "Unchanging Friend." In a letter to him (April, 1785) Lee said: "There is nothing in this life that would give me more happiness than to see and converse with you in Boston."[36]

Richard Henry and John Adams not only worked together in Congress but were also brought together in pleasant social contacts.[37] This friendship continued without interruption until the end of Lee's career. Writing to brother Arthur in May, 1778, he said: "I have found ample cause to love and esteem Mr. [John] Adams in our joint labors for the public good." When Adams received the appointment as minister to the court of London, Lee (April 14, 1785) congratulated his "old and excellent friend" on the honor, but he also congratulated the country on having a minister of such wisdom, patriotism, and diligence.[38] Statements made by John Adams in his letters and autobiography show that he also held Lee in "great and sincere esteem."[39]

There were no political parties in the Continental Congress, in the present-day sense of the term. Members who were in general agreement on policy worked together, consulted each other at informal meetings, and planned joint action on important measures pending in the House. The Lees, the Adamses, and their friends seem to have been the center of such a group, which was designated by their contemporaries as the "Junto."

A contemporary view of this political club was expressed in a letter (June 24, 1779) sent from Philadelphia to the Baltimore *Advertiser* and signed "O Tempora! O Mores!" Reprinted in several other newspapers, it was probably written by Edward Langworthy of Georgia, a recent member of Congress, or by someone equally conversant with the proceedings of Congress. According to this article, the foundation of the "Junto" had been laid during the sitting of the First Congress, and it had functioned effectively during the entire first period of Lee's membership in the Second Continental Congress. The members met regularly as a caucus and debated upon and adjusted the manner of their proceedings. Although a small minority, they managed to keep some of their outstanding leaders continuously in the House and as members of important federal agencies. Since Congress was fluctuating in membership and the "Junto" was a continuous body, the latter exerted an influence beyond what would be expected from the size of its membership.[40]

Later, the *Connecticut Courant* published a reply to this article signed by "A Friend to Truth and Fair Play." The author said that the nameless writer of the above-mentioned letter might perhaps think that he had done God service, but he certainly had used the devil's means. He intimated that there was no proof of the existence of a Junto in Congress. It was hardly possible, he continued, since the membership of Congress was so changeable, that a nucleus could have continued in control for five years.[41] There are other contemporary references to the "Junto," especially by Lee's enemies,[42] and historians of our day also refer to it as if there was such a clique. It is true that Lee, the Adamses, and others generally agreed on the main issues discussed in Congress; and although adequate evidence has not been found in this study of the sources to warrant the assertion that they acted as an organized club and formulated policies in caucus meetings, they were in such marked agreement that they constituted virtually a unified party.[43]

The effective cooperation between the Lees and the Adamses was helpful in securing the adoption by Congress of measures that they advocated. On the other hand, it subjected Richard Henry and Francis Lightfoot to an unjust criticism. Owing to their close association with John and Samuel Adams, whose disagreement with Washington was branded as "disloyalty," the two Lees were naturally painted with the same brush.[44] Moreover, the desire to please these two friends may have influenced Richard Henry in one or two instances to support an unwise policy. It was doubtless due to his friendship for John Adams that Lee on one occasion voted in Congress in a way that was not in keeping with his normal attitude. When John Hancock retired from the presidency of Congress, a motion was passed expressing thanks for his efficient discharge of his duties as president. Richard Henry voted against the motion, although the other members of the Virginia delegation, including Francis Lightfoot, voted for it. Richard Henry gave as a reason for his negative vote that it was not proper for Congress to thank Hancock since such an honor had not been accorded Hancock's predecessors on their retirement; but it may have been that he was acting to please John Adams, who was not kindly disposed toward Hancock.[45]

Lee gave a very high rating to the political leaders from New England. At one time (November 29, 1778) he said that, in his opinion, the ship of state could best be steered by Eastern pilots. He even expressed a preference for New England as a place of residence over his own Southland. Writing to John Adams (October, 1779), he declared that he yet hoped to be able to spend the remainder of his days in the free republic of Massachusetts Bay. "The hasty unpersevering, aristocratic genius of the South," he said, "suits not my disposition, and is inconsistent with my ideas of what must constitute social happiness and security."[46] He once spoke of his fellow patricians in the South as "a dissipated aristocracy."[47]

It is difficult to believe that one reared in Virginia would have such an attitude; but it may be explained in part by the fact that his teeth had been set on edge by the sour grapes that he had been forced to eat by the Virginia House of Delegates.[48]

One mooted question as to the relations of Lee with his colleagues is that of his feeling for and attitude toward Washington. Some of his contemporaries accused him of hostility to and even intrigue against Washington. This accusation likely would have been ignored had not historians in later years attached such importance to it.

John C. Fitzpatrick, collector and editor of the Washington papers, maintained that it was hostility to Washington that prompted the New England-Virginia coalition to have General Gates put at the head of the Board of War and to arrange the Canadian expedition with Lafayette in command. The purpose was to ruin the French influence (how this was to be done was not stated) and separate Lafayette from Washington. The expedition, it was suggested, whether it failed or succeeded, would have inured to the advantage of the coalition.[49] In the documents examined in this study no sign of evidence has been found to support this accusation.[50]

One among the causes of the alleged breach between Lee and Washington was the part played by Lee in the "Conway Cabal" and in the controversy between Washington and General Charles Lee (no relation of the Virginia Lees). During the winter of 1777-78, after Gates' victory over Burgoyne, there was a persistent rumor regarding an alleged intrigue in the army and an effort in Congress to remove Washington and put Gates in supreme command. According to this report, the leaders of the army plot were Thomas Conway, an Irish-born French officer in the American service, Thomas Mifflin, Dr. Benjamin Rush, and General Gates.[51] The supposed leaders in Congress were James Lovell, the Adamses—John and Samuel—and the Lees—Francis Lightfoot and Richard Henry. The chief villain in the Congressional drama, it was charged, was Richard Henry. Even Lafayette at one time considered him and the Adamses responsible for the Congressional part of the cabal.[52]

Lee's old enemy, Benjamin Harrison, helped to spread this rumor. In a letter to Robert Morris (December 18, 1777), he said:

> We have a story circulating here that there has been a motion made in Congress to divide the command of the army and that R.H.L. was at the bottom of it.[53] It makes much noise, and if true, will effectually do his business, we are also informed that Genl. Washington's character had been attack'd publicly by S. & J. Adams, and that the Genl. has been so inform'd. Your being sent to Camp gives me some reason to fear that these reports may be true, and that my worthy Friend suspects such treatment.[54]

There is no doubt that this charge was brought to Washington's attention. In a letter to Washington (January 6, 1778), Dr. James Craig, at Port Tobacco, Maryland, wrote that he had been informed by a true friend of the former that a strong faction was forming against him in the new Board of War in Congress. All along his journey from Lancaster and Bethlehem, Pennsylvania, to Port Tobacco, he heard this rumor repeated. No one gave particulars but all seemed to believe it. It was said, he continued,

> that some of the Eastern and Southern Members were at the bottom of it, particularly one who has been said to be your enemy before, but denied it, R.H.L. [Richard Henry Lee]. . . . The Method they are taking is by holding up General G——s to the people and making

215

them believe that you have had three or four times the number of the Enemy, and have done nothing. That Philadelphia was given up by your Mismanagement and that you have missed many opportunities of defeating the Enemy, and many other things as ungenerous and unjust.[55]

Although the statements in these letters are based on hearsay, Conway made a statement in a letter to General Gates (June 7, 1778) which Fitzpatrick considered compromising evidence against Lee and Samuel Adams. In this letter Conway reported that he had been coldly received when he appeared before Congress except by Lee, Samuel Adams, and a few others, who were favorably affected to Gates. It is quite possible, however, that the cordiality of Lee and Adams toward Conway was inspired by pity for a defeated man who later repented of his mistake and wrote Washington to that effect.[56] Lafayette, whose respect and affection for Washington were beyond question, declared that Conway was a good officer, and he went so far as to ask (in a letter to Lee, June 8, 1778) that Congress grant Conway a certificate indicating its evaluation of his services. "My being," he said, "the warmest friend and the first admirer of our great general will not prevent me to speak in favour of a gentleman [Conway], whose conduct I was very far from approving [as to Washington] and other respects."[57]

Washington may have had the feeling that behind all this smoke there was some fire. This feeling could have been back of a reference to a rumor which he made in a letter to his brother Lund early in 1778. This letter has been lost but we have Lund's reply to it:

> . . . Colonel Mason (who I showed your letter of the 16th of January) tells me he was informed of the cabal against you, before he left Williamsburg and some had hinted to him that R. H. Lee was one suspected of having a hand in it, and as they knew the intimacy existing between them, begged that he would talk to Lee and discover whether anything of the sort was in agitation or not. He did so. Lee declared no such thing or even a hint has ever been mentioned in Congress, and that he should look upon it as one of the greatest misfortunes that could befall this continent, should you by any means whatever give up the command of the Army

for fully convinced he was in his own opinion no other man upon this continent was equal to the task; that he had often lamented the heavy burden you bare, and the difficulties you had to surmount more than any man ever had before.[58]

In his letters and in the Journal of Congress there is no hint of adverse criticism of Washington by Lee but numerous expressions and actions indicating satisfaction with his leadership.

Another charge that was brought against Richard Henry was that he took the side of General Charles Lee against Washington in the controversy between these two leaders brought on by the former's retreat at Monmouth.[59] Colonel Walter Stewart, a bitter enemy of Richard Henry, stated in a letter to General Greene (January, 1779) that Richard Henry had been industrious in the attempt to make the American people believe "that General Lee was the Salvation of our [the American] Army at Monmouth." (This alleged appraisal of General Lee's tactics at Monmouth, it should be added, seems to be in keeping with the verdict of recent scholarship.)[60]

It is undoubtedly true that Richard Henry and General Lee were on very friendly terms, nor did this friendship end with the general's disgrace. Sometime after his court-martial (apparently several years) General Lee put Richard Henry first in a list of the leading men who were his friends and advocates. In one of his letters to Richard Henry, General Charles spoke of him as one of the best members of Congress. General Lee's high regard for Richard Henry evoked a warm response. He felt that America was under lasting obligation to the General for the great service he had performed in her behalf. "His military talents are considerable," he said, "and his zeal in the American cause is equal to his martial accomplishments."[61] But Richard Henry's friendship for General Lee did not necessarily carry with it enmity to Washington.

Lee was also accused of hostility to Washington because he had such cordial relations with the Adamses. In the opinion of John Fitzpatrick, it was impossible for one to have been "a warm friend of John and Samuel Adams and George Washington at one and the same time, and Lee was certainly a warm friend of the Adamses."[62] That John and Samuel Adams and the three Lees (Richard Henry, Arthur, and Francis Lightfoot) cooperated as personal friends and political allies is well established.[63] This group was accused of being opposed to Washington's continued leadership of the military forces. But the charge that Lee used the influence of this connection to oppose Washington is not supported by reliable evidence. On the other hand, there is an impressive array of evidence against this accusation.

It is difficult to believe that the Adamses were bitter toward Washington when we remember that John Adams first suggested that Washington be appointed commander-in-chief of the American forces. In referring to the charge that he was an enemy of Washington, John Adams said in his autobiography that it was "utterly false and groundless."[64] And when we recall that Samuel Adams supported the resolution that made Washington a near-dictator in the crisis of 1777, his "hostility" certainly becomes suspect. In a letter to Richard Henry Lee (August 29, 1789) Samuel Adams denied that he had ever been concerned in an attempt to remove Washington from command. In this letter he said: "I have always had a very high Esteem for the late Commander in Chief of our Armies; and I now most sincerely believe that while President Washington continues in the chair he will be able to give all good Men a satisfactory reason for every instance of his public Conduct."[65]

Another alleged cause of ill feeling between Washington and Lee was the latter's opposition to the Constitution. One of Lee's contemporaries, Oliver Ellsworth, in his pamphlet, *Letters of a Landholder,* made the following statements:

> The factious spirit of R.H.L., his implaceable [sic] hatred to General Washington, his well-known intrigues against him in the late war, his attempts to displace him and give the command of the American army to General Lee, is so recent in your minds it is not necessary to repeat them. He is supposed to be the author of most of the scurrility poured out in the New York papers against the new Constitution.

In another one of the *Letters,* Ellsworth says:

> In Virginia the opposition wholly originated in two principles; the madness of Mason, and the enemity [sic] of the Lee faction to General Washington. Had the General not attended the convention nor given his

sentiments respecting the constitution, the Lee party would undoubtedly have supported it, and Col. Mason would have vented his rage to his own negroes and to the winds.[66]

Yet instead of opposing, Lee favored Washington's participation in the Constitutional Convention. When he learned that Washington and Mason had gone as delegates to the Constitutional Convention, Lee wrote to Mason stating that he was pleased to know that he and Washington would be representatives of Virginia in the Philadelphia Convention.[67]

This evidence points to the soundness of the conclusion reached by Dr. Bernhard Knollenberg, who says: "In the course of a long and painstaking search, I have found no evidence whatsoever that Lee was anything but loyal to Washington."[68] Furthermore, apparently no effort was ever made by anyone to have Washington superseded by Gates.[69] In this study no record of a motion to that effect has been found in the *Journals* of Congress or in the letters of the members who were in attendance during the period of the alleged conspiracy. This negative evidence is supported by statements made by members of Congress who would have known of any intrigue against Washington by their colleagues.[70] It seems, therefore, that the traditional story of the so-called Conway Cabal is in the main a classic myth.

Correspondence between Lee and Washington began in 1774 and continued off and on until Lee's death. Washington wrote the first letter (August 7) inviting Lee to stop at Mount Vernon on his way to the first Continental Congress and ride with him and Patrick Henry to Philadelphia. There seems, however, to have been a lull in their correspondence in the middle or late 1770's. In writing to Washington (June 12, 1781) Lee spoke of their correspondence as having been long interrupted. He hoped, however, "that our friendship never will [suffer] notwithstanding the arts of wicked men who have endeavored to create discord and dissension among the friends of America." The reason given for this interruption in his letter writing was that he had had little but his good wishes to send to him.[71]

Washington answered this letter on July 15, 1781. The delay, he said, was due to his preoccupation with urgent affairs. He had not supposed that Lee had changed the favorable sentiments for him which he had expressed, since he (Washington)

219

was unconscious of having given Lee just cause for such a change in sentiment; ". . . and," he continued, "as I never suffer reports, unsupported by proofs, to have weight in my mind I know no reason why our correspondence should cease, or become less frequent than heretofore" except that his affairs were becoming more complex and demanding so much attention that he did not have much leisure for writing. On August 26, 1781, Lee wrote another very cordial letter to Washington in which he made the following statement: "You may be assured Sir, that as I do not take up friendships upon trival grounds, . . . I never lay them down for slight causes. I have been happy to find that the principles which attached me to you have increased, not diminished."[72]

Another cause of the temporary interruption in their correspondence may have been the charges against Lee, possibly arousing in Washington a questioning of Lee's loyalty to him. One must remember too that Washington disapproved of Lee's opposition to the Constitution and thought that by this attitude he had injured his reputation in Philadelphia and Virginia. Washington also attributed George Mason's stand against the Constitution to Lee's influence.[73] Although this criticism of Lee by Washington indicated that he may have been irritated by Lee's position on the Constitution, there is no evidence to show that Lee harbored ill will toward Washington.[74] Furthermore, Washington's dissatisfaction with Lee's opposition to the Constitution could not have led to a permanent breach in their friendship, for later their personal relations were apparently quite cordial. When Washington was recovering from a severe attack of influenza (May, 1790), Lee was the first person except his physician and members of his family who was received by the President in his private chamber.[75]

This mutual friendship was not confined to personal relations but was also carried over into public affairs. While he was in the Continental Congress Lee served as a sort of representative of Washington, acting as a liaison agent between him and Congress. On several occasions Washington appealed to him to secure favorable congressional action on his military policies. Washington's commission as commander-in-chief of the American forces was framed by a committee of three of which Lee was first-named and John Adams a member. On December 26,

1776, Congress appointed a committee of three, with Lee as first-named, to take into consideration the state of the army. The report was made next day and a plan presented on which Washington would be given almost dictatorial powers. This part of the report was in Lee's handwriting and was doubtless written by him. On the following day a committee of three (Lee, James Wilson, and Samuel Adams, named in this order) was selected to prepare a circular letter to the states explaining the reasons for conferring such large powers on Washington and requesting them to cooperate with the commander-in-chief and give him all the aid in their power. The letter was drafted by Lee.

On the eve of the surrender of Burgoyne at Saratoga and just after the defeat of the Americans at Germantown, Congress voted unanimously (October 8, 1777) "That the thanks of Congress be given to General Washington, for his wise and well concerted attack upon the enemy's army near Germantown. . . ." This resolution seems (the record is not clear) to have been based on a recommendation made by a committee of which Lee was first-named.[76] Later, as a member of the United States Senate, Lee gave Washington whole-hearted support in his foreign policy, and showed a strong inclination to cooperate with the Administration in domestic affairs wherever his strong states' rights principles would permit.

The good will that existed between these two great men was too strong to be permanently disturbed by misunderstandings. The cordial letters that were exchanged during Lee's last illness show that this friendship was based on affection as well as respect. The last letter written by Lee that has come down to us was a long one to Washington. This was an appropriate end to an association of two patriots and co-workers in the cause of liberty.[77]

Chapter XVII

Personal Traits and Home Life

Widely read in the classics,[1] Lee used to advantage in his public career the information and breadth of view derived from these historical and literary sources. In his letters are many quotations from French and Latin works in the original.[2] For illustrations in his speeches and writings he drew on Greek and Roman mythology. He also showed a knowledge of the history and governmental practices of countries of both the modern and ancient world. He seems to have been well-versed in the history of Greece, Rome, and England, and in his letters there are references to the history of Macedonia, Germany, Carthage, Tyre, and Scythia. His knowledge of the two last-named countries was probably obtained from Herodotus.[3]

Lee deprecated, however, the tendency of his time to neglect the study of English for that of Latin.[4] He was fond of the English classics, especially Shakespeare. In one of his letters he used an argument from Adam Smith's *Wealth of Nations*, which suggests an acquaintance with this classic in economic theory.[5] Among his chief interests were works on legal principles and political theory. In pursuit of this interest he read Montesquieu, Blackstone, and Locke, along with other noted authorities on these subjects.[6] He was especially interested in Locke, who in his justification of the English revolution of 1688 had advocated some of the liberal doctrines later embodied in the Declaration of Independence. Richard Henry not only accepted this philosophy, but agreed with Locke's conservative attitude in favor of sound money and the financial integrity of the government. There are also in his letters and official papers references to and quotations from the Bible.[7]

He had a real interest in science and a deep appreciation of its importance despite the fact that his education in this direction had been very rudimentary. In an undated letter to L. H. Girardin, a scientist, he expressed his attitude toward science as follows: "I do not pretend to have gone farther toward the Temple of Science than to the threshold. The glance at the glories and beauties within has left an impression which irresistibly impels me to desire [your] friendship." He was deeply interested and widely read in medical treatises, probably urged on by the search for remedies for his frequent illnesses.[8]

Lee was largely indebted to his wide reading for the polished style of his oratory, in which field he was regarded by his contemporaries as ranking next to Patrick Henry. By them Henry was considered the Demosthenes and Lee the Cicero of Virginia, and there were some who preferred the polished style of Cicero to the rugged manner of Demosthenes.[9]

At the time the House of Burgesses was discussing the creation of a standing Committee of Correspondence, among those who heard Lee's speech was Judge St. George Tucker. Tucker was at that time in his twentieth year and was a student at the College of William and Mary. He was very favorably impressed with the personal appearance of "the harmonious Richard Henry Lee, whose acquiline nose and Roman profile" struck him "more forcibly than that of Mr. Henry, his rival in eloquence." In this oration, he said, Lee combined the fine polish of language with a harmonious voice and made an effective use of gestures. While under the spell of this eloquence at times he fancied that he "was listening to some being inspired with more than mortal powers of embellishment."[10]

Although some of Lee's speeches may have been the product of careful study, many of them were impromptu. Dr. Lyon G. Tyler, an authority on early American history, rated him as "the most finished orator of the first American Congress."[11]

He owed his success as a speaker to his easy command of English, his chaste language, his graceful manner, his clear and melodious voice, and his effective gestures. According to Judge Tucker, he would lean forward "a little with his *hat in his hand* on the back of the front seat." His maimed hand, kept neatly bandaged in black silk with the thumb protruding, was used in such a way as to make his gestures more impressive. "I think," continued Judge Tucker, "his eloquence approach'd more nearly to that of Cicero . . . than any other I ever heard."[12]

In later years, Patrick Henry and Lee displayed in the Virginia House of Delegates the eloquence which had won them such fame in the House of Burgesses, the Virginia conventions, and the Continental Congress. With two such noted speakers in the same branch of the Assembly, there was often a display of oratorical fireworks, and outsiders would often come to witness the performance. According to a report made by Judge Spencer Roane, who had served in the Virginia House of Delegates for two sessions with both Henry and Lee, they were (in the middle 1780's) the outstanding leaders in that body and at that time were usually opposed to each other. There were, he said, "many great men in the House, but, as orators, they cannot be named with Henry and Lee." Lee's language "was always chaste, and although somewhat too monotonous, his speeches were always pleasing; yet he did not ravish your senses, nor carry away your judgment by storm." "He was like a beautiful river, meandering through a flowery mead, but which never overflowed its banks. It was Henry who was the mountain torrent that swept away everything before it."[13] John Adams also eulogized his friend Richard Henry as a public speaker, saying "he had a fluency as easy and graceful as it was melodious, which his classical education enabled him to decorate with frequent allusion to the finest passages of antiquity."

One reason for the popularity of Lee's oratory was that he did not tire his hearers with long harangues. Dr. Benjamin Rush spoke of the brevity of his speeches as follows: "I never knew so great an orator whose speeches were so short. Indeed, I might almost say that he could not speak long. He had conceived his subject so clearly, and presented it so immediately to his hearers, that there appeared nothing more to be said about it."[14]

Lee's portraits indicate that he was not blessed with handsome facial features. He was tall and spare[15] and had a Roman profile, red hair, and a fair complexion.[16] The student of his career, however, gets the impression that he had exceptional charm. Reared as he was in a family of high social rank, Lee was from childhood schooled in the amenities of polite society. But his refinement went far beyond a surface polish. It sprang from an inner kindliness and affection that imparted to it an exceptional charm. This impression cannot be pinned down by specific references, but the reader imbibes it from the atmosphere that permeates his correspondence.

The general tone of his letters and the deep affection that his brothers and his friends had for him show that he was an exceptionally likable person. Writing to Richard Henry in 1766 (month and day not given), Arthur made this high appraisal of his beloved brother:

> Possessed, as you are, of a benevolence which every one feels of wisdom which every one admires, exalted very high in the opinion of men as a member of the legislation [*sic*] beloved as a relation, esteemed as a friend and admired as a man. . . .[17]

A considerable portion of this encomium should be credited to hero worship for an older brother; but after a due allowance has been made it still shows that Richard Henry enjoyed the warm affection and deep respect of this brilliant brother. A like respect and affection for him was also shown by his other brothers and doubtless by his sisters also, but our knowledge of his relations with his sisters is based more on inferential than on direct evidence. He must also have enjoyed exceptional popularity in his home county for he won in every one of his county election contests.

Being human, he, of course, had some corresponding faults stamped on the obverse side of his virtues. One of his bitter critics, William Maclay, his colleague in the Senate, spoke of him as being "certainly ambitious and vainglorious" but also as being one who sought gratification of his ambitions in serving the public.[18] Even Landon Carter pointed out one or two shortcomings. He said: "I confess R. H. Lee has a private failing or two, which I wish he could see. I am certain then that from his principles of Public Virtue he would leave them off. One is he is always open to flattery; and though he is really clever; in this he is eternally wounded by such sycophants. I know one always large in his Praise yet secretly his violent opposer". But even underneath the imperfections that are common to humanity there ran a strain of redemptive goodness. It was this quality that his son-in-law, Charles Lee, noted when, on leaving his sick bed after his last visit, he said: "When I left Chantilly, it was without hope of ever again seeing the best of men."[19] His character was briefly but correctly appraised by John Adams as follows: "He was a gentleman of fine talent, of amiable manners, and of great worth."[20] He had in his favor one infallible test of character—those who knew him best admired him most.

His tastes and social practices were like those of his associates, with a leaning toward a fondness for luxury. He wore expensive clothes, used snuff, smoked, and drank, preferring Havana "segars" and good wines. While acting as president of Congress he was glad to note that in New York the "champaign [sic], Claret, Madiera [sic] and Muscat" were good. He kept his cellar at Chantilly bountifully supplied with wines or liquors or both, such as apple brandy, French brandy, whiskey, sherry, claret, and Lisbon and Madeira wines. Especially partial to Madeira, he bought on one occasion (March, 1792) 108 gallons of this wine.[21]

The preference that Lee once expressed for New England over his own section and his advocacy in Congress on one occasion of measures that called for strict self-denial might lead to the impression that he was a Puritan living in Babylon. But it was the needs of the army and not a Puritan philosophy that caused him to advocate a policy of rigid economy. In his private affairs his actions were in keeping with the Cavalier rather than the Puritan tradition. Certainly he was not acting like a Puritan when he engaged in the practice of buying lottery tickets. In one of these gambling ventures he and his daughter each drew a prize of $500. He used the money to purchase more lottery tickets.

One trait in Lee's personality stands out conspicuously in his letters and public utterances—that of dignity. He never descended to trivialities. But unfortunately, this fine quality led him into a stiff formality in his correspondence even with his relatives and close friends. In writing to his brother Francis Lightfoot, he refers to the latter's wife as Mrs. Lee. Some of his letters to his nephew, Thomas Lee Shippen, have a slight human touch, but the others sound as if they were intended for publication. He seems, however, to have had a sense of humor, for he greatly enjoyed the facetiousness of the Rev. Isaac W. Giberne. There are also in his letters a few attempts at joking. He once called his wife "Mrs. Chantilly," and at another time referred to her as the ruler of his home, as he said, is the case with all men. But his sense of humor was kept under strict restraint by his dignity. It was so carefully guarded that there is not a single hearty laugh in all his known writings.[22]

Since the extant letters of Lee are concerned mainly with public affairs they do not give us a clear insight into his inner spiritual life. There are, however, occasional statements in which he uses the language of piety, such as: "I pray God to have you in His holy keeping," and "God bless you." In one of his letters he speaks of a friend who had recently died as being "far happier than those he has left upon this turbulent wicked stage." He also on one occasion thanked God for the recovery of his health and on another he thanked Him that his family and the one at Stratford had recovered from the measles. In writing to James Madison (November, 1784) he deprecated the fact that avarice was destroying religion.[23] Whether in these utterances he was merely repeating conventional platitudes or giving expression to deep feeling we are unable to say. It is evident, however, that he considered religion as an essential aid to right living.

According to Bishop Meade, who as a young man served as an assistant to Lee's former family tutor, the Rev. Alexander Balmaine, the latter often spoke in the highest terms of Lee as a Christian and patriot. We have a clearer idea as to his attitude toward the outer framework of religion. He was a member of the Nomini Anglican Church, of Cople Parish, and for a number of years served on its vestry.[24] He also held family worship services in his home on Sundays.[25]

One serious gap in our knowledge of Richard Henry Lee is our lack of information regarding his home life. The scanty documents that bear on this question give us only tantalizing hints about what went on at Chantilly and the part played by Lee's family in the social activities of the Westmoreland patriciate. Although Richard Henry was married twice and had nine children, there is not in all the documents studied, one letter to or from either of his wives.[26]

In the education of his children Lee followed the practice of the Virginia gentry of his day by having them first tutored at home. His daughters were also doubtless taught, along with their brothers, by the same tutor. One of his tutors, Alexander Balmaine, a young Scotchman, was sent over from London by Arthur Lee as being both a pious man and a friend of America. Later he became an Anglican minister and an active leader in the Revolutionary cause.[27] Apparently, the tutorial system afforded the daughters the only opportunity they had for a formal education. All four of the sons, however, were sent away for further schooling.

Lee's opposition to British policy did not cause him to lose faith in the English educational system; he sent his two oldest sons, Thomas and Ludwell, to England for instruction. The reason given by him for so doing was that the cost of their education would be less in England than in America unless they went to the College of William and Mary, and he could never think of sending them there because at William and Mary, so he thought, they paid too little attention both to the learning and the morals of the boys. There was in Virginia at that time (1772) a comparative lull in the contest with the mother country; and so the boys, in keeping with the family tradition, were sent to the homeland for their education.[28]

Thomas and Ludwell were fourteen and twelve, respectively, when they sailed for England, along with Mr. Balmaine, their tutor, in their Uncle William's ship, loaded with tobacco. They were, said their father, "good scholars" (meaning pupils) but had not yet learned arithmetic. They were placed in the school of St. Bees, at Warrington, in Lancashire County.[29]

Such high-spirited youths, sons of a leading rebel and outspoken advocate of the patriot cause, could not be happy, even if safe, in England while the war was going on. After the war had warmed up, Richard Henry was deeply concerned for their safety in England, "where," he said, "every consideration of virtue and justice is sacrificed to wicked resentment and views of Tyranny." So in writing to Arthur (February 17, 1777) he begged him to get his "poor boys" back home "in the quickest and safest manner." Instead of sending them back to America, Arthur had them come to him in France, where they remained for some time under the care first of Arthur and afterwards of William.[30] Later (June, 1777) in a letter to William, Richard Henry stated that it would be impossible for him to make remittances to cover the expense of their stay in Europe. The ports were so blocked by British cruisers that exports from Virginia were for the time being nearly at an end. If William could not make advances for them, the boys should be sent home.[31] Arthur and William, however, assumed the responsibility of financing them and they remained in France until July 8, 1780, when in company with Uncle Arthur they set sail for America.[32]

While they were still in England Richard Henry wrote his sons a joint letter (December 30, 1775) instructing them to study French, Greek, Latin, mathematics, writing and dancing. He also advised them to read once a day from some good English book, such as the *Spectator,* Locke on *Government,* Rollins' *Ancient History,* and Rapin-Thoyras' *History of England.* By the time his sons arrived in France, Richard Henry had formed plans for their careers. He wanted Ludwell to be instructed in military affairs while in France, or more especially in eloquence and natural law, so that he might turn either to war or the law. Thomas should be employed as a clerk or secretary to William or in some other profitable work while he was in France. In a second letter (June 14, 1776) Richard Henry gave further instructions as to the studies which he expected the boys to pursue.[33]

In his answer to these letters (October 5, 1777) Ludwell assured his father that he would try to carry out his instructions. His Uncle Arthur, he said, "is exceedingly good to me in every respect." He had Ludwell memorize speeches in both English and Latin and recite them to him for his correction. Arthur gave a very favorable report of Ludwell's progress. "He is as good," he said, "and improves as much as we can possibly wish. . . . In less than 3 quarters has learned fencing extremely well, dances decently, and has made great progress in the Mathematics and French."[34] William was also pleased with the conduct of the boys while they were under his care, though he felt that Thomas was inclined toward extravagance. In a report to their father he said: "These boys behave well and I hope will prove a comfort to you and protectors of their infant relatives."[35]

By the time his sons had returned home, Lee had changed his unfavorable attitude toward William and Mary. He even went so far as to send Ludwell to the college to study law under Professor George Wythe. Richard Henry explained this move not only as a consideration of Wythe's friendship for him and his son, but also because of the propriety of preferring the institutions of his own country to those of other states.[36] Ludwell had been at William and Mary for only a short time when he withdrew to enter the army on Lafayette's staff; he was present at the surrender of Cornwallis at Yorktown. He later (March, 1783) returned to William and Mary to resume his law studies under Wythe.[37]

Ludwell must have made a very favorable impression on Lafayette, for their association led to a warm mutual friendship. In writing to Richard Henry (June 13, 1779), Lafayette referred to his son in most endearing terms.[38] Ludwell also enjoyed the high esteem of Patrick Henry, who, in a letter to Richard Henry (January, 1790) spoke of Ludwell as follows: ". . . make my best regards to my friend, your son Ludwell, when you see him. I did not know of his abilities till of late, or I should have congratulated you sooner on having such a son."[39]

Cassius was sent to Princeton College and was there at the time of his death. George Washington Parke Custis, his roommate at Princeton, thought of him as being of "an amiable disposition and very well informed." He was "perfectly agreeable and very engaging" and was "a remarkable moral, modest and clever young man."[40]

Francis Lightfoot was sent to a boarding school at an early age, but it is not known where this school was located or how long he was in attendance. He was only about twelve years old at the time of his father's death, and he probably did not go to college.[41]

Ludwell and Thomas carried on the Lee tradition to the extent of serving for some years in public life. Ludwell was a member of the Virginia House of Delegates for three sessions (1787-88, 1789, 1790) and was in the State Senate continuously for eight years (1792-1800). He was also Speaker of the Senate for three sessions. He was a Federalist, and retired from politics after the Federalist Party was defeated in the National election of 1800.[42] Thomas was for four sessions also a member of the Virginia Senate.[43]

The sons and daughters of Richard Henry made connections by marriage with the Washingtons and other prominent Westmoreland families.[44]

Richard Henry was very fond of his nephew, Thomas Lee Shippen, son of Dr. William Shippen, Jr. Their relationship was more like that of father and son than that of uncle and nephew. Not only were they bound together by a strong tie of mutual affection, but they were also closely associated by business activities. Lee relied on young Shippen for the performance of numerous errands, such as making purchases for his family, finding living quarters in Philadelphia for his servant and himself, having his clothes tailored, and sending his horses and chair to him at his home in New York.[45]

Although Lee spent a great deal of time away from home in the performance of his public duties, he took a deep interest in his plantation affairs. Farming operations were carried on at Chantilly very much as they were at other plantations in the Northern Neck. Tobacco was the principal crop, but corn, wheat, cotton, peas, and barley were also raised in large amounts. A gardener supervised the cultivation of the flowers and table vegetables, such as Irish and sweet potatoes, cabbage, celery, and beans. As a rule, Lee seems to have sold his farm products or at least a good portion of them at Dumfries or in other Virginia markets, but on one occasion at least he shipped his tobacco to France. He may also have often sent the latter crop to European markets, since his brother William was interested in the foreign shipping business. It would seem that owing to the difficulty of harvesting and threshing wheat, the raising of this crop could not have been very profitable. References in Lee's *Account Book* to sickles and the absence of any reference to cradles indicate that the former was used in harvesting the grain. Threshing was also a slow and tedious process. At one time (July-August, 1784) it took eight days to thresh and clean 147 bushels of wheat.

The raising and caring for livestock was also an important part of the farm economy. In the *Account Book* there were listed on January 6, 1777, at Chantilly twenty-five head of beef cattle, eight work oxen, four milk cows, and eight calves. In the winter of 1788 nineteen hogs were killed. At one time (April, 1780) there were thirty-two old sheep and nine lambs on the plantation.

An overseer directed the work of the slaves and had general management of the farming operations. Lee had a considerable number of slaves, apparently more than he needed for work on the plantation, for from time to time he hired out one or more of them to neighboring planters. One year (1785) he leased nine of his Negroes to others.[46] In his *Account Book* a great deal of space is devoted to the listing of livestock and farm products with the prices received from the sale of them.[47]

The mansion at Chantilly was a "handsome and commodious wooden" structure on a circular eminence overlooking the Potomac which is nine miles wide at this point. Chantilly was not so pretentious in appearance as Stratford, but it was up to the standard generally demanded by the Virginia gentry. There was a large living room and other rooms well-suited for the comfort of members of the family and the numerous guests that came for long visits. Outbuildings gave additional aid in meeting the business and social needs of plantation life. An important room in the mansion was the one that housed the library, which contained a large collection of law books and works of general interest, many of which "were bound in rich and costly style." There were also numerous legal documents, state and county papers, and letters from officers in the Continental army and statesmen of the Revolution.[48]

The approach to the mansion was by a narrow, densely shaded road which wound through the surrounding forest. The mansion commanded a fine view of the nearby cleared land and the forest beyond. This forest, extending for miles up and down the river and inland, was a paradise for those like Lee who were fond of hunting, for in it abounded deer, wild turkeys, foxes, and other game animals and birds.

A partial insight into the activities at Chantilly is afforded by the journal of a young lady who in the fall of 1782 made a long visit to her relatives in northern Virginia. This interesting observer was Lucinda Lee (afterwards Mrs. Orr), a niece of Richard Henry. The Lee daughters were very cordial to her and with them she took walks, rode in the "Chariot," and went horseback riding. She enjoyed the walks and the "airing in the Chariot," but at least one of the horseback trips was unsatisfactory because she was on "a very hardgoing horse." She also noted the religious atmosphere of her uncle's home, for on Sunday the family were "collected in the Chamber, reading the Lessons of the day."

On one occasion she was greatly embarrassed when Corbin Washington, husband of cousin Hannah (Richard Henry's daughter), took advantage of his privilege as an in-law "kissin cousin." She describes this experience as follows: She and Molly were going to take a long walk (October 11) "but were prevented by the two horrid mortals, Mr. Pinkard and Mr. Washington who seized me and kissed me a dozen times in spite of all the resistance I could make. They really think, now they are married, they are privaliged [sic] to do anything."[49]

Another account of the home life of the Lee family is one that Thomas Lee Shippen gave in a letter to his father after his visit at Chantilly in September, 1790. He spoke in glowing terms of the family of his Uncle Richard Henry and their mode of living, but he left it to our imagination to fill in the details. Of the family he said, "They are everything I could wish." His account of his uncle's home at Chantilly was as follows:

> Chantilly . . . commands a much finer view than Stratford by reason of a large bay into which the Potomac forms itself opposite to Chantilly, and a charming little creek whose windings spread across and water the space which lies before Chantilly and the river. . . . At Chantilly, you have everything that is most excellent in fish, crabs, wild fowl, and exquisite meats, the best of liquors, and a most hearty welcome. The house is rather commodious than elegant. The sitting room which is very well ornamented is 30 feet by 18 and the dining room 24 feet by 20. My uncle has a charming little daughter whom you remember he mentioned to us—his little beauty. Her name is Sally and she is everything her friends could wish. The pleasures which so many agreeable circumstances necessarily afforded me at Chantilly were not a little interrupted by the extreme indisposition of the family—Excepting Sally there was not one of them perfectly well. You were very frequently mentioned and wished for. We never sat down to a fine rock fish soft crab or wild duck without my uncle R's wishing for you to partake of it.[50]

On social occasions dancing and other forms of amusement were enjoyed, and conversation was practiced as a fine art. The men would sharpen their wits by the moderate use of good wine or other liquors, and at times excessive drinking, though frowned upon, may have been indulged in.[51] The Lees were connected by kinship or marriage with a number of the most prominent families of Virginia, such as the Harrisons, the Ludwells, the Corbins, the Fitzhughs, and the Washingtons. Especially close were the family connections between the Lee and Washington families.[52]

In keeping with the custom of the time, Richard Henry and his family exchanged lengthy visits with their aristocratic friends and relatives. These included, in addition to the Washingtons, the families of Robert Carter of Nomini Hall, Landon Carter of Sabine Hall, George Mason of Gunston Hall, and other "barons of the Potomac."

The social attractions of Chantilly seem to have been especially appealing to George Mason, for one of his visits lasted a week or longer and delayed Lee's preparations for going to attend a session of Congress.[53]

In the Northern Neck, as elsewhere in Tidewater Virginia, dancing was the most popular of all amusements. Among the upper-class families, learning to dance was considered an important part of education, and dancing masters were much in demand. From the diary and letters of Philip Fithian, a tutor at Nomini Hall, we get a good idea as to the large place dancing had in the social life of the Virginia patriciate during the middle 1770's.

He describes the activities of a dancing master, a Mr. Christian, who was employed to teach the young people of several families, including those at Chantilly, Nomini Hall, and Stratford. He went from one mansion to another, giving lessons at every place to all his pupils. At each home the instruction usually ended in a general dancing party at night. As a rule, the party began with minuets, danced by some or all of the couples. Then came the country dance, in which the whole group took part. ". . . it was indeed beautiful to admiration to see such a number of young persons, set off by dress to the best advantage, moving easily, to the sound of well performed Music and with perfect regularity, tho' apparently in the utmost Disorder." On one occasion the dance gave way early in the evening to the game of *Button*. Fithian took part in this game and proved a lucky winner; for, as he said, "in the course of redeeming my pauns, I had several kisses of the Ladies!"[54]

It was the practice of the gentry, as well as the yeomanry, to spend a considerable amount of time in the churchyard both before and after the weekly service, in enjoyable, neighborly conversation. Fithian's reference to this custom was as follows: "It is not the Custom for Gentlemen to go into Church til Service is beginning, when they enter in a Body, in the same manner as they come out; I have known the Clerk to come out and call them in to prayers.—They stay also after the Service is over, usually as long, sometimes longer, than the Parson was preaching."[55]

These social pleasures must have had a strong appeal for Lee, and yet his public activities left him only limited opportunity for enjoying them. His official duties also took him away from

234

his family for far too great a proportion of his time. During the periods of his membership in the House of Burgesses, the Virginia conventions, and the House of Delegates, none of his family seems to have been with him. When he was in attendance at Congress Mrs. Lee and the children usually remained at home, though once she spent six months with him while he was serving in Congress. Writing to John Page (March 8, 1777), he said that he had arrived at Chantilly the day before, after six days of disagreeable travel through the snow, bringing Mrs. Lee, anxious to see her children, home with him after an absence of six months.[56] Such a long absence from her children must have been a severe deprivation, and apparently she never repeated the experience. In November, 1778, Lee spoke of having been away from his family from six to seven months. Even during the year of his presidency of Congress (1784-85), when he was living in such state in New York, Mrs. Lee was not present to preside over the social responsibilities that went with this honored position. At the end of his term he said that he was returning home after an absence of thirteen months from his family.[57]

On one occasion he spoke of being happy at Chantilly since "we have neither wicked, perverse or foolish Politicians here whose misconduct makes us fear for the safety of the Country." He was very fond of his children and enjoyed their winsome prattle. In one of his letters (November, 1778), he referred to his reluctance to give up domestic enjoyment at the call of duty. "I have not yet," he said, "been able to quit the entertainment of my prattling fireside; when I have heard every little story and settled all points, I shall pay a visit to Williamsburg where our Assembly is now sitting."[58]

One problem—often a serious one—that confronted the Virginia gentry was that of financing the high standard of living. An English traveller in America in the early 1770's thought that in "most articles of life, a great Virginia planter makes a greater show, and lives more luxuriently than a country gentleman in England, on an estate of three or four thousand pounds a year."[59] Since Lee, in keeping with the high standard of the gentry, had to meet the demands of a large family and the expenses incurred in sending his four sons away from home for schooling, this problem must have at times presented considerable difficulty. It is true that he had income from extensive farming operations at Chantilly and from his leased lands in Fauquier County. But the amount of rent received from the latter was very small during the years of inflation.[60]

His compensation as a member of the House of Burgesses, the Virginia House of Delegates, and the Continental Congress, did not, in all probability, add much to his net income. His pay as a member of Congress, however, was fairly liberal and seems to have been in specie or paper money valued in specie. There also were adequate allowances for travel to and from the places of meeting of Congress.[61] But his expenses must have eaten up the greater part, if not all, of this compensation.[62] These expenses included the charge for the care of his horses and board and room for himself and servant while he was in attendance at the sessions. He seems not to have taken along his servant when he attended the First Continental Congress and so had only one horse to pay for. At some and probably all of the later attendances at Congress he kept with him a servant and two horses.[63] During the year of his presidency he had with him several of his slaves and a head servant sent up to New York from Philadelphia. At this time he also had his carriage in New York. Even when at York he had his chair with him.[64]

In his long career of public service Lee's greatest handicap was ill health. Dr. Rush said of him that "his mind was like a sword, which was too large for its scabbard." His most persistent ailment was gout, that plague of the well-fed colonial aristocracy. The medicine he used in treating his complaint was wine and Jesuit bark, and he felt very dependent upon both. In writing to General James Warren on one occasion he thanked the general for sending him a parcel of bark. "This is a medicine," he said, "rendered necessary in my family from situation and climate which expose us to intermittent fevers. Indeed long habit has made its constant use indispensable to me."[65]

Gout was not the only type of illness with which he was afflicted.[66] In August, 1779, he was "extremely indisposed" with a severe cold for which he was bled four times. Next year in July he returned from Richmond with a severe cold and fever. Gout also troubled him in January and February of 1780 and again in September, 1781. Next year he had to employ an amanuensis because of illness. In June, 1785, he speaks of his convalescence from a severe intestinal trouble which he attrib-

236

uted to gout. He even had a special type of shoe made for his gouty feet.[67] His activity as United States Senator was at times halted by illness including a serious case of influenza.

These attacks of illness started at the end of his twenties and returned periodically during the rest of his life. They frequently prevented his full attendance at the legislative assemblies to which he had been chosen and kept him for two months away from his duties as president of the Continental Congress. His chronic enemy, gout, probably along with some other complaint, finally brought his public career to an end and later ended his life (June 14, 1794), after some months of confinement in his home at Chantilly.[68]

Not only did Lee suffer, off and on, during a good part of his life from bad health, but he was also the victim of two serious accidents and one or two minor ones. He was able to change the results of the most serious one into a helpful asset; his maimed hand, artistically bandaged, was used to give added grace to his oratory. Even the alleged danger to his health from being in Richmond he turned to good account; it gave him an excuse for not seeking a seat in the Virginia Convention, which was to pass on the federal constitution. In this way he was spared the unpleasant experience of a fight foredoomed to defeat.[69]

In the evening of his life he could look back upon a record of achievement. He had been prominent in local affairs in his home county as president of the county court and commander of the Westmoreland militia; had distinguished himself in the Virginia House of Burgesses by his oratory, his fight for clean government, and his championship of American rights; had played a leading part in opposing the Stamp Act, in originating the system of intercolonial correspondence, in giving birth to the union, in declaring American independence, in forming the French alliance, in supervising and directing military affairs, in transferring the postal system from British to American control, and in adopting the first federal constitution. He also had a minor role in the initiation of our public land policy and the plan of government for the territories, the designing of the Virginia commonwealth, and the launching of our national government. In his last term of national service, he was a leader in the movement which led to the adoption of the Bill of Rights.

237

Lee and his contemporaries blazed unexplored trails through what was mainly a conservative age. Mistakes were inevitable, solutions often were temporary, and friendships were constantly threatened with disagreements and conflicts. But Lee could go to his reward with the certainty that his contributions had been important ones and his role among the most significant that his generation could record.

Appendix

The Association of Westmoreland

The following articles prepared and offered by RICHARD HENRY LEE were passed by the patriots of that day at LEEDS-TOWN, Virginia, on the 27th day of February, 1766.

"ROUSED BY DANGER, and alarmed at attempts, foreign and domestic, to reduce the people of this country to a state of adject and detestable slavery, by destroying that FREE and happy constitution of government, under which they have hitherto lived,—WE, who subscribe this paper, have associated, and do bind ourselves to each other, to GOD, and to our country, by the firmest ties that RELIGION and virtue can frame, most sacredly and punctually to stand by, and with our lives and fortunes, to SUPPORT, MAINTAIN, and DEFEND each other in the observance and execution of these FOLLOWING ARTICLES:—

FIRST. We declare all due allegiance and obedience to our lawful Sovereign; George the Third, King of Great Britain. And we determine to the utmost of our power to preserve the laws, the peace and good order of this Colony, as far as is consistent with the preservation of our Constitutional rights and liberty.

SECONDLY. As we know it to be the Birthright privilege of every British subject, (and of the people of Virginia as being such) founded on Reason, Law, and Compact; that he cannot be legally tried, but by his peers; and that he cannot be taxed, but by a consent of a Parliament, in which he is represented by persons chosen by the people and who themselves pay a part of the tax they impose on others. If therefore, any person or persons shall attempt, by any action or proceeding, to deprive this Colony of those fundamental rights, we will immediately regard him or them, as the most dangerous enemy of the community; and we will go to any extremity, not only to prevent the success of such attempts, but to stigmatize and punish the offender.

THIRDLY. As the Stamp Act does absolutely direct the property of the people to be taken from them without their consent expressed by their representatives and as in many case it deprives the British American Subject of his right to trial by jury; we do determine, at every hazard, and, paying no regard to danger or to death, we will exert every faculty, to prevent the execution of the said Stamp Act in any instance whatsoever within this Colony. And every abandoned wretch, who shall be so lost to virtue and public good, as wickedly to contribute to the introduction or fixture of the Stamp Act in this Colony, by using stampt paper, or by any other means, we will, with the utmost expedition, convince all such profligates that immediate danger and disgrace shall attend their prostitute purposes.

FOURTHLY. That the last article may most surely and effectually be executed, we engage to each other, that whenever it shall be known to any of this association, that any person is so conducting himself as to favor the introduction of the Stamp Act, that immediate notice shall be given to as many of the association as possible; and that every individual so informed, shall, with expedition, repair to a place of meeting to be appointed as near the scene of action as may be.

FIFTHLY. Each associator shall do his true endeavor to obtain as many signers to this association, as he possibly can.

SIXTHLY. If any attempt shall be made on the liberty or property of any associator for any action or thing to be done in consequence of this agreement, we do most solemnly bind ourselves by the sacred engagements above entered into, at the risk of our lives and fortunes to restore such associate to his liberty, and to protect him in the enjoyment of his property."

In testimony of the good faith with which we resolve to execute this association we have this 27th day of February 1766, in Virginia, put our hands and seals hereto.

Richard Henry Lee,
Will. Robinson,
Lewis Willis,
Thos. Lud. Lee,
Saml. Washington,
Chas. Washington,
Moore Fauntleroy,
Francis Lightfoot Lee,
Thomas Jones,
Rodham Kenner,
Spencer M. Ball,
Richard Mitchell,
Joseph Murdock,
Richd. Parker,
Spence Monroe,
John Watts,
Robt. Lovell,
John Blagge,
Charles Weeks,
Willm. Booth,
Geo. Turberville,
Alvin Moxley,
Wm. Flood,
John Ballatine, Jr.,

William Lee,
Thos. Chilton,
Richard Buckner,
Jos. Pierce,
Will Chilton,
John Williams,
William Sydnor,
John Monroe,
William Cocke,
Willm. Grayson,
Wm. Brockenbrough,
Saml. Selden,
Richd. Lee,
Daniel Tibbs,
Francis Thornton, Jr.,
Peter Rust,
John Lee, Jr.,
Francis Waring,
John Upshaw,
Meriwether Smith,
Thos. Roane,
Jas. Edmondson,
Jas. Webb, Jr.,
John Edmondson,

Jas. Banks,
Smith Young,
Laur. Washington,
W. Roane,
Richd. Hodges,
Jas. Upshaw,
Jas. Booker,
A. Montague,
Richd. Jeffries,
John Suggett,
John S. Woodcock,
Robt. Wormeley Carter,
John Blackwell,
Winder S. Keener,
Wm. Bronaugh,
Wm. Pierce,
John Berryman,
John Dickson,
John Broone,
Edwd. Sanford,
Charles Chilton,
Edward Sanford,
Daniel McCarthy,
Jer. Rush,
Edwd. Ransdell,
Townshend Dade,
John Ashton,
W. Brent,
Francis Foushee,
John Smith, Jr.,
Wm. Ball,
Thos. Barnes,
Jos. Blackwell,
Reuben Meriwether,

Edw. Mountjoy,
Wm. J. Mountjoy,
Thos. Mountjoy,
John Mountjoy,
Gilbt. Campbell,
Jos. Lane,
John Beale, Jr.,
John Newton,
Will Beale, Jr.,
Chs. Mortimer,
John Edmondson, Jr.,
Charles Beale,
Peter Grant,
Thompson Mason,
Jona. Beckwith,
Jas. Samford,
John Belfield,
W. Smith,
John Augt. Washington,
Thos. Belfield,
Edgcomb Suggett,
Henry Francks,
John Bland, Jr.,
Jas. Emerson,
Thos. Logan,
Jo. Milliken,
Ebenezer Fisher,
Hancock Eustace,
John Richards,
Thos. Jett,
Thos. Douglas,
Max Robinson,
John Orr.

Donated to Westmoreland County through the Circuit Court by Mrs. Emily Steelman Fisher, Reedville, Virginia, a Daughter of the American Revolution. Genl. La Fayette Chapter Atlantic City, New Jersey.

241

Notes

1. *Lee Chronicle*, 10, 17, 18, 28-29; Montague, "Richard Lee, The Emigrant," *Va. Mag. Hist. and Biog.*, LXII, 6-11, 13-15, 14 n.

2. The Council acted as the governor's cabinet and was the superior court of the colony and the upper house of the Assembly. See Ch. II, p. 16.

Other positions in the public service held by him were clerk of the Quarter Court, sheriff of York County, member of the House of Burgesses, and justice of the peace for Northumberland County. *Va. Mag. Hist. and Biog.*, I, 456; VIII, 107; XI, 37, 284; XII, 205; LXII, 13; *Mag. of Lees*, I, 110; *Lee Chronicle*, 45-46.

3. There is also strong evidence to support the claim that Lee in 1650, after the execution of Charles I, went to Brussels and received from the exiled Stuart prince (afterwards Charles II) a new commission to Berkeley as governor. Tradition also relates that Lee invited Charles to come to Virginia and there set up his throne. Lee, *Lee of Va.*, 60; Gibbon, *Introductio* (Photo., VHS); Hogg, *Geneal. Mag.*, XIII, 333.

4. Montague, "Richard Lee," 24, 25; Charles Campbell, *Hist. of Va.*, 216-218.

5. Montague, "Richard Lee," 39; Ballagh, *White Servitude*, 33 ff.; Lee, *Lee of Va.*, 70; *Lee Chronicle*, 24.

6. Montague, "Richard Lee," 28, 34-37, 44-45, 45 n., 46, 48; Lee, *Lee of Va.*, 62 (will of Richard Lee I).

7. *Lee Chronicle*, 25, 55; Wright, *First Gentlemen of Va.*, 213-214, 217 ff.

8. Lee, *Lee of Va.*, 74; Hendrick, *Lees of Va.*, 33; *Lee Chronicle*, 55-56.

9. Hendrick, *Lees of Va.*, 39-41; *Lee Chronicle*, 57.

10. Lee, *Lee of Va.*, 75; Brock, *Spotswood Letters*, I, 178; Wright, *First Gentlemen of Va.*, 213 (quoted).

11. *Lee Chronicle*, 55-58, 65, 105; Hendrick, *Lees of Va.*, 50-51.

12. *Lee Chronicle*, 58; *North. Neck Mag.*, IV, 292, 293; Harrison, *Landmarks*, I, 146; Brown and Brown, *Virginia*, 81.

The "Northern Neck" was that part of Virginia between the Rappahannock and Potomac rivers. Charles II had granted this extensive area to two of his favorites, Lords Arlington and Culpeper. Lord Culpeper bought out the rights of his associate and thus became sole proprietor. This proprietorship later descended by inheritance to Lord Thomas Fairfax.

13. Lee, *Lee of Va.*, 104-109; Hendrick, *Lees of Va.*, 64-65.

14. An informal organization of the Ohio Company of Virginia had been agreed upon in 1747 but the formal official organization was not made un-

til the next year. James, *Ohio Co.*, 10, 15-16, 23, 45; Bailey, *Ohio Co.*, 18; Livermore, *Early Amer. Land Companies*, 75-82, 77a; Morton, *Colonial Va.*, II, 573.

15. Lee, *Lee of Va.*, 103; *Jour. H. of B.*, *1727-34*, pp. viii, viii n., 173; *Ex. Jour. Va. Council*, IV, 307; V, 299-300.

Thomas Lee had also succeeded his father as Naval Officer for the Potomac. *Lee Chronicle*, 66.

16. *Ibid.*, 62-64.

17. *Ibid.*, 58, 64-65, 67; *Md. Gazette*, February 4, 1729.

George Lee, only son of Richard III of London, inherited Machodoc and he built a second residence on this plantation at a different location. This new house he called Mount Pleasant, a name that was afterwards applied to the whole estate. Adjoining the site of the original dwelling is the Lee graveyard, known as Burnt House Field, which has been the burial place of many of the Lee family.

18. *Lee Chronicle*, 64, 65, 66; *Va. Mag. Hist. and Biog.*, XXXIV, 105; Mason, *Jour. of Young Lady of Va.*, 23.

19. Armes, *Stratford Hall*, 91, 92; Hendrick, *Lees of Va.*, 85-86.

20. Thomas and Hannah Lee had eight sons and three daughters. One of the sons, John, died the day of his birth, and another, Richard, the first born, died unmarried before his father's death. One daughter, Lucy, was apparently never married, and no record has been found of her except that of her birth. She was born in 1730; and as she is not mentioned in her father's will (dated February 22, 1749), she doubtless died at an early age. Lee, *Lee of Va.*, 113, 125-127.

21. *Ibid.*, 120-123 (will of Thomas Lee).

22. Philip Ludwell Lee's election to the House of Burgesses was contested, but he resigned his seat in the House, before the contest was decided, to accept an appointment to the Council (1757). *Jour. H. of B.*, *1756-1758*, 390, 392, 416; *Leg. Jour. Va. Council*, III, 1159; *Lee Chronicle*, 72.

23. For the text of the *Westmoreland Association*, see Appendix.

24. Ballagh, *Letters*, I, 403; *Lee Chronicle*, 73; Brenaman, *Hist. Va. Conven.*, 28, 35; *Jour. H. of B.*, *1758-61*, *1761-65*, *passim*; *1773-76*, 20, 164; Lee, *Account Book*, 10; Adams, *Works of John Adams*, III, 32; Swem and Williams, *Reg. Va. Assembly*, 398.

25. On the inside of the cover of his Bible, Richard Henry copied the birth list from Thomas Lee's Bible. According to this list Thomas Ludwell was born December, 1731, and Richard Henry, January 20, 1732. At that time and until 1752 the old calendar was still in use in Virginia, and by it the new year began on March 25. In making the change from the old to the new calendar, all dates between January 1 and March 25 had to be advanced one year and eleven days. Richard Henry and possibly Thomas Ludwell, as well as all the younger children, were born at Stratford; the older ones were born at Machodoc. According to tradition, the room of Richard Henry and Francis Lightfoot's birth was the one in which Robert

E. Lee was born. Richard Henry Lee's Bible (VHS); Burnett, "Richard Henry Lee," *DAB;* Freeman, *R. E. Lee,* I, 12; *Columbia Encyclopedia* (3rd ed.), 317.

26. Hendrick, *Lees of Va.,* 86-87; *Cal. Inner Temple Rec.,* IV, sec. I, 585.

27. He also took notes on his reading. Some of these notes—those on Greek history, the Tudor period of English history, and Locke and Puffendorf—are in the *Lee Papers* in the Alderman Library. See No. 6642.

28. *Coppett Collection* (PUL); *Lee Chronicle,* 71, 81, 122, 143.

29. The children by the first wife were Thomas, Ludwell, Mary, and Hannah; by the second, Anne, Henrietta, Sarah, Cassius and Francis Lightfoot. *Ibid.,* 71, 81, 122, 142; Lee, *Lee of Va.,* 206; *Va. Mag. Hist. and Biog.,* IV, 474; Ballagh, *Letters,* I, 40.

For an account of his family and home life see Ch. XVII.

30. Nomini Church was burned by the British in 1814, and the present building does not have this monument. Armes, *Stratford Hall,* 107; *W. and M. Quar.* (1), IX, 25; *Westmoreland Papers* (Montross).

31. About the time Lee was building his home, the young Prince of Condé was occupying the chateau of Chantilly, near Paris. Lee probably named his home after this chateau. Armes, *Stratford Hall,* 104, 106.

32. Lee, *Account Book,* 106, 158, 197, 298.

33. Lee, *Lee of Va.,* 173, 205; Ballagh, *Letters,* I, 39-40; *Tyler's Magazine,* II, 92-93.

On January 6, 1763, Philip Ludwell signed an agreement with Richard Henry leasing him the Chantilly estate. The lease was for the lifetime of Richard Henry and that of his wife and his second son, Ludwell. The lessee was to pay all taxes and quitrents and keep all the buildings repaired. The annual rental was 2,650 pounds of tobacco. However, Richard Henry may have been living here under a temporary arrangement several years before this lease was signed, for the lease speaks of outbuildings, gardens, orchards, and the dwelling house that Richard Henry had built. A modern authority on the Lees says that Richard Henry moved to Chantilly early in the 1760's. If this statement is correct then he remained at Stratford for more than three years after his marriage before settling at his permanent home. *Westmoreland Co. Deeds and Wills, 1761-1768* (VSL), 187-191; Armes, *Stratford Hall,* 104.

34. *Lee Chronicle,* 73-74.

35. Eckenrode, "Francis Lightfoot Lee," *DAB;* Brenaman, *Hist. Va. Conven.,* 17, 28, 35.

36. Rush, *Autobiography,* 115.

37. Adams, *Works of John Adams,* II, 422; *Tyler's Mag.,* X, 196; Armes, *Nancy Shippen,* 22; Lee, *Lee of Va.,* 112.

38. Ballagh, *Letters,* I, II, *passim;* also *Lee Papers* (Houghton), I, No. 63; II, Nos. 1, 9, 17, 22, 33, 35, 36; V, No. 75; VI, No. 39; Lee, *Account Book,* 53, 54, 55, 57, 67, 390.

39. Rowland, *George Mason,* I, 152; Ballagh, *Letters,* II, 7-9; Ford, *Letters of William Lee,* I, 157-158.

40. See p. 112.

41. Hendrick, *Lees of Va.,* 347-348.

42. Lee, *Memoir*, I, 57 n.; Jones, *Amer. Members Inns of Court*, XIII, 23, 87, 122-123; *William Lee MS*. (LC); *Lee Papers* (AL).

43. Arthur to Richard Henry Lee, March 20, 1765, *Lee Papers* (AL).

44. Swem and Williams, *Reg. Va. Assembly*, Index, 397; Burnett, *Letters*, VI, 11; VII, p. LXXVII; *Jour. Cont. Cong.*, XXVIII, 232 n.; XXIX, 582; XXXIV, 576.

45. See Ch. VIII, p. 112.

46. *Lee Papers* (AL), *passim*.

In a letter to Richard Henry (November 8, 1761) Arthur spoke of the former's "noble and godlike Passions, which I have often contemplated with equal Pleasure and admiration." He also referred to the generosity of his mind and the extreme benevolence of his disposition.

47. See pp. 110-114.

48. William Lee to Thomas Ludwell Lee, November, 1770, *Lee Chronicle*, 223.

49. In his reply to his sister's letter Richard Henry stated that he had no objection to extending to women property owners the suffrage franchise. It has not been allowed either in England or America, he continued, probably because it was thought to be out of character for women to press into the tumultuous assemblages of men where the business of choosing representatives was conducted. Besides, it might not have been considered necessary since the taxes levied by their representatives would apply to themselves as well as to their constituents. Ballagh, *Letters*, I, 392-393.

50. *Westmoreland Co. Orders, 1761-1764*, May 29, 1764.

51. R. H. Lee to Hannah Corbin, March 22, 1766, *Peckatone Papers;* Beale, *Stratford*, 211.

52. Corner, *William Shippen, Jr.*, 96; Duncan, *Medical Men in Amer. Rev.*, 22, 116, 276.

53. Fitzpatrick, *Washington's Diaries*, II, 162, 163, 166; III, 224; Fitzpatrick, *Writings of Washington*, II, 331, 331 n., 454; Fithian, *Journal*, 235 n.; *Jour. Cont. Cong.*, V, 562; Lee, *Account Book*, 235, 238, 239, 264, 266, 267, 268.

54. Corner, *William Shippen, Jr.*, 96 n.; Adams, *Works of John Adams*, II, 363.

55. Trevelyan, *Amer. Rev.*, IV, 443 n. (quoted).

CHAPTER II (Pages 14-27)

1. Lee is listed as justice, apparently for the first time, at a court held on July 24, 1755. *Westmoreland Co. Order Book*, 287.

Westmoreland County is noted as the birthplace of famous men. Prominent among its native sons were George Washington, Bushrod Washington, the five Lee brothers of Revolutionary fame, "Light-Horse Harry" Lee, James Monroe, and Robert E. Lee. Wright, *Westmoreland County Va.*, 11-12.

2. Chitwood, *Justice in Colonial Va.*, 80, 91-92.

3. Lee, *Memoir*, I, 12; *Lee Chronicle*, 122; *Ex. Jour. Va. Council*, Oct. 14, 1756 (photo., AL).

4. Greene, *Quest for Power*, 201-202, 381.

5. Ballagh, *Letters*, I, 19.

6. Griffith, *Va. H. of B.*, 16-18, 53, 60, 61, 64; *Jour. H. of B., 1752-58*, 3.

7. Griffith, *Va. H. of B.*, 18-20.

8. Sydnor, *Polit. Leadership*, 4, 5; Hening, *Statutes*, IV, 475-78. For an unfavorable, humorous account of a Burgess election by a contemporary who had served in the House, see Hubbell and Adair, editors, "Munford's The Candidates," *W. and M. Quar.* (3), V, 227-257.

9. Greene, "Foundations," *W. and M. Quar.* (3), XVI, 485, 487-488, 490-491.

St. George Tucker, a contemporary observer of the procedure of the House of Burgesses, said that he had never seen in this body anything "that bore the appearance of party spirit." *Ibid.*, 487; (1), XXII, 252-257.

10. *Jour. H. of B., 1758-61*, pp. VII-VIII; *Leg. Jour. Va. Council*, III, 1184, 1189.

11. Flippin, *Royal Govt. in Va.*, 155-157, 161, 182; Hening, *Statutes*, V, 227; VII, 527.

12. Lee, *Memoir*, I, 13-15.

13. Ballagh, *Letters*, I, 2-4, 52; Arthur Lee to Richard Henry Lee, London, Feb. 14, 1773, *Lee Papers* (Har., photo AL); Sachse, *Colonial American in Britain*, 149; William Lee to R. H. Lee, Sept. 30, 1772, *Lee-Ludwell Papers* (VHS).

14. Burnaby, *Travels*, 4-5.

15. For a sketch of some of these historic buildings, with a picture of each, see Carson, *Histor. Shrines of Va.*, 45, 49, 51.

16. He was a member of the Committee on Privileges and Elections during the entire period of his attendance in the House. He served on the Committee of Propositions and Grievances for seven sessions and on the Committee for Courts of Justice from 1766 to the end of his membership in the House, except for one session when he was not in attendance. He was chairman of the last-named committee apparently during the entire time of his service on it. He was a member of the Committee on Religion for four sessions. The other permanent committees on which he served were Public Claims (two sessions) and Trade (one session). On three of these permanent committees he was at one time or another associated with his brother, Francis Lightfoot, and apparently at one time he, Francis Lightfoot, and Thomas Ludwell were all working together on the same committee. In the two volumes that give a meager report of the proceedings of the House of Burgesses from 1761 to 1769, there are in the index 148 references to Richard Henry Lee.

17. *Jour. H. of B., 1758-61*, 141, 148, 149, 150-151, 284-285; Hening, *Statutes*, VII, 388.

18. The text of this speech as we now have it is in all probability the same as the one delivered by Lee, for it was found among his papers. This is the only one of his orations that has been preserved in complete original form. Lee, *Memoir*, I, 17-19 (text of the speech); *Lee Chronicle*, 123-125.

19. Ballagh, *Letters*, I, 11-12, 383.

20. See pp. 19, 162.

21. See pp. 19, 175.

22. *Va. Mag. Hist. and Biog.,* X, 232; *Westmoreland Co. Per. Prop. Rec.,* *1782,* 232; 1791 (photo VSL); *Westmoreland Papers* (Montross).

23. Ballagh, *Letters,* I, 75-76.

It ought to be added that at that time men of the highest standing promoted lotteries for the disposal of real and personal property, including slaves. This was in effect selling slaves on commission. In the *Virginia Gazette* (Purdie and Dixon) for December 1, 1768, there is an advertisement of a lottery to dispose of lands, slaves, and stock belonging to Bernard Moore. The managers of the lottery were eighteen gentlemen, all prominent in the public affairs of the colony. In the list were three who later were signers of the Declaration of Independence. Prominent among the managers were Richard Henry Lee, Edmund Pendleton, and George Washington.

24. Donnan, *Documents,* IV, 151-152.

25. Hening, *Statutes,* VIII, 343-344.

26. *Jour. H. of B., 1770-72,* 256-257, 283-284.

27. Arthur Lee to Richard Henry Lee, London, February 14, 1773, *Sparks MSS.,* 32, vol. 2, *Harvard Photo* (AL).

28. William Lee to Richard Henry Lee, London, February 23, 1773, *Lee-Ludwell Papers* (VHS).

29. Richard Henry Lee to William Lee, May 13, 1773, *Chamberlin Collection* (BPL).

30. Matthews, "Richard Henry Lee," 11-12; *Jour. H. of B., 1761-65, passim,* especially 96-97, 138; Hening, *Statutes,* IV, 475; VII, 518-519, 521.

31. *Jour. H. of B., 1761-65,* pp. XXVII, 105, 148, 151, 181, 188; Hening, *Statutes,* VII, 549 ff., 643.

32. *Jour. H. of B., 1761-65,* 203, 205-207, 212; Ballagh, *Letters,* I, 4; Mays, *Edmund Pendleton,* I, 151.

33. *Jour. H. of B., 1761-65,* 227-228, 241, 249-250, 252.

34. *Jour. H. of B., 1766-69,* p. VII; Abernethy, "John Robinson," *DAB;* Randolph, "Hist. of Va.," Part I, 110-111 (VHS); Mays, *Edmund Pendleton,* I, 178; Fauquier to the Board of Trade, May 11, 1766, *Bancroft Transcripts* (LC).

35. Mays, *Edmund Pendleton,* I, 358-375.

36. Richard Henry Lee and Patrick Henry owed only small amounts to the treasury, the former only $12 and the latter slightly less. Lee, *Memoir,* I, 22-23; Meade, *Patrick Henry,* 212-213; Mays, *Edmund Pendleton,* I, 363, 364.

37. Randolph, "Hist. of Va.," Part I, 110-111.

38. *Jour. H. of B., 1761-65,* 176-178.

39. *Ibid.,* 305, 356; Eckenrode, *The Randolphs,* 85; Hendrick, *Lees of Va.,* 110; Mays, *Edmund Pendleton,* I, 177.

40. *Jour. H. of B., 1766-69,* pp. XXI-XXII, 14.

41. *Ibid.,* pp. XIII, XXI-XXII, 14, 23, 24; Randolph, "Hist. of Va.," Part I, III (VHS).

247

42. The above summary is based on and the quotations are taken from a rather lengthy "Fragment" (as it is termed) of a speech to be delivered by Richard Henry Lee in the House of Burgesses. The original manuscript in the handwriting of Lee is in the Alderman Library. It has also been printed in the *Southern Literary Messenger* for August, 1858.

43. *Jour. H. of B., 1766-69,* 24.

44. Fauquier to Board of Trade, April 7, 1776, *P.R.O., C. O.,* 5, 1331, pp. 132-133; Richard Bland to Richard Henry Lee, May 22, 1766; Robert Carter Nicholas to Richard Henry Lee, May 23, 1766, *Lee Papers* (AL).

CHAPTER III (Pages 28-43)

1. Sanderson, *Signers Dec. Ind.,* III, 285-286; Alvord, *Miss. Valley in Brit. Politics,* I, 95; II, 93; Abernethy, *Western Lands,* 20, 47, 216; Livermore, *Early Amer. Land Companies,* 102-105; Knollenberg, *George Washington. Va. Period,* 88-90; Ballagh, *Letters,* I, 106.

2. In 1755 the Assembly had passed an act with these same provisions except that this latter act was to be in effect for ten months only. No action was taken against this measure. Wirt, *Patrick Henry,* 24-25; Hening, *Statutes,* VI, 568-569; VII, 240-241.

3. Perry, *Va. Church Papers,* 509-511.

4. *Ibid.,* 497, 498, 514; Maury, *Mem. of Huguenot Family,* 418-424; Brydon, *Virginia's Mother Church,* II, ch. XIV.

5. For the text of this paper see Charles Campbell, *Hist. of Va.,* 512-513. See also *So. Lit. Mess.,* February, 1860, 126-128.

6. Chitwood, *Colonial Amer.,* 624; Bogart and Thompson, *Readings,* 143-144; Kalm, *America of 1750,* 461.

7. One of the older authorities (G. L. Beer) says that the troops were needed to put down the Pontiac rebellion. Dr. Bernhard Knollenberg, a late authority on this period, shows that this was not the case, for the decision to increase the army in America had been made before the Pontiac uprising had started or was expected. Beer, *Brit. Col. Policy,* 261-262; Knollenberg, *Origin Amer. Rev.,* 88-89.

8. *Ibid.,* 89-91, 152, 190; Ford, *Writings of John Dickinson,* II, 243; *N. Y. Col. Doc.,* VII, 713-714; *Conn. Courant,* Sept. 16, 1775.

9. Knollenberg, *Origin Amer. Rev.,* 94-96.

10. *Jour. H. of B., 1761-65,* 303.

11. Hart, *Contemporaries,* II, 381-382; Beer, *Brit. Col. Policy,* 284-285; Knox, *Claim of Colonies,* 5, 7, 198-199.

12. The policy proposed was generally objectionable to the colonials and in some of the colonies there was strong opposition to it. This opposition was expressed in written statements made by prominent leaders and also in resolutions passed by the popular branch of the assemblies. Knollenberg, *Origin Amer. Rev.,* pp. XVI-XIX.

13. Ballagh, *Letters,* I, 5-7.

14. *Jour. H. of B., 1761-65,* 256-257, 279, 289, 291, 294, 299-304.

15. In a letter to the *Va. Gazette,* July 25, 1766, Lee clearly implies that

he first moved for the address to the King and the memorials to the Lords and Commons. Ballagh, *Letters*, I, 16-18.

16. Thomas Jefferson said that the Address to the King was written by Peyton Randolph. On the other hand, Dr. Lyon G. Tyler, an authority on colonial Virginia history, said that it is known that Lee was the author both of the Address to the King and the Memorial to the Lords. In support of this view is the statement of Lee's grandson (Richard H. Lee) that among the Richard Henry Lee papers in his possession were the original manuscripts of these two documents, and that the text of these manuscripts corresponded with the text given in the Journal of the House of Burgesses. According to Dr. Tyler, the Remonstrance to the Commons was drafted by Landon Carter. Lee, *Memoir*, I, 29-30; *W. and M. Quar.* (2), XV, 288; *P.R.O., C.O.*, 5, 113 ff.

17. For the full texts of these documents, see *Jour. H. of B., 1761-65*, pp. LIV-LVIII.

18. Howard, *Preliminaries*, 136; *Commons Jour.*, XXX, 97-101, 192-193, 235; *Jour. H. of B., 1761-65*, p. LIV; Knollenberg, *Origin Amer. Rev.*, 225.

19. Van Tyne, *Amer. Rev.*, 7; Morgan, *Prologue*, 27.

Grenville said that the tax on Americans provided for by the Stamp Act was very much lower than the stamp taxes paid by the British. Gipson, "Repeal of the Stamp Act," *Pa. Mag. Hist. and Biog.*, LXXXVI, 20-21.

20. For the text of the act, see Pickering, *Statutes at Large*, XXVI, 179-204.

21. Soame Jenyns, in his *Objection to Taxation of American Colonies* (1765), argues in favor of the British position. In referring to the suggestion that the colonies be represented in Parliament he made this facetious comment: The American leaders have lately displayed such great powers of speech that if this oratory were suddenly imported into England it would greatly endanger the safety and government of the country. Revenue acquired in this way would not be a measure of frugality, for it would "be much cheaper for us to support their army than their Orators." Jenyns, *Objection to Taxation*, 15-16, 18-24; Morison, *Sources and Documents*, 18-24; Van Tyne, *Amer. Rev.*, 11.

22. Howard, *Preliminaries*, 137-138; Sparks, *Franklin's Works*, X, 430.

23. See pp. 36-37.

24. Among these were George Wythe and Peyton Randolph, later the first president of the Continental Congress. Wirt, *Patrick Henry*, 51; Randolph, "Hist. of Va.," Part I, 107; *Amer. Hist. Rev.*, XXVI, 745.

25. *Jour. H. of B., 1761-65*, 359-360; Landon Carter, *Diary*, II, 1063.

For the text of the five resolutions originally passed, and two others that were offered and not passed, along with a lengthy discussion as to the exact words used by Henry in his final sentence, see Meade, *Patrick Henry*, 170-182; Morgan, *Prologue*, 44-50.

26. Knollenberg, *Origin Amer. Rev.*, 192; Morgan, *Prologue*, 49-62; Morison, *Oxford History*, 186-187.

27. Ballagh, *Letters*, I, 5-7, 9-10.

28. Morgan, *Stamp Act Crisis*, 166, 169-177, 177 n.; *Pa. Jour.*, III, 50;

Conn. Courant, Nov. 1, 1765; Va. Gazette (Purdie), March 21, 1766; Matthews, "Richard Henry Lee," 20.

29. Ballagh, Letters, I, 15.

30. While Lee prior to that time may not have been informed of the intention of Parliament to levy a stamp tax on the colonies, he had heard some months earlier that the House of Commons had declared its intention to tax British subjects in America. Ibid., I, 5.

31. Va. Gazette (Rind), Aug. 8, 1766; Lee Papers (APS), I, 11-13.

32. Richard Henry and Arthur were both admirers of John Wilkes, the English radical. They, as well as Francis Lightfoot and John and Samuel Adams, were also members of an English organization known as the "Supporters of the Bill of Rights." Miller, Origins Amer. Rev., 151, 186.

33. This account of the procession was given by John Mercer, the father of George. The author was, of course, very bitter toward Lee, but he gives the statement of an eyewitness as the authority for his description of the procession. Md. Gazette, October 17, 1765.

34. Va. Gazette (Rind), Aug. 8, 1766.

35. Va. Gazette (Purdie and Dixon), October 31, 1765.

After Mercer resigned his agency Captain Stirling took on board the Rainbow all the stamps brought over by Mercer. Governor Fauquier to the Board of Trade, November 8, 1765, P.R.O., C. O., 5, 1331, pp. 97 ff., III.

36. This alleged "confession" of Lee (which was in some respects like the report he shortly afterwards published) must have been based on oral statements made by him, for in the course of this study no letter or publication of a date prior to that of this letter has been found which refers to his application for the stamp agency. Va. Gazette (Purdie and Dixon), July 18, July 25, Sept. 26, Oct. 3, 1766.

37. See note 31.

38. Va. Gazette (Purdie and Dixon), Oct. 3, Nov. 20, 1766.

39. Richard Parker to R. H. Lee, Feb. 23, 1766; Lee Papers (AL); Ballagh, Letters, I, 14.

40. Va. Gazette (Rind), May 16, 1766; Tyler's Magazine, XVI, 111-114; The Commonwealth, May, 1957, 27-28.

41. Va. Gazette (Rind), May 16, 1766.

For a good account of the part played by Richard Henry in the Lee, Mercer, and Ritchie affair see a recent article by Dr. John C. Matthews in The Old Dominion, Darrett Rutman, editor, Ch. VI, 96-108.

42. The opposition of the Lee brothers to the stamp tax involved them in an event that occurred after the repeal of the act. A Mr. Caul (apparently in Essex County) refused to join the general rejoicing over the repeal of the Stamp Act. John Sears, of the same county, resented this unpatriotic attitude and in so doing apparently resorted to illegal methods, for a judgment was issued against him. As a token of approval of his conduct and as a means of indemnifying him for the cost of meeting the judgment, a fund was raised for Mr. Sears by subscription. Richard Henry headed the list of ten subscribers with a pledge of twenty pounds, and four of his brothers came in with liberal amounts. The four brothers listed

were those who were active in the Revolutionary cause—Thomas Ludwell, Francis Lightfoot, William and Arthur Lee. Lee, *Memoir*, I, 37-39; *Lee Papers* (APS), I, 55.

43. For an excellent account of the debate in the House of Commons preceding the repeal of the Stamp Act, based on contemporary accounts, see Gipson, *Pa. Mag. Hist. and Biog.*, LXXXVI, No. 1 (1962), *passim*, especially 10-11, 14, 19, 21, 21 n., 27, 40; Pickering, *Statutes*, XXVIII, 19-20 (text of the Declaratory Act).

44. *Jour. H. of B.*, 1766-69, 13, 26, 53, 59.

45. Ballagh, *Letters*, I, 22-26, 36, 69-70, 92, 394; Rowland, *George Mason*, I, 153; *Va. Histor. Reg.*, I, 68; Edmund Jennings to R. H. Lee, August 15, 1769, *Westmoreland Papers* (Montross), 51.

46. Bancroft, *Hist. U. S.*, III, 112.

CHAPTER IV (Pages 44-59)

1. Franklin expressed this opinion when he was before the Committee of the Whole House of Commons testifying as to the attitude of the colonials toward taxes levied against them by Parliament. Gipson, "Repeal of Stamp Act," *Pa. Mag. Hist. and Biog.*, LXXXVI, 34.

2. Pickering, *Statutes*, XXVII, 447-449, 505-572, 600-605 (text of the Townshend Acts).

3. Chitwood, *Colonial Amer.*, 528-529; Callender, *Selections*, 149-151.

4. *Jour. H. of B.*, 1766-69, 145, 146.

5. *Ibid.*, 151, 157, 158, 165-171; *Leg. Jour. Va. Council*, III, 1383-1384.

6. *Jour. H. of B.*, 1766-69, 136; Ballagh, *Letters*, I, 27, 27 n.

7. *Pa. Chronicle*, Dec. 2, 1767—Feb. 15, 1768; *Va. Gazette* (Rind), Feb. 25-April 27, 1768; Ford, *Dickinson's Writings*, II, 307-406.

8. The title of the pamphlet was *The Farmer's and Monitor's Letters* (1769).

9. He was mistaken, however, in thinking that Dickinson's *Letters from a Farmer in Pennsylvania* had appeared only in newspapers, for they had been published in pamphlet or book form. For a recent edition of Dickinson's *Letters from a Farmer in Pennsylvania* see *Empire and Nation* edited by William E. Leuchtenberg and Bernard Wishy (1962).

10. Lee, *Farmer's and Monitor's Letters*, Preface.

11. Flippin, *Royal Govt. in Va.*, 60, 136.

12. *Jour. H. of B.*, 1766-69, 187, 188-189, 190-200; *Va. Gazette* (Purdie and Dixon), May 11, 1769.
Another pleasing announcement made by the governor was that the Proclamation issued by the King in 1763 declaring the region west of the Allegheny Mountains an Indian reservation had been annulled and that this area was now open to occupation by the colonials. Chitwood, *Colonial America* (3rd ed.), 499-500.

13. Ballagh, *Letters*, I, 30-31.

14. *Jour. H. of B.*, 1766-69, 214-216.

15. *Ibid.*, 218.

After the House was dissolved Richard Henry Lee wrote to Lord Shelburne defending the action of the House. Ballagh, *Letters*, I, 37; Meade, *Patrick Henry*, 271.

16. Nineteen names were later added to the list of signatories. Boyd, *Jefferson's Papers*, I, 27-31; Ballagh, *Letters*, I, 34, 45.

17. *Ibid.*, I, 37.

18. *Jour. H. of B.*, *1766-69*, 227, 233-234.

19. *Va. Gazette* (Purdie and Dixon), Dec. 14, 1769.

20. Ballagh, *Letters*, I, 45-46.

21. *Jour. H. of B.*, *1770-72*, 85.

22. *Ibid.*, pp. XXVII ff.; Mays, *Edmund Pendleton*, 258-259; *Va. Histor. Reg.*, III, No. 1, 18-24 (text of the Association).

23. *Jour. H. of B.*, *1770-72*, p. XXXI.

24. *Ibid.*, 101-102.

In the brief report of the proceedings of the House given in its journal there is no hint as to the reason for this reversal of their action by the Burgesses. In the time between the two acts of the assembly Arthur Lee had written a letter to Richard Henry (May 20, 1770). The latter may have received and used this letter. If so, it may have caused a change in the position of the Burgesses, even of those who were classed as conservatives. In this letter Arthur Lee reported Lord Hillsborough as declaring in Parliament that "all hope of reconciliation with America were vain, unless the whole Authority of this Country were given up." Arthur also declared that the friends of America in England were afraid that the colonials would not abide by their nonimportation agreements, on which all hope of the reestablishment of their rights depended. *Lee Papers* (APS), I, 165.

25. He and Francis Lightfoot, in cooperation with two other planters, made an unsuccessful effort to establish a cooperative store. Matthews, "Richard Henry Lee," 59-60; Ballagh, *Letters*, I, 42, 56.

26. *Jour. H. of B.*, *1770-72*, 173, 188, 249; Brydon, *Virginia's Mother Church*, II, 377, Appendix, IV, 548-551 (text of the proposed bill).

27. *Jour. H. of B.*, *1773-76*, 225.

28. In the interval between the death of Lord Botetourt and the arrival of Dunmore, William Nelson, president of the Council, was acting as governor.

29. *Jour. Commrs. Trade and Plantations*, LXXVII, 218; Hening, *Statutes*, VIII, 597-598, 600.

30. Ballagh, *Letters*, I, 162.

31. *W. and M. Quar.* (1), XIX, 236-237; Van Tyne, *Causes*, 371-372.

32. Lee, *Memoir*, I, 86-89.

33. Richard Parker to R. H. Lee, March 1, 1773, *Lee Papers* (AL).

Shortly before the meeting of the Assembly, Lee, in response to a request of Thomas Cushing, had the *Virginia Gazette* publish without comment "a flaming declaration of colonial grievances" by the town meeting of Boston (January 21, 1773). Schlesinger, *Prelude to Independence*, 153; *Va. Gazette* (Purdie and Dixon), February 25, 1773.

34. Ford, *Jefferson's Autobiography*, 9-10.

35. *W. and M. Quar.* (1), XIX, 236-237; XXII, 99-113; *Jour. H. of B.*, *1773-76*, 28 (text of the resolves); Leake, *Va. Committee System*, 85-88.

36. *Jour. H. of B.*, *1773-76*, 41.

37. Before this important step had been taken by the Virginia Assembly a committee of correspondence had been organized in Massachusetts, in November, 1772. This earlier committee, however, was not intended primarily for communication with other colonies but to conduct correspondence between the towns of Massachusetts. *W. and M. Quar.* (1), XXII, 102-104; Collins, "Committees of Correspondence," *An. Rept. Amer. Hist. Asso.* (1901), I, 247-249, 250-260.

38. Ballagh, *Letters*, I, 29.
Colonel Gadsden of South Carolina stated that in the year 1768 he had been invited by Richard Henry Lee to become a member of a corresponding society, "the object of which was to obtain a mutual pledge from the members to write for the public journals or papers of their respective colonies, and to converse with, and inform the people on the subject of their rights and wrongs, and upon all seasonable occasions to impress upon their minds the necessity of a struggle with Great Britain for ultimate establishment of independence." Sanderson, *Signers Dec. Ind.* (quoted), 649.

39. Howard, *Preliminaries*, 258; Ballagh, *Letters*, I, 83-84.

40. William Lee to R. H. Lee, January 1, 1774, *Lee Papers* (AL).

41. An act passed by the British Parliament (effective May, 1773) gave the East India Company a monopoly of the tea trade in America. Under this act the American merchants could not compete with the Company in the sale of tea in the colonies. In protest to this measure, a mob boarded the Company's ships in Boston harbor and threw all the tea overboard. To punish Boston for the "Tea Party," Parliament passed (1774) some coercive measures against Massachusetts, one of which closed the harbor of Boston (the Boston Port Bill) to all trade except in necessaries until the tea was paid for. Chitwood, *Colonial Amer.*, 533-536; Knollenberg, *Origin Amer. Rev.*, 244-245.

42. Quoted in *W. and M. Quar.* (1), XIX, 239.

43. Ford, *Jefferson's Works*, I, 9, 11-12; Landon Carter, *Diary*, II, 817-819.

44. *Jour. H. of B.*, *1773-76*, pp. XV-XVI, 124, 132; *Va. Gazette* (Purdie and Dixon), May 26, 1774; Randolph, "Hist. of Va.," Part II, 25; *W. and M. Quar.* (1), XXII, 107-108; Conway, *Edmund Randolph*, 15; Meade, *Old Churches*, II, 440.

45. *W. and M. Quar.* (1), XXII, 108-109; Boyd, *Jefferson's Papers*, I, 107-109 (text of the resolution and list of signatories); Ford, *Jefferson's Autobiography*, 12-13; *Jour. H. of B.*, *1773-76*, pp. XIII-XIV.

46. Ballagh, *Letters*, I, 111-112, 115 n. (text of the resolutions).

47. Boyd, *Jefferson's Papers*, I, 105-112.

48. The Assembly did not meet, however, until June 1, 1775, having been prorogued a number of times by the governor. *Jour. H. of B.*, *1773-76*, 165-173.

49. For important articles of this agreement, see Brenaman, *Hist. Va. Conven.*, 12-15.

50. *Va. Gazette* (Purdie and Dixon), August 11, 1774.

By this time there was a widespread feeling throughout the colonies in favor of a general congress and suggestions for such a body had been made in a number of colonies. *W. and M. Quar.* (1), XXII, 109.

51. Schlesinger, *Colonial Merchants*, 365-367.

52. *Va. Gazette* (Purdie and Dixon), June 30, 1774. For the text of these resolutions see Wright, *Westmoreland County, Va.*, 48-50.

During this eight-year period (1766-1774) the Virginia Assembly was concerned mainly, but not entirely, with the issues that had been raised by the British government. It had also, of course, to deal with local problems, such as that of providing relief (July, 1770) to tobacco growers who had suffered loss from a flood. A committee was appointed, of which Lee was a member, to frame a relief measure. The House of Burgesses also adopted a plan for the redemption of the paper money issued in 1769 and 1771. It chose a committee of six, of which Lee was a member, to prepare a bill in line with this plan. *Va. Gazette* (Rind), July 18, 1771, March 11, 1773.

CHAPTER V (Pages 60-75)

1. *Jour. Cont. Cong.*, I, 13-14, 15-24; *Amer. Papers, Bancroft Transcripts* (NYPL), II, 49-55.

On some of the ballots it is said that individual notations suggested that Peyton Randolph be made president of the Congress; Patrick Henry and Lee display their oratory; Washington command the army if one should be raised; Richard Bland make use of his rich store of colonial learning; Benjamin Harrison utter plain truths; and Edmund Pendleton be the penman for business.

2. Randolph, "Hist. of Va.," Part II, 26; Boyd, *Jefferson's Papers*, I, 141-143; Niles, *Principles and Acts*, 275-276.

3. Fitzpatrick, *Washington's Diaries*, II, 162.

4. *Lee Papers*, I, 83 (APS); *Lee Chronicle*, 146.

5. Adams, *Works of John Adams*, II, 362.

6. Butterfield, *Adams Papers* (Diary), II, 119-120.

7. *Ibid.*, 121.

If Lee was "very high" on this occasion, it must have been an exceptional experience for him since he was not addicted to excessive drinking; or it may have been that Adams' lingering puritanism might have mistaken Lee's natural effusion for alcohol-induced gaiety.

8. Adams, *Works of John Adams*, II, 381, 382, 386; Burnett, *Letters*, I, 54 n., 74, 81, 82.

9. Burnett, *Cont. Cong.*, 31-32; Burnett, *Letters*, I, 2; Butterfield, *Adams Papers* (Autobiography), III, 371.

A young contemporary (William Bradford) in a letter to James Madison (January 4, 1775), expressed the following high opinion of the Virginia delegates: The representatives were highly celebrated for their zeal. "Your province," he continued, "seems to take the lead at present; that silent spirit of Courage which is said to reign there has gained you more credit than you can imagine." *Bradford Letter Book* (Histor. Soc. of Pa.), 36-37.

10. Burnett, *Letters*, I, 27.

11. Roger Atkinson, a fellow Virginian, said of Lee (October, 1774): ". . . I know his value as true a trout as ever swam, as staunch a hound as ever ran." *Lee Chronicle*, 145.

12. Burnett, *Letters*, I, 28-29; Meade, *Patrick Henry*, 326 (quoted).

13. Jensen, *Art. of Confed.*, 166; Adams, *Works of John Adams*, II, 371.

14. *Lee Chronicle*, 147.

15. *John Adams Papers* (microfilm), reel No. 2.

16. *Jour. Cont. Cong.*, I, 25-26.

17. Burnett, *Cont. Cong.*, 36-38; Burnett, *Letters*, I, 12.

18. *Ibid.*, 14, 69; Adams, *Works of John Adams*, II, 367.

19. *Jour. Cont. Cong.*, I, 26, 27-29, 28 n.

20. Burnett, *Letters*, I, 20-21; Burnett, *Cont. Cong.*, 41-42; Adams, *Works of John Adams*, II, 370-372.

21. *Jour. Cont. Cong.*, I, 42, 63 ff.

22. For the text of the Declaration of Rights, see *ibid.*, 63-73; or Morison, *Sources and Documents*, 118-122.

23. Galloway, *Reflections on Amer. Rebellion*, 66-67.

24. *Jour. Cont. Cong.*, I, 31 ff., 39; Burnett, *Letters*, I, 33-34; Smith, *John Adams*, I, 176.

25. Lee, *Memoir*, I, 109-110; *Amer. Heritage, Book of Rev.*, 72. Galloway, however, stated that two members offered protests against endorsement and that these protests were ignored and the request for their inclusion in the minutes was refused. Burnett, *Letters*, I, 34-35, 55-56; *Jour. Cont. Cong.*, I, 39, 39 n., 40 n.

26. Morison, *Sources and Documents*, 116-118; *Jour. Cont. Cong.*, I, 49-51.

27. Burnett, *Letters*, I, 52, 53, 54, 57, 59; *Mag. Amer. Hist.*, I, 441, 442; Adams, *Works of John Adams*, II, 389; Mays, *Edmund Pendleton*, I, 290.

28. Lee, *Memoir*, I, 112. The original paper is in the *Lee Papers* (AL).

29. *Jour. Cont. Cong.*, I, 54-55, 54 n.

30. Chitwood and Owsley, *Short History*, I, 186.

31. *Jour. Cont. Cong.*, I, 41.

32. *Ibid.*, 43; Burnett, *Letters*, I, 48-50.

33. *Jour. Cont. Cong.*, I, 51-52, 52 n.; Adams, *Works of John Adams*, II, 385 n.

34. *Jour. Cont. Cong.*, I, 53.

35. *Ibid.*, I, 62, 74, 75-81; Burnett, *Cont. Cong.*, 55.

36. This delay in nonexportation would enable the Chesapeake colonies and the Carolinas to market the crop of 1774.

37. *Jour. Cont. Cong.*, I, 75-81 (text of the Association).

38. *Ibid.*, 62, 62 n., 81, 90; Lee, *Memoir*, I, Appendix, III, 270-271.

39. *Jour. Cont. Cong.*, I, 90-101 (text of the Memorial).

40. *Ibid.*, 102-103.

41. By this act the boundaries of Quebec were extended southward to include the territory between the Ohio and Mississippi rivers and the Great Lakes. French law was to be used in the decision of civil suits, which meant that such cases were to be tried without juries. Religious freedom was guaranteed to the Catholics, and their clergy were allowed to collect tithes. The administration of the province was centralized under the control of the King. Pickering, *Statutes*, XXX, 549-554.

42. *Jour. Cont. Cong.*, I, 103, 105-113 (text of the address).

43. *Amer. Papers, Bancroft Transcripts* (NYPL), II, 125-131.

44. Burnett, *Letters*, I, 79 n.

45. *Lee Papers*, (Houghton), VIII, No. 4 (text of this document in Lee's handwriting).

46. *Jour. Cont. Cong.*, I, 75, 81, 82-90 (text of Jay's draft).

47. Burnett, *Letters*, I, 79 n.; Grigsby, *Va. Conven. of 1776*, 132.

48. *Jour. Cont. Cong.*, I, 53, 54-55, 102; Stillé, *John Dickinson*, I, 145-146.

49. Wirt, *Patrick Henry*, 85 n., 104, 113; *Va. Gazette* (Purdie and Dixon), Dec. 22, 1774.

50. *Jour. Cont. Cong.*, I, 104-105, 121-122.

51. Arthur Lee to R. H. Lee, Lee, *Life of Arthur Lee*, I, 211-213; also *Coppett Collection* (PUL), Dec. 24, 1774.

Arthur Lee also showed the petition to Lord Chatham, friend of America, who approved it "exceedingly," stating in a letter to Arthur: "I have not words to express my satisfaction that the Congress had conducted this most arduous and delicate business, with such manly wisdom and calm resolution, as does the highest honor to their deliberations." "The whole of your countrymen's conduct has manifested such wisdom, moderation, and manliness of character, as would have done honor to Greece or Rome in their best days." Arthur Lee to Richard Henry Lee, December 26, 27, 1774, *Lee Papers*, Har. photo (AL).

52. Burnett, *Cont. Cong.*, 57-58; *Jour. Cont. Cong.*, I, 102, 114.

CHAPTER VI (Pages 76-90)

1. Burnett, *Cont. Cong.*, 57.

2. Harwell, *Com. of Safety, Westmoreland and Fincastle*, 14-15, 27-31, 27 n., 30 n.

3. *Ibid.*, 32-36, 38, 42 n., 43.

4. Burnett, *Cont. Cong.*, 57.

5. *Va. Gazette* (Dixon and Hunter), Feb. 3, 1775; Freeman, *George Washington*, III, 401.

6. Brenaman, *Hist. Va. Conven.*, 16-18.

7. *Proceedings Va. Conven.* (March, 1775), 5; Brenaman, *Hist. Va. Conven.*, 19; Wirt, *Patrick Henry*, 90-95; Force, *Amer. Archives*, 4th series, II, 165-171.

8. Brown, *Truths*, 23-25 (text of Henry's speech).

9. Randolph, "Hist. of Va.," II, 31.

10. Wirt, *Patrick Henry*, 95 n.

It will be observed that his recollection of this quotation from Shakespeare is slightly inaccurate. Shakespeare, *Henry VI*, Part II, Act III, Sc. 2, line 232.

11. *Proceedings Va. Conven.* (March, 1775), 6-7.

12. Force, *Amer. Archives*, 4th series, II, 170-171; *Proceedings Va. Conven.* (March, 1775), 7-8.

13. Hansard, *Parl. Hist.*, XVIII, 319-320, 338, 358; *Jour. Cont. Cong.*, II, 202, 203, 224-234.

14. Eckenrode, *Rev. in Va.*, 53-54; *Jour. H. of B.*, *1773-1776*, 173, 175, 188, 190, 191; Miller, *Triumph of Freedom*, 42; Ballagh, *Letters*, I, 136.

15. Mays, *Edmund Pendleton*, II, 13-14; *P.R.O.*, *C. O.*, 5, 1353, f. 276; Force, *Amer. Archives*, 4th series, II, 1227.

16. *Va. Gazette* (Purdie), May 12, 1775; Burk, *Hist. of Va.*, III, 411; Michael Wallace to G. B. Wallace, May 14, 1775, *Wallace Papers* (AL); Charles Campbell, *Hist. of Va.*, 608-610; Harrower, "Diary," *Amer. Histor. Rev.*, VI, 95.

17. Mays, *Edmund Pendleton*, II, 14, 15; Alden, *South in Rev.*, 185; Madison to William Bradford, May 9, 1775, *Bradford Letterbook*, quoted by Brant, *James Madison*, I, 181; Marshall, *Life of George Washington*, II, 209 n.

18. Ballagh, *Letters*, I, 108-110.

19. *Va. Gazette* (Dixon and Hunter), May 13, 1775; Henry, *Patrick Henry*, I, 280-283; John W. Campbell, *Hist. of Va.*, 156-157.

20. Andrews, *Virginia*, 284 ff.

21. *Jour. H. of B.*, *1773-1776*, 280, 283.

22. Brenaman, *Hist. Va. Conven.*, 18, 20; Burnett, *Cont. Cong.*, 64-65.

23. Fitzpatrick, *Washington's Diaries*, II, 194.

24. Roche, *Joseph Reed*, 61, quoting Samuel Curwen, *Journal and Letters*, 28.

25. Burnett, *Cont. Cong.*, 64-67; *Jour. Cont. Cong.*, II, 11, 12, 44-45, 48-50, 58-59; Ballagh, *Letters*, I, 134.

26. *Jour. Cont. Cong.*, II, 89-93, 96, 99-101.

Among the numerous committees on which Lee served during this first half-year of the second Congress, those charged with the following duties might be mentioned: to report on Lord North's motion of February 20, 1775; to draw up instructions for General Schuyler; and to answer Washington's letters. *Ibid.*, II, 202, 261; III, 317, 420.

27. See pp. 71-72.

28. *Jour. Cont. Cong.*, II, 80, 110, 126, 127.

For the text of the Petition to the King, see *ibid.*, 158-161; for the text of the Address to the Inhabitants of Great Britain, 163-170.

29. Lee, *Memoir*, I, 268-269.

30. *Jour. Cont. Cong.*, II, 80, 157, 163-170; Ballagh, *Letters*, I, 141-143, 143 n.

The original of this document (apparently on scratch paper) in the handwriting of Richard Henry Lee is in the *Lee Papers*, I, 139 (APS).

31. Richard Penn and Arthur Lee to Congress, London, September 2, 1775, *Lee Papers*, Harvard Photo (AL); Cadbury, "Richard Penn," *DAB*.

32. *Jour. Cont. Cong.*, II, 203, 208-209, 224-234.

33. Chitwood, *Colonial Amer.*, 389-392.

34. *Ibid.*, 589; Fitzpatrick, *Spirit of Rev.*, 237.

35. Adams, *Works of John Adams*, II, 467.

36. *Jour. Cont. Cong.*, II, 71, 208-209.

37. Chitwood, *Colonial Amer.*, 590; Fitzpatrick, *Spirit of Rev.*, 238.

38. *Jour. Cont. Cong.*, II, 177.

In the *Papers of the Continental Congress* one of these reports is in the handwriting of Franklin (No. 24, folio 7) and one in the handwriting of Richard Henry Lee (No. 36, IV, folio 167). Both of these papers are given in *Jour. Cont. Cong.*, II, 200-201. These two papers are only slightly different in substance (except that the one prepared by Lee is more aggressive in tone than the one written by Franklin).

39. Adams, *Works of John Adams*, II, 464.

40. *Jour. Cont. Cong.*, III, 308, 314, 315.

41. *Pa. Misc. Papers* (LC).

42. Dunaway, *Hist. of Pa.*, 155.

43. Ballagh, *Letters*, I, 147; *Proceedings Va. Conven.* (July-August, 1775), 14.

44. Brenaman, *Hist. Va. Conven.* (July-August, 1775), 23, 23 n.; *Proceedings Va. Conven.* (July-August, 1775), 16, 53.

45. Matthews, "Richard Henry Lee," 141; Ballagh, *Letters*, I, 149-151.

46. *Jour. Cont. Cong.*, 274, 293-294, 312-313; Ballagh, *Letters*, I, 154-155.

47. Burnett, *Letters*, I, 216 n., 217 n.; *Jour. Cont. Cong.*, III, 420, 425-426, 428, 443.

48. Ballagh, *Letters*, I, 160 ff.

CHAPTER VII (Pages 91-103)

1. *W. and M. Quar.* (1), XIX, 248.

2. Force, *Amer. Archives*, 4th Series, III, 240-241.

3. Hendrick, *Lees of Va.*, 207; Pickering, *Statutes*, XXXI, 135 ff., 154; Jensen, *Art. of Confed.*, 90-91; *Annual Register, 1776*, 109, 110, 111; Burnett, *Letters*, I, 406.

4. Chitwood, *Colonial Amer.*, 550.

5. *W. and M. Quar.* (1), XVI, 258; XIX, 253.

6. *Lee Papers* (AL); Commager and Morris, *Spirit of Seventy-Six*, I, 272.

7. Ballagh, *Letters*, I, 173.

8. *Ibid.*, 176-179; Nevins, *Amer. States in Rev.*, 144; Richard Henry Lee to Robert Carter Nicholas (or Thomas Jefferson, not clear), April 30, 1776, *Jefferson Papers, Coolidge Collection.*

9. Ballagh, *Letters*, I, 182-183; Force, *Amer. Archives*, 4th Series, V, 794.

10. *Jour. Cont. Cong.*, IV, 342; Adams, *Works of John Adams*, III, 44, 46; Burnett, *Letters*, I, 443, 443 n.; *John Adams Papers, Autobiography* (microfilm), reel 180.

11. Hazelton, *Dec. of Ind.*, 72, 73.

For letters showing sentiment in favor of independence, see *So. Lit. Messenger*, XXVII, 186, 187, 188, 255, 326; *Lee Papers* (AL), Nos. 96, 100.

In one of these letters the writer (General Charles Lee) says that "the spirit of the People (except a very few in these lower parts whose little blood has been sucked out by musquitoes) cry out for this Declaration."

12. Mays, *Edmund Pendleton*, II, 103-110; *Proceedings Va. Conven. 1776*, 15-16, 167; Rowland, *George Mason*, I, 222, 223; *W. and M. Quar.* (1), XIII, 65; XIX, 254-255; Grigsby, *Va. Conven. of 1776*, 17-18; Brenaman, *Hist. Va. Conven.*, 35-36; *Va. Gazette* (Purdie and Dixon), May 17, 1776.

For the text of the resolution see *Genesis of the Declaration of Independence*, photostat (LC).

13. Thomas Ludwell Lee to Richard Henry Lee, May 18, 1776, *Lee Papers* (AL).

14. In a letter to General Charles Lee (May 27, 1776), Richard Henry said: "The sensible and manly resolve of Virginia of the 15th instant has gladdened the hearts of all wise and worthy Men here." *Coppett Collection* (PUL); Ballagh, *Letters*, I, 195, 198-199.

15. Richard Henry Lee to Robert Carter Nicholas, April 30, 1776, *ibid.*, 184.

16. Brant, *James Madison*, I, 261-262, 432; *Va. Gazette* (Purdie), May 10, 1776; John Augustine Washington to R. H. Lee, April 22, 1776, *Lee Papers* (AL); *John Adams Papers, Autobiography* (microfilm), reel 180.

17. *Jour. Cont. Cong.*, IV, 397.

18. *Ibid.*, V, 425.

19. The journal of Congress contains the text of the resolutions offered by Lee but does not state who made and who seconded the motion. John Adams attributed this omission to the influence of John Hancock, president of Congress, Benjamin Harrison, chairman of the committee of the whole, and Charles Thomson, secretary of Congress. Hancock and Harrison were hostile to Lee, and Thomson was a cousin of John Dickinson. But evidence to sustain the assumption that Lee and Dickinson were on unfriendly terms (as here intimated) has not been found in the course of this study. Butterfield, *Adams Papers (Autobiography)*, III, 392.

20. Botta, *War of Independence*, I, 345-350 (text of the alleged speech).

Botta did not claim that in this report of American orations he used the exact wording of the speaker. He admitted that he sometimes added phrases of his own.

21. *Jour. Cont. Cong.*, V, 426, 426 n., 427, 428-429, 507; Burnett, *Letters*, I, 476-477.

22. *Jour. Cont. Cong.*, V, 504-507.

23. Burnett, *Cont. Cong.*, 184-185 (quoted).

24. *Jour. Cont. Cong.*, V, 431.

25. Ballagh, *Letters*, I, 203.

26. Lee, *Memoir*, I, 173; Lee, *Lee of Va.*, 178.

27. In one of his letters he said: "The desire of being here [Williamsburg] at the formation of our new Government brought me from Philadelphia the 13th of this month." Ballagh, *Letters*, I, 203.

In a letter to Samuel Adams (July 6, 1776) he said that his fortnight's stay in Williamsburg "has enabled me to assist my Countrymen in finishing our form of Government—the mighty work is now done. . . ." *Samuel Adams Papers* (NYPL).

28. Lee, *Memoir*, II, 200 (quoted).

29. Rowland, *George Mason*, I, 226-227; *Lee Transcripts*, IV (VHS), 212.

30. F. L. Lee to R. H. Lee, April 13, 1776, *Lee Papers* (AL); Thomas Ludwell Lee to R. H. Lee, May 18, 1776, *So. Lit. Messenger*, XXVII, 325.

31. Henry, *Patrick Henry*, I, 411; *Lee Chronicle*, 156, 157 (quoted).

32. Hilldrup, *Va. Conven. of 1776*, 242-248, *passim;* Force, *Amer. Archives*, 6th Series, IV, 748-754.

33. Ballagh, *Letters*, I, 190; Matthews, "Richard Henry Lee," 174-175.

34. Ballagh, *Letters*, I, 203, 207; *Proceedings Va. Conven., 1776*, 167.

35. *Jour. Cont. Cong.*, V, 510-515.

For the original text as prepared by Jefferson and the emendations made by Congress, see Becker, *Dec. of Ind.*, 174-184.

36. *Jour. Cont. Cong.*, V, 590-591, 626; Becker, *Dec. of Ind.*, 192-193.

37. On one occasion Lee indicated a little jealousy of Jefferson when he declared that the Declaration was copied from Locke's treatise on government. This statement was not fair to Jefferson, for while the ideas of the Declaration were not original with Jefferson, and some of them were borrowed from Locke, he "turned," he said, "to neither book nor pamphlet while writing it." Ford, *Jefferson's Autobiography*, 31 n.

38. Jefferson to R. H. Lee, July 8, 1776, *Lee-Ludwell Papers* (VHS); Ballagh, *Letters*, I, 210, 210 n.

39. In the opinion of a leading authority on Thomas Jefferson (Dr. Dumas Malone), it was fortunate that Lee was not assigned the task of preparing the Declaration. He thinks that Lee's effectiveness as a public speaker did not carry over into his writing, and if he had written this noted document it would not have had the literary quality which was imparted to it by Jefferson. Lee, *Memoir*, I, 178-179; Malone, *Dec. of Ind.*, 67.

40. Gipson, "Va. Debts before Amer. Rev.," *Va. Mag. Hist. and Biog.*, LXIX, 259 ff.; Boyd, *Jefferson's Papers*, X, 27.

41. Evans, "Planter Indebtedness," *W. and M. Quar.* (3), XIX, 530-531; Fitzpatrick, *Writings of Washington*, III, 229-234.

42. Hening, *Statutes*, XI, 76.

43. Harrell, *Loyalism in Va.*, 129-130; Campbell, *Bland Papers*, 278; Rowland, *George Mason*, II, 46.

44. *Jour. Cont. Cong.*, XXVI, 23, 28-29, 30-31.

The resolution did not make specific mention of debts to British creditors, but the obligation to pay them was implied in the recommendation that all state laws be repealed that interfered with the restoration of the rights and property of British subjects.

45. *Jour. Va. H. of D.*, June, 1784, 41.

46. *Ibid.*, 1787, 79-80, 91, 94, 95; Hening, *Statutes*, XII. 528.

47. Tate, "Coming of the Revolution," *W. and M. Quar.* (3), XIX, 337.

48. See Ch. I, *passim.*

49. Gipson, *Coming of Rev.*, 215.

CHAPTER VIII (Pages 104-119)

1. Ballagh, *Letters*, II, 259; Lee. *Memoir*, I, 217, 223.

During this period he was in attendance from August 27, 1776, to February 27, 1777; April 2 or 3 to June 15, 1777; August 12 to December 6, 1777; May 1 to October 31, 1778; and February 20 to May 24, 1779. Burnett, *Letters*, II, p. LXXI; IV, p. LXV; Lee, *Account Book*, 15, 406, 414, 431.

2. *Jour. Cont. Cong.*, II, 253; III, 392; Adams, *Works of John Adams*, III, 3.

3. *Jour. Cont. Cong.*, XIX, 43-44, 64; Bemis, *Dip. Amer. Rev.*, 32.

The Committee of Correspondence soon added to its title the word "Secret." On April 17, 1777, the name Committee of Secret Correspondence was changed by act of Congress to that of the Committee for Foreign Affairs. Burnett, *Cont. Cong.*, 118; *Jour. Cont. Cong.*, VI, 274; *Cal. Franklin Papers*, I, 189, 200, 307, 314, 421, 422, 443-444; IV, 403.

4. Burnett, *Letters*, II, 129-131, 181-183, 224, 232-233; III, 234-239, 242, 470, 471; *Jour. Cont. Cong.*, VI, 1067; *Com. on For. Affairs, Letters* (Nat. Ar.), *passim;* Lee Papers (Houghton), III, No. 9; IV, Nos. 123-126, 152; Lee, *Memoir*, I, 285-293.

5. *Jour. Cont. Cong.*, V, 827.

6. *Ibid.*, 792-797; Burnett, *Letters*, IV, 172; Fell, *Diary* (LC), April 21, 1779; Ballagh, *Letters*, II, 160-161.

7. Burnett, *Letters*, I, 274; Burnett, *Cont. Cong.*, 141.

8. *Ibid.*, 142-143.

9. Bemis, *Dip. Amer. Rev.*, 35, 35 n.; Stillé, *Beaumarchais*, 28-29; Stephenson, *Amer. Histor. Rev.*, XXX, 277.

10. Burnett, *Cont. Cong.*, 242; Fitzpatrick, *Washington's Writings*, VIII, 74-76; Ballagh, *Letters*, I, 293-295; Hendrick, *Lees of Va.*, 304.

11. Ballagh, *Letters*, I, 364-365.

12. *Jour. Cont. Cong.*, V, 738, 738 n.; Butterfield, *Adams Papers (Autobiography)*, 429, 429 n.; Burnett, *Letters*, II, 75, 82.

13. *Atlantic Monthly*, LXXVII, 759-762.

14. Burnett, *Cont. Cong.*, 207-208; *Jour. Cont. Cong.*, V, 768 ff. For the text of the plan see *Secret Jour. Cong.*, II, 7-25.

15. *Jour. Cont. Cong.*, IX, 947 n.; *Papers Cont. Cong.*, No. 19, III, folio 165 (Nat. Ar.); Ballagh, *Letters*, I, 355.

16. Burnett, *Letters*, II, ·129-131, 197; *Secret Jour. Cont. Cong.*, II, 31, 35; *Lee Papers* (Houghton), Nos. 71-72, 74.

17. *Jour. Cont. Cong.*, XI, 418, 419-444 (text of the treaties in French and English).

18. *Papers Cont. Cong.*, item 102, vol. II, 54 (Nat. Ar.); Richard Henry

Lee to John Page, ————, 1778, *Personal Papers Misc.* (LC); Lee, *Memoir*, I, Appendix, 295.

19. *Jour. Cont. Cong.*, XI, 418, 457.

20. *Ibid.*, 457-458, 467-468; Burnett, *Letters*, III, 223, 223 n.

21. *Papers Cont. Cong.*, No. 78, XI, folio 299 (text of Lord Howe's letter); *U. S. Rev. Papers* (LC), (text of Clinton's letter).

22. *Jour. Cont. Cong.*, XI, 572-575; Ballagh, *Letters*, I, 411; *Lee Papers* (AL), No. 9.

23. Burnett, *Letters*, III, 295 n.; *Papers Cont. Cong.*, No. 23, folio 43; *Jour. Cont. Cong.*, XI, 614-615 (text of the answer).

24. Among the terms offered by the British commissioners, the following should be noted: "a cessation of hostilities both by sea and land"; a restoration of free intercourse and a revival of mutual affection; and the extension of "every freedom of trade that our respective interests can require." No British troops would be kept in the colonies without the consent of Congress or the particular colonial assemblies. It was also suggested that each state be allowed a voting representative in Parliament and Great Britain be allowed like representation in each state convention (note the term "state" is used instead of "colony"). Pitkin, *Hist. U. S.*, II, 38-39.

25. Ballagh, *Letters*, I, 414-416; *Lee Papers* (APS), II, 128, No. 36; Burnett, *Letters*, III, 280, 296-297; *Lee Papers* (AL), No. 309.

26. Burnett, *Letters*, III, 472; Ballagh. *Letters*, I. 447.

27. *Jour. Cont. Cong.*, XI, 683, 685; Burnett, *Letters*, III, 329-330, 333, 342, 347.

28. Ballagh, *Letters*, I, 423, 427.

29. See pp. 97-98.

30. *Jour. Cont. Cong.*, XI, 688.

31. *Ibid.*, 695, 696-697, 698-701, 703, 707-708, 733.

32. Tower, *LaFayette*, II, 30.

33. Burnett, *Letters*, III, 363; *Papers Cont. Cong.*, No. 25, I, folio 53; Doniol, *Histoire*, III, 268-269.

For the text of Gérard's letter to Count Vergennes describing his reception by Congress, see *ibid.*, 269 n.–271 n.

Later (September 10, 1778) Lee was first-named on a committee of five to confer with Gérard respecting the future operations of the French fleet. *Jour. Cont. Cong.*, XII, 897.

34. *Ibid.*, IX, 946-947, 975, 988; Burnett, *Letters*, III, Preface, XXXI.

35. Burnett, *Cont. Cong.*, 361; *Deane Papers*, 486; *Jour. Cont. Cong.*, XI, 726; Burnett, *Letters*, III, 417.

36. Burnett, *Cont. Cong.*, 361-362.

37. In February, 1777, Franklin and Deane had Arthur Lee "to go to Spain to seek the recognition and alliance of that country." Lee failed in this endeavor, but he was able to get promises of secret aid which were afterwards carried out. His fellow commissioners also persuaded Lee to go on a fruitless mission to Prussia. He was not received by the King and while he was at dinner in Berlin the British envoy contrived to have his door forced and his papers stolen. Bemis, *Dip. Amer. Rev.*, 52-53, 115, 115 n.

38. Ford, *Letters of William Lee*, II, 683-684.

39. Arthur Lee was on very friendly terms with Lord Shelburne and was entertained by his lordship at his home, "Bowood." *Lee Papers* (Houghton), I, No. 58; VII, No. 23.

40. Ballagh, *Letters*, II, 33.

It is true that in a letter to John Page in 1778 (month not given) Lee said that if England were wise she would immediately acknowledge American independence and make a treaty with the United States without going to war with France. This letter was probably written before England and France were at war, and if so, the Americans could have made a treaty with Great Britain without violating commitments to their ally. Later, after France had become deeply involved in the conflict with England, he was strongly opposed to a separate treaty with Great Britain without the consent of France. In a letter to Arthur (February 11, 1779) he made the following statement: "As to the noise about its being said that the United States might make treaty with England with [without] the consent of their Ally if war was not declared—I do not believe that any one Man of sense or member ever said or thought anything like it. 'Tis mere pretense. For myself I know that I would sooner cease to live than I would agree in any manner or for any pretext to desert our Ally for whom I feel infinite gratitude and reverence." *Lee Papers, Misc.* (NYPL); Ballagh, *Letters*, II, 33.

41. *Coppett Collection* (PUL).

42. Burnett, *Cont. Cong.*, 365-366; *Jour. Cont. Cong.*, XII, 1202-1206; Wallace, *Life of Henry Laurens*, 320-328.

43. Ballagh, *Letters*, II, 80.

44. *Ibid.*, I, 355.

45. Burnett, *Letters*, III, 231.

46. Ballagh, *Letters*, I, 446.

47. *Ibid.*, II, 105, 120-21.

48. *Ibid.*, I, 458-460; II, 11-26, 31, 169; Van Doren, *Secret Hist. Amer. Rev.*, 107 (quoted).

49. Ballagh, *Letters*, I, 458-460; II, 31, 169; Van Doren, *Secret Hist. Amer. Rev.*, 107 (quoted).

50. Burnett, *Letters*, IV, 391.

51. *Jour. Cont. Cong.*, XIV, 542-543; Burnett, *Letters*, IV, 193, 196 n.; Fell, *Diary* (LC), April 25-May 3, 1779.

52. *Jour. Cont. Cong.*, XIV, 712.

The vote was unanimous as to states and there were only two individual votes in the negative.

53. Burnett, *Letters*, IV, 385, 385 n.; James Lovell to Arthur Lee, July 17, 1779, *Lee Papers*, Har. (photo. AL).

54. Ballagh, *Letters*, II, 164, 172.

55. Harlow, "Silas Deane," *DAB*.

56. Boyd, "Silas Deane," *W. and M. Quar.* (3), XVI, 165-187, 318-342, 515-550.

57. Burnett, *Cont. Cong.*, 369.

58. Arthur Lee seems to have come out of this controversy without any serious permanent injury to his reputation, for he was afterwards elected

to Congress by the Virginia Assembly. Congress also honored him by putting him on the board of the treasury and appointing him commissioner to treat with the Western Indians. By February, 1785, Richard Henry was able to say that Arthur had settled his affair with Congress to his entire satisfaction. Burnett, *Letters*, VI, p. LIII; Lee, *Memoir*, II, 225 n.; Ballagh, *Letters*, II, 328.

59. Deane was not so happy in his later career. The long delay in giving him a hearing caused him to lose confidence in Congress and to despair of the success of the American cause. He spent his later years in exile in Europe and while there he wrote some letters in pessimistic vein advising the Americans to come to terms with the British without insisting on independence. That laid him open to the charge of disloyalty if not of treason. Harlow, "Silas Deane," *DAB*.

60. Ballagh, *Letters*, II, 98, 130, 145, 147, 151.

61. *Ibid.*, II, 30, 176.

62. *Jour. Cont. Cong.*, XIV, 861-862.

63. Burnett, *Letters*, IV, 227-228. See also Ch. IX.

64. Ballagh, *Letters*, II, 119-120, 131.

65. See pp. 93-94.

This false accusation was repeated by a modern authority on the Lee Family (B. J. Hendrick). This author says that at first Richard Henry Lee and John Adams were opposed to an alliance with France, taking the position that America must win her own independence. He quotes Arthur Lee as saying: "American liberty must be of American fabric." Richard Henry also gave expression to a similar view in a letter to an unknown correspondent (January 15, 1778). He expected France to come to the aid of the Americans but felt that they should "rely not at all upon the aid of others, but trust to our [their] own wise and manly exertions." By this statement he did not mean that he was opposed to the French alliance but was urging the Americans to make their own forces stronger. Hendrick, *Lees of Va.*, 232; *Waterston Autographs* (MHS), III; Ballagh, *Letters*, I, 191, 378-380 (quoted).

66. *Ibid.*, 177-178.

67. *Ibid.*, 211.

68. *Jour. Cont. Cong.*, VI, 1039.

69. Ballagh, *Letters*, II, 33-34.

70. *Ibid.*, 142, 153, 158.

CHAPTER IX (Pages 120-135)

1. Matthews, "Richard Henry Lee," 372; *Jour. Cont. Cong.*, VI, 1065, 1067; Burnett, *Letters*, II, 129, 131; Ballagh, *Letters*, I, 231, 241, 243, 423, 425, 429, 442, 444.

2. *Jour. Cont. Cong.*, IV, 330, 369-370, 383-384, 391; VI, 1065-1067; VII, 271-272, 294, 318; VIII, 648; XI, 656.

3. On December 3, 1777, the Committee on Indian Affairs reported the draft of a speech to be made to the Six Nations. This was written by Richard Henry Lee. *Ibid.*, IX, 994-998.

4. Burnett, *Cont. Cong.*, 232 (quoted); *Jour. Cont. Cong.*, VI, 1027, 1027 n.

5. Burnett, *Letters*, II, 178, 179, 214; Ballagh, *Letters*, I, 166.

6. Burnett, *Cont. Cong.*, 233-234; Burnett, *Letters*, II, 209, 240.

7. Burnett, *Cont. Cong.*, 234; *Jour. Cont. Cong.*, VI, 1028-1029; Ballagh, *Letters*, I, 265.

8. *Jour. Cont. Cong.*, VI, 1027, 1043, 1045-1046.

9. *Ibid.*, 1047, 1049-1050, 1053.

10. *Ibid.*, VII, 65, 93-94.

11. Burnett, *Letters*, II, 251, 252-253; Burnett, *Cont. Cong.*, 235.

12. *Jour. Cont. Cong.*, VII, 88, 93-94, 124-125.

13. *Ibid.*, XI, 569-570, 578-579.

14. *Ibid.*, III, 628; VII, 169-247; Burnett, *Letters*, II, p. LXXI.

15. See Ch. X.
He did not return to Congress, however, until August 12. On November 15, he was excused from attendance by Congress on account of ill health but he did not leave until December 6. *Jour. Cont. Cong.*, VIII, 631; IX, 928; Ballagh, *Letters*, I, 381.

16. *Jour. Cont. Cong.*, VIII, 666.

17. In his letter to President Hancock, Hamilton said: "If Congress have not yet left Philadelphia, they ought to do it immediately without fail: for the enemy have the means of throwing a party this night into the city." Mitchell, *Alexander Hamilton*, I, 120-121 (quoted); *Jour. Cont. Cong.*, VIII, 742, 754, 755-756; Burnett, *Letters*, II, 525.

18. Krout, "Philip John Schuyler," *DAB;* Burnett, *Letters*, II, 377; *Jour. Cont. Cong.*, VII, 364; VIII, 375, 604.

19. Ballagh, *Letters*, I, 313-314.

20. *Ibid.*, 322, 325-326, 328, 372-373; Trevelyan, *Amer. Rev.*, IV, 278 (quoted).

21. *Jour. Cont. Cong.*, VIII, 756; XI, 662; Ballagh, *Letters*, I, 325.

22. Montross, *Reluctant Rebels*, 210-211; Ballagh, *Letters*, I, 332 n.

23. Montross, *Reluctant Rebels*, 321-322; Prowell, *Hist. York Co., Pa.*, 289-298.

24. *Jour. Cont. Cong.*, IX, 851, 854-855 n.; *Papers Cont. Cong.* (Nat. Ar.), No. 24, folio 431.

25. This letter was only advocating cooperation of the colonies by committees of correspondence, but it was an important step toward political confederation. Ballagh, *Letters*, I, 29; *Jour. Cont. Cong.*, V, 425, 433.

26. *Ibid.*, 546-555, 546 n.

27. Ballagh, *Letters*, I, 308.

28. Burnett, *Letters*, II, 32; *Secret Jour. Cong.*, I, 304-315.

29. *Jour. Cont. Cong.*, IX, 780-782, 803-804; *Secret Jour. Cong.*, I, 317-321.

30. *Jour. Cont. Cong.*, V, 548.

31. *Ibid.*, IX, 801, 807-808; *Secret Jour. Cong.*, I, 325-326.

32. Burnett, *Letters*, II, 345-346.

33. *Jour. Cont. Cong.*, IX, 885, 887, 893-894, 895, 899-900.

34. *Ibid.*, 900, 902, 907.

35. *Ibid.*, 932-934; *Secret Jour. Cong.*, I, 362-365.

36. The need of adopting the Articles of Confederation was considered so great that there was a move to federate with fewer than thirteen states. Virginia took the lead in this attempt and instructed her delegates (December 19, 1778) to make such a proposal to Congress. Connecticut also gave similar instructions to her delegates. Fortunately, this proposed compromise in favor of a rump union was not accepted Burnett, *Cont. Cong.*, 493-494; Ballagh, *Letters*, I, 417; II, 200.

37. *Ibid.*, I, 452-453.

38. *Ibid.*, II, 200-201.

39. *Jour. Va. H. of D.*, Jan. 2, 1781, 80-81.

40. Jensen, *New Nation*, 351; Burnett, *Cont. Cong.*, 597.

41. *Jour. Cont. Cong.*, XXV, 559-564; XXVI, 112-116.

42. Burnett, *Letters*, IV, 6; *Jour. Cont. Cong.*, XIII, 236; XIX, 213 ff.

43. In October, 1776, Lee was chosen chairman of a committee of three to devise ways and means for supplying the treasury with a further sum of money. By August, 1778, the continental currency was well on the road to rapid depreciation and Congress was deeply concerned over the seriousness of the situation. A committee of five, of which Lee was a member, was appointed (August 27) to make an examination of financial conditions. One proposal made by this committee was for the states to cede their unsettled western lands to the confederation, which would receive the money accruing from the sale of these lands. Burnett, *Cont. Cong.*, 381-382; *Jour. Cont. Cong.*, VI, 874; XI, 843.

44. Ballagh, *Letters*, I, 451-452; II, 65.

45. *Jour. Cont. Cong.*, XII, 1001-1003, 1018.

46. *Ibid.*, XXXIII, 449-450.

47. Burnett, *Letters*, IV, 262.

48. See p. 135.

49. *Ibid.*, II, 65-67; *So. Lit. Messenger*, XXVII, 260.

50. Ballagh, *Letters*, II, 54-55.

CHAPTER X (Pages 136-148)

1. Richard Henry was a member of the following Virginia conventions: the first (August 1-6, 1774); the second (March 20-27, 1775); the third (July 17-August 26, 1775); and the fifth (May 6-July 5, 1776). Brenaman, *Hist. Va. Conven.*, 14, 18, 23, 35.

2. Apparently the republican General Assembly of Virginia had not inherited the decorum that characterized the House of Burgesses under the chairmanship of John Robinson. A German tourist gave this report: "It is said of the Assembly: It sits; but this is not a just expression, for these members show themselves in every possible position rather than that of sitting still, with dignity and attention. . . . During the visits I made I saw this estimable assembly quiet not 5 minutes together; some are leaving, others coming in, most of them talking of insignificant or irrelevant matters. . . ." Schoepf, *Travel in Confederation*, II, 55.

3. *Lee Transcripts* (VHS), IV, 309-310.

4. Thomas Lee to R. H. Lee, Dec. 6, 1776, *Lee Papers* (AL); Ballagh, *Letters*, I, 300.

In fact Lee had opposed the policy of secrecy on the part of Congress. Burnett, *Letters*, IV, 172; Ballagh, *Letters*, II, 160-161.

5. *Ibid.*, I, 297-302.

6. *Fauquier Co. Rec. Deed Book* (VSL), No. 2, Part 2, 424-427.

The first courthouse in Fauquier County was located on Lee's land. The county seat was at first called Fauquier Court House, but later was named Warrenton, apparently in honor of General Joseph Warren, the hero of Bunker Hill. In 1790 Lee had surveys made and streets located and named in the town that as yet existed only on paper. Groome, *Fauquier During Proprietorship*, 145-166, 210-211, 212-213; *Lee Chronicle*, 127-128.

7. Ballagh, *Letters*, I, 298-300.

8. James Blackwell to R. H. Lee, Jan. 16, 1777, *Lee Papers* (AL); Matthews, "Richard Henry Lee," 207-208 (quoted).

9. *Lee Transcripts* (VHS), V, 57; Matthews, "Richard Henry Lee," 195-196 (quoted).

10. Later (October 17) the measure was changed to provide that no delegate in Congress could serve more than three years in any term of six. *Jour. Va. H. of D.*, May 5-June 28, 1777, 8, 10, 13, 22, 23; *Jour. Va. Senate*, May 25-June 28, 1777, 5, 6, 8, 10; Hening, *Statutes*, IX, 299, 388.

11. Henry, *Patrick Henry*, I, 523-525.

12. According to his latest biographer, Jefferson, in offering this bill, was acting on his own previously expressed convictions as to the advisability of rotation in office. Malone, *Jefferson*, I, 249; *Jour. Va. H. of D.*, 1777, 21.

13. *Ibid.*, 24-27.

14. *Lee Papers* (AL), June 10, 1777.

It is significant that Benjamin Harrison, who was then a member of the Virginia delegation in Congress, did not join his colleagues in this act of protest.

15. Rowland, *George Mason*, I, 284; *Jour. Va. H. of D.*, 1777, 84.

16. Ballagh, *Letters*, I, 295-296; Henry, *Patrick Henry*, I, 76, 77.

17. *Jour. Va. H. of D.*, June 20, 1777.

18. Rowland, *George Mason*, I, 284; *Bland Papers*, I, 57-58.

19. *Jour. Va. H. of D.*, June, 1777; Grigsby, *Va. Conven.*, 1776, 140.

20. *Jour. Va. Senate*, June 21, 1777.

21. Photostatic copy of Lee's letter, ms. in Leland Stanford Library (VHS).

22. *Jour. Va. H. of D.*, 1777, 93-94.

After winning his victory in the Virginia Assembly, Richard Henry went to "Greenspring," William's estate near Jamestown, to investigate conditions on his brother's plantation. In a long letter to William (written at "Greenspring" June 30, 1777) and in one of the same date to Arthur he made no mention of the recent action of the Assembly regarding himself. This silence would seem to indicate that he was still not very happy as to the action of the Assembly. *Richard Henry Lee Papers* (Huntington Library, photo).

23. Ballagh, *Letters*, I, 304, 334-337.

24. *Ibid.*, 376.

25. *Jour. Va. H. of D.*, October, 1777–January, 1778, *passim*.

26. *Ibid.*, Oct. 20, 1777 – Jan. 24, 1778, 120, 123, 127, 130, 132.

27. Governor Henry to R. H. Lee, June 18, 1778, *Official Letters of Va. Governors*, I, 291-292.

28. Hening, *Statutes*, IX, 85-86; *Jour. Va. H. of D.*, May-July, 1780, 1, 2.

29. Stanard, *Richmond*, 38.

On May 9, 1765, a bill was presented to the House of Burgesses to "prevent the raising of Hogs, and suffering them to run at large in the town of Richmond." *Jour. H. of B., 1761-1765*, 330.

Johann David Schoepf, a German traveler in the United States in 1783-1784, said that according to a recent estimate the number of houses in Richmond was 280 and the number of inhabitants about 2,000. Schoepf, *Travel in Confederation*, II, 49 n.

30. *Jour. Va. H. of D.*, May-July, 1780, 1, 2, 6, 14, 44, 67.

31. *Jour. Cont. Cong.*, XVI, 262 ff.

32. *Jour. Va. H. of D.*, May-July, 1780, 36-39, 59; Armentrout, *Va. Finance*, 35-37; Tyler, *Letters and Times*, I, 73-75.

Owing to the delay of the Congressional plan in going into effect, Virginia was driven to a new issue of paper money.

33. Ford, ed., *Letters of Joseph Jones*, 55; Armentrout, *Va. Finance*, 41-42; Hening, *Statutes*, X, 347-350; *Jour. Va. H. of D.*, Dec., 1780, 41.

In a later session of the Assembly, Lee and Henry were on opposing sides regarding an act which permitted debts contracted on a specie basis to be paid in paper money. Lee considered this act as a violation of honesty and good faith, holding that without honesty and virtue no republic could exist. It would have been better, he declared, to have remained "the honest slaves of Great Britain than to become dishonest freemen." Lee, *Memoir*, I, 235-236.

34. *Jour. Va. H. of D.*, session Oct. 1, 1781-June 5, 1782, 21.

35. Burnett, *Letters*, V, 538 n.-539 n.

36. *Jour. Va. H. of D.*, March 1-22, 1781, 6; Hutchinson and Rachal, *Madison Papers*, III, 3, 4 n., 36 n.

37. *Jour. Va. H. of D.*, May-June, 1781, 3, 10; Ballagh, *Letters*, II, 233-234.

38. *Jour. Cont. Cong.*, XIX, 102-103, 110, 112-113.

39. *Jour. Va. H. of D.*, May-June, 1781, 9, 11, 12, 16, 18; Hening, *Statutes*, X, 409-410.

40. Jensen, *New Nation*, 58.

There was also a meeting of the Assembly in May, 1782, in Richmond, with Richard Henry Lee in attendance; but the imperfect record gives us no satisfactory information as to what was done at this session. *Minutes Va. H. of D.*, 1781-83; *Reg. Va. Assembly*, 16.

41. *Jour. Va. H. of D.*, October 21-December 28, 1782, 9.

42. Richard Henry was again made chairman of the committee on Privileges and Elections and was put on two other permanent committees—

those of Propositions and Grievances and of Religion. He was also appointed to a number of special committees, and was chairman of some of them. *Ibid.*, 4-6, 9, 14, *passim*.

43. *Ibid.*, October-December, 1782, 55, 58; *Jour. Cont. Cong.*, XXXIV, 96; *Papers Cont. Cong.* (Nat. Ar.), No. 75, folio 373.

44. Jensen, *New Nation*, 412; Benjamin Harrison to Washington, March 31, 1783, *Washington Papers* (LC).

45. Burnett, *Letters*, VII, 21 n.; Governor Randolph to James Madison, Feb. 3, 7, 1783, *Madison Papers* (LC), III.

46. Ballagh, *Letters*, II, 284.

In a letter to George Mason (May 15, 1787) Lee declared that it was necessary for Congress to have the power to levy an impost for a period of time, but the revenue should be used only for the payment of the state debts. He also thought that the right to issue paper money should "be exclusively vested in Congress." *Ibid.*, 421.

47. It should be remembered that Richard Henry was not on friendly terms with his fellow Virginians, James Mercer and Meriwether Smith.

48. *Jour. Va. H. of D.*, October-December, 1782, 72, 76.

About this same time the enemies of Lee in Congress made a futile attempt to censure him. See pp. 136-143.

49. *Ibid.*, May-June, 1783, 4; October-December, 1783, 16, 66; *Reg. Va. Assembly*, 18; Ballagh, *Letters*, II, 286.

50. There are two references to Richard Henry in the House *Journal*, but these may be clerical or typographical errors and intended for Richard Lee. Richard Henry's name does not appear as a member of any permanent or special committees and is not given in any lists of ayes and nays.

51. *Jour. Va. H. of D.*, May-June, 1784, 44, 45, 51, 58.

52. Nevins, *Amer. States in Rev.*, 193-194.

53. Rives, *James Madison*, I, 556-559 (quoted from Madison's *Letters*); *Jour. Va. H. of D.*, May-June, 1784, 70-71.

54. *Ibid.*, November 7, 1786.

Randolph's opponents in the election were Theoderick Bland and Richard Henry Lee. The vote was as follows: Randolph, 73; Bland, 28; and Lee, 22. Hunt, *Madison's Writings*, II, 284; Conway, *Edmund Randolph*, 59.

CHAPTER XI (Pages 149-156)

1. Lee, *Memoir*, I, 234.

2. *Jour. Va. H. of D.*, October, 1777—January, 1778, 127, 132-133; Matthews, "Richard Henry Lee," 279-281 (quoted); Ballagh, *Letters*, I, 369-370.

3. *Ibid.*, II, 72-75, 81-82, 268.

4. *Ibid.*, 72-75, 81-82.

5. *Ibid.*, 82-86.

This plan was very similar to, or virtually the same as, the one adopted by the Assembly a year and a half earlier. The renewal of the proposal, together with the activity of the British ships on the Potomac River, indicates that the resolutions adopted early in 1778 were not carried out. Apparently, Lee's advice was not taken, for in the course of this study no evidence has been found showing that it was favorably acted upon.

6. Eckenrode, *Rev. in Va.*, 264; Ballagh, *Letters*, II, 212-213.

7. *Ibid.*, II, 217.

8. *Ibid.*, 220, 223; Lee, *Memoir*, I, 234-235.

9. Ballagh, *Letters*, II, 230; *Chamberlin Collection* (BPL); Carson, *Histor. Shrines of Va.*, 65-66.

10. Ballagh, *Letters*, II, 230.

11. Weedon also leaned heavily on Lee for information as to the location of the enemy forces and in carrying out his plans. On one occasion Weedon said that his and Lafayette's movements would be determined by Lee's reports. General George Weedon to R. H. Lee, Jan. 28, July 31, 1781; General Weedon to General Nelson, Jan. 29, 1781; *Weedon Papers* (Brown); *Weedon Papers* (APS).

12. Ballagh, *Letters*, II, 230, 233-238; Malone, "Thomas Jefferson," *DAB;* Hutchinson and Rachal, *Madison Papers*, III, 157-158.

13. Fitzpatrick, *Writings of Washington*, XXII, 382-384, 382 n.

14. Ballagh, *Letters*, II, 239-240.

15. *Ibid.*, 253, 257.

16. Lee, *Memoir*, I, 214, 298-299 (letter).

17. Ballagh, *Letters*, II, 249-250, 251.

18. *Ibid.*, 262-263; R. H. Lee to Governor Nelson, Oct. 9, 1781, *Signers Dec. Ind. Collection* (PUL); R. H. Lee to Governor Nelson, Sept. 21, 1781, *Misc. Papers* (MHS).

19. Lee, *Memoir*, I, 179; Sanderson, *Signers Dec. Ind.*, 657.

20. Ballagh, *Letters*, II, 263; Cresson, *James Monroe*, 61-62 (quoted); *W. and M. Quar.* (2), XX, April, 1940 (p. 246).

21. Two hundred Westmoreland militiamen had been sent to Gloucester County as a prospective reinforcement to Washington's army at Yorktown. After the surrender of Cornwallis they were deprived of their military equipment and sent home unarmed. Ballagh, *Letters*, II, 264, 270-273.

22. It was apparently in response to this appeal that the Council of State voted (July 16, 1782) to send 100 stands of arms to the County Lieutenant (Lee) of Westmoreland. *Jour. Va. Council*, III, 123, 270-271, 272-273, 276.

23. In his reply to this letter (September 15, 1782) Governor Harrison expressed strong resentment against the statement in the last sentence. The Executive, he said, was not to blame because the legislature had taken this power out of its hands. Besides, the funds appropriated for the navy had been inadequate. He gave Lee a rap on the knuckles in saying that if he meant his censure for the Executive it was "injurious and more particularly so from a Gentleman who had so great a share in taking this Business out of their Hands." *Ex. Letter Book*, 281-283.

CHAPTER XII (Pages 157-169)

1. Ballagh, *Letters*, II, 206.

2. *Jour. Cont. Cong.*, XVI, 326.

3. Burnett, *Letters*, V, 12, 12 n.

4. Ballagh, *Letters*, II, 277.

5. *Jour. Va. H. of D.*, Session May-June, 1784, 72; Burnett, *Letters*, VII, p. LXXVII.

6. *Jour. Cont. Cong.*, XXVII, 641, 649, 710; Burnett, *Cont. Cong.*, 612.

7. Ballagh, *Letters*, II, 322; Burnett, *Letters*, VIII, 9, 9 n.

8. Ballagh, *Letters*, II, 356, 368, 408; Wright and Tingling, *Quebec to Carolina*, 133, 138, 161, 191.

9. *Jour. Cont. Cong.*, XXVII, 693-695, 705-706.

10. Burnett, *Letters*, VII, 632-633; *Madison Papers* (LC), Monroe to Madison, Dec. 18, 1784, *Jour. Cont. Cong.*, XXVIII, 134.

11. *Ibid.*, XXVII, 700-704.

12. Burnett, *Cont. Cong.*, 634.

13. Burnett, *Letters*, VIII, 181, 186, 186 n.–187 n.; Ballagh, *Letters*, 383-384.

14. *Jour. Cont. Cong.*, XXIX, 810-812.

15. Fitzpatrick, *Writings of Washington*, XXVIII, 11-12; Ballagh, *Letters*, II, 317.

16. *Jour. Cont. Cong.*, XXVII, 446-453; XXVIII, 114, 165, 165 n., 251-256, 264, 284-285, 292-296, 316-317, 319, 327, 329, 342, 375; Burnett, *Letters*, VIII, 130; Burnett, *Cont. Cong.*, 624 (quoted).

17. Chitwood, *Colonial Amer.*, 612; Ballagh, *Letters*, II, 353, 359, 365, 370; Burnett, *Letters*, VIII, 174; *Jour. Cont. Cong.*, XXVIII, 375-381 (text of the land ordinance as finally passed).

18. Burnett, *Letters*, VIII, 193 n., 200; *Jour. Cont. Cong.*, XXIX, 631, 787; Ballagh, *Letters*, II, 384-386.

19. See p. 158, note 15; *Pa. Mag. Hist. and Biog.*, XVII, 76-82; Lee, *Lee of Va.*, 184 (quoted).

20. *Jour. Cont. Cong.*, XXXII, 310; Burnett, *Letters*, VIII, 510; *Jour. Va. Senate*, October, 1785-January, 1786, 13.

21. Ballagh, *Letters*, II, 434-435.

22. *Jour. Cont. Cong.*, XXVI, 275-279; Chitwood, *Colonial Amer.*, 612.

23. *Jour. Cont. Cong.*, XXVI, 275-279; XXVIII, 164-165.

24. *Ibid.*, XXXI, 669-672; XXXII, 274, 292-297, 310 n., 313-320; *Com. Book, Papers of Cont. Cong.* (Nat. Ar.), No. 190, p. 151.

25. Burnett, *Letters*, VIII, 621-622; *Jour. Cont. Cong.*, XXXII, 313, 320, 334, 343.

26. According to George Bancroft, the clause in the Ordinance which prohibits the passage of any measure in violation of contracts "bears in every word the impress of the mind of Richard Henry Lee." Bancroft, *Formation of the Cons.*, II, 113.

27. Chitwood, *Colonial Amer.*, 613-614.
For the text of the Ordinance of 1787 see *Jour. Cont. Cong.*, XXXII, 334-343, or *Old South Leaflets*, No. 13.

28. Ballagh, *Letters*, II, 430.

29. *Jour. Cont. Cong.*, XXXIII, 419-420.

30. *Ibid.*, 451-453.

31. *Ibid.*, XXXII, 174, 174 n.; *Com. Book, Papers Cont. Cong.* (Nat. Ar.), No. 190, p. 145.

32. *Jour. Cont. Cong.*, XXXIII, 415-418.

33. *Ibid.*, 517-520.

34. *Ibid.*, 521-522; XXXIV, 40-41; Adams, *Works of John Adams*, I, 437-438; *Papers Cont. Cong.* (Nat. Ar.), No. 93, IV, p. 43.

35. Mrs. William Smith, daughter of John Adams, while on a visit to New York spoke of Congress as follows: "Congress are sitting; but one hears little more of these than if they were inhabitants of a newly-discovered planet." Monaghan, *John Jay*, 247 (quoted).

36. Ballagh, *Letters*, II, 307, 320.

37. Burnett, *Letters*, VIII, pp. XXXV-VI.

38. Burnett, *Cont. Cong.*, 668.

39. *Jour. Cont. Cong.*, XXXII, 71-74; XXXIII, 723-724 (Madison's Notes).

The statement in Madison's *Notes* is not in entire agreement with the record given in the *Journal*.

40. Ballagh, *Letters*, II, 415, 415 n., 456, 457.

Lee was selected after General Nelson had declined the appointment. The objection to Lee's "unfederal opinions was so urgently pressed that the council consisting of eight were equally divided." Governor Edmund Randolph cast the deciding vote in his favor because, as he expressed it, he hoped that Lee and "his friends might be attached to the Union on those principles which can alone support it." He also acted in consideration of the "conspicuousness" of Lee's character and the respect due his past services. Edmund Randolph to James Madison, March 22, 1787; Robinson, *Edmund Randolph*, 66 (quoted).

41. Ballagh, *Letters*, II, 424.

42. *Ibid.*, 441-444.

There is some disagreement, in minor details, between the account in Ballagh and that given in Burnett's *Letters*, VIII, 648-649. The document as it appears in Ballagh's *Letters* is a copy of a paper in the *Lee Papers* (AL), written in Lee's hand. For a fuller list of principles that Lee wished to include in his bill of rights.

43. Madison to Washington, September 30, 1787, Burnett, *Letters*, VIII, 650-652.

44. Ballagh, *Letters*, II, 449-455.

45. *Jour. Cont. Cong.*, XXXIII, 540-541, 549; Burnett, *Letters*, VIII, p. XLVII.

46. *Ibid.*, VII, 647, 665.

CHAPTER XIII (Pages 170-182)

1. Ballagh, *Letters*, II, 419-422.

2. *Ibid.*, 441.

3. *Ibid.*, 444-447.

In suggesting that Congress be given power to regulate trade Lee was reversing a position which he had formerly taken, for in the previous May he had expressed opposition to granting this power to Congress. *Ibid.*, II, 420.

The correspondence between Samuel Adams and Lee shows that they held very similar views as to the Constitution. It is not unlikely that Lee was influenced as to his opposition to the Constitution by the position taken by the Massachusetts leader. Samuel Adams to R. H. Lee, December 3, 1787, Bancroft, *Calendar Samuel Adams Papers* (NYPL); Adams to R. H. Lee, April 22, July 14, August 29, September —, *Samuel Adams Papers* (NYPL).

4. Ballagh, *Letters*, II, 450 ff.; Fitzpatrick, *Writings of Washington*, XXIX, 234; McDonald, *We the People*, 285; Main, *The Antifederalists*, 223, 223 n.

5. Ballagh, *Letters*, II, 449; Washington to Madison, October 10, 1787; Fitzpatrick, *Writings of Washington*, 285.

6. Ballagh, *Letters*, 469-474; *Va. Histor. Reg.*, II, 100-103.

So anxious was Lee for amendment that shortly before the Virginia Convention met, he wrote (May 7, 1788) to his old friend and ally, George Mason, asking his opinion as to the advisability of six or eight friends of amendments meeting privately to consider strategy in getting amendments. Apparently, nothing came of this suggestion, though the Virginia convention did propose a long list of amendments it did not make acceptance of them a condition for ratification. Rowland, *George Mason,* II, 215.

7. Lee, *Letters*, I, Preface.

8. According to a modern authority the *Letters* were a powerful influence in bringing about the first ten amendments to the Constitution (the Bill of Rights). Spiller, *Lit. Hist. of U. S.*, 142-143.

One of the authors of the *Federalist* [apparently Alexander Hamilton] considered these works of Lee as the "most plausible" of all the writings in opposition to the Constitution. Syrett and Cook, *Hamilton Papers*, IV, 586, 586 n.

9. Lee, *Letters*, I, 8-10.

10. *Ibid.*, II, 46-47.

11. *Ibid.*, I, 3, 4.

12. *Ibid.*, II, 158-159.

13. *Ibid.*, I, 3, 7, 14, 15.

14. *Ibid.*, I, 9, 34-35; II, 35, 50, 80-81.

He had now changed his position as to the power of Congress to regulate commerce. In a letter to George Mason (May, 1787) he had opposed giving Congress the exclusive power of regulating trade, since it might result in a monopoly of the carrying trade by the eight northern states to the great detriment of the five staple states. Ballagh, *Letters*, II, 420-421.

15. Lee, *Letters*, I, 20, 30; II, 179.

The statement as to the precedence of national over state law is apparently contradicted in another letter in which he lists as an objection the clause in the Constitution which makes federal law the supreme law of the land.

16. *Ibid.*, II, 162.

17. *Ibid.*, II, 63, 72-73.

18. *Ibid.*, I, 5, 7, 18-20, 98, 114-116; II, 13, 89, 91-93, 95, 180.

19. *Ibid.*, I, 9, 22-23, 130-142, 148; II, 18, 163, 173, 177.

20. *Ibid.*, I, 122-130.

21. *Ibid.*, II, 174-175, 178-182.

22. *Ibid.*, I, 24-25, 170-172.

23. *Ibid.*, II, 82, 83, 143, 145.

24. *Ibid.*, II, 117, 181.

25. *Ibid.*, I, 48.

26. Ballagh, *Letters*, II, 475; *Lamb Papers* (NYHS).

27. Edward Carrington, in a letter to General Knox (January 12, 1788), said that owing to his opposition to the Constitution, Richard Henry was "finding that even his own family have separated from him." *Knox Papers* (MHS), box XXI.

28. Fitzpatrick, *Writings of Washington*, XXIX, 372.

29. Arthur Lee to R. H. Lee, February 19, 1788, *Lee Papers* (AL).

30. Ballagh, *Letters*, II, 507-508.

CHAPTER XIV (Pages 183-195)

1. Ballagh, *Letters*, II, 479.

2. Henry, *Patrick Henry*, II, 426 ff.

3. *Madison Papers* (LC), X, 28, 50; *Va. Mag. Hist. and Biog.*, LVI, 144-145.

4. Fitzpatrick, *Writings of Washington*, XXX, 125-126.

5. Brant, *James Madison*, III, 241.

6. The day after he took his seat, Lee was appointed a member of two important committees—one to bring in a bill for organizing the judiciary of the United States, and one for preparing rules covering the business of the Senate and that of the two houses acting in conference. *Annals of Congress*, I, 15-17, 18, 22; *Jour. U. S. Senate, Ex. Proceedings*, I, 11.

7. Ballagh, *Letters*, II, 482-483.

8. Adams, *Works of John Adams*, VIII, 493; Brant, *James Madison*, III, 256.

According to William Maclay, this "whole silly business" was the "work of Mr. Adams and Mr. Lee." "He [Lee] labored on the subject of titles with a diligence worthy of a better cause." Maclay, *Journal*, 1, 25, 29; *Gazette of U. S.* (N. Y.), May 9, 16, 20, 1789.

9. *Jour. U. S. Senate*, I, 16-17, 24, 25; *Annals of Congress*, I, 24, 33-36; Ames, *Works of Fisher Ames*, I, 36-37.

10. Fitzpatrick, *Writings of Washington*, XXX, 363 n.

The Virginia Antifederalists were somewhat embarrassed by Lee's vigorous support of Adams in the title dispute. Freeman, *George Washington*, VI, 203 n.; Ames, *Works of Fisher Ames*, I, 36-37; *Madison Papers* (LC), XI, 48.

11. *Annals of Congress*, I, 25-27.

12. Stanwood, *Amer. Tariff Controversies*, I, 39 ff.; *Annals of Congress*, 38-39, 49, 381; Maclay, *Journal*, 87.

13. *Ibid.*, 49-50, 53-54, 55-57, 70.

Lee opposed secret Senate sessions and in obedience to instructions of the Virginia Assembly, in April, 1790, made a futile attempt to have the doors of the Senate opened to the public. Later, in March, 1792, he supported his colleague, James Monroe, in another unsuccessful effort. *Acts Va. General Assembly,* 1789, 45; Ballagh, *Letters,* II, 546; *Cal. Va. State Papers,* V, 443; *Jour. U. S. Senate,* I, 125, 415; *Annals of Congress,* I, 113.

14. Maclay, *Journal,* 49-50, 53-54, 55-57, 70.

15. *Annals of Congress,* I, 47, 48, 49, 51; *Jour. U. S. Senate,* I, 42.

Later (September 17, 1789) Lee reported for his committee a bill to regulate processes in the Federal courts. *Annals of Congress,* I, 82.

16. *Ibid.,* 440-441, 685-691, 730, 808-809; Brant, *James Madison,* III, 264.

17. *Annals of Congress,* I, 77-80, 86, 90.

18. See p. 202.

19. Brant, *James Madison,* III, 270-271, 273; *Annals of Congress,* I, 783-784; *Cons. of U. S., Amend. I; Jour. U. S. Senate,* I, 71.

The United States Supreme Court has recently (June 25, 1962) ruled that the First Amendment, "as reinforced by the provisions of the Fourteenth Amendment, imposes upon the state legislatures the same restrictions as to religious legislation as it does on Congress." *N. Y. Times,* June 26, 1962, 16.

20. Ballagh, *Letters,* II, 487-488, 499, 502, 503.

21. *Ibid.,* 507-508; *Va. Misc. Records* (LC), Sept. 28, 1789.

22. Ballagh, *Letters,* II, 500-501, 524-525.

23. *Jour. U. S. Senate,* I, 71.

24. Ballagh, *Letters,* II, 505; *Annals of Congress,* 262; Smith, *John Adams,* II, 774-775; *John Adams Papers* (microfilm).

25. *Annals of Congress,* I, 18, 20, 24, 30, 42, 46, 52.

26. On May 15, 1789, the Senate divided its membership by lot into three classes as stipulated in the Constitution. Grayson drew a two-year term and Lee a four-year term. *Jour. U. S. Senate,* I, 25.

William Grayson died March 12, 1790, and Governor Beverley Randolph appointed John Walker to the interim vacancy. Later, James Monroe was elected junior Senator from Virginia and he took his seat December 6, 1790. *Biog. Direct. of Cong.,* 969, 1765.

27. *Jour. U. S. Senate,* I, 101, 131.

28. Ballagh, *Letters,* II, 510, 513-516, 523, 539.

29. *Annals of Congress,* I, 89.

30. Schouler, *Hist. U. S.,* I, 152-154.

31. *Annals of Congress,* I, 1039-1040; II, 1678-1680, 2234-2235; Ballagh, *Letters,* II, 531.

32. Brant, *James Madison,* III, 306, 308; Madison to Randolph, March 14, 1790, *Madison Papers,* XII (LC).

33. *Annals of Congress,* I, 1019, 1025, 1026; II, 1629; Maclay, *Journal,* 321.

34. *Annals of Congress,* I, 1028, 1049, 1050, 1054, 1055; II, 1712; Maclay, *Journal,* 330.

35. Hunt, *Madison,* 197-200; Ford, *Jefferson's Works,* VII, 224-227.

Before the final passage of the bill an important concession had been made to Virginia, by giving as the amount to be assumed for her three and one half million dollars, more than the amount of her indebtedness. Ballagh, *Letters,* II, 534.

36. ·Brant, *James Madison,* III, 197-200.

37. Ballagh, *Letters,* II, 535.

38. *Jour. U. S. Senate,* I, 269; Ballagh, *Letters,* II, 541.

39. *Annals of Congress,* II, 1738, 1745, 1748, 1755.

40. Ballagh, *Letters,* II, 541-542.

41. *Annals of Congress,* II, 1051, 1769.

Lee voted against a proposal to fund the continental currency at the rate of forty to one.

An authority on the Revolution (John Chester Miller) says that Richard Henry Lee in later years switched to the party of Hamilton. No evidence, however, has been found in the course of this study to support this view but much to oppose it. Lee expressed opposition to Hamilton's national banking policy and voted against the assumption of the debts of the states by the Federal government. See pp. 191-192; Miller, *The Federalist Era,* 102.

42. *Annals of Congress,* III, 9, 140.

43. Ballagh, *Letters,* II, 543, 544.

44. *Annals of Congress,* III, 51, 74, 79, 94, 95, 103, 108, 113; *Lee Chronicle,* 174; Lee, *Account Book,* 268.

45. See note 13, above.

46. *Annals of Congress,* III, 32, 46-47, 49-50, 191, 200, 208-210.

47. *Ibid.,* 93, 105, 106, 403, 407, 414, 415-416, 418.

48. Ballagh, *Letters,* II, 547.

Lee and Monroe voted in favor of a defeated motion that the Senate recede from all its amendments.

49. Freeman, *George Washington,* VI, 345-347; *Annals of Congress,* III, 539.

50. *Ibid.,* 120, 540-541, 543-549.

51. *Ibid.,* 80, 84, 88, 89, 91, 92-93.

52. *Ibid.,* 125, 140.

53. Richard Henry Lee to the Speaker of the Va. House of Delegates, October 8, 1792, *Lee Papers, Misc.* (NYPL).

He was thus relinquishing his seat nearly five months before the end of his four-year term. John Taylor was elected as his successor. *Cal. Va. State Papers,* VI, 103-104.

54. Lee, *Memoir,* I, 243-244.

CHAPTER XV (Pages 196-205)

1. Burnett, *Cont. Cong.,* 433-434; *Jour. Cont. Cong.,* XIV, 896-897.

2. Bemis, *Dip. Amer. Rev.,* 101; *Jour. Cont. Cong.,* XIV, 896-897, 959-960.

3. Ballagh, *Letters,* II, 60, 62, 98.

4. *Ibid.,* 97, 103, 156, 184.

5. N. Y. *Evening Post,* July 9, 1779.

6. Lee, *Memoir,* I, 238.

7. Ballagh, *Letters,* II, 426-427.

8. *Ibid.,* 299-300.

9. *Ibid.,* 315, 333, 334.

10. *Ibid.,* 409.

11. *Ibid.,* 362.

12. See pp. 136, 141-142.

13. *Ibid.,* 369-370.

14. *Ibid.,* 405.

15. *Ibid.,* 405, 501, 557.

16. R. H. Lee to General Washington, October 3, 1793; *Gratz Autograph Collection* (Histor. Soc. Pa.).

17. Ballagh, *Letters,* II, 563-575.

18. *Ibid.,* 576-577.

19. When Lee and his colleagues went to Philadelphia to attend the First Continental Congress, Robert Pleasants, an influential Virginia Quaker, wrote to prominent Friends in Philadelphia, giving a very favorable report of the Virginia delegates. He referred to Richard Bland, Patrick Henry, and Richard Henry Lee "as great speakers in our House of Assembly . . . and very able advocates for us at the time we made application for relief from militia fines." *W. and M. Quar.* (2), I, 176.

20. Ballagh, *Letters,* II, 304-305.

21. *Jour. Va. H. of D.,* October, 1784-January, 1785, 82; article by Gaillard Hunt in *An. Rept. Amer. Histor. Asso.* (1901), I, 165-171; Brant, *James Madison,* II, ch. XXII; James, *Doc. Hist.,* 134-140.

For the text of this remonstrance, see Rosenberger, *Va. Reader,* 300-306.

22. Eckenrode, *Separation Church and State in Va.,* 75 (quoted).

23. See pp. 202-203.

24. Ballagh, *Letters,* II, 388, 400-401.

25. *White Mss.* (NYHS), I, No. 117.

26. Ballagh, *Letters,* II, 157; *Fields Papers.*

For Jefferson's plan for public education see Ford, *Jefferson's Notes,* 146-149.

Lee also offered a bill in the Virginia House of Delegates (June, 1780) "for the more general diffusion of Knowledge." Apparently no action was taken by the Assembly to carry out this suggestion. *Jour. Va. H. of D.,* sess. May-July, 1780, 44.

27. Meade, *Old Churches,* II, 141.

28. Groome, *Fauquier During Proprietorship,* 213.

29. Ballagh, *Letters,* II, 411-412.

30. James Mercer to R. H. Lee, March 5, 1789, *Lee Papers* (AL), No. 417; Lee, *Account Book,* 81, 186.

31. Ballagh, *Letters,* II, 471.

32. *Ibid.,* 343-344, 441-442.

33. *Ibid.,* 65, 266, 544.

1. See pp. 23-25.

2. See pp. 136-137.

Richard Henry seemed to take the criticism of his enemies as a matter of course and did not allow it to upset his equilibrium. In one of his letters (May, 1788) he said: "I like to reason with a reasonable man, but I disdain to notice those scribblers in the newspapers altho' they have honored me with their abuse—My attention to them will never exist whilst there is a Cat or Spaniel in the house." *Va. Histor. Reg.*, II, 104; *Lee Papers* (Houghton), No. 65.

3. Interview at Williamsburg, Va., November, 1957.

4. Burnett, *Letters*, IV, 379 n.; Ballagh, *Letters*, II, 70-71.

5. At one time, when Richard Henry was facing the false charge in the Virginia Assembly of belonging to a pro-British party, Smith tried to furnish evidence against him. See p. 147.

Lee also had an unfavorable opinion of Gouverneur Morris, and when Washington appointed Morris plenipotentiary to France, Lee voted against his confirmation. Ballagh, *Letters*, II, 198; *Jour. U. S. Senate, Exec. Proceedings*, I, 96.

6. William Bradford to James Madison, June 2, 1775, *Bradford Letter Book* (Histor. Soc. Pa.).

7. Ballagh, *Letters*, II, 123, 198; Burnett, *Letters*, V, 362 n.

8. Ballagh, *Letters*, II, 202-203.

According to Bernard Fay, Lee by 1785 had either abandoned or dissembled his wrath toward Franklin, although he termed Lee Franklin's "dearest, most faithful" and "most patient enemy." When Franklin returned to the United States that year, Lee as President of Congress came to Franklin to express "in his own name and in the name of Congress . . . his high regard for him and the joy which his fortunate arrival gave him. They embraced with tears." Fay, *The Two Franklins*, 69.

9. Both Richard Henry and Arthur Lee were accused of trying to ruin Robert Morris. This enmity was due, as was alleged, to the fact that the Secret Committee of Congress, dominated by Morris, had mainly supported Deane and Franklin in their controversy with Arthur Lee. Richard Henry Lee to Charles Lee, August 31, 1779, *Lee Papers, Misc.* (NYPL).

As has been seen, the enmity between Lee and James Mercer, which started with Lee's action at Montross against George Mercer, persisted to trouble their relations in later years. See Chapter III, pp. 28-43; Burnett, *Letters*, IV, 482, 489.

10. *Ibid.*, 309, 349.

11. Ballagh, *Letters*, I, 256, 256 n., 347; II, 205, 219, 274, 283, 306-307; *Mercy Warren Papers* (BPL), box 1; *Lee Papers* (Houghton), III, No. 60. R. H. Lee to General Nathanael Greene, Sept. 3, 1781, *Greene Papers;* Thayer, *Nathanael Greene*, 334, 428, 436.

12. Lee, *Memoir*, II, 156; Ballagh, *Letters*, II, 291.

13. *Ibid.*, I, 441-442.

Owing to a misprint in this reference, "Francis Lightfoot" is improperly used for "William."

14. Lee, *Memoir*, II, 109-110.

15. See p. 140.

16. Ballagh, *Letters*, I, 12, 127, 172-173, 199.

17. Morton, *Robert Carter, passim.*

18. Ballagh, *Letters*, II, 422-423.

19. *Ibid.;* Lee, *Memoir*, II, 225-227 (quoted).

It is true that on one occasion Monroe suspected Lee of acting on a selfish motive, and yet at other times he spoke of him in very complimentary fashion. See pp. 158-159.

20. See pp. 139, 210.

21. *Lee-Ludwell Papers* (VHS); Jefferson to R. H. Lee, February 7, 1768, Ballagh, *Letters*, II, 357.

22. *Ibid.,* 60, 82-83, 86.

23. *Fields Papers.*

24. Ballagh, *Letters*, I, 395; II, 115, 374, 542.

25. Cappon, *Adams-Jefferson Letters*, II, 612.

26. Brant, *James Madison*, I, 175; Boyd, *Jefferson's Papers*, VI, 266.

27. See p. 147.

28. Henry, *Patrick Henry*, I, 111.

29. See pp. 78-79, 183.

30. Ballagh, *Letters*, II, 331.

31. Morgan, *Patrick Henry*, 287 (quoted).

32. Boyd, *Light-Horse Harry Lee*, 164-165.

Of the other Virginians who were kindly disposed toward Lee, mention should be made of Thomas Marshall, father of the Chief Justice, George Wythe, John Augustine Washington, John Page, and Mann Page, Jr. In the *Southern Literary Messenger* (XXVII, 254, 260 ff., 328 ff.) there are listed eight letters from John Augustine Washington to Lee, and ten letters and excerpts from thirteen letters to him from John Page and Mann Page, Jr., respectively. He regarded George Wythe as one of the "chosen few of his friends." Ballagh, *Letters*, I, 265, 337.

33. *Ibid.,* II, 64.

34. Conway, *Writings of Thomas Paine*, I, 395-408; *Pa. Packet*, December 15, 1778; Ballagh, *Letters*, I, 462; II, 182, 194, 293, 579.

Richard Henry also spoke (September 24, 1780) of his "worthy friend, Tench Coxe." *Ibid.,* II, 556.

35. *Lee Chronicle*, 178; Ballagh, *Letters*, I, 82-83.

36. *Ibid.,* 345, 483.

37. For John Adams' account of his association with Richard Henry Lee during the first session of the Continental Congress and the impression he formed of him, see pp. 61-63.

38. *Ibid.,* I, 410; II, 347.

39. Dr. Page Smith, in his authoritative biography of John Adams, lists Richard Henry Lee as among the friends John Adams had loved and esteemed and had lost in the political battles of thirty years. It may be that the name "Richard Henry Lee" was intended for "Henry Lee," the mistake being a clerical or typographical error, for no evidence has been found in this study of the sources to show that there was ever any breach

in their friendship. Smith, *John Adams*, II, 906; Cunningham, *Jeffersonian Republicans*, 97.

40. Burnett, *Letters*, IV, 307-309, 307 n.

41. *Conn. Courant*, August 10-September 7, 1779; *Va. Gazette* (Purdie and Nicolson), July 17, 1779.

42. *Deane Papers*, III, 342.

43. John Adams on one occasion referred to "our phalanx." Adams, *Works of John Adams*, III, 49; Burnett, *Letters*, IV, 162.

44. Ward, *War of Rev.*, II, 560 ff.; Fitzpatrick, *George Washington Himself*, 345, 350.

45. *Jour. Cont. Cong.*, IX, 851, 853.

One of Lee's New England admirers was Nathan Dane, who expressed his high opinion of him as follows: ". . . his character serves at least in some degree to check the effect of the feeble habits and lax mode of thinking of some of his countrymen." Other Northern friends of Lee were Governor Ward of Rhode Island and Joseph Reed of Pennsylvania. Dr. Benjamin Rush and Lee were also on cordial terms for a while; but later Dr. Rush had a quarrel with Lee's brother-in-law, Dr. William Shippen, Jr., and the friendship between Lee and Dr. Rush cooled off. Butterfield, *Letters of Benjamin Rush*, I, 120-130, 121 n.; Butterfield, *Adams Papers*, III, 371.

46. Ballagh, *Letters*, I, 453-454; II, 155.

47. See p. 226.

48. See pp. 137-142.

49. Fitzpatrick, *George Washington Himself*, 350. See also Alden, *Amer. Rev.*, 199; Morison, *Oxford History*, 238.

50. See Knollenberg, *Washington and the Revolution*, 76.

51. Sparks, *Washington's Writings*, V, 493, 495-497, 510-511, 511 n.; Fitzpatrick, *George Washington Himself*, 347; Fitzpatrick, *Washington's Writings*, XI, 164-165, 493.

52. Burnett, *Cont. Cong.*, 284-285.

53. John Page in a letter to Lee (May 6, 1778) said that he had often heard that Richard Henry had made a motion against Washington. He constantly denied belief in this rumor on the ground that even if Lee had any pique against Washington, he was too good a politician and Whig to attempt to remove him from command. He believed it was a state trick of the Tories. *Lee Papers* (AL).

54. *Fields Papers;* transcript of a letter originally in the *Papers of Robert Morris*.

For a statement by Samuel Adams that might be construed as a criticism of Washington, see Cushing, *Writings of Samuel Adams*, III, 386-388.

55. James Craig to Washington, Jan. 6, 1778, *Washington Papers*, LXIV (LC).

Colonel John Fitzgerald of Washington's staff in a letter to Washington (March 17, 1778) said that he had had an interview with Charles Carroll, a member of Congress, who had heard, he said, only one of his colleagues speak disrespectfully of Washington and he was quickly silenced by the warm replies of other members. Carroll did not give the name of this would-be critic, but Fitzgerald thought that it was Washington's "friend from this State [Virginia] whose good intentions you have for some time suspected." The "friend" referred to was in all probability Richard Henry Lee. Freeman, *George Washington*, IV, 609, 609 n.; *Washington's Papers* (LC), LXIX, 115.

56. Sparks, *Life of Gouveneur Morris*, I, 169; Fitzpatrick, *George Washington Himself*, 350; Sparks, *Washington's Writings*, V, 517.

57. Lee, *Memoir*, II, 105 (quoted).

58. *Toner Transcripts, Papers of Washington* (LC), vol. 730, 293-297.

59. *Lee Transcripts*, IV, 246-247 (VHS).

60. General Lee's biographer, John Richard Alden, states that Lee at Monmouth "did his best for the American army" and that his retrograde movement there "prevented Clinton from delivering a smashing counter-attack." Alden, *General Charles Lee*, 239.

61. *Lee Papers*, I, 203, 232, 362, 367, 440, 442; II, 25, 31, 97, 237, 238; IV, 11; VI, 237 (AL); Freeman, *George Washington*, IV, 79; Ballagh, *Letters*, I, 189, 256.

62. Fitzpatrick, *Washington Himself*, 345.

63. See pp. 211-212.

64. Butterfield, *Adams Papers (Autobiography)*, III, 371.

65. *Samuel Adams Papers* (NYPL).

66. Ford, *Essays on the Constitution*, VI, 161, 177.

67. Ballagh, *Letters*, II, 419.

68. Knollenberg, *Washington and the Revolution*, 198.

It ought to be added, however, that some present-day historians of the Revolution still represent Richard Henry Lee as having been on friendly terms with Thomas Mifflin, General Horatio Gates, James Lovell, and others accused of the alleged cabal, as well as with the Adamses, reputed to be hostile to Washington. Another present-day author (John Richard Alden) thinks that it is possible that James Lovell, Samuel Adams, and Richard Henry Lee made an attempt in Congress to have Washington supplanted by Gates. Burnett, *Cont. Cong.*, 285.

69. William Gordon, when collecting material for his history of the American Revolution, after having gone through the papers of General Gates, reported that he did not find in these papers "any one letter to or from him [Gates] that contained the most distant hint of any design to remove G. W-n, and put either him [Gates] or M[ifflin] at the head of the army, nor anything of the kind in any other of his papers." Henry Steele Commager and Richard B. Morris, in their collection of documents—*The Spirit of Seventy-Six*—state as their final conclusion that there was no real plot against Washington although they include Richard Henry Lee in the list of Washington's critics. Rossman, *Thomas Mifflin and Amer. Rev.*, 135 (quoted); *Mass. Histor. Soc. Proceedings*, LXIII, 472; Commager and Morris, *The Spirit of Seventy-Six*, I, 651-652.

70. Burnett, *Letters*, III, 29; Knollenberg, *Washington and the Revolution*, 75-77.

71. Fitzpatrick, *Writings of Washington*, III, 236; Ballagh, *Letters*, I, 266, 338; II, 233.

72. *Gratz Autograph Collection* (Histor. Soc. of Pa.).

73. Fitzpatrick, *Writings of Washington*, XXIX, 285; *Pa. Packet*, October 14, 1787.

74. E. J. Lee, in his biography of Richard Henry, says that during the fight for the ratification of the Constitution there developed a coldness between Lee and Washington and the latter spoke of his old friend in "uncomplimentary fashion"; but when Washington became President the old feeling of friendship was restored. However, he does not support this statement with documentary evidence. Lee, *Lee of Va.*, 183; Bancroft, *Formation of the Cons.*, II, 443.

75. Ballagh, *Letters*, II, 517.

76. *Jour. Cont. Cong.*, II, 97; VI, 1041, 1045-1056; IX, 783-785; Lee, *Memoir*, I, 186-188.

77. Ballagh, *Letters*, II, 580-583.

CHAPTER XVII (Pages 222-238)

1. See Ch. I, p. 8, and note 27.

2. Ballagh, *Letters*, I, 13, 20, 167, 316, 320; II, 297, 396, 446, 564, 566, 567.

According to his grandson and biographer, Lee also had a reading knowledge of Greek, though confirmatory evidence of this claim has not been noted in his correspondence or other writings. Lee, *Memoir*, I, 250-251.

3. Ballagh, *Letters*, I, 195, 372-373; II, 217, 218, 261, 267, 530.

He read Mrs. Macaulay's *History of England* as each volume came from the press. Ms. letter belonging to the late Rev. Edmund Jennings Lee.

4. Ballagh, *Letters*, I, *passim*, especially 179, 313; II, *passim*, especially 81, 107, 198.

5. *Ibid.*, II, 542.

6. Among other writers mentioned are Beccaria, Delome, Hale, Holt, and Mansfield. *Ibid.*, *passim*.

7. *Ibid.*, 107, 249, 342.

8. *Lee Papers, Misc.* (NYPL); Lee, *Memoir*, I, 247, 247 n.

9. See Ch. V, p. 62; Ch. VI, pp. 78-79; Ch. XVII, p. 223. Henry, *Patrick Henry*, I, 163-164.

10. *Ibid.*

11. *Tyler's Magazine*, II, 96.

12. *W. and M. Quar.* (1), XXII, 256.

His fingers on the left hand had been shot off by an accidental discharge of a gun while he was hunting.

13. Judge Spencer Roane's *Memorandum*, in Morgan, *Patrick Henry*, 442-443 (quoted).

14. Lee, *Lee of Va.*, 190-191 (quoted); Cappon, *Adams-Jefferson Letters*, II, 369.

Lee also used a good style—clear and sometimes colorful—in his public papers and in some of his letters. His spelling and grammatical constructions were exceptionally accurate, although some misspelled words and a few slips in grammar have been noted in his letters. Thomas Jefferson, however, considered Lee's style "loose, vague, frothy, rhetorical."

15. Adams, *Works of John Adams*, II, 362.
16. Arthur Lee to R. H. Lee, May 31, 1761, *Lee Papers* (AL).
17. *Lee Papers* (AL).
18. Maclay, *Journal*, 36, 57, 70.
19. *Mag. of Lees*, IX, 75 (quoted); Carter, *Diary*, II, 1102.
20. *Lee Chronicle*, 179 (quoted).

In reading Lee's letters and official papers and in following his public career, one gets the impression that this characterization of him (by a modern writer) is correct: "Lee represented what the classically trained revolutionary generation meant when it spoke of Roman virtues." Spiller, *Lit. Hist. of U. S.*, I, 143.

21. Ballagh, *Letters*, II, 292, 368; Lee, *Account Book*, 65, 71, 83, 172, 175, 177, 183, 203-203b, 241.
22. Ballagh, *Letters*, I, 249; II, 51, 104, 162-163, 225, 393, 407.
23. *Ibid.*, II, 49-50, 304, 393, 395, 397, 495.
24. Meade, *Old Churches*, II, 141, 152; Morton, *Robert Carter*, II, 231.
25. See p. 232.
26. There are still extant a few letters that passed between Lee and his two oldest sons, Thomas and Ludwell, and they are the only record we have of the correspondence between him and his children.
27. Meade, *Old Churches*, II, 285-286, 319; Ballagh, *Letters*, I, 384.
28. *Ibid.*, 70-71.
29. *Mag. of Lees*, I, 48.
30. Ballagh, *Letters*, I, 258, 287-288.
31. *Lee Papers* (Huntington Library, photo, Library WVU).
32. William Shippen, Jr., to R. H. Lee, August 28, 1780, *Lee Papers* (AL); *Lee Chronicle*, 215.
33. *Mag. of Lees*, XI, 49-50; Ballagh, *Letters*, I, 280, 288.
34. *Stevens, Facsimiles and Transcripts* (LC). Great Britain. Auchland MSS. October 4, 5, 1777.
35. Ford, *Letters of William Lee*, I, 241, 243.
36. Ballagh, *Letters*, II, 199, 289.
37. *Mag. of Lees*, I, 49-50.
38. *Franklin Papers* (AL, typed), II, 43, 156.

In speaking of Ludwell, after his first meeting with him, Lafayette said that he had seen him for only a few minutes but that he knew "enough of him to be very desirous of making him my [his] friend."

39. Henry, *Patrick Henry*, III, 414.
40. G. W. P. Custis to George Washington, June 8, July 7, 1797, *Va. Mag. Hist. and Biog.*, XX, 300.
41. *Lee Account Book* (Huntington Library, microfilm), 288.
42. *Reg. Va. Assembly*, 38, 41, 43, 45, 47, 49, 50, 52, 54; *Mag. of Lees*, I, 50.

According to some recent authorities on this period, Richard Henry in his last years switched his allegiance to the party of Hamilton. The sources examined in this study do not affirm but strongly deny this contention. While in the Senate, Lee opposed Hamilton's proposals for a national bank and the assumption of the debts of the states. In fact he did not support any of the controversial measures of Hamilton's financial policy. Miller, *The Federalist Era*, 7, 102. See Ch. XIV, pp. 191-192.

43. *Reg. Va. Assembly,* 23, 25, 28, 30.

The sources examined give us very little information as to the career of Francis Lightfoot the younger. He seems never to have been active in public affairs.

44. The first wife of Thomas (1758-1805) was Mildred Washington, daughter of John Augustine Washington, a brother of the General. His second wife was Eliza Ashton Brent.

Ludwell (1760-1836) married Flora Lee, the daughter of his uncle, Philip Ludwell Lee.

Mary (1764-1792) married William Augustine Washington, son of Augustine Washington, half-brother of George.

Hannah (ca. 1766—ca. 1801) married Corbin Washington, son of John Augustine Washington.

Anne (1770-1804) married her third cousin, Charles Lee, the brother of "Light-Horse Harry." Her husband was an eminent lawyer and served as counsel in the case of *Marbury vs. Madison* and in the trial of Aaron Burr. He was also United States Attorney General for a while under both Washington and Adams.

Henrietta (1773-1803 or 1804) married first, Richard Lee Turberville; secondly, the Rev. William Moffett of South Carolina.

Sara (1775-1798) married her third cousin Edmund Jennings Lee.

Cassius (1779-1798) died unmarried.

Francis Lightfoot (1782-1850) married two sisters, Elizabeth and Jane Fitzgerald. *Lee Chronicle,* 181, 182-183; *Shippen Papers, Scrap Book* (LC); *Mag. of Lees,* IV, 70; Fitzpatrick, *Writings of Washington,* XXII, 30.

45. Ballagh, *Letters,* II, *passim.*

46. *Ibid.,* 466; *Lee Papers* (YL, Xeroxed), *Account of Estate,* 19-21, 44; Lee, *Account Book, passim.*

There was a notice in the *Virginia Gazette* (Rind), November 29, 1770, of two runaway indentured servants, one of whom belonged to Richard Henry Lee. The notice was signed by Daniel Morgan, doubtless Lee's manager.

47. At one time (1776 and probably also later) Lee was engaged in the manufacture of salt from water taken from the creek at Chantilly. *Lee Transcripts* (VHS), II, 45; Lee, *Account Book,* 32, 42, 52, 79.

48. There were five rooms on the first floor, including a large hall furnished as a sitting room. On the second floor, there were four large rooms and one small one; and on the third floor, two rooms. The outbuildings included barns, a sheep pen, a blacksmith shop, and apparently a tannery and a distillery for making apple brandy. Armes, *Stratford Hall,* 106, 283-284; Lee, *Account Book,* 106, 158, 197, 198.

At the death of Philip Ludwell Lee, his daughter Flora inherited the Chantilly estate. It was afterwards sold to "Light-Horse Harry" Lee, who sold it to Joseph Watson. The house was later dismantled and razed, and a tree is all that now marks its site. Armes, *Stratford Hall,* 283; *Westmoreland Court Papers* (VSL), Sept. 22, 1797.

49. Mason, *Jour. of Young Lady of Va.*, 22-23, 25-29, 45, 50.

50. Thomas Lee Shippen to Dr. William Shippen, Jr., *Shippen Papers, Scrap Book* (LC).

51. Fithian, *Journal*, 38, 164, 222, 233, 264.

On one occasion Fithian seemed to have been bored by the conversation carried on by his young associates. He complained that the talk of the evening was mainly about dogs and horses, with "Toddy constantly circulating."

52. See p. 5 and note 44 above.

53. Ballagh, *Letters*, I, 375-376.

54. Fithian, *Journal*, 42-46, 68, 117, 164, 165, 250, 251-252; Wilstach, *Potomac Landings*, 233-234.

Several years later (1781) Lee noted in his account book a payment to be made to Mr. Christian for teaching dancing to his own children and one made for teaching his two nieces at Stratford, for whom he had been acting as guardian since the death of their father, Philip Ludwell Lee. Lee, *Account Book*, 390.

55. Fithian, *Journal*, 38.

56. *Fields Papers;* Ballagh, *Letters*, I, 265.

57. *Ibid.*, II, 30, 408.

One of his sons was with him for a while during the latter part of his year as president. See p. 158.

58. *Ibid.*, I, 454.

59. Carman, *American Husbandry*, I, 242-245; quoted by L. H. Gipson, *Va. Mag. of Hist. and Biog.*, LXIX, 260.

60. See pp. 9, 137-138.

61. *Cont. Cong. Expenses of Delegates* (Mss, VSL).

62. In a letter to brother Arthur (February 11, 1779) he said, "My family suffers immensely by my absence," and in writing to Patrick Henry a few months later he declared that his public service was rendered at a financial sacrifice. Ballagh, *Letters*, II, 34-35.

63. He was probably without a servant when he was in Williamsburg and Richmond.

64. Lee, *Account Book*, *passim*, especially 15, 406, 408, 427.

In November, 1778, he paid the lady at whose house he was lodging 540 dollars for eighteen weeks of board for his servant, his horses, and himself.

65. Rush, *Autobiography*, 151; *Mercy Warren Papers* (BPL).

66. As early as 1761, Arthur, in a letter to Richard Henry, spoke of him as suffering from epilepsy. This must have been a wrong diagnosis, however, for no further reference to this affliction has been found in any of the later documents or contemporary accounts. Arthur Lee to R. H. Lee, *Lee Papers* (AL).

67. Ford, *Letters of William Lee*, II, 490; Ballagh, *Letters*, II, *passim;* Lee, *Account Book*, 221.

68. See p. 194.

69. See p. 180.

Bibliography

The lists given below include only those works and sources to which reference is made in the footnotes. The abbreviations on the left are those used in the footnotes. Many of the citations to the secondary sources are to source materials which appear in these works as quotations or excerpts from the documents.

NEWSPAPERS

Conn. Courant. The Connecticut Courant and Weekly Intelligencer.
Gazette of U. S. The Gazette of the United States (New York).
Md. Gazette. The Maryland Gazette.
N. Y. Evening Post. The New York Evening Post.
N. Y. Times. New York Times (1962).
Pa. Chronicle. The Pennsylvania Chronicle.
Pa. Packet. The Pennsylvania Packet or General Advertiser.
Richmond Examiner. The Richmond Examiner.
Va. Gazette (Dixon and Hunter). The Virginia Gazette (Dixon and Hunter).
Va. Gazette (Purdie). The Virginia Gazette (Purdie).
Va. Gazette (Purdie and Dixon). The Virginia Gazette (Purdie and Dixon).
Va. Gazette (Purdie and Nicolson). The Virginia Gazette (Purdie and Nicolson).
Va. Gazette (Rind). The Virginia Gazette (Rind).

MANUSCRIPTS

John Adams Papers (microfilm).
Samuel Adams Papers (NYPL).   The Papers of Samuel Adams. New York Public Library.
Amer. Papers. Bancroft Transcripts (NYPL).   American Papers. Bancroft Transcripts, 3 vols. New York Public Library.
Bancroft Calendar, Samuel Adams Papers (NYPL).   Bancroft's Calendar of Samuel Adams Papers. New York Public Library.
Bancroft Transcripts (LC).   Bancroft Transcripts.   Board of Trade Papers. Official Correspondence, 1752-1753. Library of Congress.
Bradford Letter Book (Histor. Soc. of Pa.).   Letters of William Bradford, Jr., to and from James Madison, Jr., Historical Society of Pennsylvania.
Carter, *Diary* (AL).   Diary of Colonel Landon Carter.   Alderman Library.
Chamberlin Collection (BPL).   The Chamberlin Collection. Boston Public Library.

286

Com. Book, Papers of Cont. Cong. Committee Book, Papers of the Continental Congress. National Archives.

Com. on For. Affairs Letters. Letters of the Committee [of the Continental Congress] on Foreign Affairs . . ., 1776-1782, vol. I, National Archives.

Cont. Cong. Expenses of Delegates (VSL). The Continental Congress. Expenses of Delegates. Virginia State Library.

Coppett Collection (PUL). The Andre de Coppett Collection. Library of Princeton University.

Emmett Collection (NYPL). The Emmett Collection of Manuscripts. New York Public Library.

Ex. Jour. Va. Council (AL). Executive Journal of the Virginia Council. Photostatic copy of a manuscript in the British Public Record Office. Alderman Library.

Fauquier Co. Rec. Deed Book (VSL). Fauquier County Records. Deed Book No. 2 (photostat). Virginia State Library.

Fell, *Diary* (LC). John Fell, Diary, November 29, 1778-November 29, 1779. Library of Congress.

Fields Papers. Lee Papers in possession of Dr. J. E. Fields, Joliet, Illinois.

Franklin Papers (AL). Franklin Papers. American Philosophical Society, Philadelphia. Typed copy, Alderman Library.

Genesis Dec. of Ind. (LC). Genesis of the Declaration of Independence (photo). Library of Congress.

Gibbon, *Introductio* (VHS). John Gibbon, Introductio ad Latinam blasoniam (1682). Photographic extract in the Library of the Virginia Historical Society.

Gratz Autograph Collection (Histor. Soc. of Pa.). Simon Grantz Autograph Collection. Historical Society of Pennsylvania.

Greene Papers (Clements). Nathaniel Greene Papers. The Clements Library, University of Michigan (films).

Jefferson Papers. Coolidge Collection (MHS). Jefferson Papers. Coolidge Collection. Massachusetts Historical Society.

Knox Papers (MHS). Knox Papers. Massachusetts Historical Society.

Lamb Papers (NYHS). Lamb Papers. New York Historical Society.

Lee, Account Book (Huntington Library). Account Book of Richard Henry Lee. Henry E. Huntington Library (microfilm).

Lee, Fragment (AL). Liberal fragments of a speech written by R. H. Lee. Alderman Library.

Lee Bible (VHS). Bible of Richard Henry Lee. (Birth list of Thomas Lee's children) Virginia Historical Society.

Lee Letter (Shepherdstown, W. Va.). Letter of R. H. Lee borrowed from the late Rev. Edmund Jennings Lee of Shepherdstown, West Virginia.

Lee Letter (VHS). Photo. Letter of Richard Henry Lee to the president of the Virginia Senate. Manuscript in Leland Stanford Library. Photostat in Library of Virginia Historical Society.

Lee MSS (LC). William Lee Manuscripts. Library of Congress.

Lee Papers (AL). Lee Papers. Alderman Library.

Lee Papers (APS). *Correspondence of Richard Henry Lee and of Arthur Lee.* Library of American Philosophical Society, Philadelphia.

Lee Papers. Har. (photo. AL). *Lee Papers.* Library of Harvard University. Photostats in the Alderman Library.

Lee Papers (Houghton). *Lee Papers.* Houghton Library, Harvard.

Lee Papers (Huntington Library, photo.). *Richard Henry Lee Papers.* Henry E. Huntington Library, photostats, West Virginia University Library.

Lee Papers, Misc. (NYPL). *Lee Papers, Miscellaneous Collection.* New York Public Library.

Lee Papers (YL, Xeroxed). *Lee Papers. Executor's Account of Richard Henry Lee's Estate* (Yale Library, Xeroxed).

Lee Transcripts (VHS). *Transcripts of the Lee Family Papers, 1761-1882,* 6 vols. Library of the Virginia Historical Society.

Lee-Ludwell Papers (VHS). *Lee-Ludwell Papers.* Library of Virginia Historical Society.

Madison Papers (LC). *The Papers of James Madison, 1723-1846,* 90 vols. Library of Congress.

Mason Papers (photo., LC). *George Mason Papers.* Photostats, Library of Congress.

Memoranda (VSL). *Memoranda* in Virginia State Library.

Misc. Papers (MHS). *Miscellaneous Papers.* Massachusetts Historical Society.

Papers Cont. Cong. (Nat. Ar.). *Papers of the Continental Congress.* National Archives.

Pecatone Papers (VHS). *Pecatone Papers, 1758-1898.* Library of Virginia Historical Society.

Pa. Misc. Papers (LC). *Pennsylvania Miscellaneous Papers.* Library of Congress.

Personal Papers, Misc. (LC). *Personal Papers, Miscellaneous.* Library of Congress.

P.R.O., C.O., 5, 1331. British *Public Record Office. Colonial Office,* Class 5, No. 1331.

Randolph, "Hist. of Va." Edmund Randolph, "Manuscript History of Virginia." Library of the Virginia Historical Society.

Shippen Papers. Scrap Book (LC). *The Shippen Papers. Scrap Book.* Library of Congress.

Signers Dec. Ind. Collection (PUL). *Signers of the Declaration of Independence Collection.* Library of Princeton University.

Sparks Mss. Har. (photo., AL). *Sparks Manuscripts.* Library of Harvard University, photostats, Alderman Library.

Stevens Facsimiles and Transcripts (LC). *B. F. Stevens's Collection of Facsimiles and Transcripts of Manuscripts in the Archives of England, France, Holland and Spain Relating to America, 1763-1783.* Library of Congress and other libraries.

Toner Transcripts, Papers of Washington (LC). *Toner Transcripts of the Papers of George Washington.* Library of Congress.

Unclassified ms. photo (VHS). *Unclassified manuscript.* photo.
Virginia Historical Society.

U. S. Congress Papers (microfilm). *United States Congress Papers.* Clements Library. Microfilm, West Virginia University Library.

U. S. Rev. Papers (LC). *United States Revolution Papers.* Library of Congress.

Va. Misc. Records (LC). *Virginia Miscellaneous Records.* Library of Congress.

Wallace Papers (AL). *Wallace Papers.* Alderman Library.

Mercy Warren Papers (BPL). *Mercy Warren Papers.* Boston Public Library.

Washington Papers (LC). *The Papers of George Washington.* Library of Congress.

Waterston Autographs (MHS). *The Waterston Autographs.* Massachusetts Historical Society.

Weedon Papers (APS). *George Weedon Papers.* Library American Philosophical Society, Philadelphia.

Weedon Papers (Brown). *The Weedon Papers.* Annmary Brown Library, Brown University.

Westmoreland Co. Deeds and Wills (VSL). *Westmoreland County Deeds and Wills, 1761-1768* (photostats). Virginia State Library.

Westmoreland Co. Order Book (VSL). *Westmoreland County Order Book, 1752-1755* (photostats). Virginia State Library.

Westmoreland Co. Orders (VSL). *Westmoreland County Orders, 1761-1764* (photostats). Virginia State Library.

Westmoreland Court Papers (VSL). *Westmoreland Court Papers* (photostats). Virginia State Library.

Westmoreland Papers (Montross). *Westmoreland Papers.* Clerk's Office, Montross, Virginia.

Westmoreland Per. Prop. Rec. 1782 (VSL). *Westmoreland County Personal Property Records, 1782.* Original ms., Virginia State Library.

White Mss. (NYHS). *William White Manuscripts* (Protestant Episcopal Church Archives), New York Historical Society.

DOCUMENTS AND OTHER SOURCE MATERIALS

Acts Va. General Assembly. *Acts Passed at a General Assembly of the Commonwealth of Virginia; Begun October 19, 1789.*

Adams, Works of John Adams. Charles Francis Adams, ed., *The Works of John Adams,* 10 vols. (1850-1856).

American Husbandry. Harry J. Carman, ed., *American Husbandry* (1775, 1939).

Ames, Works of Fisher Ames. Seth Ames, ed., *The Works of Fisher Ames with a Selection from his Speeches,* 2 vols. (1854).

Annals of Congress. Joseph Gales, comp., *The Debates and Proceedings in the Congress of the United States* (1834).

Annual Register. *The Annual Register of World Events.*

Armes, *Nancy Shippen.* Ethel Marie Armes, *Nancy Shippen: Her Journal Book* (1935).

Ballagh, *Letters.* James Curtis Ballagh, ed., *Letters of Richard Henry Lee,* 2 vols. (1911-1914).

Bland Papers. The Bland Papers, a selection from the manuscripts of Colonel Theodorick Bland, Jr., edited by J. W. Campbell, 2 vols. (1840).

Bogart and Thompson, *Readings.* E. L. Bogart and C. M. Thompson, *Readings in the Economic History of the United States* (1916).

Boyd, *Dec. of Ind.* Julian P. Boyd, *The Declaration of Independence* (1945).

Boyd, *Jefferson's Papers.* Julian P. Boyd, ed., *The Papers of Thomas Jefferson* (in progress, 1950——).

Brock, *Official Letters of Alexander Spotswood.* R. A. Brock, *The Official Letters of Alexander Spotswood* (Virginia Historical Society Collection, Vol. I), 1882.

Brown, *Truths.* S. J. Brown, *We Hold These Truths* (1948).

Brydon, *Virginia's Mother Church.* George Maclaren Brydon, *Virginia's Mother Church,* 2 vols. (1947-1952).

Burk, *Hist. of Va.* John Daly Burk, *The History of Virginia,* 4 vols. (1804-1816). Petersburg, Va.

Burnaby, *Travels.* Andrew Burnaby, *Travels through the Middle Settlements in North America in the Years 1759 and 1760* (1775, reprinted 1960). Ithaca, N. Y.

Burnett, *Letters.* Edmund C. Burnett, ed., *Letters of Members of the Continental Congress,* 8 vols. (1921-1936). Washington, D. C.

Butterfield, *Adams Papers.* Lyman Henry Butterfield, *et al.,* editors, *The Adams Papers: Diary and Autobiography of John Adams,* 4 vols. (1961).

Butterfield, *Letters of Benjamin Rush.* Lyman Henry Butterfield, ed., *Letters of Benjamin Rush, 1745-1813,* 2 vols., (1951).

Cadbury, "Richard Penn," *DAB.* Henry J. Cadbury, "Richard Penn," *Dictionary of American Biography.*

Cal. Franklin Papers. Calendar of the Papers of Benjamin Franklin, 5 vols. (1908).

Cal. Va. State Papers. Calendar of Virginia State Papers and Other Manuscripts, from January 1, 1782, to April 15, 1869, 11 vols. (1883-1893).

Cappon, *Adams-Jefferson Letters.* Lester Jesse Cappon, *The Adams-Jefferson Letters* (1959).

Carter, Landon. Jack P. Greene, ed., *The Diary of Landon Carter of Sabine Hall, 1752-1778,* 2 vols. (1965).

Commons Jour. Journal of the House of Commons.

Connor, *Autobiography of Benj. Rush.* George W. Conner, ed., *The Autobiography of Benjamin Rush* (1948).

Cons. of U. S. The Constitution of the United States.

Conway, *Writings of Thomas Paine.* Moncure Daniel Conway, *The Writings of Thomas Paine,* 2 vols. (1894).

Curwen, *Journal. The Journal and Letters of Samuel Curwen, 1715-1802,* ed. by George Atkinson Ward (1842).

Cushing, *Writings of Samuel Adams.*   Harry Alonzo Cushing, *The Writings of Samuel Adams,* 4 vols. (1904-1908).

Deane Papers.   *The Deane Papers, 1774-1790,* 5 vols. New York Historical Society *Collections,* vols. XIX-XXIII (1886-1890).

Dickinson, *Farmer's Letters.*   John Dickinson, *Letters from a Farmer in Pennsylvania to the Inhabitants of the British Colonies* (1768).

Donnan, *Documents.*   Elizabeth Donnan, *Documents Illustrative of the Slave Trade to America,* 4 vols. (1930-1935).

Ex. Jour. Va. Council.   *The Executive Journal of the Virginia Council.*

Ex. Letter Book.   *Executive Letter Book.*   *Letter Book of Governor Benjamin Harrison, 1781-1782.*

Fithian, *Journal.*   Hunter Dickinson Farish, ed., *Journal and Letters of Philip Vickers Fithian* (1943).

Fitzpatrick, *Washington's Diaries.*   John Clements Fitzpatrick, ed., *The Diaries of George Washington, 1748-1799,* 4 vols. (1926).

Force, *Amer. Archives,* 4th series.   Peter Force, *American Archives,* 4th series, 6 vols. (1837-1853).

Ford, *Dickinson's Writings.*   Paul Leicester Ford, *The Writings of John Dickinson* (1895).

Ford, *Essays on the Constitution.*   Paul Leicester Ford, *Essays on the Constitution of the United States* (1892).

Ford, *Jefferson's Autobiography.*   Paul Leicester Ford, ed., *Autobiography of Thomas Jefferson, 1743-1790.*

Ford, *Jefferson's Work.*   Paul Leicester Ford, ed., *The Works of Thomas Jefferson,* 12 vols. (1904-1905).

Ford, *Letters of Joseph Jones.*   Worthington C. Ford, ed., *Letters of Joseph Jones of Virginia, 1777-1787* (1889).

Ford, *Letters of William Lee.*   Worthington Chauncey Ford, ed., *Letters of William Lee, 1766-1783,* 3 vols. (1891).

Galloway, *Reflections on Amer. Rebellion.*   Joseph Galloway, *Historical and Political Reflections on the Rise and Progress of the American Rebellion* (1780).

Genealogist's Mag.   *Genealogist's Magazine.*

Goodwin, *Williamsburg.*   Rutherford Goodwin, *Williamsburg in Virginia* (1940).

Hansard, *Parl. Hist.*   T. C. Hansard, *The Parliamentary History of England from the Earliest Period to the Year 1803,* XVI (1803).

Harrower, *Diary, Amer. Histor. Rev.*   "The Diary of John Harrower," *American Historical Review,* VI, 65-107.

Hart, *Contemporaries.*   Albert Bushnell Hart, *American History Told by Contemporaries,* 4 vols. (1897-1901).

Harwell, *Com. of Safety, Westmoreland and Fincastle.*   Richard Barksdale Harwell, ed., *The Committees of Safety of Westmoreland and Fincastle. Proceedings of the County Committees, 1774-1776* (1956).

Hening, *Statutes.*   William Waller Hening, comp., *The Statutes at Large of Virginia from 1619 to 1808,* 13 vols. (1819-1823).

Hogg, *Geneal. Mag.*   O. F. G. Hogg,   "The Lees of Virginia," *The Genealogist's Magazine,* vol. XIII.

Hunt, *Madison's Writings.* Gaillard Hunt, ed., *The Writings of James Madison,* 9 vols. (1900-1910).

Hutchinson and Rachal, *Madison Papers.* *The Papers of James Madison,* edited by William T. Hutchinson and William M. E. Rachal (1962----).

James, *Doc. Hist.* Charles J. James, *Documentary History of the Struggle for Religious Liberty in Virginia* (1900).

Jenyns, *Objection to Taxation.* [Soame Jenyns], *The Objection to the Taxation of our American Colonies by the Legislature of Great Britain Briefly Considered* (1765).

Jour. Commrs. Trade and Plantations. *Journal of the Commissioners for Trade and Plantations,* January, 1754-December, 1758, Public Record Office, vol. 65.

Jour. H. of B. *Journals of the House of Burgesses of Virginia, 1619-1776,* 13 vols. (1905-1915).

Jour. U. S. Senate. *Journal of the Senate of the United States of America* (1820).

Jour. U. S. Senate, Ex. Proceedings. *Journal of the Executive Proceedings of the Senate of the United States of America,* vol. I.

Jour. Va. H. of D. *Journal of the House of Delegates of the Commonwealth of Virginia.* (The session in each case is indicated in the footnote references.)

Jour. Va. Senate. *Journal of the Senate of Virginia.*

Jour. Cont. Cong. *Journals of the Continental Congress, 1774-1789,* 34 vols. (1904-1938).

Jour. Va. Council. *Journals of the Council of State of Virginia,* 3 vols. (1931-1932).

Kalm, *America of 1750.* Adolph B. Benson, ed., *The America of 1750; Peter Kalm's Travels in North America,* 2 vols. (1937).

Knox, *Claim of Colonies.* [Wm. Knox], *The Claim of the Colonies to an Exemption from Internal Taxes Imposed by Authority of Parliament Examined* (1765).

Lee, *Farmer's and Monitor's Letters.* Richard Henry Lee, *The Farmer's and Monitor's Letters to the Inhabitants of the British Colonies* (1769).

Lee, *Letters,* I. Richard Henry Lee, *Letters from the Federal Farmer to the Republican* (1787).

Lee, *Letters,* II. Richard Henry Lee, *Additional Letters from the Federal Farmer to the Republican* (1788).

Leg. Jour. Va. Council. *Legislative Journals of the Council of Colonial Virginia,* 3 vols. (1918-1919).

Maclay, *Journal.* Edgar S. Maclay, ed., *The Journal of William Maclay, 1789-1791* (1927).

Mag. Amer. Hist. *Magazine of American History.*

Mag. of Lees. *Magazine of the Society of the Lees of Virginia,* eleven vols. bound as three.

Mason, *Jour. of Young Lady of Va.* Emily V. Mason, ed., *Journal of a Young Lady of Virginia* (Mrs. Lucinda Lee Orr), 1782 (1788).

Maury, *Mem. of Huguenot Family.* Ann Fontaine Maury, *Memoirs of a Huguenot Family,* translated and compiled from the autobiography of

Rev. James Fontaine and other family papers (1852, revised by W. M. L. Hutchinson, 2 vols., 1915).

Minutes Va. H. of D., 1781-83.   *Minutes of the Virginia House of Delegates, 1781-83.*

Morgan, *Prologue to Revolution.*   Edmund S. Morgan, *Prologue to Revolution: Sources and Documents on the Stamp Act Crisis* (1959).

Morison, *Sources and Documents.*   S. E. Morison, ed., *Sources and Documents Illustrating the American Revolution, 1764-1788, and the formation of the Federal Constitution* (1923).

"*Munford's The Candidates.*"   John B. Hubbell and Douglas Adair, editors, "Robert Munford's *The Candidates: or the Humors of a Virginia Election* (1770)," *William and Mary Historical Quarterly,* third series, V.

N. Y. Colonial Doc.   *New York Colonial Documents.*

Niles, *Principles and Acts.*   Hezekiah Niles, *Principles and Acts of the Revolution in America* (1822).

Old South Leaflets.   *Old South Leaflets.*

Official Letters of Va. Governors.   *Official Letters of the Governors of the State of Virginia,* July, 1776-February 1, 1783, 3 vols. (1926-1929).

Pendleton, "*Autobiography.*"   Edmund Pendleton's "Autobiography," *Richmond Examiner,* April 11, 1928.

Pa. Mag. Hist. and Biog.   *Pennsylvania Magazine of History and Biography.*

Perry, *Va. Church Papers.*   William Stevens Perry, ed., *Papers Relating to the History of the Church in Virginia, 1650-1776* (1870).

Pickering, *Statutes.*   Danby Pickering, *Statutes at Large* (1762-1807).

Proceedings Va. Con. (March, 1775).   *The Proceedings of the Convention of Delegates for the Colony of Virginia.*   March 20-27, 1775.   Reprint in 1816.

Proceedings Va. Con. (July-Aug., 1775).   *Proceedings of the Virginia Convention held at Richmond, July 17-August 26, 1775.*

Proceedings Va. Conven. of 1776.   *The Proceedings of the Convention of Delegates Held . . . in the Colony of Virginia . . . 1776.*

Rosenberger, *Va. Reader.*   Francis Coleman Rosenberger, *Virginia Reader* (1948).

Sanderson, *Signers Dec. Ind.*   John Sanderson, *Sanderson's Biography of the Signers to the Declaration of Independence.* Revised edition by Robert T. Conrad (1865).

Schoepf, *Travel in Confederation.*   Johann David Schoepf, *Travel in the Confederation* (1783-1784), edited by Alfred J. Morrison, 2 vols. (1911).

Secret Jour. Cong.   *Secret Journal of the Acts and Proceedings of Congress,* 4 vols. (1821).

So. Lit. Messenger.   *Southern Literary Messenger.*

Sparks, *Franklin's Works.*   Jared Sparks, ed., *The Works of Benjamin Franklin* (1856).

Sparks, *Rev. Dip. Cor.*   Jared Sparks, *The Diplomatic Correspondence of the American Revolution,* 12 vols. (1929).

Sparks, *Washington's Writings.*   Jared Sparks, ed., *The Writings of George Washington,* 12 vols. (1834-1847).

Syrett, *Hamilton Papers.* Harold C. Syrett and Jacob E. Cook, editors, *The Papers of Alexander Hamilton* (1961———).

Tyler, *Letters and Times.* Lyon G. Tyler, *Letters and Times of the Tylers,* 3 vols. (1884-1896).

Tyler's Magazine. Tyler's Historical and Genealogical Magazine.

Va. Histor. Reg. William Maxwell, *The Virginia Historical Register and Literary Advertiser.*

Va. Mag. Hist. and Biog. Virginia Magazine of History and Biography.

Watson, *Men and Times of Rev.* Winslow C. Watson, ed., *Men and Times of the Revolution or Memoirs of Elkanah Watson,* 2nd ed. (1856).

Westmoreland Association. The Westmoreland Association.

W. *and M. Quar.* (1) (2) (3). *William and Mary Historical Quarterly,* First series (1), Second series (2), Third series (3).

Wright and Tingling, *Quebec to Carolina.* Louis B. Wright and Marion Tingling, eds., *Quebec to Carolina in 1785-1786; Being the Travel Diary and Observations of Robert Hunter, Jr., A Young Merchant of London* (1943).

SECONDARY SOURCES

Abernethy, "John Robinson," *DAB.* Thomas Perkins Abernethy, "John Robinson," *Dictionary of American Biography.*

Abernethy, *Western Lands.* Thomas Perkins Abernethy, *Western Lands and the American Revolution* (1937).

Alden, *Amer. Rev.* John Richard Alden, *The American Revolution, 1775-1783* (1954).

Alden, *General Charles Lee.* John Richard Alden, *General Charles Lee: Traitor or Patriot?* (1951).

Alden, *South in Rev.* John Richard Alden, *The South in the Revolution, 1763-1789* (1957).

Alvord, *Miss. Valley in Brit. Politics.* Clarence Wentworth Alvord, *The Mississippi Valley in British Politics,* 2 vols. (1917).

Amer. Heritage: Book of Rev. The American Heritage: Book of the Revolution (1958).

Amer. Histor. Rev. The American Historical Review.

Andrews, *Virginia.* Matthew P. Andrews, *Virginia, the Old Dominion* (1937).

An. Rept. Amer. Histor. Asso. Annual Report of the American Historical Association (1901), I.

Armentrout, *Va. Finance* (AL). Mary Travers Armentrout, "A Political Study of Virginia Finance, 1781-1789." Maunscript dissertation, Alderman Library, University of Virginia.

Armes, *Stratford Hall.* Ethel Marie Armes, *Stratford Hall, the Great House of the Lees* (1936).

Atlantic Monthly. The Atlantic Monthly, LXXVII.

Bailey, *Ohio Co.* Kenneth P. Bailey, *The Ohio Company of Virginia* (1939).

Ballagh, *White Servitude.*   James Curtis Ballagh, *White Servitude in the Colony of Virginia* (1895).

Bancroft, *Formation of the Cons.*   George Bancroft, *History of the Formation for the Constitution of the United States of America,* 2 vols. (1882).

Bancroft, *Hist. U. S.*   George Bancroft, *History of the United States of America,* 6 vols., (1876, 1883).

Beale, *Stratford.*   George Beale, *Stratford: The Great House.*

Becker, *Dec. of Ind.*   Carl L. Becker, *The Declaration of Independence* (1922).

Beer, *Brit. Col. Policy.*   G. L. Beer, *British Colonial Policy* (1907).

Bemis, *Dip. Amer. Rev.*   Samuel Flagg Bemis, *The Diplomacy of the American Revolution* (1935).

Biog. Direct. of Cong.   *Biographical Directory of the American Congress, 1774-1961* (1961).

Botta, *War of Independence.*   Charles Botta, *History of the War of the Independence of the United States of America,* 2 vols. (1826).

Boyd, *Light-Horse Harry Lee.*   Thomas Boyd, *Light-Horse Harry Lee* (1931).

Boyd, "Silas Deane," *W. and M. Quar.* (3).   Julian P. Boyd, "Silas Deane: Death by a Kindly Teacher or Treason," *William and Mary Quarterly,* 3rd series, vol. XVI (1959).

Brant, *James Madison.*   Irving Brant, *James Madison,* I (1941), III (1950).

Brenaman, *Hist. Va. Conven.*   J. N. Brenaman, *A History of Virginia Conventions* (1902).

Brown and Brown, *Va.*   Robert E. and B. Katherine Brown, *Virginia, 1705-1786; Democracy or Aristocracy?* (1964).

Brydon, *Virginia's Mother Church.*   George Maclaren Brydon, *Virginia's Mother Church,* 2 vols. (1947-1952).

Burnett, *Cont. Cong.*   Edmund Cody Burnett, *The Continental Congress* (1941).

Burnett, "Richard Henry Lee," *DAB.*   Edmund Cody Burnett, "Richard Henry Lee," *Dictionary of American Biography.*

Cadbury, "Richard Penn," *DAB.*   Harry J. Cadbury, "Richard Penn," *Dictionary of American Biography.*

Campbell, *Hist. of Va.*   Charles Campbell, *History of the Colony and Ancient Dominion of Virginia* (1860).

Carson, *Histor. Shrines of Va.*   William Edward Carson, *Historic Shrines of Virginia* (1933).

Chitwood, *Colonial Amer.*   Oliver P. Chitwood, *A History of Colonial America*   (1961).

Chitwood, *Justice in Colonial Va.*   O. P. Chitwood, *Justice in Colonial Virginia* (1905).

Chitwood and Owsley, *Short History.*   O. P. Chitwood and Frank L. Owsley, *A Short History of the American People,* I (1955).

Commager and Morris, *Spirit of 'Seventy-Six.*   Henry Steele Commager and Richard B. Morris, *The Spirit of 'Seventy-Six; the Story of the American Revolution as Told by Contemporaries,* 2 vols. (1958).

The Commonwealth. *The Commonwealth, The Magazine of Virginia.*

Conway, *Edmund Randolph.* Moncure Daniel Conway, *Omitted Chapters of History Disclosed in the Life and Papers of Edmund Randolph* (1888).

Corner, *William Shippen, Jr.* Betsey Copping Corner, *William Shippen, Jr., Pioneer in Medical Education* (1934).

Cresson, *James Monroe.* William Penn Cresson, *James Monroe* (1946).

Cunningham, *Jeffersonian Republicans.* Noble Cunningham, *Jeffersonian Republicans* (1957).

D.A.B. *The Dictionary of American Biography.*

Doniol, *Histoire.* Henri Doniol, *Histoire de la Participation de la France à l'establissement des Etats-Unis d'Amerique,* 5 vols. (1886-1892).

Dunaway, *Hist. of Pa.* Wayland Fuller Dunaway, *A History of Pennsylvania* (1935).

Eckenrode, "Francis Lightfoot Lee," *DAB.* Hamilton J. Eckenrode, "Francis Lightfoot Lee," *Dictionary of American Biography.*

Eckenrode, *The Randolphs.* Hamilton J. Eckenrode, *The Randolphs* (1946).

Eckenrode, *Rev. in Va.* Hamilton J. Eckenrode, *The Revolution in Virginia* (1916).

Eckenrode, *Separation Church and State.* Hamilton J. Eckenrode, *The Separation of Church and State in Virginia* (1910).

Evans, "Planter Indebtedness," *W. and M. Quar.* (3). Emory G. Evans, "Planter Indebtedness and the Coming of the Revolution in Virginia," *William and Mary Quarterly,* series 3, XIX (1962).

Fay, *The Two Franklins.* Bernard Fay, *The Two Franklins: Fathers of American Democracy* (1933).

Fitzpatrick, *George Washington Himself.* John C. Fitzpatrick, *George Washington Himself* (1933).

Fitzpatrick, *Spirit of Rev.* John C. Fitzpatrick, *The Spirit of the Revolution* (1924).

Flippin, *Royal Govt. in Va.* Percy Scott Flippin, *The Royal Government in Virginia, 1624-1775* (1919).

Freeman, *George Washington.* Douglas Southall Freeman, *George Washington, A Biography,* 7 vols. (1948-1957).

Freeman, *R. E. Lee.* Douglas Southall Freeman, *Robert E. Lee,* 4 vols. (1934-1936).

Frothingham, *Rise of Republic of U. S.* Richard Frothingham, *Rise of the Republic of the United States* (1910).

Gipson, "Colonial War Debts," *Va. Mag. Hist. and Biog.* Lawrence Henry Gipson, "Liquidation of Colonial War Debts: Southern Colonies," *The Virginia Magazine of History and Biography,* LXX (1962).

Gipson, *Coming of Rev.* Lawrence Henry Gipson, *The Coming of the Revolution, 1763-1775* (1954).

Gipson, "Repeal of Stamp Act," *Pa. Mag. Hist. and Biog.* Lawrence Henry Gipson, "The Great Debate in the Committee of the Whole House of Commons on the Stamp Act, 1766, as Reported by Nathaniel Ryder." *The Pennsylvania Magazine of History and Biography,* LXXXVI (1962).

Gipson, "Va. Debts before Amer. Rev.," *Va. Mag. Hist. and Biog.* Lawrence H. Gipson, "Virginia Planter Debts before the American Revolution," *The Virginia Magazine of History and Biography,* LXIX (1961).

Greene, "Foundations," *W. and M. Quar.* (3). Jack P. Greene, "Foundations of Political Power in the Virginia House of Burgesses, 1720-1776," *William and Mary Quarterly,* series 3, XVI (1959).

Greene, *Quest for Power.* Jack P. Greene, *The Quest for Power. The Lower Houses of Assembly in the Southern Royal Colonies, 1689-1776* (1963).

Griffith, *Va. H. of B.* Lucille Blanche Griffith, *Virginia House of Burgesses, 1750-1774* (1963).

Grigsby, *Va. Conven., 1776.* Hugh Blair Grigsby, *The Virginia Convention of 1776* (1855).

Groome, *Fauquier During Proprietorship.* H. C. Groome, *Fauquier During the Proprietorship* (1927).

Harlow, "Silas Deane," *DAB.* Ralph V. Harlow, "Silas Deane," *Dictionary of American Biography.*

Harrell, *Loyalism in Va.* Isaac Samuel Harrell, *Loyalism in Virginia* (1926).

Harrison, *Landmarks.* Fairfax Harrison, *Landmarks of Old Prince William,* 2 vols. (1924).

Hazelton, *Dec. of Ind.* John Hampden Hazelton, *The Declaration of Independence; Its History* (1906).

Hendrick, *Lees of Va.* Burton J. Hendrick, *The Lees of Virginia* (1935).

Hilldrup, *Va. Convention of 1776.* Robert Leroy Hilldrup, "The Virginia Convention of 1776." Manuscript dissertation, University of Virginia. (AL).

Howard, *Preliminaries.* George Elliott Howard, *Preliminaries of the Revolution, 1763-1765* (1905).

Hunt, *An. Rept. Amer. Histor. Asso.* Gaillard Hunt, "James Madison and Religious Liberty," *Annual Report of the American Historical Association,* 1901, I.

Hunt, *James Madison.* Gaillard Hunt, *The Life of James Madison* (1902).

James, *Ohio Co.* Alfred J. James, *The Ohio Company: Its Inner History* (1959).

Jensen, *Art. of Confed.* Merrill Jensen, *The Articles of Confederation* (1948).

Jensen, *New Nation.* Merrill Jensen, *The New Nation* (1950).

Johnson, *Va. Experiment.* Alf Johnson, *The Virginia Experiment; the Old Dominion's Role in the Making of America, 1607-1781* (1957).

Jones, *Amer. Members Inns of Court.* Edward Alfred Jones, *American Members of the Inns of Court* (1924).

Kellogg, "Dunmore," *DAB.* Louise Phelps Kellogg, "Dunmore, John Murray, Earl of," *Dictionary of American Biography.*

Knollenberg, *George Washington.* Bernhard Knollenberg, *George Washington, The Virginia Period* (1964).

Knollenberg, *Origin Amer. Rev.* Bernhard Knollenberg, *Origin of the American Revolution, 1759-1766* (1960).

297

Knollenberg, *Washington and the Revolution*. Bernhard Knollenberg, *Washington and the Revolution, a Reappraisal* (1940).

Krout, "Philip John Schuyler," *DAB*. John A. Krout, "Philip John Schuyler," *Dictionary of American Biography*.

Leake, *Va. Committee System*. James Miller Leake, *The Virginia Committee System and the American Revolution* (1917).

Lee, *Lee of Va*. Edmund Jennings Lee, *Lee of Virginia, 1642-1892* (1895).

Lee, *Life of Arthur Lee*. Richard Henry Lee, *Life of Arthur Lee*, 2 vols. (1829).

Lee, *Memoir*. Richard H. Lee, *Memoir of the Life of Richard Henry Lee and His Correspondence*, 2 vols. (1825).

Lee Chronicle. Cazenove Gardner Lee, Jr., and Dorothy Mills, *Lee Chronicle.. Studies of the Early Generations of the Lees of Virginia* (1957).

Lingley, *Transition in Va*. Charles Ramsdell Lingley, *The Transition in Virginia from Colony to Commonwealth* (1910).

Livermore, *Early Amer. Land Companies*. Shaw Livermore, *Early American Land Companies* (1939).

McDonald, *We the People*. Forrest McDonald, *We the People: The Economic Origins of the Constitution* (1958).

Mag. of Amer. History. *Magazine of American History*.

Mag. of Lees. *Magazine of the Lees*.

Main, *The Antifederalists*. Jackson Turner Main, *The Antifederalists: Critics of the Constitution, 1781-1788* (1961).

Malone, *Dec. of Ind*. Dumas Malone, *The Story of the Declaration of Independence* (1954).

Malone, *Jefferson*. Dumas Malone, *Jefferson and His Time* (1948-   ).

Malone, "Thomas Jefferson," *DAB*. Dumas Malone, "Thomas Jefferson," *Dictionary of American Biography*.

Marshall, *Life of Washington*. John Marshall, *The Life of George Washington*, 5 vols. (1804-1807).

Matthews, "Richard Henry Lee." John C. Matthews, "Richard Henry Lee and the American Revolution." Doctoral dissertation, University of Virginia, 1939. Alderman Library.

Matthews, "Two Men on a Tax." John C. Matthews, "Two Men on a Tax," *The Old Dominion*, Darrett B. Rutman, editor (1964).

Mays, *Edmund Pendleton*. David John Mays, *Edmund Pendleton, 1721-1803*, 2 vols. (1952).

Meade, *Old Churches*. William Meade, *Old Churches, Ministers, and Families of Virginia* (1857, 1878).

Meade, *Patrick Henry*. Robert Douthat Meade, *Patrick Henry, Patriot in the Making* (1957).

Miller, *Triumph of Freedom*. John Chester Miller, *Triumph of Freedom* (1948).

Mitchell, *Alexander Hamilton*. Broadus Mitchell, *Alexander Hamilton*, 2 vols. (1957-1962).

Monaghan, *John Jay*. Frank Monaghan, *John Jay* (1935).

Montague, *Va. Mag. of Hist. and Biog.* Ludwell Lee Montague, "Richard Lee, the Emigrant, 1613?-1664," *Virginia Magazine of History and Biography,* LXII (1954).

Montross, *Reluctant Rebels.* Lynn Montross, *The Reluctant Rebels* (1950).

Morgan, *Patrick Henry.* George Morgan, *The True Patrick Henry* (1907).

Morgan, *Stamp Act Crisis.* Edmund S. and Helen M. Morgan, *The Stamp Act Crisis* (1953).

Morison, *Oxford History.* Samuel Eliot Morison, *The Oxford History of the American People* (1965).

Morton, *Colonial Va.* Richard Lee Morton, *Colonial Virginia,* 2 vols. (1960).

Morton, *Robert Carter.* Louis Morton, *Robert Carter of Nomini Hall* (1941).

Munford, *Virginia's Attitude.* Beverly Bland Munford, *Virginia's Attitude toward Slavery and Secession* (1915).

Nevins, *Amer. States in Rev.* Allan Nevins, *The American States During and After the Revolution, 1775-1789* (1927).

North. Neck Mag. The Northern Neck of Virginia Magazine.

Pa. Mag. Hist. and Biog. Pennsylvania Magazine of History and Biography.

Phillips, *West in Dip. of Rev.* Paul Chrisler Phillips, *The West in the Diplomacy of the American Revolution* (1913).

Pitkin, *Hist. U. S.* Timothy Pitkin, *A Political and Civil History of the United States of America . . .* (1828).

Prowell, *Hist. York Co., Pa.* George R. Prowell, *History of York County, Pennsylvania,* 2 vols. (1907).

Reg. Va. Assembly. Earl G. Swem and John W. Williams, editors, *A Register of the General Assembly of Virginia, 1776-1918, and of the Constitutional Conventions* (1918).

Rives, *James Madison.* William Cabell Rives, *History of the Life and Times of James Madison,* 3 vols. (1868-1873).

Robinson, *Edmund Randolph.* Morgan P. Robinson, *Edmund Randolph.*

Roche, *Joseph Reed.* John Francis Roche, *Joseph Reed, a Moderate in the American Revolution* (1957).

Rossman, *Thomas Mifflin and Amer. Rev.* Kenneth P. Rossman, *Thomas Mifflin and the Politics of the American Revolution* (1952).

Rowland, *George Mason.* Kate Mason Rowland, *The Life of George Mason, 1725-1792,* 2 vols. (1892).

Rutman, ed., *Old Dominion.* Darrett B. Rutman, editor, *The Old Dominion, Essays for Thomas Perkins Abernethy* (1964).

Sachse, *Colonial American in Britain.* William L. Sachse, *The Colonial American in Britain* (1956).

Schlesinger, *Colonial Merchants.* Arthur Meier Schlesinger, Sr., *Colonial Merchants and the American Revolution, 1763-1776* (1939).

Schlesinger, *Prelude to Independence.* Arthur M. Schlesinger, Sr., *Prelude to Independence: The Newspaper War on Britain, 1764-1776* (1958).

Schouler, *Hist. of U. S.* James Schouler, *History of the United States under the Constitution,* 7 vols. (1897-1913).

Shakespeare, *Henry VI.*

Smith, *John Adams.* Page Smith, *John Adams,* 2 vols. (1962).

Sparks, *Life of Gouverneur Morris.* Jared Sparks, *The Life of Gouverneur Morris,* 3 vols. (1832).

Spiller, *Lit. Hist. of U. S.* Robert E. Spiller, *et al.,* editors, *Literary History of the United States,* 3 vols. (1949).

Stanard, *Richmond.* Mary Newton Stanard, *Richmond: Its People and Its Story* (1923).

Stanwood, *Amer. Tariff Controversies.* Edward Stanwood, *American Tariff Controversies in the Nineteenth Century* (1903).

Stephenson, *Amer. Histor. Rev.* O. W. Stephenson, "The Supply of Gunpowder in 1776," *American Historical Review,* vol. XXX.

Stillé, *John Dickinson.* Charles J. Stillé, *The Life and Times of John Dickinson* (1891).

Swanstrom, *U. S. Senate.* Roy Swanstrom, *The United States Senate, 1787-1801* (1962).

Sydnor, *Polit. Leadership.* Charles Sackett Sydnor, *Political Leadership in Eighteenth Century Virginia* (1951).

Tate, "Coming of Revolution," *W. and M. Quar.* (3). Article by Thad W. Tate, "The Coming of the Revolution in Virginia: Britain's Challenge to Virginia's Ruling Class, 1763-1776," *William and Mary Historical Quarterly,* Third series, XIX (1962), pp. 323-343.

Thayer, *Nathanael Greene.* Theodore Thayer, *Nathanael Greene: Strategist of the American Revolution* (1960).

Tower, *La Fayette.* Charlemagne Tower, *The Marquis de La Fayette in the American Revolution,* 2 vols. (1901).

Trevelyan, *Amer. Rev.* Sir George Otto Trevelyan, *The American Revolution to 1778,* 4 vols. (1926-1939).

Van Doren, *Secret Hist. Amer. Rev.* Carl Clinton Van Doren, *Secret History of the American Revolution* (1941).

Van Tyne, *Amer. Rev.* Claude Halstead Van Tyne, *The American Revolution* (1905).

Ward, *War of Rev.* Christopher Ward, *The War of the Revolution,* edited by J. R. Alden (1952).

Wilstach, *Potomac Landings.* Paul Wilstach, *Potomac Landings* (1920, 1937).

Wirt, *Patrick Henry.* William Wirt, *Sketches of the Life and Character of Patrick Henry* (revised edition, 1850).

Wright, *First Gentlemen of Va.* Louis Booker Wright, *The First Gentlemen of Virginia* (1949).

Wright, *Westmoreland County, Va.* Thomas R. B. Wright, *Westmoreland County, Virginia* (1912).

Index

Custis, George Washington Parke, 230.

Dane, Nathan, 162, 208.
Dartmouth, William Legge, Earl of, 75.
Deane, Silas, 62, 89, 105-106, 107, 111-117, 206-208, 211.
Debtors, 21-23, 100-101.
Debts and the revolution, 100-101.
Declaration of Independence, 10, 75, 95, 96-99, 102, 222.
Declaration of Rights, 64-65, 75.
Defense, Virginia, 149-153, 154-156.
Delaware River, 121.
DeLolme, Jean Louis, 173.
Desertions, French, 153-154.
D'Estaing, Charles Henri, Comte, 110.
Dickinson, John, opinions of, 31, 88, 96; writings of, 46, 74, 83, 128; Lee letters to, 48, 55, 127-128.
Digges, Dudley, 55, 153.
Dissenters, Protestant, 52.
District of Columbia, 159, 178.
Douglass, William, 6.
Dunmore, John Murray, Earl of, 52, 56, 58, 76, 77, 80-81.
Duties, miscellaneous, 31, 44, 185-186; slaves, 17-19, 20; tea, 44, 50, 51. *See also* Taxes.

East India Company, 57, 69, 253 n. 41.
Education, 203-204.
Ellery, William, 157.
Ellsworth, Oliver, 218-219.
English Toleration Act, 51-52.
Episcopal Church, 202-203. *See also* Anglican Church.
Estaing, Charles Henri, Comte d', 110.

Fairfax family, 4.
"Farmer's Letters," 46.

Fauquier, Francis, 14, 22, 44, 45; opinions, 18, 23, 27.
Federal Court of Appeals, 157.
Federal district, 159; Lee on, 178.
Federalist, The, 171-172, 179.
Fisheries, 196-198.
Fithian, Philip, 234.
Foreign affairs, 175, 207-208; France and French alliance, 104-108, 110-111, 117-118, 152, 200, 201; Committee of Secret Correspondence, 104-105, 137; British peace proposals, 108-109; Spain, 118-119, 201; Portugal, 120; piratical states, 163-164; foreign debts, 190-191; England, 196-199, 201.
Foreign Affairs, Committee for, 104.
Foreign Affairs, Secretary of, 104, 164.
France, relations with U. S., 105, 152, 200.
Franklin, Benjamin, 75; Stamp Act, 34, 44; Continental Congress II, 82, 84-85, 87, 97, 106, 126; French mission, 107, 158-159, 207-208.
Fredericksburg Academy, 204.
Freedom of press, 204.
French Alliance, 104, 107-108, 117-118.
French and Indian War, 23, 30.
French Revolution, 200-201.
Funding of debts, 190-191.

Galloway, Joseph, 65.
Galloway Plan, 66.
Gaskins, Thomas, 9.
Gaspee affair, 53.
Gates, General Horatio, 120, 126, 208, 214-215, 219.
General Advertiser, 114.
Genêt, Edmond Charles, 201.
George III, 75, 92.
Gérard de Rayneval, Conrad Alexander, 109-110, 117, 196, 206.
Gerardin, L. H., 222.

303

Germantown, battle of, 126, 221.
Giberne, Isaac W., 226.
Gipson, Lawrence Henry, 102.
Glasgow Journal, 77.
Goddard, William, 86.
Gooch, William, 5.
Government (Locke), 229.
Grasse, Francois Joseph Paul, Comte de, 154.
Graves, Admiral Thomas, 149.
Grayson, William, 159, 168, 183, 186, 188.
Great Bridge, battle of, 81.
Greene, General Nathanael, 106, 168, 183, 186, 188, 217.
Grenville, George, 31, 33.
Griffin, Samuel, 147.
Gwatkin, Rev. Mr., 56.

Hale, Sir Matthew, 193.
Hamilton, Alexander, 125, 179, 193; financial policies of, 190-197.
Hancock, John, 82, 127, 213-214.
Hardy, Samuel, 159.
Harnett, Cornelius, 127.
Harrison, Benjamin, 61, 74, 82; positions, 24, 60, 145; opinions of, 72, 88, 180, 206, 215.
Hay, Anthony, 49.
Henry, Patrick, 143, 202, 205, 219; House of Burgesses, 24, 25, 29, 34-35, 56; and Revolution, 43, 49, 54, 81; Congress, 60, 63, 64, 66, 74, 88; oratory of, 62, 223-224; Virginia Convention, 78, 79; Lee letters to, 92-93, 131, 133, 137; Virginia Assembly, 98, 101, 144-145, 146-147; Constitution, 148, 166, 181, 183; and Lees, 210-211, 230.
Henry, William Wirt, 139, 210.
Herodotus, 222.
History of England (Paul de Rapin-Thoyras), 229.
Holt, Sir John, 173.
Holten, Samuel, 161.
House of Burgesses, composition

and nature, 14-16; and slavery, 20-21; and debtors, 21-22; and defense, 22; and paper money, 23-24; and Stamp Act, 32-36, 42; dissolved, 48-49, 56, 82; and Townshend Duty Act, 45, 47-51; and *Gaspee* affair, 53-56; and peace proposals, 79-80; end of, 82.
House of Delegates, 136, 183; and debts, 100-101; and RHL, 125, 139-143, 147, 210; and western lands, 131-132; and state capital, 143; and currency, 143-144; flees British army, 145; and federal finances, 145-147; and religion, 202.
House of Representatives, apportionment of, 193-194.
Howe, Admiral Richard, Earl, 108, 109.
Howe, General William, 106, 121, 125.
Hunter, Robert, 158, 161.

Inauguration, of Washington, 184, 185.
Independence, resolution for, 91-96; movement for, 99-103.
Inflation, 123-124.
Inner Temple, 7.
Intelligence, Committee for, 120.

Jacobins, 211.
James II, 3.
Jay, John, and Congress, 71, 72, 75; opinions of, 113, 164, 193; *Federalist* papers, 179.
Jefferson, Thomas, 6, 100; Virginia Assembly, 34, 49, 54, 56, 139, 146; and Lee, 72, 99, 209-210; Virginia Convention, 78; Congress, 82, 88, 162, 192; Declaration of Independence, 97; diplomat, 107, 158, 159; Lee letters to, 134-135, 150-151, 203; Governor, 152-153.
Jennings, Edmund, 4, 43.

Johnson, Samuel, 34.
Jones, John Paul, 90.
"Junto," 212, 213.

Knox, General Henry, 106.

Lafayette, Marquis de, 152, 158; and Lees, 208-209, 230; "Conway Cabal," 214-216.
Lamb, General John, 180.
Lancaster, 125.
Land Ordinance of 1784, 162.
Land Ordinance of 1785, 159-161, 165.
Land speculation, 3, 28, 37, 242 n. 14.
Langdon, John, 85, 184.
Langworthy, Edward, 212.
Laurens, Henry, 113, 134, 147, 157; Lee letters to, 117, 197, 207; and Lee, 208, 211.
League of Nations, Lee proposal of, 199.
Lee, Ann Constable, great-grandmother of RHL, 1.
Lee, Anne Aylett, wife of RHL, 8.
Lee, Anne Pinckard, wife of RHL, 9, 235.
Lee, Arthur, brother of RHL, 28, 46-47, 128-129, 158; and Lee family, 10, 11, 20-21, 225, 229-230; Lee letters to, 15, 18, 113, 151, 152, 157, 188; agent in England, 75, 84-85; Deane controversy, 105-106, 111-117, 197, 211.
Lee, Cassius, son of RHL, 230.
Lee, General Charles, 208, 215, 217-219, 225.
Lee, Elizabeth Bendy, great-great-grandmother of RHL, 1.
Lee, Francis Lightfoot, brother of RHL, 9, 10, 28, 41; House of Burgesses, 16, 25, 54, 98; Declaration of Independence, 98; attacks on, 112, 215; Congress, 123, 139, 140, 143, 180; Lee letters to, 79-80, 211, 226.

Lee, Francis Lightfoot, son of RHL, 230.
Lee, Hannah, sister of RHL, 11.
Lee, Hannah Ludwell, mother of RHL, 5.
Lee, Henry, "Light-Horse Harry," second cousin, nephew-in-law of RHL, 139, 193, 204, 208; Congress, 165; Constitution, 168, 180.
Lee, John, 2-3.
Lee, Ludwell, son of RHL, 99, 208, 209, 228, 229-230.
Lee, Philip Ludwell, brother of RHL, 5, 7, 8, 11, 12, 13, 149.
Lee, Richard, the emigrant, 1-2.
Lee, Richard, grandfather of RHL, 3-4.
Lee, Richard, member Virginia House of Delegates, 148, 211.
Lee, Richard, uncle of RHL, 4.
Lee, Richard Bland, 200.
Lee, Richard Henry, ancestry, British, 1; early life, 7-9; marriages, 8-9; justice of peace, 14; Virginia suffrage, 15-21; slavery, 17-21; currency, 22; Robinson speakership, 24-27; Mississippi Co. of Va., 28; Parson's Cause, 29; Stamp Act, 32, 34-36, 37-40, 42-43; Westmoreland Association, 11, 40-41; "Address to the Good People of Virginia," 41; Townshend Acts, 44-48, 50-51; religion, 52; *Gaspee*, 52-53; committee of correspondence, 54-55, 59; Boston Port Bill, 56-57; continental congress, suggested, 57; associations for non-importation, 49-51, 58;

First Continental Congress, delegate, 61-64; Declaration of Rights, 64-65; Galloway Plan, 66; quartering of troops, 66-67; Continental Association, 68-69; memorial to British people, 70; Quebec Act, 71; address to people of Britain, 71-74; address to the King, 75; Westmoreland Co.

305

Maryland Journal and Baltimore Advertiser, 86.
Mason, George, 16, 49, 101, 144; and Lee, 97, 134-135, 219, 220, 233, 234; in Congress, 139-140; and Constitution, 166, 170, 172, 180-181.
Mason-Dixon line, 88.
Maury, Rev. James, 29.
Meade, Bishop William, 227.
Medical School of the College of Philadelphia, 13.
Memorial to Lords and Commons, 32-33, 249 n. 16.
Mercer, George, 37, 38.
Mercer, James, 38, 39, 147, 204.
Mercer, John, 38, 147.
Middleton, Henry, 75.
Mifflin, Thomas, 61, 120, 121, 208, 215.
Military affairs, 178-179, 189.
Mississippi Company of Virginia, 28, 37.
Mississippi River, 197-198.
"Monitor's Letters," 47.
Monmouth, battle of, 217.
Monroe, James, 6, 209; in Congress, 158-159, 160; in Senate, 192, 193, 194.
Monroe, John, 39.
Montesquieu, 173, 222.
Montross, 37, 39, 43.
Morris, Gouverneur, 108, 278 n. 5.
Morris, Robert, 122, 215.
Mount Vernon, 60.
Murray, John. *See* Dunmore.
Murray, William. *See* Mansfield.

National bank, 191, 192.
Navigation rights, 196-198.
Navy, federal, 89, 120; Virginia, 149.
Neale, Thomas, 85.
Nelson, Thomas, 95, 128, 139, 155, 272 n. 40.
Nelson, William, 51, 252 n. 28.
New England, 137, 187, 196, 214, 226.

Newfoundland fisheries, 196-198.
Newspapers, 46, 77, 86, 111-112, 114, 197, 212, 213. *See also Virginia Gazette.*
New York, 158-159.
New York *Evening Post,* 197.
Nicholas, Robert Carter, 55, 56.
Nomini Anglican Church, 227.
Non-importation of goods. *See* Trade.
North, Lord Frederick, Earl of Guilford, 63, 79, 86.
Northwest Ordinance of 1787, 19, 162-163, 165.

Ohio Company of Virginia, 3, 37, 242 n. 14.
Ordinance of 1784, 162.
Ordinance of 1787 (Northwest Ordinance), 19, 162-163, 165.
Orr, Lucinda Lee, 232.
Ott, Louis Guillaume, 13.

Page, John, 92, 97, 108, 140, 235, 279 n. 32.
Page, Mann, 80, 140, 145, 147, 279 n. 32.
Paine, Robert Treat, 86.
Paine, Thomas, 92, 94, 211.
Parker, Richard, 138.
Parson's Cause, 29-30.
Peace negotiations, 106, 108-109; treaty, 101, 156.
Peale, Charles Wilson, 43.
Pendleton, Edmund, 94, 172, 206; House of Burgesses, 22, 24-25, 32; Continental Congress, 60, 64, 72.
Penet, Pierre, 105.
Pennsylvania boundary dispute, 88.
Pennsylvania Chronicle, 46.
Pennsylvania Packet, 111-112, 114.
"Petition to the King," 83, 84.
Philadelphia, 60, 61, 89, 121-122, 126, 127.
Pinckard, Thomas, 9.
Pinkard, Mr., 232.
Pitt, William, 33, 42-43, 59.

307

308